INTELLECTUAL HUMILITY

Intellectual Humility: Theory, Science, and Practice
Free Online Courses

These completely free and open online mini-courses introduce students to the philosophy and science of intellectual humility. The mini-courses will be composed of a total of ten lectures, each focusing on a big question surrounding the theme of intellectual humility. The lectures will be given by leading researchers on the science, philosophy, and theology of intellectual humility .

The first mini-course will focus on the theory of intellectual humility and focus on questions like: What is intellectual humility? What is an intellectual virtue? How do we know who is intellectually humble?

The second mini-course will focus on the science of intellectual humility and focus on questions like: How do we become intellectually humble? What can human cognition tell us about intellectual humility? Are some people born humble? How do emotions affect our ability to be intellectually humble?

And the last mini-course will focus on applied issues surrounding intellectual humility and focus on questions like: Can you believe what you hear? How should we handle disagreement? What does intellectual humility tell us about religion?

Find more information and signup for the courses
at www.coursera.org.

Taught by Prof Jason Baehr; Dr Ian Church; Dr Katherine Dormandy; Prof Catherine Elgin; Prof Peter Graham; Prof John Greco; Prof Peter C. Hill; Prof Frank Keil; Prof Cristine Legare; Prof Victor Ottati; Prof Vasu Reddy; Dr Peter L. Samuelson; Prof John Schellenberg; Prof Eleonore Stump

INTELLECTUAL HUMILITY

An introduction to the philosophy and science

IAN M. CHURCH AND

PETER L. SAMUELSON

Bloomsbury Academic

An imprint of Bloomsbury Publishing Plc

B L O O M S B U R Y
LONDON · OXFORD · NEW YORK · NEW DELHI · SYDNEY

Bloomsbury Academic

An imprint of Bloomsbury Publishing Plc

50 Bedford Square
London
WC1B 3DP
UK

1385 Broadway
New York
NY 10018
USA

www.bloomsbury.com

BLOOMSBURY and the Diana logo are trademarks of Bloomsbury Publishing Plc

First published 2017

British Library Cataloguing-in-Publication Data

A catalogue record for this book is available from the British Library.

ISBN: HB: 978-1-4742-3673-7
PB: 978-1-4742-3674-4
ePDF: 978-1-4742-3676-8
ePub: 978-1-4742-3675-1

Library of Congress Cataloging-in-Publication Data

Names: Church, Ian M., author. | Samuelson, Peter L., author.
Title: Intellectual humility: an introduction to the philosophy and science
/ Ian M. Church and Peter L. Samuelson.
Description: London, UK; New York, NY: Bloomsbury Academic, an imprint of
Bloomsbury Publishing, Plc, [2016] | Includes bibliographical references
and index.
Identifiers: LCCN 2016029223 (print) | LCCN 2016039266 (ebook) | ISBN
9781474236737 (hardback) | ISBN 9781474236744 (pbk.) | ISBN 9781474236768
(ePDF) | ISBN 9781474236751 (ePub) | ISBN 9781474236768 (epdf) | ISBN
9781474236751 (epub)
Subjects: LCSH: Humility. | Thought and thinking. | Intellectual life.
Classification: LCC BJ1533.H93 C48 2016 (print) | LCC BJ1533.H93 (ebook) |
DDC 179/.9–dc23
LC record available at https://lccn.loc.gov/2016029223

Cover design: Avni Patel
Cover image © Robert A. Waller Memorial Fund/The Art Institute of Chicago

Typeset by Deanta Global Publishing Services, Chennai, India

For my children.

Ian Church

To my father and mother, Paul and Edith Samuelson,
who taught intellectual humility by their example, and to
my wife, Debra, for her constant support.

Peter Samuelson

CONTENTS

ACKNOWLEDGMENTS

Over the last four years, the John Templeton Foundation has generously funded a number of major projects on intellectual humility: "The Science of Intellectual Humility" project at the Fuller Graduate School of Psychology, "The Philosophy and Theology of Intellectual Humility" project at Saint Louis University, and, most recently, the "Intellectual Humility Massive Open Online Course" project at the University of Edinburgh. We are tremendously grateful to have been involved with all of these projects, and this book is one of the outputs of our involvement. This book simply would not have been possible without the generous support of the John Templeton Foundation.

The person who deserves the greatest thanks for the completion of this book is Justin Barrett. As the Director of the Thrive Foundation for Human Development and the Principal Investigator of the "Science of Intellectual Humility" project, Justin was the first one to bring us together to work on the philosophy and science of intellectual humility. Justin gave us valuable feedback on many of the ideas within this book. But what is more, Justin has proved to be a fantastic mentor and friend.

Unfortunately, we can't mention everyone who gave us feedback and support on this project (though we are very grateful to everyone); however, there are a few individuals we would like to thank directly: in particular, J. Adam Carter, Ariel Celeste, Scott Cleveland, Don Davis, Matthew Frise, John Greco, Bob Hartman, Peter Hill, Joshua Hook, Ross Inman, Matthew Jarvinen, Jesper Kallestrup, Jim McCollum, Tom Paulus, Maura Priest, Duncan Pritchard, Jonathan Reibsamen, Matthew Siebert, Rebecca Sok, Julia Stewart, and Eleonore Stump.

Substantial portions of the research in this volume have been carried out and presented at several institutions and conferences. We are exceedingly grateful for the helpful feedback we received at the *American Philosophical Association Pacific Division Meeting* (2015); Biola University; Calvin College; the Fuller Graduate School of Psychology; the *Intellectual Humility Capstone Conference*; the *Intellectual Humility: Its Nature, Value, and Implications* seminar; the *Joint Session of the Aristotelian Society and the Mind Association* (2015); the University of Edinburgh; the University of Western Kentucky; and the *World Congress of Philosophy* (2013).

Nothing is so difficult as not deceiving oneself.

—*Culture and Value*

Ludwig Wittgenstein (1980, 34e).

PART ONE

THEORY

1

What is intellectual humility? (and why should we care?)

Intellectual humility is important. To see the incredible need for intellectual humility—the need to understand something about what it is, how it might be developed, and how it can be applied—consider the closing remarks of Dr. Jacob Bronowski (1973) in the monumental, thirteen-part documentary *The Assent of Man*, as he walks into a pond at the Auschwitz concentration camp:

> There are two parts to the human dilemma. One is the belief that the end justifies the means. That push-button philosophy, that deliberate deafness to suffering, has become the monster in the war machine. The other is the betrayal of the human spirit: the assertion of dogma that closes the mind, and turns a nation, a civilization, into a regiment of ghosts—obedient ghosts, or tortured ghosts.
>
> It is said that science will dehumanize people and turn them into numbers. That is false, tragically false. Look for yourself. This is the concentration camp and crematorium at Auschwitz. This is where people were turned into numbers. Into this pond were flushed the ashes of some four million people. And that was not done by gas. It was done by arrogance. It was done

by dogma. It was done by ignorance. When people believe that they have absolute knowledge, with no test in reality, this is how they behave. This is what men do when they aspire to the knowledge of gods.

Science is a very human form of knowledge. We are always at the brink of the known, we always feel forward for what is to be hoped. Every judgment in science stands on the edge of error, and is personal. Science is a tribute to what we can know although we are fallible. In the end the words were said by Oliver Cromwell: "I beseech you, in the bowels of Christ, think it possible you may be mistaken."

I owe it as a scientist to my friend Leo Szilard, I owe it as a human being to the many members of my family who died at Auschwitz, to stand here by the pond as a survivor and a witness. We have to cure ourselves of the itch for absolute knowledge and power. We have to close the distance between the push-button order and the human act. We have to touch people.

All too often, when faced with difficult questions, people are prone to dismissing and marginalizing dissent. Around the world, politics is incredibly polarizing and, in many parts of the world, extremely dangerous. And whether it's Christian fundamentalism, Islamic jihadism, or militant atheism, religious dialogue remains tinted by a terrifying and dehumanizing arrogance, dogma, and ignorance.

So on the face of it, the world needs more people who are sensitive to their own intellectual failings, who are more likely to "think it possible" that their political, religious, and moral beliefs "may be mistaken." The world needs more intellectual humility. But the significance of intellectual humility is not merely practical; it has important theoretical and scientific implications and is central to various projects in both philosophy and psychology.

What are some ways intellectual humility will be important to philosophy? Recent work in philosophy has highlighted the theoretical importance of intellectual humility in the context of the broader subject of "virtue epistemology." Virtue epistemology focuses on the process by which beliefs are formed, looking specifically at whether or not the belief was formed by an *intellectually virtuous knower*. Some have claimed that intellectual humility is among these core intellectual virtues. In this way, intellectual humility can be seen as foundational to knowledge itself. What is more, intellectual humility might seem incompatible with the notion that one might stick to his or her guns (intellectually speaking) when faced with others who are equally intelligent and well informed but who hold opposing, even incompatible views. And yet, while sticking to your guns and being intellectually humble seem incompatible, even paradigmatically intellectually humble individuals sometimes (quite justifiably) maintain their positions in the face of such disagreement. The epistemic import of peer disagreement is a hot topic in contemporary epistemology and directly relevant to intellectual humility (and vice versa).[1]

What are some ways intellectual humility will be important to psychology? Well, we could begin our investigation into intellectual humility by recognizing it as the opposite of intellectual arrogance, for we have evidence that this vice is deeply rooted in human psychology. First, human beings are notoriously (and naturally) disposed to overestimate their intellectual strengths and underestimate their weaknesses; indeed, the evidence is clear that there is a strong tendency even to underestimate our liability to such biases! Do these biases show a natural tendency away from intellectual humility? Furthermore, we are susceptible to all sorts of biases that make intellectual humility difficult. For example, we tend to favor evidence or data received early in our inquiries (primacy bias) and we tend to discount the weight of evidence that counts against hypotheses we endorse (confirmation bias). Second, evolutionary psychologists have offered some intriguing arguments that these dispositions are embedded within our cognitive architecture in ways that can systematically lead us to biased thinking, in some cases for adaptive reasons. Does this mean that intellectual arrogance is both an epistemic vice and a "biological virtue"?

Third, some clinicians have argued that intellectual arrogance is necessary for maintaining mental health. The intellectually humble, who see themselves and their condition with unmitigated clarity, are more susceptible to forms of depression, for example. Presumably, however, viewing intellectual humility merely as the opposite of intellectual arrogance gives us an incomplete picture. For example, evidence indicates correlations between intellectual humility and important morally salient traits such as a willingness to forgive others, a lack of aggression, and helpfulness. Moreover, psychologists have discovered traits and behaviors associated with intellectual humility that facilitate learning, personal growth, and social interaction. What other positive, or negative, correlations exist between intellectual humility and other aspects of human flourishing?

No doubt then, intellectual humility has enormous practical import and is an important subject for academic work in psychology and philosophy. *The problem, however, is that a robust conceptual, theoretical, and empirical understanding of intellectual humility—the sort of understanding that is going to be most valuable for projects like those noted above—is surprisingly difficult to come by.* Intellectual humility has sometimes been explicitly delineated as a subset of concepts such as humility and wisdom. For example, research into folk conceptions of wisdom reveals that components such as open-mindedness, not being afraid to admit and correct a mistake, and listening to all sides of an issue (what Sternberg [1985] calls "sagacity") resonate with intellectual humility,[2] but there have been no such investigations to date that deal with intellectual humility as a stand-alone concept. There are, no doubt, an enormous number of projects that intellectual humility can speak to; however, if we do not understand precisely what intellectual humility *is*, we will be unable to explore the full significance of intellectual humility (both practical and academic) with much precision.

Prima facie, humility is the virtuous mean between something like arrogance, on the one hand, and self-deprecation or diffidence, on the other. The humble person, to put it roughly, doesn't value herself too much (arrogance) nor does she value herself too little (diffidence or self-deprecation). Instead, she thinks of herself—her value, her status among her peers, her abilities—as she ought.[3]

Building off of this extremely simple and basic view of humility, an intuitive account of intellectual humility seems to follow. We might imagine that *intellectual* humility is the virtuous mean between *intellectual* arrogance and *intellectual* diffidence. The intellectually humble person, then, doesn't overly value her beliefs (intellectual arrogance) nor does she undervalue them (intellectual diffidence). Instead, she values her beliefs, their epistemic status, and her intellectual abilities as she ought. Given its focus on beliefs, this rough approximation of intellectual humility is what we will be calling *the doxastic account of intellectual humility.*

In this chapter, we will try to unpack and defend this simple, intuitive account of intellectual humility. While recent empirical research suggests that intellectual humility might be a multifaceted and multilayered virtue—complete with moral dimensions, interpersonal dimensions, intrapersonal dimensions, etc.—we will be defending a fundamentally *doxastic* account of intellectual humility (see Samuelson et al., 2014). Whatever social or moral dimensions the virtue of intellectual humility might have, we will suggest that it needs to be built upon or understood within this basic, doxastic account.

§1: Problems with the current, seminal accounts of intellectual humility

The account of intellectual humility developed by Robert Roberts and Jay Wood (2003, 2007) is currently the seminal one in the literature. In developing their account of intellectual humility, Roberts and Wood (2003) begin by defining humility *simpliciter* by contrasting it with vices like arrogance and vanity. As they explain:

Like many other epistemic virtues, humility has a wider than merely intellectual sphere. So our strategy will be first to explore it in its broader moral application, and then to carry what we have learned into a discussion of the intellectual life.... Often, virtues are best described in connection with their vice-counterparts, and this is especially important with humility.... Humility is opposite a number of vices, including arrogance, vanity, conceit, egotism, grandiosity, pretentiousness, snobbishness, impertinence (presumption), haughtiness, self-righteousness, domination, selfish ambition, and self-complacency. (pp. 257–58)

And so, Roberts and Wood (2003) explicate intellectual humility by working from an understanding of humility in general,[4] generated by contrasting it with vices approximately summarized as "improper pride" (p. 258).[5] And in this way, Roberts and Wood (2003) go on to define intellectual humility as

an unusually low dispositional concern for the kind of status that accrues to persons who are viewed by their intellectual communities as intellectually talented, accomplished, and skilled, especially where such concern is muted or sidelined by intrinsic intellectual concerns—in particular, the concern for knowledge with its various attributes of truth, justification, warrant, coherence, precision, and significance. (p. 271)

According to Roberts and Wood, intellectual humility is a virtue that can be negatively defined by its opposition to intellectual variants of vices such as arrogance, vanity, snobbishness, and domination. One way of understanding many of these kinds of vices is as those that are often focused on the social well-being of the possessor. Thus, according to Roberts and Wood (2007), intellectual humility must be something quite the opposite: as they put it more recently, "a striking or unusual unconcern for social importance, and thus a kind of emotional *insensitivity* to the issues of status" (p. 239). The important nuance here being that the possessor of intellectual humility is not *unaware* of his or her status, excellence, or importance, but that he or she is largely *unconcerned* with the issue and is motivated to pursue epistemic goods to something beyond social status.

The first concern for such an account is that it is not at all clear that intellectual humility is just the opposite of intellectual arrogance. We can easily imagine a person who is *too humble*—a person who is so intellectually diffident that they fail to appropriately recognize and appreciate their own intellectual achievements. Consider the following case:

> BOTANIST: Susan is a highly acclaimed botanist with a litany of scientific achievements and an almost unmatched knowledge of orchids; however, Susan cares nothing for social status or the accolades of her peers. Frank, on the other hand, is a novice botanist at best but is wildly obsessed with his status amongst his peers and how much they think of him. To make matters worse, Frank is an idiot. Susan and Frank know each other (and each other's accomplishments) very well; and being obsessed with status and intimidated by Susan's accomplishments, Frank is regularly antagonistic toward Susan. Susan and Frank are at a botanical garden when they have a disagreement about the scientific name of a certain species of orchid. Caring nothing for her intellectual status and accolades (or Frank's negative status), Susan takes Frank's dissent seriously and treats him as an intellectual peer.

According to the Roberts and Wood (2003, 2007) account, Susan in BOTANIST exhibits intellectual humility; she is not at all concerned about her intellectual social importance or her academic status. That said, our intuition in a case like this is that she is not being virtuous. For a highly acclaimed and accomplished botanist like Susan to take the dissent of a botanical dunce like Frank seriously—where (caring nothing for her status or Frank's) she views him as a peer—seems intellectually *vicious*. Our intuition here is that Susan is simply being *too humble*. Arguably, intellectual humility is best conceived as a *virtuous mean* in between the vices of *intellectual arrogance,* on the one side, and *intellectual diffidence,* on the other. This latter dimension, however, is completely missing in the Roberts and Wood account.

Second, the Roberts and Wood (2003, 2007) account of intellectual humility seems to lead to strange asymmetries when it comes to nonsocial scenarios where intellectual status within a community is simply not possible. Consider the following case:

> STRANDED: Tragedy has befallen Frank—the ignorant, yet arrogant wannabe botanist—and he has been shipwrecked on a small deserted island. He is entirely alone. And with no social status to care about, Frank can no longer be obsessed with his status amongst his peers and how much they think of him.

In STRANDED, with no social status to be gained or lost, Frank cannot help but be intellectually humble. He can have no concern for his social status because there is no social status to be concerned about. And even though he might sit on his island, endlessly telling himself that all of his botanical judgments are right and true, he simply cannot be intellectually arrogant—at least not according to the Roberts and Wood account. This is problematic on at least two fronts: first of all, it is extremely odd that the Roberts and Wood account affords asymmetric scenarios where someone cannot help but be virtuous and vice is conceptually impossible. After all, if someone cannot help but be intellectually humble, is that really a virtue? Second, STRANDED seems to be a counterexample to the Roberts and Wood account. As Frank endlessly tells himself that all of his botanical judgments are right and true, it sure seems like he is being intellectually arrogant. But that goes against what the Roberts and Wood (2003, 2007) account would allow.

Perhaps a different, more recent account of intellectual humility might fare better. In their paper "Intellectual Humility: Owning Our Limitations," Whitcomb et al. (2015) have proposed a new definition: intellectual humility is "proper attentiveness to, and owning of, one's intellectual limitations." Perhaps the most striking feature of this limitations-owning account of intellectual humility is that in order to be intellectually humble, one need be *only* attentive to and own one's intellectual limitations; being attentive to and owning one's intellectual *strengths*, according to Whitcomb et al., is a different virtue altogether, namely, *proper pride*. With such a distinction, intellectual humility *qua* intellectual humility is blind to intellectual strengths. As Whitcomb et al. (2015) admit, their account of intellectual humility "says nothing about one's orientation or stance toward one's intellectual strengths" (p. 20).

And as Whitcomb et al. (2015) noted, this can lead to some bizarre conclusions. Imagine someone who is duly attentive to and owning of her intellectual *limitations* but radically overestimates and brags about her intellectual *strengths*. Then, insofar as someone is intellectually arrogant if they radically overestimate and brag about their intellectual strengths, it looks like the limitations-owning account leads to this odd conclusion: it's possible for someone to "be at once intellectually humble and intellectually arrogant" (p. 20). And that seems like a reason to reject the view outright. The inability to rule out the possibility of someone being at once intellectually arrogant and intellectually humble is a limitation that we don't want to own in accounts of intellectual humility.

In response, Whitcomb et al. (2015) argue that such a result is metaphysically impossible for an agent who is *fully internally rational*. They suggest that strengths and weaknesses are on a continuum. To use their example, if someone is attentive to and owns the limitations of their memory—that it's worse than 5 percent of people in the world—then, if they're fully internally rational, it won't be possible for them to overestimate the strengths of their memory—that it's better than 95 percent of people in the world. If someone is appropriately attending to and owning their intellectual limitations, then, *if they're fully internally rational*, they simply can't overestimate their intellectual strengths. Conversely, if someone is overestimating their intellectual strengths, then, *if they're fully internally rational*, they simply can't be intellectually humble—they can't appropriately attend to and own their intellectual limitations.[6]

Of course, for anyone who isn't fully internally rational—which is most everyone—it's still possible to be at once both intellectually humble and intellectually arrogant on the limitations-owning view. Attending to and owning intellectual limitations might generally go hand in hand with attending to and owning strengths in non-fully internally rational people; however, "if someone is internally irrational in a suitable way, then it might well turn out that she owns her limitations but over-owns her strengths, in which case she will be both intellectually humble and intellectual [*sic*] arrogant" (Whitcomb et al., 2015, p. 25). But that's a limitation they are willing to own. To soften the blow, Whitcomb et al. (2015) note that "perhaps [such a result] should not be all that surprising. When irrationality is on the scene—as it can be in the human mind—seemingly incompatible mental states can coexist" (p. 25).

But, what Whitcomb et al. (2015) don't seem to appreciate is that *that's still a serious limitation of the view.* Pre-theoretically, we take being intellectually humble to be simply incompatible with being intellectually arrogant. Imagine someone said this to you: "You need to meet Richard! He's such a kind and humble guy. Watch out, though, he's an arrogant jerk." You'd think whoever said this just contradicted themselves. You wouldn't think, "Well, I guess Richard must be less than fully internally rational." You'd think that whoever said such a thing is either using "humble" and "arrogant" in an extremely unusual, unorthodox way, or that they simply don't understand the words that they're using. It seems like there is something wrong or counterintuitive with a definition of intellectual humility that does not preclude someone—even a less than fully internally rational someone—being at once intellectually humble *and* intellectually arrogant. And if the limitations-owning view gives us such a definition, then that's a serious strike against it.

In any case, there is another worry lurking in the neighborhood, which Whitcomb et al. (2015) don't seem to consider. Even if a fully internally rational person can't appropriately attend to and own their limitations while *overestimating* their strengths, it's not at all clear that a fully internally rational person can't appropriately attend to and own their limitations while simply *failing to attend to their strengths*. It may be right that a fully internally rational person can't appropriately attend to and own that their memory is worse than 5 percent of people while overestimating the strengths of their memory, that it's better than 95 percent of people in the world, say; however, it's not at all clear that a fully internally rational person cannot appropriately attend to and own the limitations of their memory *and simply fail to consider their corresponding strengths*. There is nothing irrational about not attending to the logical consequences of one's beliefs.

So here's the other worry: even if it's right that the limitations-owning view of intellectual humility can avoid cases where someone is at once intellectually humble and intellectually arrogant just so long as that person is fully internally rational, the view still allows for cases where someone (even a fully internally rational someone) can be at once intellectually humble and, to use Whitcomb et al.'s (2015) term, "intellectually servile." By Whitcomb et al.'s reckoning, if someone does not appropriately attend to and own their intellectual strengths enough, then they are intellectually servile. Intellectual servility is the complete opposite of intellectual arrogance, the intellectual vice on the other side of the virtuous mean of intellectual humility. And here again, since Whitcomb et al. insist on limiting the scope of intellectual humility to intellectual *limitations*—such that intellectual humility is blind to intellectual strengths—we get another odd result: someone can be at once intellectually humble and intellectually servile. And here appeals to fully internally rational agents don't seem to mitigate the problem.

But maybe a defender of the limitations-owning account of intellectual humility will want to push back on this point. Perhaps we could defend the limitations-owning account by arguing that intellectual limitations and intellectual strengths are *so* intertwined and interconnected that it's somehow impossible for a fully internally rational agent to appropriately attend to and own one's limitations and not appropriately attend to and own their strengths. But remember, since proper pride requires the conjunction of appropriately attending to *and* owning one's intellectual strengths, then to be intellectually servile someone only needs to fail to appropriately *attend* their strengths. So, insofar as there is nothing irrational about attending to and owning intellectual limitations without attending to intellectual strengths, this line of defense is hopeless. In other words, the only way to get this line of defense off the ground is to claim that appropriately attending to and owning intellectual limitations necessarily entails appropriately attending to and owning intellectual strengths, such that a fully internally rational agent couldn't do one without doing the other.

There are at least three reasons this is a bad defense of the limitations-owning view. First of all, even if successful, this only prevents fully internally rational agents from being at once intellectually humble and intellectually servile. For non-fully internally rational agents like us, this remains a problem. And as we noted earlier, this is still a serious drawback to the view. Second, such a defense seems at odds with experience. It sure seems like we can attend to our limitations without attending to our strengths, and it's hard to see how there is anything irrational about that. And third, this line of defense seems to simply undermine the limitations-owning view. If appropriately attending to and owning intellectual limitations is so closely tied to appropriately attending to and owning intellectual strengths—such that attending to the one necessarily entails attending to the other—then we might wonder why we should pull them apart to begin with. If intellectual limitations and intellectual strengths are *that* intertwined, then the distinction between intellectual humility and proper pride seems to disappear and with it the distinguishing feature of the limitations-owning view.

§2: Folk theories of intellectual humility

No doubt, the Roberts and Wood (2003, 2007) account and the Whitcomb et al. (2015) account have a great deal to commend them. The Roberts and Wood (2003, 2007) account, for example, seems to rightly capture an important social aspect of intellectual humility, and it is surely right that one can get valuable insights into intellectual humility by contrasting it with vices like intellectual arrogance—in many ways, it is intuitive and elegantly prescriptive. To be sure, Roberts, Wood, and Whitcomb et al. are traditional philosophers, and as such there is a tremendous amount of work still to be done explicating the *empirical* dimensions of intellectual humility. That said, they have all done a great deal to further our conceptual and theoretical understanding of intellectual humility.

But even so, there is still an enormous amount of theoretical work to be done; as we've seen, there are serious worries facing both accounts of intellectual humility—worries that might motivate us to explore other, perhaps more viable, accounts. But where should we start? To be sure, we could easy settle into our armchairs and produce valuable and informed accounts of intellectual humility from there; however, since intellectual humility might be a somewhat foreign concept—with academic research really taking off only in the last few years—perhaps a survey of what most people (or "the folk") think of when they think of intellectual humility (and related virtues and vices) might help inform our armchair theorizing. Of course, the folk's conception of intellectual humility might be way off—we can cither take it or leave it—but even so, an understanding of the folk conception of intellectual humility can serve as an excellent backdrop to continued research and theorizing.

While most people, save some philosophers and psychologists, have probably not given intellectual humility much thought, it turns out they have a fairly sophisticated understanding of what an intellectually humble person is like. They hold these theories about many things that, like intellectual humility, are complex and hard to define. They may not be able to quickly define it, but they know it when they see it. There is a famous statement made by U.S. Supreme Court justice Potter Stewart who, in admitting he had trouble defining hard-core pornography, said: "I know it when I see it" ("Justice Stewart's Legacy," NY Times Opinion Page Published: December 9, 1985). Intellectual humility is a little like that. Not like pornography, but like other complex and hard-to-define concepts—say intelligence or creativity—that we have a sense of but have difficulty articulating exactly what it is, or who has it.

Psychologists call such notions "implicit theories." They have studied such complex notions as "intelligence," "creativity," and "wisdom," to name a few. We initiated a study to discover the implicit theory of an intellectually humble person, following a process that begins with asking people to think of words and phrases (descriptors) that characterize an intellectually humble person. In this case, we asked 116 people to give us a list of 10 descriptors of an intellectually humble person, then another 117 people gave us 10 descriptors for characteristics of a wise person, and finally another 117 people did the same for an intellectually arrogant person.

Now we have a list of over 1,150 descriptors for each of these three types of people (or "person-concept"). We boiled this list down, eliminating duplicates, separating phrases that contained two distinct descriptors (e.g., humble and modest), eliminating modifiers ("very honest" became "honest"), and collapsing words (or phrases) we judged to be synonymous. Finally, we eliminated words or phrases that occurred less than three times. We ended up with a list of just over hundred words for each type of person we were interested in (101 for the intellectually humble person, 108 for the wise person, and 101 for the intellectually arrogant person).

Next, we gave people the list of descriptors for an intellectually humble person and asked the following question: "Rate on a scale of 1–7 how characteristic the following descriptors are of an 'intellectually humble' person." One hundred and twelve people completed this task. One hundred and eleven different people rated the descriptors of a wise person and a different 112 people did the same tasks with the list of descriptors of an intellectually arrogant person. Now we have a rank order of these descriptors—those rated the most characteristic of an intellectually humble person and those rated the least. Here are the top ten descriptors of an intellectually humble person:

humble*	(17)
not a showoff	(3)
doesn't brag	(3)
modest	(45)
intelligent***	(30)
smart***	(72)
thinker*	(4)
humility	(4)
love of learning	(3)
intellectual*	(7)

The number in the parenthesis is the number of times the word was nominated in the first go-around when people came up with the list of ten descriptors. A single asterisk by the word means it was also a word nominated to describe a wise person. A triple asterisk means it was nominated for all three person-concepts.

Finally, we took the top fifty rated words and phrases describing an intellectually humble person and asked a group of people (113 to be exact) to sort the descriptors into categories according to how similar they were to each other. They could sort the descriptors into as many categories as they chose. Through a statistical procedure called Hierarchical Cluster Analysis (HCA), we aggregated the number of times words were paired with each other, which gave us a sense of how many distinct clusters of words there were for an intellectually humble person. Next, we plotted the position of these words in three-dimensional space through a process called Multi-Dimensional Scaling (MDS). Two words often associated with each other would end up located close to each other on the graph. Combining HCA and MDS, we created a "semantic map" of the relationship of these words to each other according to how similar

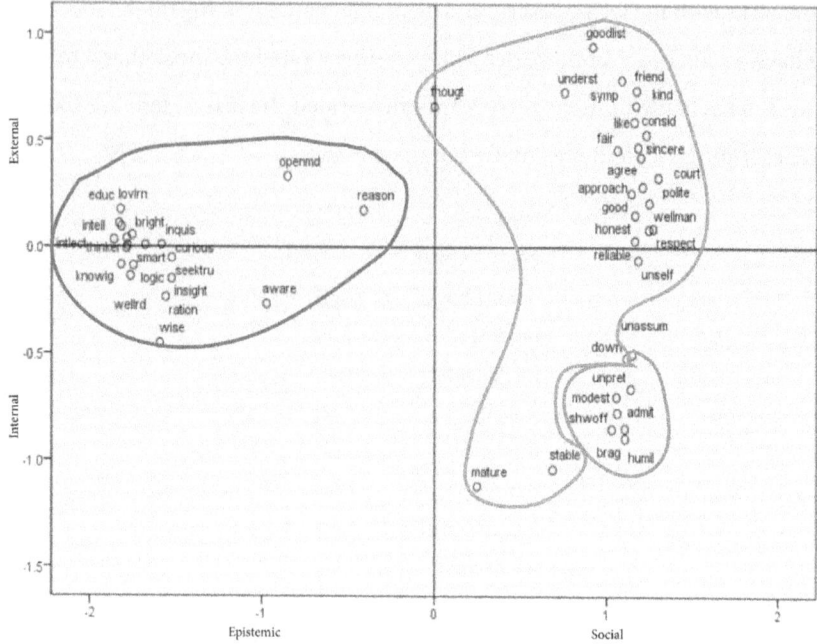

FIGURE 1.1[7] *Semantic Map of an Intellectually Humble Person.*

they were perceived to be. We discovered three distinct clusters of descriptors within the folk idea of an intellectually humble person, which we labeled as follows: Intelligence/Love of Learning (the cluster on the left side of Figure 1.1); Humility/Modest (the small cluster on the lower-right side of Figure 1.1); Respectful/Considerate (the larger cluster on the right side of Figure 1.1).

What this analysis revealed is that the concept of an intellectually humble person, in the folk mind, is a complex combination of epistemic, self-oriented, and other-oriented dimensions. The Intelligence/Love of Learning (epistemic) cluster included descriptors like smart, bright, and intelligent combined with elements such as curiosity, inquisitiveness, and love of learning that described the epistemic dimension of intellectual humility. The Humility/Modest (self-oriented/intrapersonal) cluster contained words and phrases that describe a person's quality of being before others like modest, not-a-showoff, and doesn't brag, while the Respectful/Considerate (other-oriented/interpersonal) cluster had descriptors like polite, honest, reliable, and unselfish, which indicate how a person interacts with others.

A comparison with the concept of a wise person yields some interesting results. The wise person-concept had four distinct dimensions: Intelligent/Learned; Respectful/Listens-to-both-sides; Reflective/Perceptive; Experienced/Rational. As you might be able to tell from the shared words in the titles of the dimensions, the concepts of an intellectually humble person and a wise person shared descriptors along epistemic and interpersonal lines. Thus, a wise person and an intellectually humble person were both described in epistemic terms as bright, intellectual, intelligent, knowledgeable, and smart, and in interpersonal terms as good listeners, honest, mature, respectful, thoughtful, and understanding. However, we see a particular quality in the intellectually humble person-concept that is not found in the wise person-concept that might be described as the desire for knowledge. Descriptors unique to an intellectually humble person such as love of learning, curious, and inquisitive clustered in the epistemic dimension. These words were not found in the epistemic dimension of the wise person. By the same token, there are many external social qualities of an intellectually humble person that have to do with respectful sharing of information that were shared with a wise person (good listener, thoughtful, understanding, etc.), but the unique internal social qualities of the intellectually humble person were more interpersonal, even pro-social in nature (kind, considerate, unselfish, etc.). The humility/modesty dimension was also unique to the idea of an intellectually humble person. Those words did not cluster in the same way in the wise person-concept.

Finally, we found that the dimensions of the concept of the intellectually arrogant person were largely the opposite of those of an intellectually humble person in the folk mind. Thus, three dimensions emerged: Educated/Proud (Epistemic); Opinionated/Jerk (Interpersonal); Arrogant/Know-it-all (Intrapersonal). However, the intellectual humility person-concept is not merely the opposite of the intellectual arrogance person-concept. Proud is closely associated with being educated and is found in the epistemic dimension of the intellectually arrogant person-concept, whereas being educated is associated with love of learning and other epistemic goods (knowledgeable, curious, inquisitive, etc.) in the intellectually humble person-concept.

Intellectual humility in the folk mind has a clear and robust social status dimension that describe a person's stance as knowledgeable before others (which Roberts and Wood [2003, 2007] account for, but Whitecomb et al. [2015] haven't), but it also has a unique epistemic dimension having to do with curiosity and love of learning along with additional social descriptors that indicate a preference for civility. It also has significant correspondence to existing folk constructions of wisdom, while retaining many unique qualities, especially in the epistemic dimension. Finally, in the folk mind, an intellectually arrogant person links pride with intellect, while intellect drives curiosity and love of learning in an intellectually humble person.

§3: The doxastic account of intellectual humility

Whatever worries one might have about the Roberts and Wood (2003, 2007) account of intellectual humility or the limitations-owning account of intellectual humility, they are nevertheless the seminal, focused accounts within the contemporary literature. But, as we argued in §1, both accounts face some serious difficulties. Our goal now is to explore an *alternative* account of intellectual humility—a doxastic account—that might better serve as a starting place for explicating this virtue. This account will put a particularly strong emphasis on the epistemic dimension of intellectual humility pointed to by the folk; whatever social or moral dimensions the virtue of intellectual humility might have (whether identified by the folk or by theorists), we will suggest that it needs to be built upon or understood within the doxastic account.

The alternative account that we want to explore is what we're calling *the doxastic account of intellectual humility* (DA). Again, intellectual humility intuitively seems to be the virtuous mean between intellectual arrogance and intellectual diffidence. The intellectually humble person, as we said before, doesn't overly value her beliefs nor does she undervalue them; instead, she regards her beliefs, their epistemic status, and her intellectual abilities as she ought. Or, as a rough first approximation:

DA: Intellectual humility is the virtue of valuing one's own beliefs as he or she ought.

Now, we might easily think that this *valuing* amounts to how firmly someone holds a given belief, how resilient a given belief is to revision or relinquishment. And to some extent, this makes a lot of sense. After all, it seems right to think that an intellectually arrogant person would be someone who is completely unwilling to change her belief in the face of disagreement, threat, or defeat. Likewise, it seems right to think that an intellectually diffident person would be someone who holds his beliefs loosely and revises or changes them at the proverbial drop of a hat. Intellectual humility, then, would amount to holding beliefs as firmly as you ought.[8]

That said, there are cases that suggest that belief firmness—a belief's resilience to revision or relinquishment—is not a relevant metric for intellectual humility. Consider the following case:

MOTHER: Conner has been charged and convicted of a series of extremely heinous crimes. And there is manifold evidence suggesting that Conner is indeed guilty. There is surveillance footage of Conner committing the crimes. There is Conner's personal journal that explains in detail his criminal plans, motivation, and intent. There are several eyewitnesses to Conner's crimes. Conner even confesses in full. All in all, Conner's trial is an easy, open-and-shut case. Nevertheless, Conner's mother, who loves him dearly, simply cannot bring herself to believe that Conner is guilty. She's seen the surveillance footage, she's read the diary, she's availed herself of all the relevant evidence against her son; indeed, she does not blame the judge, the jury, or the judicial system for convicting him. Nevertheless, her love for her son bars her from believing that her son is guilty of such heinous crimes.

Conner's mother believes that her son is innocent, and this belief is extremely resistant to change or relinquishment. Indeed, there seems to be absolutely nothing that anyone could say or do to convince her that her son is guilty. Conner's mother knows full well that her belief in her son's innocence has no justification or warrant, but, nevertheless, she cannot help but believe it. Is she being intellectually arrogant, then? We don't think so. As MOTHER makes clear, she adequately appreciates the manifold reasons why the jury found her son guilty as charged; but it is the psychological inflexibility caused by her love that simply won't allow her to believe it.

So how one "values his/her beliefs" should not simply be a function of belief firmness. What cases like MOTHER seem to suggest, however, is that the value should actually track something like justification or warrant or, to be entirely nonpartisan, *positive epistemic status*.[9] No doubt, how much positive epistemic status one attributes to their beliefs will often go hand in hand with how firmly they believe it. It seems natural to think that the intellectually arrogant person attributes far more positive epistemic status than she should. Likewise, it seems natural to think that the intellectually diffident person attributes far less positive epistemic status than she should. But what cases like MOTHER show is that attributions of positive epistemic status and belief firmness can and do occasionally come apart; and when they do, it seems like what really matters when it comes to intellectual humility is the former.

But just what do we mean by positive epistemic status? We don't intend to commit ourselves or the doxastic account of intellectual humility on this score.

For now, let's let a thousand flowers blossom. Whether it's safety, sensitivity, evidence, reliability, character virtues, justification, defeasibility, or whatever, if it can give a belief positive epistemic status—or at the very least, positive epistemic status that really matters—then DA should track it. With this in mind, perhaps we can now think of DA in terms of the following:

DA': Intellectual humility is the virtue of attributing positive epistemic status to one's own beliefs as he or she ought.

Imagine two freshwater aquarium hobbyists, Peter and John. Peter has an aquarium with *astronotus ocellatus* (or "oscar" fish) in it. Upon seeing his oscars eat some goldfish and generally bully the other fish in the aquarium, Peter comes to believe very strongly that (or attributing high amount of positive epistemic status to the belief that) oscars are one of the meanest freshwater fish. John also keeps oscars, which are a members of the *cichlid* family of fish; however, after perusing the back-alleys of the internet, reading blogs that suggest that oscars are actually goldfish (which are not cichlids) that have been mutated by the government, John is no longer all that sure that oscars are members of the cichlid family. Given that watching an oscar eat goldfish and bully a few other fish is, at best, very weak evidence for thinking oscars are one of the meanest freshwater fish, then, DA' would predict that Peter is intellectually *arrogant* in holding his belief as strongly as he does. And given that back-alley blogs should not in any way upset establish biological research, DA' would predict that John is being intellectually diffident in holding his belief as weakly as he does. Neither John nor Peter is being intellectually humble; neither one seems to be accurately tracking the positive epistemic status of his belief.

But there are still a couple of problems (at least) facing DA'. First of all, it would be nice if we could say a bit more about the normative component— what determines the positive epistemic status that a given belief *ought* to be attributed with. And relatedly, it's not entirely clear that the *attribution* of positive epistemic status is really what is at issue; it's not clear that *attribution* is really what we *ought* to be concerned about when it comes to intellectual humility. After all, *attributing positive epistemic status to a belief* seems like a highly reflective activity requiring explicit, controlled (System 2) cognitive processing,[10] and it's not obvious that intellectual humility should only be relegated to that domain.

First of all, it seems like the positive epistemic status one *ought* to attribute to their own beliefs is the positive epistemic status such beliefs *actually have*. So, at the very least, perhaps a doxastic account of intellectual humility should be most concerned with whether or not someone is accurately tracking—be it consciously or subconsciously—the positive epistemic status that their beliefs actually enjoy. And, what is more, *accurately tracking* positive epistemic status, perhaps unlike *attributing* positive epistemic status, does not seem to require highly reflective activity; *accurately tracking* positive epistemic status, perhaps unlike *attributing* positive epistemic status, seems like the sort of thing that can be done implicitly and subconsciously.[11] All that said, we can modify our doxastic account of intellectual humility accordingly:

> DA″: Intellectual humility is the virtue of accurately tracking the positive epistemic status of one's own beliefs.

Helpfully, like DA′, DA″ allows us to rightly attribute intellectual arrogance to Peter in his belief about oscar aggression, and it allows us to rightly attribute intellectual diffidence to John in his weak belief about oscars being a part of the cichlid family. And it does all this without being completely normatively underdescribed or inadvertently demanding highly reflective cognition.

That said, we might need to make some sort of caveat with DA″ in order to account for situations where someone has been non-culpably deceived. Consider the following case:

> LIE: Mary has known Martha for many years and has always found her to be extremely trustworthy. One day, Martha is feeling a bit cheeky and decides

to tell Mary a lie. Feigning a panic, Martha runs up to Mary and tells her that Mary's house is on fire. Naturally enough, since Mary has never known Martha to be anything but entirely honest, Mary non-culpably, yet falsely, believes that her house is on fire and takes such a belief to have a lot of positive epistemic status (via Martha's testimony). And as such, Mary heads home in a hurry.

In order for DA″ to rightly handle cases like LIE, we need Mary's strong belief (i.e., belief which is taken to have a lot of positive epistemic status) to not count as intellectual arrogance simply because she was non-culpably deceived. However, someone might worry that—depending on how we cash out *positive epistemic status*, an enterprise we're trying to avoid right now—the fact that Mary's belief is false means that it enjoys far less positive epistemic status than Mary imagines. To avoid such a worry, we'll make a final adjustment to our doxastic account of intellectual humility:

DA‴: Intellectual humility is the virtue of accurately tracking what one could non-culpably take to be the positive epistemic status of one's own beliefs.

And since Mary is non-culpable in believing Martha's testimony, DA‴ helps guarantee that Mary won't be wrongfully ascribed with intellectual arrogance.

According to DA‴, intellectual humility is assessed along two axes: how much positive epistemic status a given belief enjoys, and how much positive epistemic status a given agent *thinks* it enjoys. Consider the following figure:

As such, if a belief enjoys only a very marginal amount of positive epistemic status (perhaps the belief that a thousand angels can dance on the head of a pin), then intellectual humility requires that a given agent track that modest positive epistemic status accordingly. In contrast, if a given belief enjoys a tremendous amount of positive epistemic status (as in the belief that $2 + 2 = 4$), then the intellectually humble agent will value such a belief—tracking its positive

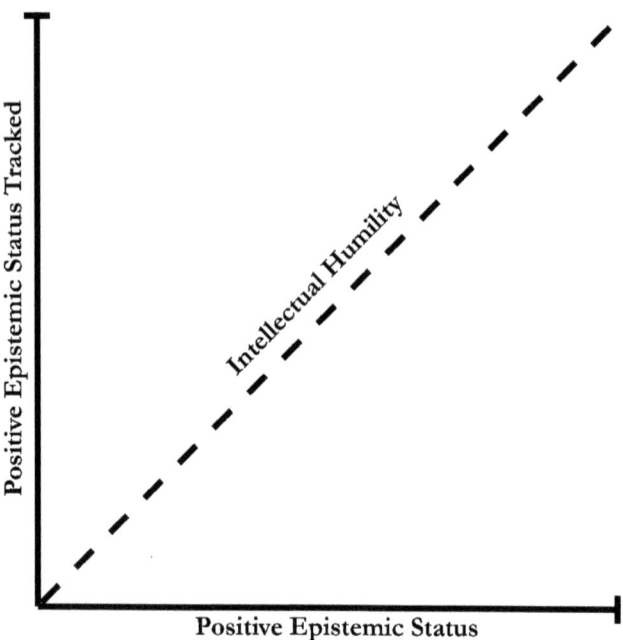

FIGURE 1.2[12] *The Doxastic Account of Intellectual Humility.*

epistemic status—accordingly. Ascribing too much positive epistemic status to a given belief would be vicious (intellectually arrogant, upper left-hand corner of Figure 1.2), as would ascribing too little (intellectual diffidence, lower right-hand corner of Figure 1.2).

Now that we have developed this doxastic account of intellectual humility, DA‴, we can see how it fares against the worries that threatened the seminal Roberts and Wood (2003, 2007) account of intellectual humility and the limitations-owning account of intellectual humility. Since someone can take a belief to have more or less positive epistemic status than it actually has, then intellectual humility, on this account, is a virtuous mean. In BOTANIST, Susan was presumably not virtuous because she is not accurately tracking the substantial positive epistemic status of her belief, valuing her belief far less than she ought. Conversely, Frank, as seen in STRANDED, was presumably not virtuous because he values his beliefs far too much, failing to track the modest positive epistemic status they actually enjoy. And, what is more, DA''' does not afford strange, asymmetric scenarios where someone cannot help but be virtuous and where vice is conceptually impossible. Frank can be either virtuous or vicious on his deserted island. If Frank is sitting alone on his deserted island believing that all of his beliefs about orchids are right and true, a claim that far outstrips what his beliefs' positive epistemic status afford, then he is intellectually arrogant. And finally, unlike the limitations-owning view, DA''' does not afford counterintuitive scenarios where someone can be at once both intellectually arrogant (or intellectually servile) and intellectually humble.

The doxastic account of intellectual humility does not seem to fall victim to the same problems facing other accounts, but that doesn't mean that it doesn't face its own unique problems. In the next section, we'll consider some of these and try to defend the view against them.

§4: Addressing some objections

We suggest (humbly, of course) that this doxastic account is the best way to think about intellectual humility. But while the doxastic account is not vulnerable to the same worries that face the Roberts and Wood (2003, 2007) account or the limitations-owning account (Whitcomb et al., 2015), it does seem to face its own objections or worries. In this section, we try to address three of the major worries someone might have against the doxastic account of intellectual humility, arguing that we need not worry about them.

Worry 1: Is intellectual humility really a virtuous mean? Some philosophers (like Roberts and Wood) might object to the idea that intellectual humility (or humility) is really best conceived of as a virtuous mean.[13] And one reason we might think intellectual humility *isn't* a virtuous mean is because it seems like we'd have to encourage someone who is extremely self-deprecating or intellectually diffident to be *more* humble, and that feels like an odd result. So it might seem as though we have conflicting intuitions here. On the one hand, it seems right (we suggest) to say that someone can be *too* humble. On the other, it might seem odd to encourage someone who is already really down on themselves that they need to be more humble.

We suggest that we can explain away this latter intuition. Consider the virtue of courage. We take it that most people agree that courage is the virtuous mean between cowardice and foolhardiness. But even so, like humility and intellectual humility, it might feel odd to encourage someone who is recklessly foolhardy to be more courageous. Why is this? First of all, this might feel odd because, more often than not, people are cowardly. (After all, if someone were to confess that they lack courage, we imagine almost everyone would assume that they are cowardly.) So if we are accustomed to telling people to "take courage" when they are being cowardly, telling someone who is foolhardy to "take courage" might seem odd. And secondly, we might often assume that whatever property makes someone courageous is in overabundance in someone who is foolhardy, so telling a foolhardy person they need to be more courageous might sound like we are encouraging them to have more of the property they already have too much of. That said, just because it might seem odd to encourage a foolhardy person to be more courageous, that doesn't mean that courage isn't actually best conceived of as a virtuous mean between foolhardiness and cowardice.

The same thing can be said about intellectual humility and humility. While it might very well seem odd that we might encourage someone who is extremely self-deprecating to be more humble, this does not mean that humility isn't really best conceived as a virtuous mean. Like courage, this might feel odd because, more often than not, people are arrogant. (After all, if someone were to confess that they lack humility, we imagine almost everyone would assume that they are arrogant.) So if we are accustomed to telling people to "humble thyself" when they are being arrogant, telling someone who is self-deprecating or diffident to "humble thyself" might very well seem odd. And secondly, also like courage, we might easily assume that whatever property makes someone humble is in overabundance in someone who is self-deprecating or overly diffident. As such, telling a self-deprecating person that they need to be more humble might sound like we are encouraging them to have more of a property they already have too much of. So it might seem odd to encourage someone who is self-deprecating to be more humble, but we think we can see why this might be the case: such oddness does not seem to legitimately undermine the intuition that intellectual humility is best conceived of as a virtuous mean. This oddness, we propose, can be explained away.

Worry 2: Are we really talking about intellectual humility? People can disagree about nearly anything. So if someone finds something to criticize in our work, we tend not to worry (unless, of course, it just seems like a crushing objection.) However, when we find that people are systematically, across contexts and audiences, clustering around the same criticism, then we really start to worry. And there is such a criticism facing the doxastic account—a worry that people do indeed seem to cluster around—and we are truly concerned. Here's the worry: *Are we really talking about intellectual humility?*

When we've tried to cash out our account of intellectual humility, people like Jason Baehr (2015), Bob Roberts (2012), and Jay Wood (2012) all seem to have the same sort of worry (though there are important differences). All of them have suggested that perhaps we are not really talking about intellectual humility at all—that perhaps we are talking about another virtue and just calling it intellectual humility. Some have worried that perhaps our account highlights a feature of intellectual virtues in general and that we are not picking out intellectual humility in particular. Or if we are picking out something specific, perhaps we're really just talking about intellectual *honesty* and not intellectual humility. Similarly, in a Big Questions Online discussion, Jay Wood (2012) suggested that something close to our proposed account is actually honing in on a virtue like intellectual *accuracy* or intellectual *firmness*, but not intellectual humility.

So, does this mean we should consider giving up on our account of intellectual humility as an *actual* account of intellectual humility? We don't think so, not yet anyway. The philosophy of intellectual humility is currently something like a wild frontier. As Bob Roberts (2012) noted in his discussion summary for the Big Questions Online piece, "What is it to be Intellectually Humble?": "One of the most striking things to emerge from our discussion of intellectual humility is the lack of consensus on what 'humility' and 'intellectual humility' mean." As the conversation develops, it has become manifestly clear that there is no shared or even entirely dominant view of intellectual humility in the literature; the Roberts and Wood (2003, 2007) view is different from Whitcomb et al.'s (2015) view, which is different from our view, etc. So it seems like the state of play right now is to try to stake a claim and defend it as best you can! And that's what we're doing.[14]

Of course, if there was consensus regarding what we're confusing intellectual humility *with*, then perhaps we should still back off from our account. For example, if it was manifestly clear to everyone but us that we were really talking about open-mindedness and not intellectual humility, then (even if there was no consensus regarding what intellectual humility actually is) we might yet worry that we've got something wrong. But, as we've already noted, that's not our situation. There is no consensus regarding what we might be confusing intellectual humility with.

Worry 3: What about the folk conception of intellectual humility? As we saw in §2, there were some noticeable disconnects between the Roberts and Wood (2003, 2007) account of intellectual humility, the limitations-owning account of intellectual humility (Whitcomb et al., 2015), and intellectual humility as it is collectively understood by the folk. For example, to the folk conception, intellectual humility has a distinct and significant social dimension—a dimension that seems underdeveloped in the limitations-owning account. And according to the folk conception, intellectual humility does not seem to merely be the opposite of intellectual arrogance, which seems to directly conflict with the Roberts and Wood (2003, 2007) account. If we take folk conceptions to be authoritative, then these accounts of intellectual humility seem to face a new worry: that they are not in keeping with the folk understanding of intellectual humility.

And if all this is right, then it seems like a similar worry faces the doxastic account of intellectual humility. While the doxastic account does not view intellectual humility as the mere opposite of intellectual arrogance (in keeping with the folk), interpersonal and intrapersonal dimensions of intellectual humility seem entirely underdeveloped. In focusing so much on the *epistemic* dimension of intellectual humility, we might worry that we have neglected the interpersonal and intrapersonal dimensions that seem so central to the folk conception of intellectual humility. So again, if we take folk conceptions to be authoritative, then the doxastic account would also seem to be in trouble.

Thankfully, however, I don't think we need folk conceptions to be authoritative. After all, contrasted with experts, the folk understanding of concepts often seems misguided, wrong, or ill-informed. So, just as we wouldn't expect the folk understanding of gravity to upset the established understanding of gravity within the professional scientific literature, perhaps we shouldn't expect the folk understanding of intellectual humility to upset the theoretically robust conceptions of intellectual humility developed by professional philosophers and psychologists. While an appreciation of the folk understanding of intellectual humility is a good starting place for understanding such a virtue, it is in no way obvious that the folk understanding of intellectual humility is especially authoritative—certainly not to the point to where it could undermine divergent theories.

But it is worth noting that even if we *did* take the folk conception of intellectual humility to be authoritative, it's not obvious that the doxastic account of intellectual humility couldn't incorporate interpersonal or intrapersonal elements within it. While research on the folk understanding of intellectual humility might suggest that intellectual humility is a multifaceted and multilayered virtue—with moral dimensions, interpersonal dimensions, intrapersonal dimensions, etc.—we would like to suggest that such facets can be built upon or understood within the doxastic account. After all, our account of positive epistemic status is extremely open-ended. If intellectual character virtues are included as at least a part of the positive epistemic status (which we think they should be), and if interpersonal and intrapersonal considerations are built within such virtues (which they often are), then there is a straightforward way for the doxastic account of intellectual humility to account for such dimensions.

Intellectual humility has become an increasingly important and vibrant area of philosophical and scientific research. As such, understanding what intellectual humility is has become increasingly important. Thus far, we have suggested that intellectual humility is the virtue of accurately tracking what one could non-culpably take to be the positive epistemic status of one's own beliefs. We argued that the seminal accounts of intellectual humility in the literature—the Roberts and Wood (2003, 2007) account and the limitations-owning account (Whitcomb et al., 2015)—face some serious worries, and we (humbly) suggest that perhaps the doxastic account might serve as a better starting place for understanding this virtue.

§5: Book outline

While we think that the doxastic account of intellectual humility might serve as the best starting point for thinking about this virtue, we certainly understand that this isn't the final word in this debate. Plenty of smart, knowledgeable people have and *do* disagree with our assessment of intellectual humility. And we have no doubt that the alternative accounts of intellectual humility that we criticized could be cogently defended, and that powerful objections to our view are still lurking around the corner. Nevertheless, the doxastic account of intellectual humility is the view that we find to be the most viable and intuitive, so that's the view that we're going to give special (though certainly not exclusive) attention.

Thankfully, the rest of the book does not hang on whether or not the doxastic account of intellectual humility is ultimately correct. While we will frequently refer back to the doxastic account—that is, after all, our preferred view—the majority of what we want to say about, for example, intellectual humility and testimony or intellectual humility and human cognition can be said regardless of the specific account of intellectual humility we're espousing. Perhaps, then, this is a bit of a strange book. There isn't a grand thesis that we are ultimately arguing for. Each chapter aims to address a big question regarding intellectual humility, but each chapter explores its own terrain. As such, this book isn't a "building" project as much as it is an "exploratory" project. Chapters are not meant to build upon the foundation laid in previous chapters; instead, each chapter is aimed at exploring another piece of the terrain, another big question regarding intellectual humility.[15]

This book is composed of ten chapters. The first two chapters, including this one, focus on the theoretical undergirding of intellectual humility. The big questions they respectively focus (or in the case of this chapter, *have* focused) on are:

1 What is intellectual humility? And why should we care?

2 What is an intellectual virtue?

The next five chapters will focus on the science of intellectual humility. *And it's worth noting that the goal of these chapters isn't to argue for a specific view, but to primarily survey the growing body of literature. Where Chapter 1 and Chapter 2, for example, are more philosophical—where we might be arguing for various theses—the chapters on the science of intellectual humility are primarily aimed at reporting, through a review of the relevant literature, what scientific research is discovering.* The big questions they will respectively focus on are as follows:

1 How do we know who is intellectually humble?

2 How do we become intellectually humble?

3 What can human cognition tell us about intellectual humility?

4 Are some people born humble?

5 How do emotions affect our ability to be intellectually humble?

And the last three chapters will focus on applied issues surrounding intellectual humility. *These chapters are, again, philosophical. While we will certainly try to draw from the growing body of relevant philosophical and theological literature, our primary aim in these closing chapters is to argue for a specific view or theses.* The big questions to be considered are:

1 Can you believe what you hear?

2 How should we handle disagreement?

3 What does intellectual humility tell us about religion?

Before diving in, let's briefly outline each of the forthcoming chapters, so as to have a better sense of what we should expect.

(The rest of) Part 1: The theory

- **Chapter 2: What is an intellectual virtue?** While the nature of intellectual virtues is a topic of ancient interest, contemporary philosophy has experienced unparalleled energy and concern for the topic over the last thirty years. This chapter will introduce this expansive body of literature and highlight some of the implications for our theoretical understanding of intellectual humility.

Part 2: The science

- **Chapter 3: How do we know who is intellectually humble?** Before we can encourage or facilitate personal growth in intellectual humility, we need to know how such a virtue can be identified and measured in people. This chapter addresses these issues and the potential hurdles to a scientifically valid measure of intellectual humility.

- **Chapter 4: How do we become intellectually humble?** If we have a sense of what intellectual humility is and how it can be measured, what steps can we take to encourage intellectual humility in others and ourselves? This chapter introduces recent research in social and developmental psychology and how they address these issues.

- **Chapter 5: What can human cognition tell us about intellectual humility?** A major hurdle for intellectual humility may be our own cognition. Recent research in cognitive science has shown that humans are woefully prone to a litany of cognitive heuristics and biases. This chapter introduces that literature and considers how heuristics and biases might be overcome and shape our ability to be intellectually humble.

- **Chapter 6: Are some people born humble?** There are certain cognitive dispositions and personality traits that might give some people an edge at being more intellectually humble than others. This chapter will detail some of these traits and dispositions and explore whether these are stable from birth, learned habits, or available to everyone but enhanced in certain situations.

- **Chapter 7: How do emotions affect our ability to be intellectually humble?** The Platonic vision of the passions being subjected to the authority of reason is difficult to sustain in light of contemporary, psychological research on the emotions. This chapter highlights that research and the constraints emotion places on intellectual humility.

Part 3: The application

- **Chapter 8: Can you believe what you hear?** We rely on testimony. Whether it's a friend, a witness to a crime, or an expert in a given field, we depend on what other people tell us. But sometimes people lie or mislead. Sometimes being open-minded—perhaps with a politician, a salesperson, etc.—is tantamount to the intellectual vice of gullibility. In this chapter, we will explore some of the philosophical difficulties surrounding testimony, and their implications for intellectual humility.

- **Chapter 9: How should we handle disagreement?** People can disagree on just about any subject. And disagreement among peers— interlocutors who are equally familiar with the relevant data and just as intelligent, clever, rational, etc.—can be found in almost every realm of inquiry. This chapter will highlight the problems posed by disagreement and explore the practical import of intellectual humility.

- **Chapter 10: What does intellectual humility tell us about religion?** As the world grows increasingly interconnected, the problems posed by religious pluralism are becoming increasingly urgent. This chapter will explore these issues and whether or not a commitment to intellectual humility precludes religious fidelity or certain theological commitments.

In sum, once we agree that we need intellectual humility, that it's a topic worth our consideration, a host of questions present themselves to us. First of all, what is intellectual humility? And why should we care? These are questions we've considered in this chapter. But beyond this, we will want to know whether or not intellectual humility is an intellectual virtue (Chapter 2). We'll also want to know how we can tell when someone's humble (Chapter 3), and how we might become more humble ourselves (Chapter 4). Of course, given our proclivity to heuristics and biases, we might wonder whether intellectual humility is something human beings are truly capable of (Chapter 5). We'll wonder whether some people are more inclined toward intellectual humility (or intellectual arrogance) from birth (Chapter 6), and we will wonder what role our emotions and our ability to regulate them might play in all of this (Chapter 7). And once we have an understanding of the theory and science behind intellectual humility, we will want to know more about how we might apply intellectual humility in our lives. How does intellectual humility affect when and why we listen to the testimony of some people but not that of others (Chapter 8)? How can we be intellectually humble in the face of peer disagreement (Chapter 9)? And does intellectual humility preclude firm religious commitments (Chapter 10)? We've got our work cut out for us, so we better get started.

2

What is an intellectual virtue?

In the previous chapter, we suggested that intellectual humility is a critically important subject with tremendous significance in the real world. And we proposed a plausible account of what intellectual humility might be—the doxastic account of intellectual humility. And in all of this we assumed, naturally enough, that intellectual humility is an *intellectual virtue*. But what is an intellectual virtue anyway? In this chapter we are going to turn to some of the seminal work in *virtue epistemology* to help us answer this question.[1]

Virtue epistemology, as philosophers like Jason Baehr (2015) define it, "is a collection of recent approaches to epistemology that give epistemic or intellectual virtue concepts an important and fundamental role" (para. 1). This chapter will be broken down into five sections. In §1, we will briefly sketch the contours of virtue epistemology *in general*. In §2, §3, and §4, we will consider some specific virtue epistemologies in greater detail. And finally, in §5, we will return to intellectual humility and consider whether it really is an intellectual virtue and how it might fit within virtue epistemology's accounts of intellectual virtues.

§1: Virtue epistemology in general

One of the most promising ways to understand intellectual virtues is by exploring recent work in virtue epistemology and virtue-theoretic accounts of knowledge. Distinctively, virtue epistemology places intellectual virtue at the heart of knowledge. In this section, we will first note the defining characteristics of virtue epistemology, and then briefly elucidate the two dominant account of intellectual virtue found within the relevant literature.[2]

Over the last thirty years, virtue epistemology has developed into a multitude of positions; nevertheless, every variant of virtue epistemology holds to two basic resolutions: (1) that epistemology is a normative discipline and (2) that "intellectual agents and communities are the primary source of epistemic value and the primary focus of epistemic evaluation" (Greco and Turri, 2011, para. 1). The former amounts to (a) a rejection of Quine's (1969) proposal in "Epistemology Naturalized" that epistemologists should give up on attempts to discern what is reasonable to believe in favor of projects within cognitive psychology, and (b) a call for epistemologists to "focus their efforts on understanding epistemic norms, value and evaluation" (Greco and Turri, 2011, §1; see also Quine, 1969; McDowell, 1994, p. 133; Sosa, 1991, pp. 100–05; Zagzebski, 1996, pp. 334–38). To better understand the second resolution, think of virtue *ethics'* niche within moral philosophy. For the two titans of moral philosophy, Kantian deontology and utilitarianism, the starting place for moral evaluation is *action*. For Kantians and utilitarians, the question to ask when doing ethics is "What should I do?" (Kantians answer: "Act in accord with what you can will to be a universal maxim"; utilitarians answer: "Act in accord with what brings about the greatest happiness for the greatest number.") For virtue ethicists, however, the starting place for moral evaluation, where the rubber meets the road, so to speak, is the *agent*—his or her character—and, consequently, the virtue ethicist asks a different question: "How should I live?"[3] To put it roughly, instead of focusing on the beliefs of agents (whether or not they are justified, rational, etc.), virtue epistemologists predominantly focus on the agent himself or herself: whether he or she has the right sort of epistemic character, the right sort of cognitive faculties, and whether he or she is epistemically virtuous or not. To be sure, other theories of knowledge will give some account of epistemic virtues, norms, and values—good memory, intellectual courage, etc.—but usually ancillary to other epistemic terms or concepts. The radical claim that virtue-theoretic accounts of knowledge make, however, is that epistemic virtues, norms, and values should be the primary focus of epistemology (see Pritchard, 2005, p. 186; Greco, 2010, pp. 17–46).

So defined, virtue epistemology has developed by and large into two distinct schools: agent-reliabilism and responsibilism (or, neo-Aristotelianism). The primary difference between the schools is their application of "virtue" terminology. Agent-reliabilism, being modeled along reliabilist lines, applies virtue terminology in regard to faculties in the same way we might talk about a virtuous knife. In other words, just as we might call a knife virtuous if it does what it is supposed to do (cut things, be sharp, etc.), agent-reliabilism calls various cognitive faculties such as memory, perception, etc., virtuous insofar as they are reliably functioning the way they are supposed to. That is, agent-reliabilism focuses on the reliable functioning (virtuous functioning) of a given agent's cognitive faculties. Neo-Aristotelianism or responsibilism, on the other hand, applies virtue terminology in a way that is perhaps more familiar: in terms of specific character traits such as open-mindedness, intellectual courage, intellectual perseverance, etc.

Agent-reliabilism virtue epistemologies developed out of a dissatisfaction with what is called process-reliabilism: the view that, to put it roughly, S knows a true proposition p if and only if p was formed by a reliable process. There are some serious concerns for such a view (e.g., the "generality problem");[4] however, the agent-reliabilists' primary concern was that knowledge ascriptions based on reliable processes do not always appropriately involve a given agent—that process-reliabilism seems to allow agents to "possess knowledge even though the reliability in question in no way reflects a cognitive achievement on their part" (Pritchard, 2005, p. 187). One way this occurs is when a given reliable process does not appropriately relate to facts. For example, consider the following case by John Greco (1999):

RENÉ AND THE GAMBLER'S FALLACY: René thinks he can beat the roulette tables with a system he has devised. Reasoning according to the Gambler's Fallacy, he believes that numbers which have not come up for long strings are more likely to come up next. However, unlike Descartes' demon victim, our René has a demon helper. Acting as a kind of epistemic guardian, the demon arranges reality so as to make the belief come out as true. Given the ever-present interventions of the helpful demon, René's belief-forming process is highly reliable. But this is because the world is made to conform to René's beliefs, rather than because René's beliefs conform to the world. (p. 286; also quoted in Pritchard, 2005, p. 187)

Though René's beliefs happen to be based on a reliable process—reasoning according to the Gambler's Fallacy with the aid of a helper demon—it is completely accidental. Intuitively, he does not have knowledge.[5]

Another way that knowledge ascriptions based on reliable processes do not always appropriately involve a given agent is in the case of reliable cognitive malfunctions. Consider a case originally developed by Alvin Plantinga (1993a) in which our protagonist has a brain lesion that causes him to believe he has a brain lesion:

BRAIN LESION: Suppose . . . that S suffers from this sort of disorder and accordingly believes that he suffers from a brain lesion. Add that he has no evidence at all for this belief: no symptoms of which he is aware, no testimony on the part of physicians or other expert witnesses, nothing.

(Add, if you like, that he has much evidence against it, but then add also that the malfunction induced by the lesion makes it impossible for him to take appropriate account of this evidence.) Then the relevant [process] will certainly be reliable but the resulting belief—that he has a brain lesion—will have little by way of warrant for S. (p. 199; also quoted in Pritchard, 2005, p. 188)

Again, though S's belief that he has a brain lesion is formed via a reliable process, we would not ascribe knowledge to it since it is only formed out of a glitch in S's cognitive equipment. It is simply accidental that the brain lesion causes S to form the said belief, and as such, S had nothing to do with its formation. Though there may be some worries as to what constitutes a given person's cognitive equipment (Why is S's brain lesion not a part of his cognitive equipment? What if he had the lesion since birth?), we nevertheless have strong intuitions that beliefs formed as a direct result of a cognitive malfunction cannot be knowledge (see Pritchard, 2005, p. 188; Greco, 2003, pp. 356–57). S's belief that he has a brain lesion cannot be knowledge simply because, though formed via reliable process, the agent (S) was not appropriately involved in its formation.

Neo-Aristotelianism virtue epistemologies, in contrast, are not modeled after reliabilism. Instead of focusing on whether or not a given agent's epistemic faculties are functioning properly and reliably, neo-Aristotelian virtue epistemologists tend to focus more on the agent's epistemic character and epistemic responsibilities. Consider the following case:

CHICKEN SEXER: Naïve and Reflective are both chicken sexers. Their job is to look at baby chickens, determine their genders, and then segregate the chickens accordingly, putting male chicks in one box and female chicks in another. Both Naïve and Reflective are equally good at their job; both are highly reliable at determining the gender of the baby chickens. There is, however, one important difference between them: Naïve has no idea how he is able to correctly determine the gender of the chicks—he "just does it." Reflective, on the other hand, is very much aware of how he makes such a judgment—by looking for a certain pattern in the chick's feathers. Does Naïve's ignorance affect his ability to know "that's a male chick," "that's a female chick," etc.?

Whereas agent-reliabilism virtue epistemologists would generally deny that Naïve's ignorance affects his ability to know (after all, his cognitive equipment is highly reliable), neo-Aristotelianism virtue epistemologists would cry foul (or fowl). In focusing on epistemic character traits instead of epistemic faculties, neo-Aristotelianism tends to "stress that agents should not only exhibit reliable cognitive traits but that they should also be in a position to take . . . reflective responsibility for their true beliefs" (Pritchard, 2005, pp. 194–95). Naïve may very well have reliable cognitive faculties but, for the neo-Aristotelianism virtue epistemologist, that is not enough; in order to be properly said to *know* the sex of the chicks, Naïve needs to exhibit more conscientiousness and take more epistemic responsibility.

This focus on epistemic responsibility ties into another common hallmark of neo-Aristotelianism, namely, a closer correspondence between epistemology and moral philosophy. As we noted earlier, the primary objects of interest for the neo-Aristotelian virtue epistemologist are not cognitive faculties (as it was with the agent-reliabilist) but, rather, intellectual character traits (intellectual courageousness, open-mindedness, etc.), whether or not a given agent is of the right sort of epistemic character. And being of the right sort of epistemic character often means (at the very least) not only reliably reaching virtuous ends/*teloi* but also being virtuously motivated. In other words, in order to be of the right sort of epistemic character, not only do you need to regularly hit upon the truth, you also need to hit upon the truth for the right reasons (e.g., because you were intellectually courageous as opposed to simply lucky). Not only is neo-Aristotelianism interested in your veritic reliability, it is also interested in what sort of person—what sort of epistemic character—you should be. And all of this gives epistemology a distinctive moral dimension. Indeed, some neo-Aristotelian virtue epistemologists (e.g., Linda Zagzebski) have even gone so far as to elucidate epistemic virtues as a subset of moral virtues.[6]

While it may seem as though the subject of intellectual humility might be best explicated in terms of neo-Aristotelianism virtue epistemology's character traits, there is no obvious reason why our concepts of intellectual humility cannot also be explicated in terms of agent-reliabilism virtue epistemology.[7] Presumably, any robust, full account of intellectual virtue will have to account for both cognitive faculty virtues as well as character trait virtues; whether one does this along the lines of agent-reliabilism or neo-Aristotelianism could be, to some extent, a matter of emphasis.

Over the last thirty years, virtue-theoretic accounts of knowledge have produced a flourishing and increasingly popular body of literature with excellent resources for cultivating a robust conceptual understanding of intellectual virtues in general and intellectual humility in particular. So, now that we've sketched two, dominant approaches to explicating intellectual virtues, agent-reliabilism and agent-responsibilism, we're in a better position to reflect on whether and how intellectual humility might be conceived of as an intellectual virtue. Straightforwardly, anyone interested in explicating intellectual humility as a *character* virtue could easily, it seems, explicate intellectual humility as an intellectual virtue. And while it isn't easy to imagine how intellectual humility could be viewed as a *faculty* virtue (the focus of agent-reliabilism), that doesn't mean it isn't a *character* virtue that agent-reliabilists might be extremely interested in. After all, whether or not someone can accurately track the positive epistemic status of their beliefs—drawing from the doxastic account of intellectual humility—might be a meta-virtue acquired by a wide range of cognitive faculties (from vision to self-reflection) functioning properly. Before saying more, however, let's look at some examples of specific virtue epistemologies in greater detail.

§2: Ernest Sosa's agent-reliabilism

Ernest Sosa's seminal work in *A Virtue Epistemology* (2007) and *Reflective Knowledge* (2009) provides a touchstone from which most contemporary agent-reliabilist virtue epistemologies have been developed and should be understood.[8] Sosa uses the example of an archer to help us understand his theory of knowledge. In assessing an archer's shot, we will be interested in three things: (1) its accuracy—whether or not the shot hits its target; (2) its adroitness—whether or not it manifests the competence of the archer; (3) its aptness—whether or not the shot's accuracy is a result of its adroitness. Then he asks: When is the accuracy of the archer's shot attributable to him? Naturally, if the accuracy of the shot had nothing to do with the archer's competence such that it was not adroit, we would not credit the shot to him; we would not, for example, credit the accuracy of a difficult shot to an inept archer who just happened to clumsily fire the arrow in the right direction. What is more, if a given shot were accurate and adroit though not apt (i.e., not accurate *because* adroit), we would not credit it to the archer either. Imagine a scenario where an expert archer takes a shot at a relatively easy target, a shot that in normal circumstances would have hit the target without difficulty. Then, imagine that while the arrow is still in the air, it is blown off target by a sudden burst of strong wind such that it is then on an inaccurate trajectory and only luckily blown back on target by another sudden burst of strong wind in the opposite direction. While the shot indeed hits the target and seemingly manifests the archer's competence (after all, in normal circumstances, it easily hits the target), it is not accurate *because of* the archer's competence—it was accurate because of the second burst of wind. As such, we would not credit such a shot to the archer. An archer's shot, then, *is* creditable to him if and only if it is accurate as a result of its being adroit. In other words, an archer's shot is creditable to him if and only if it is apt.

Beliefs, like an archer's shots, can also be evaluated according to accuracy (i.e., truth), adroitness (whether or not it manifests the agent's epistemic competence), and aptness (whether or not the belief is true as a result of its adroitness). A given true belief is knowledge, according to Sosa, if and only if it hits upon the truth (so to speak) as a result of the given agent's epistemic competence. In other words, knowledge, for Sosa (2007), is apt belief—belief that is "true *because* competent" (p. 23). Parallel to the archery example, if the accuracy of a given belief had nothing to do with the agent's cognitive competence such that it was not adroit, we obviously would not credit the belief to him as knowledge. If, for example, someone (let's call him Frank) suddenly and without reason started believing that the pope is his fourth cousin, we would not credit Frank with knowledge even if by some chance it turned out to be true. What is more, if a given belief were accurate and adroit though not apt (i.e., not accurate *because* adroit), we would not credit the pertinent agent with knowledge either. Imagine a Gettier-style scenario where Frank does a detailed investigation into his family history and comes to the calculated belief that the pope is his fourth cousin. Then, imagine that while, as a result of some bad luck, his familial calculations were fundamentally misguided (e.g., unbeknownst to him, he was adopted), his belief is, nevertheless, true for reasons his calculations would never have predicted. While his belief in such a case is true and adroit, the truth has nothing to do with the adroitness—it is not apt—and, therefore, we would not credit Frank's belief to him as knowledge.[9]

According to Sosa, S knows that *p* if and only if (i) S believes that *p* and (ii) that belief is apt, that is, true *because of* S's cognitive competency.[10] With this initial analysis in mind, Sosa distinguishes two tiers of knowledge. The first tier of knowledge is what Sosa (2007) calls "animal knowledge" and it consists simply of apt belief: a given agent possesses animal knowledge if and only if he possesses an apt belief. The second tier of knowledge, what Sosa calls "reflective knowledge," on the other hand, is more demanding. It is, according to Sosa (2007), not only apt belief but "defensibly apt belief," which is a second-order apt belief that a given belief is apt (pp. 24, 32). I may have apt belief that "that's a zebra," say, and therefore have animal knowledge. To have reflective knowledge, on the other hand, I need to believe aptly that my belief that "that's a zebra" is apt—I might be an expert zoologist who was able to inspect the zebra closely, for example.

Sosa's (2007) distinction between animal knowledge and reflective knowledge can be quite handy. Recall the CHICKEN SEXER case. Its notoriety comes from its divisiveness. Some philosophers (externalists about warrant) are typically inclined to say that Naïve's ignorance is no hurdle for knowledge. Others (internalists about warrant), on the other hand, are likely to balk at such a suggestion because Naïve seemingly does not have the right sort of reflective access to what is grounding the pertinent belief. One way to characterize this differing of opinion is through what look like conflicting intuitions. On the one hand, Naïve obviously seems to be doing something right—he is, after all, a highly reliable judge. On the other, surely Reflective's epistemic state is preferable to Naïve's—surely they are not on equal epistemic footing. One of the nice things about Sosa's analysis is that it can account for both of these intuitions. Naïve, it seems, has apt beliefs about the sex of chicks and as such has animal knowledge; Reflective, in contrast, seems to be aptly aware of his apt beliefs concerning the sex of the chicks and as such he enjoys the more exalted reflective knowledge. In this way, Sosa's epistemology, with its distinction between animal and reflective knowledge, seems to be able to satisfy some basic internalist intuitions while, nevertheless, remaining decidedly externalist—it recognizes Naïve's competence while at the same time appreciating the superiority of Reflective's epistemic state.

Despite such merits, Sosa's analysis of knowledge as apt belief seems to run into some immediate problems. Consider the following case:

FAKE BARNS: Henry is driving in the country with his son. For the boy's edification Henry identifies various objects on the landscape as they come into view. "That's a cow," says Henry, "That's a tractor," "That's a silo," "That's a barn," etc. Henry has no doubt about the identity of these objects; in particular, he has no doubt that the last-mentioned object is a barn, which indeed it is. Each of the identified objects has features characteristic of its type. Moreover, each object is fully in view, Henry has excellent eyesight, and he has enough time to look at them reasonably carefully, since there is little traffic to distract him. . . . Suppose we are told that, unknown to Henry, the district he has just entered is full of papier-mâché facsimiles of barns. These facsimiles look from the road exactly like barns, but are really just façades, without back walls or interiors, quite incapable of being used as barns. They are so cleverly constructed that travelers invariably mistake them for barns. Having just entered this district, Henry has not encountered any facsimiles; the object he sees is a genuine barn. But if the barn on that site were a facsimile, Henry would mistake it for a barn. (Goldman, 1976, pp. 772–73; also see Zagzebski, 1994, p. 66)

It is extremely lucky that Henry's belief is true; had he been looking at nearly any other barn in the area, his belief "that's a barn" would have been false. And traditionally, most epistemologists think this luckiness undermines knowledge. But if apt belief is sufficient for knowledge, then it seems like Sosa's virtue epistemology predicts that Henry knows in FAKE BARNS—a seemingly counterintuitive conclusion. If all it takes for a given belief to be knowledge is aptness, then it seemingly will not matter how lucky that aptness may be. Imagine an archer who is unknowingly in an absolutely terrible environment for archery—an environment that has been plagued by wild and irregular winds for thousands of years. If, as he takes his shot, a quasi-miracle occurs and the winds cease and his arrow is able to fly true and hit the target, the shot is, according to Sosa, creditable to the archer—after all, it seemingly hit the target as a result of the archer's competence. And if the archer's shot hit its target because of the archer's competence (i.e., if the shot was apt), the shot is creditable to him no matter how incredibly lucky it may be that the winds died down when they did. Likewise, when a given credulous subject happens to believe "that's a barn" correctly even amid a sea of barn facades, he possesses knowledge. If his belief is true as a result of his epistemic competence, he has knowledge no matter how incredibly lucky it may be that he picked a real barn. Sosa (2007) has us consider the following case, which bears obvious similarities to FAKE BARN-type scenarios just referenced:

> KALEIDOSCOPE: You see a surface that looks red in ostensibly normal conditions. But it is a kaleidoscope surface controlled by a jokester who also controls the ambient light, and might as easily have presented you with a red-light+white-surface combination as with the actual white-light+red-surface combination. (p. 31)

According to Sosa, when presented with the white-light + red-surface combination, the protagonist of KALEIDOSCOPE knows that the surface is red. In other words, so long as the protagonist's belief is true as a result of his epistemic competence, he possesses knowledge no matter how incredibly lucky it may be that the jokester was not at that moment presenting him with a red-light + white-object combination. Environmental luck of that sort does not, according to Sosa, block knowledge.

Given the broad consensus that the protagonist in cases like KALEIDOSCOPE (including cases like Fake Barns) lacks knowledge—that his belief is at the very least somehow epistemically deficient—is not such a conclusion problematic? According to Sosa (2007), not if we make use of the *animal knowledge/reflective knowledge* distinction. By Sosa's lights, the protagonists in such cases do, indeed, have first-order (or first-tier) knowledge, animal knowledge, but that is not to say that their epistemic state is not somehow deficient. They may very well have apt beliefs, but surely they lack defensible apt beliefs—in other words, surely they lack higher order reflective knowledge. According to Sosa, when the protagonists in such cases rightly identify barns or the color of surfaces using their epistemic competencies, they should be credited for doing as much even if they could have very easily got it wrong. Indeed, where most accounts will simply say that something is epistemically *wrong* in cases like KALEIDOSCOPE, perhaps it is a virtue of Sosa's account that it can also tell us what is epistemically *right*.

But why does the perceiver in the KALEIDOSCOPE case fail to have reflective knowledge? If he has animal knowledge, why should he not also have reflective knowledge? Consider Sosa's (2007) own explanation:

> The [KALEIDOSCOPE] perceiver would there be said to have apt belief and animal knowledge that the seen surface is red. What he lacks . . . is *reflective* knowledge, since this requires apt belief that he aptly believes the surface to be red (or at least it requires that he aptly take this for granted or assume it or presuppose it, a qualification implicit in what follows). Why should it be any less plausible to think that he aptly believes that he aptly believes than to think that he aptly believes *simpliciter*? Well, what competence might he exercise in believing that he aptly so believes, and how plausible might it be to attribute to that competence his being right in believing that he aptly believes? . . . It seems a kind of default competence, whereby one automatically takes the light to be normal absent some special indication to the contrary. And that is presumably what the kaleidoscope perceiver does, absent any indication of a jokester in control. So we may suppose him to retain that competence unimpaired *and* to exercise it in taking for granted the adequacy of the ambient light, so that he can aptly take the surface to be red. Since the belief that he believes aptly is a true belief, and since it is *owed* to the exercise of a competence, how then can we suppose it not to be itself an apt belief? Well, recall: the requirement for aptly believing is not just that one's belief is true, and derived from a competence. The requirement is rather that one believes *correctly* (with

truth) through the exercise of a competence in its proper conditions. What must be attributed to the competence is not just the belief's existence but its correctness. (pp. 32–33)

While the protagonist in KALEIDOSCOPE arguably has animal knowledge, he lacks reflective knowledge because the epistemic competence (that "default competence") by which he might believe his belief that the surface is red to be apt is not itself apt. Why? Because while his belief that the surface is red is apt is true and causally "owed" to the exercise of the relevant "default" competence, it is not true *because* or *through* the relevant competence. Or, as Sosa (2007) says later, the KALEIDOSCOPE protagonist's belief that his belief is apt is not apt because the relevant competence "might ... too easily have issued a false belief that the lights are normal" (p. 33).[11]

The reason the protagonist possesses animal knowledge (i.e., apt belief) in such a case is, according to Sosa (2007), that the protagonist's "faculty of color vision" is being exercised "in normal conditions for lighting, distance, size of surface, etc., in conditions generally appropriate for the exercise of color vision" (p. 31). Our hero in the KALEIDOSCOPE case has a belief that is apt, a belief that is "true because competent," simply because the competence governing its production is operating in the right sort of conditions such that the given belief could not easily be false and so based (i.e., based in the given competence operating in the relevant conditions, see Sosa, 1996, pp. 33–35). In other words, in order for a given belief to be apt, Sosa seems to require that it be produced by a cognitive competence that is operating in good conditions, where "operating in good conditions" means at the very least something like "reliably based." Likewise, the reason the protagonist in the KALEIDOSCOPE case does *not* have reflective knowledge is seemingly because the relevant competence, the "default competence" being exercised, is *not* operating under normal conditions generally appropriate for its exercise such that it would be reliably counted on to produce a true belief. In other words, the protagonist in the KALEIDOSCOPE case does not possess reflective knowledge because the conditions under which the given competence is operating is not a reliable basis for forming true belief given the presence of the jokester.

Just as we would only credit an archer with hitting the target if he hit it due to his competence as an archer, according to Sosa (2007), we should only credit someone with knowledge if he "hit upon" the given true belief as a result of his cognitive competence. Knowledge, for Sosa, is apt belief—belief that is true because competent. And from this simple definition, Sosa specifies two kinds of knowledge: the first kind, "animal knowledge," is simply apt belief; the second kind, "reflective knowledge," is apt belief aptly believed—an apt belief that one's (first-order) belief is apt. Among its various assets, this analysis of knowledge lets us, when faced with CHICKEN SEXER-style cases, to satisfy both internalist and externalist intuitions. With it, we can say why the reflective chicken sexer's cognitive state is superior to his naïve counterpart, while upholding that there is something the latter is indeed doing right. No doubt, however, when faced with cases like KALEIDOSCOPE, someone may worry about the conclusion that the given protagonist knows under such circumstances; but such worries may be assuaged by the animal/reflective distinction—by pointing out that while the KALEIDOSCOPE protagonist may indeed have animal knowledge, he surely lacks reflective knowledge.

§3: Linda Zagzebski's agent-responsibilism

Agent-responsibilism (or neo-Aristotelian) virtue epistemology stands as another dominant view in the contemporary literature that aims to provide a viable account of knowledge. And the seminal agent-responsibilist or Neo-Aristotelian account of virtue epistemology is, no doubt, Linda Zagzebski's theory of knowledge as it is explicated in *Virtues of the Mind* (1996) and

"What is Knowledge?" (1999).[12] Zagzebski's seminal work, as other scholars have noted, has given us "[the] most detailed and systematic presentation of a neo-Aristotelian view" (Greco and Turri, 2011, sec. 5.6). Like the agent-reliabilism of Sosa and Plantinga, Zagzebski's is aiming at a virtue-theoretic theory of knowledge. But instead of thinking of intellectual virtues as virtues of cognitive faculties (e.g., the proper functioning of the faculty of hearing) she—unlike Sosa and Plantinga—is primarily concerned about intellectual virtues as virtues of one's intellectual *character*. In this section, we will consider Zagzebski's agent-responsibilism approach to knowledge as arising out of intellectual character virtues.

Zagzebski's (1999) official definition of knowledge is "belief arising out of acts of intellectual virtue" or "cognitive contact with reality arising out of acts of intellectual virtue" (p. 109). To help make such a definition clearer, Michael Levin provides us with the following notation for Zagzebski's understanding of virtue:

> Let $T(V)$ be the end or telos of virtue V. Then, for Zagzebski, act A, is an "act of V" iff (i) A expresses V-ish motives, (ii) A is the sort of thing V-ish people do, and (iii) A brings about $T(V)$ because of (i) and (ii). (Levin, 2004, p. 399)

For example, the action of saving a child from drowning is an act of courage, say, if and only if (i) such an action expresses courageous motives, (ii) it is the sort of action that courageous people do, and (iii) if, in so doing, the child is actually saved. To be sure, according to Zagzebski, if I try so to save a child yet fail, I may very well have acted courageously but I did not *perform an act of courage*. To use an epistemic case, the action of thinking carefully about a given inquiry is an act of scrupulousness, say, if and only if such an action (i) expresses scrupulous motives, (ii) is the sort of thing that scrupulous people would do, and (iii) if, in so doing, the given telos (which would include the truth) is reached. Again, if I am so cognizing and yet form a false belief,

I may very well have cognized scrupulously without performing an act of "cognitive scrupulousness" (Levin, 2004, pp. 399–400). As such, a given belief is knowledge for Zagzebski if and only if it arises out of a given A that (i) expresses V-ish motives, (ii) is the sort of thing that V-ish people do, and (iii) the given telos (which would include truth) is met.

Rephrased in this way, however, it looks like Zagzebski's (1999) official definition is insufficient. Seemingly, there is nothing different in the cognitive character between Henry in a "Fake Barn territory" case and Henry in a "Real Barn territory" (good) case. In both scenarios, by hypothesis, Henry is performing identical cognitive actions—actions that have V-ish motives and that meet their telos. Seemingly, then, according to Zagzebski's official definition, Henry knows that "that's a barn" in fake barn cases—a conclusion that seems counterintuitive to most of us. To be sure, other problematic cases abound; consider the following counterexample:

> **LUCKY MARY:** Suppose that Mary has very good eyesight, but it is not perfect. It is good enough to allow her to identify her husband sitting in his usual chair in the living room from a distance of fifteen feet in somewhat dim light (the degree of dimness can easily be specified). She has made such an identification in these circumstances many times. . . . There is nothing at all unusual about either her faculties or the environment in these cases. Her faculties may not be functioning perfectly, but they are functioning well enough, so that if she goes on to form the belief "My husband is sitting in the living room," that belief has enough warrant to constitute knowledge when true and we can assume that it is almost always true. . . . Suppose Mary simply misidentifies the chair-sitter who is, let us suppose, her husband's brother. Her faculties may be working as well as they normally do when the belief is true and when we do not hesitate to say it is warranted in a degree sufficient for knowledge. . . . Her degree of warrant is as high as it usually is when she correctly identifies her husband. . . . We can now easily emend the

case as a Gettier example. Mary's husband could be sitting on the other side of the room, unseen by her. (Zagzebski, 1994, pp. 67–68)

Here again it looks like there is nothing different in the cognitive character of Mary in the above case and Mary in the nearly identical (good) case where the only difference is that she really does see her husband (call them Mary and Twin-Mary, respectively). By hypothesis, Mary and Twin-Mary are performing identical cognitive actions—actions that have V-ish motives and that meet their telos. Seemingly, then, according to Zagzebski's (1994) definition Mary knows that "My husband is sitting in the living room" in the case of LUCKY MARY—again, an intuitively unacceptable conclusion (see Pritchard, 2005, pp. 194–99).[13]

These sorts of problems arise because, according to Levin, Zagzebski's "official definition is too elaborate for its purposes" (Levin, 2004, p. 401). On the face of it, defining knowledge as "belief arising out of acts of intellectual virtue" does not seem to incorporate truth in the right sort of way (according to Zagzebski's own diagnosis of Gettier problems), such that what is doing the warranting in Zagzebski's account (the virtuous action) entails the truth of the target belief. Repeatedly, Zagzebski describes knowledge as belief that is true "because of" or "due to" an intellectual virtue—a noncausal "acqui[sition of] true belief through the virtues that brought it about"—and it is this feature that, it seems, is missing in Zagzebski's official definition (Zagzebski, 1996, p. 270; referenced in Levin, 2004, p. 399). However, it is precisely this feature of her account that she invokes to surmount cases like Mary and Her Husband. To quote Zagzebski (1996):

In the case of Mary's belief that her husband is in the living room, she may exhibit all the relevant intellectual virtues and no intellectual vices in the process of forming the belief, but she is not led to the truth *through* those virtuous processes or motives. So even though Mary has the belief she has

because of her virtues and the belief is true, she does not have the truth
because of her virtues. (p. 297—emphasis ours; also quoted in Pritchard,
2005, pp. 196–97)

As Levin (2004) points out, requiring a given belief, *B*, to "arise from some
act of virtue *A*, where *A* attains *A*'s end, truth, via good motives *A* expresses"
in order for it to be knowledge "interposes *A* between the belief and truth;
neither *B* nor *B*'s truth arises from motives good or bad—a result at variance
with Zagzebski's plain intent that it is the *truth of the relevant belief* that
must be reached via good motives (and acts) for there to be knowledge"
(p. 401—emphasis Levin's). To incorporate this feature into Zagzebski's official
definition, according to Levin (2004), we need to "bypass the middleman"
and identify the given "*A* with the formation of *B*," thus restating Zagzebski's
definition of knowledge as "belief whose attainment of truth arises from, or is
explained by, intellectually good motives" (p. 401).[14]

The question then becomes what this "arising from," "due to," or "through"
feature of Zagzebski's account consists of. According to Zagzebski, it is not
enough to form a true belief via an act of intellectual virtue—the true belief
must *arise out of* such an act. As some commentators have noted, however,
"[this] distinction is obscure . . . since it is not at all clear what it involves"—
after all, it is not at all obvious what distinguishes Mary's cognitive act in
the case where she is "Gettierized" from the case where she's not (Pritchard,
2005, p. 197). To be clear, as Levin (2004) points out, no causal explanation
is available to Zagzebski—"all causal paths from even the surest motives to
belief permit double accidents" (p. 401) and, what is more, such a move would
fundamentally change Zagzebski's account from neo-Aristotelian virtue
epistemology into motive reliabilism.

Given Zagzebski's understanding of knowledge as "belief whose attainment
of truth arises from, or is explained by, intellectually good motives," how, then,
might truth "'arise noncausally from,' or be 'due noncausally to,' or 'explained

noncausally by'" virtuous motives (Levin, 2004, p. 401)? We are not told. As we have said earlier, Zagzebski admits that she "know[s] of no account of the *because of* relation that fully captures" the link between truth and virtuous motives—adding that "[we] all have intuitions about what it means for something to happen because of something else, but this concept is in need of further analysis and I do not know of one that is adequate" (Zagzebski, 1999, p. 111; also quoted in Levin, 2004, p. 401).

For the time being, we should grant that we have an intuitive enough (and non-problematic) grasp of what it means for "something to happen because of something else" so as to proceed with Zagzebski's account of knowledge. After all, Sosa's understanding of knowledge as a belief that is *true because competent* might very well rest on a similar *because* relation.[15] For our purposes, let's put Levin's worry aside.[16]

What Zagzebski has given us is an approach to understanding intellectual virtues that affords a closer fit with moral virtues. Zagzebski thinks "intellectual virtues as epistemically relevant personality traits" with a "close connection between virtue, agency, and responsibility" (Greco and Turri, 2011, sec. 5.6). Indeed, Zagzebski's account is meant to afford a "unified account of the intellectual and moral virtues, modeled on Aristotle's account of the moral virtues" (Greco and Turri, 2011, sec. 5.6). As John Greco and John Turri (2011) helpfully explain:

> According to Aristotle, the moral virtues are acquired traits of character that involve both a motivational component and a reliable success component. For example, moral courage is the virtue according to which a person is characteristically motivated to risk danger when something of value is at stake, and is reliably successful at doing so. Likewise, we can understand benevolence as the virtue according to which a person is motivated to bring about the well-being of others, and is reliably successful at doing so. Intellectual virtues have an analogous structure, Zagzebski argues. Just as

all moral virtues can be understood in terms of a general motivation for the good, all intellectual virtues may be understood in terms of a general motivation for knowledge and other kinds of high-quality cognitive contact with reality. Individual intellectual virtues can then be specified in terms of more specific motivations that are related to the general motivation for knowledge. For example, open-mindedness is the virtue according to which a person is motivated to be receptive to new ideas, and is reliably successful at achieving the end of this motivation. Intellectual courage is the virtue according to which a person is motivated to be persevering in her own ideas, and is reliably successful at doing this. (sec. 5.6)

And it is this understanding of intellectual virtues in terms of "a general motivation for knowledge and other kinds of high-quality cognitive contact with reality" that drives her account of knowledge as true belief arising out of intellectual virtue. And mirroring moral virtues in this way allows Zagzebski's account to more easily interface with virtues in general—affording an approach to understanding intellectual virtues that arguably has a much broader applicability than an agent-reliabilist approach like Sosa's. And perhaps this will also allow Zagzebski's account to more easily give us a framework for understanding intellectual humility.

§4: Alvin Plantinga's proper functionalist agent-reliabilism

Alvin Plantinga's virtue epistemology was one of the most iconic epistemologies of the twentieth century—offering an analysis of knowledge in terms of properly functioning cognitive faculties—a view that developed throughout his monumental warrant trilogy: *Warrant: the Current Debate* (1993a), *Warrant and Proper Function* (1993b), and *Warranted Christian Belief* (2000). While a species of agent-reliabilist virtue epistemology, Plantinga's epistemology is markedly different from the agent-reliabilism of Ernest Sosa. It draws from and intersects with concepts and debates in philosophy of religion and theology and has become a touchstone for a distinct breed of agent-reliabilist virtue epistemology.[17]

In *Warrant: The Current Debate*, Plantinga (1993a) surveys several dominant accounts of warrant (i.e., that which bridges the gap between true belief and knowledge) in the contemporary literature and subsequently argues that each fails due to an inability to track virtue-theoretic intuitions across a range of cases. It is his particular focus on the *properly functioning* human knower that is meant to distinguish his account from all others. Plantinga's notion of proper function is meant to connect rightly a given agent to the facts (cf. René and the Gambler's Fallacy) and, of course, rightly preclude knowledge from cases of malfunction (cf. Brain Lesion). According to Plantinga, other theories of knowledge fail due to their inability to track knowledge ascription in accord with the proper functioning of the relevant cognitive faculties behind a given belief's genesis. Proper function is, for Plantinga, not only the key virtue-theoretic concept in his account, it is meant to be the "rock on which" competing theories of knowledge "founder" (Plantinga, 1993b, p. 4).

Knowledge, for Plantinga, is warranted true belief.[18] Plantinga's (1993b) theory of warrant can be approximately summarized as follows:

PLANTINGA'S 1993 WARRANT: A belief B is warranted for S when B is formed by cognitive faculties (of S's) that are functioning properly in the right environment in accord with a good design plan aimed at truth. (See Plantinga 1993b, p. 19.)

In other words, a given belief, B, will be warranted for Plantinga (1993b) if and only if the following four conditions are met:

1   the cognitive faculties involved in the production of B are functioning properly;

2   [the] cognitive environment is sufficiently similar to the one for which [the agent's] cognitive faculties are designed;

3   the design plan governing the production of the belief in question involves, as purpose or function, the production of true beliefs;

4   the design plan is a good one: that is, there is a high statistical or objective probability that a belief produced in accordance with the relevant segment of the design plan in that sort of environment is true. (p. 194)[19]

Although such a compendious rendering of Plantinga's theory can be sufficiently understood without further elucidation, we will, for diligence sake, unpack it a bit further.

Again, it is Plantinga's focus on the epistemically virtuous agent (i.e., the agent with mechanically sound cognitive equipment) that is the cornerstone to his epistemology. But what, then, is proper function? If proper function is meant to be the cornerstone of Plantinga's account of warrant, then one may worry that the term "proper function" is every bit as enigmatic as "warrant" and that introducing the former to explain the latter is counterproductive; however, Plantinga thinks that we all have a more or less rough-and-ready understanding of what it means for something to be functioning properly or malfunctioning (Plantinga, 1993b, pp. 5–6). We all know what it means when a car cannot go in reverse because the transmission is not (mechanically) functioning properly. We know that a properly functioning human being should generally be able to walk in a straight line without tripping or swerving and that enough alcohol impairs this proper functioning. As such, Plantinga provisionally stipulates that the relevant cognitive facilities involved in a given belief's formation must be functioning properly if the belief is to have warrant. If John is on a hallucinogenic drug, his perceptual faculties will no longer be functioning as they should; hence, his belief that the sky is melting will not have any epistemic value in terms of warrant.

Although we may indeed have a sufficient rough-and-ready grasp of proper function, it will, nevertheless, be helpful to make some general clarifications. First of all, to function properly is not to function normally (as understood in the general statistical sense). Gottlob Frege may be better at logic than the normal human being, but this does not mean that his prowess in logic is the result of some cognitive malfunction. Likewise, to use one of Plantinga's examples, if due to some disaster almost everyone on earth was blinded (such blindness would be a statistically normal condition), the few sighted individuals would not be suffering from malfunctioning perceptual faculties (Plantinga, 1993b, pp. 9–10). Secondly, not *all* of one's cognitive faculties need to be functioning properly for them to produce warranted beliefs (Plantinga, 1993b, p. 10). If my cognitive faculties associated with vision are faulty, that would not preclude my producing warranted beliefs with my auditory faculties. What is more, all that must be working are "the faculties (or subfaculties, or modules) involved in the production of the particular belief in question" to be warranted. For example, if someone is color-blind, they can still produce all sorts of warranted visual beliefs—beliefs concerning distance, the presence of people and objects, and so on. Third and finally, proper function comes in degrees (Plantinga, 1993b, pp. 10–11). Someone's running ability may not be functioning as well as it could (if, say, they chose to pursue athletics instead of academics in life), but that doesn't mean that that person's running ability is somehow malfunctioning. Likewise, someone's cognitive faculties associated with their abilities at logic may not be as good as they could be (they could spend more time working through complex proofs, memorizing truth-tables, etc.), but that person can still produce warranted beliefs based on logical deduction. How properly functioning does a given cognitive faculty need to be in order to be warrant conferring? Here, Plantinga concedes, he has no answer; however, he notes that we independently recognize that knowledge and warrant are vague to some degree. His hope, then, is that the vagueness of his theory in this instance corresponds to the vagueness of knowledge and warrant in general.

While Plantinga's focus on the mechanical proper functioning of an agent's various cognitive faculties is the cornerstone of his account, he concedes that proper function, though necessary for warrant, is not sufficient. To demonstrate, he presents us with the following case:

Alpha Centauri Elephants: You have just had your annual cognitive checkup at MIT; you pass with flying colors and are in splendid epistemic condition. Suddenly and without your knowledge you are transported to an environment wholly different from earth; you awake on a planet revolving around Alpha Centauri. There conditions are quite different; elephants, we may suppose, are invisible to human beings, but emit a sort of radiation unknown on earth, a sort of radiation that causes human beings to form the belief that a trumpet is sounding nearby. An Alpha Centaurian elephant wanders by; you are subjected to the radiation, and form the belief that a trumpet is sounding nearby. (Plantinga, 1993b, p. 6)

Your belief in such a case, though formed by properly functioning cognitive faculties, does not have warrant. What is more, even if it turned out to be true that a trumpet is sounding nearby (one is being played in a soundproof booth out of sight), your belief still wouldn't have much, if any, warrant.[20] Why? Because the environment on Alpha Centauri's planet is not congenial to your human cognitive faculties, properly functioning though they may be. A properly functioning toaster cannot be relied on to make toast underwater, because water is the wrong environment for toasters; likewise, properly functioning human cognitive faculties cannot be relied on to produce warranted beliefs on Alpha Centauri's planet (or in a vat, or under the influence of an evil demon, etc.), because the environment there is the wrong environment for human cognitive faculties.[21] What constitutes the right environment for human cognitive faculties? According to Plantinga (1997), the kind of environment that our cognitive faculties were designed for (by God, evolution, or both) is an environment like earth with "such . . . features as the presence and properties of light and air, the presence of visible objects, of other objects detectable by cognitive systems of our kind, of some objects not so detectable, of the regularities of nature, of the existence and general nature of other people, and so on" (p. 143).[22]

So, according to Plantinga (1993b), in order for the belief B to have warrant for S, it needs to be formed by cognitive faculties (of S's) that are functioning properly in the sort of environment they were designed for; however, this is not yet sufficient for warrant either. Proper function presupposes a design plan (p. 21). To assess whether or not a toaster, say, is functioning properly, we need to have an idea of how it was designed to work. Likewise, in order to assess whether or not cognitive faculties are functioning properly, we need to have some idea as to how they were designed to function (by God, evolution, or both). To be sure, the design plan for human cognitive faculties is something like "a set of specifications for a well-formed, properly functioning human being—an extraordinarily complicated and highly articulated set of specifications, as any first-year medical student could tell you" (Plantinga, 1993b, p. 14). Indeed, our cognitive faculties are so complex that they are designed to function occasionally divorced from the goal of arriving at truth. Consider how women, it seems, are designed to believe in hindsight that the pain of childbirth was less than it actually was. Similarly, people seem to be designed to optimistically believe they will survive a terrible disease far beyond what statistics vindicate. In such cases, the beliefs formed are produced by cognitive faculties that are functioning properly in the right environment according to their design plan, but are, nevertheless, unwarranted because the cognitive faculties in question are not, at least in this instance, aimed at truth; rather, they are aimed at either propagation of the species or survival. In order for a belief to be warranted, not only does it need to be produced by cognitive faculties that are functioning properly in the right environment, but it must also be produced by cognitive faculties that are functioning properly according to a design plan that is aimed at truth (Plantinga, 1993b, pp. 11–14).

Finally, as Plantinga (1993b) points out, even if S's cognitive faculties are functioning properly in a congenial environment and in accord with a design plan aimed at truth, the given belief is not necessarily warranted. Say an incompetent angel (or one of Hume's infant deities) sets out to create a species of rational persons ("capable of thought, belief and knowledge"); however, due to the angel's incompetence, the vast majority of the created persons' beliefs turn out to be absurdly false (p. 17; also see Hume, 1948, part 5). In such a case, the given people's beliefs are produced by cognitive faculties that are functioning properly in a congenial environment in accord with a design plan aimed at truth, but the design plan just turns out to be a rubbish one—despite the incompetent angel's best efforts, the subjects he created have wholly unreliable cognitive faculties. Warrant, according to Plantinga, requires reliability. More precisely, in order for a given belief to be warranted, "the module of the design plan governing the production of that belief must be such that the statistical or objective probability of a belief's being true, given that it has been produced in accord with that module in a congenial cognitive environment, is high" (Plantinga, 1993b, p. 18).[23] In other words, to use the language of PLANTINGA'S 1993 WARRANT specified earlier, the design plan of the relevant cognitive faculties must be a "good" one if a belief produced by those faculties is to have any hope for warrant.

§5: Is intellectual humility an intellectual virtue?

Now that we've outlined some of the leading virtue-theoretic approaches to knowledge—taking virtue epistemology as our starting place for understanding intellectual virtues—we're now in a position to explore whether or not intellectual humility, especially as we described it in the previous chapter, is best understood as an intellectual virtue.

Whether or not intellectual humility is conceptually best understood as an intellectual virtue will, of course, depend on what kind of intellectual virtues we are talking about. As we noted earlier, intellectual humility could very easily be classified as an intellectual virtue according to an agent-responsibilist virtue epistemology like Zagzebski's, because intellectual humility could easily be seen as a *character* virtue that might give rise to the truth in the relevant way (though, as we have seen, cashing out this "relevant way" might seem problematic). But what about agent-reliabilist virtue epistemologies like Sosa's and Plantinga's? Here, it's not as clear that intellectual humility is easily viewed as an intellectual virtue, where intellectual virtues are understood as faculty virtues, as successful or properly functioning cognitive faculties.

Consider the following scenario:

BRIAN THE BRAIN: As far as he can tell, Brian lives a fairly normal life. Unbeknownst to Brian, however, he is actually a brain floating in a nutrient bath—kept alive artificially. He has no body. He has never left the bath. All of Brian-the-brain's "normal life" experiences are merely the product of his brain being stimulated by a network of electrodes attached to his brain, programmed by a team of neuroscientists as Brian's brain floats in their lab. Brian might think that he works at a local university, has a loving wife and three small children, and all this looks and feels exactly like it would in a normal non-envatted individual. But, for Brian, as a brain in a vat, all this is simply an illusion—the product of the neuroscientists' programmed stimulations.

Brian, in BRIAN THE BRAIN, might very well enjoy various *character* virtues—the sort of intellectual virtues at the heart of agent-responsibilism—though none of them could ever give rise to the truth in a way that produces knowledge, because his cognitive life is divorced from truth. (And without truth, there can be no knowledge. You can't know things that are false.)[24] But it doesn't look like Brain enjoys any faculty virtues—the sort of intellectual virtues that are at the heart of agent-reliabilism. After all, being envatted seems to straightforwardly undermine the ability of Brian's cognitive faculties to function properly, since they'd be operating in a radically inappropriate environment (Brian's cognitive faculties were not designed to operate while floating in a nutrient bath) and they'd certainly have little hope of ever actually hitting the truth.

But, we might wonder, pre-theoretically, whether or not Brian, the envatted brain, could be intellectually humble. Can someone whose entire world is illusory, nevertheless, form beliefs and engage with his illusory interlocutors in an intellectually humble way? The answer, it seems, is yes. Sure, almost everything Brian believes is false—he is completely severed from the real world. But why couldn't he still be humble about how he engages with his illusory world? For example, if Brian imagines himself to be the world's leading soccer player—ignoring what should be strong evidence to the contrary (illusory though it may be)—it seems as though Brian is being a delusional, arrogant bastard. If Brian's envatted experience really should tell him that he's overweight, he's not particularly athletic, and that he's had relatively little experience playing soccer, then it seems as though he'd be extremely arrogant to believe he's a leading soccer player—even if his entire life is an illusion. And if that's right, then it seems like Brian could be intellectually humble as well. Brian could, for example, accurately track what he can non-culpably take to be the positive epistemic beliefs—after all, he's non-culpable in failing to know he is a brain in a vat.

If all of this is right—if someone like Brian can have character virtues but *not* faculty virtues (or at least not *most* faculty virtues) and if Brian can still be intellectually humble—then presumably intellectual humility is best conceived of as a character virtue. If we're looking to virtue epistemology to guide us in our understanding of intellectual virtues, then it looks like the best framework for understanding intellectual humility as an intellectual virtue is agent-responsibilism.

Now, does this mean that intellectual humility is more or less irrelevant to agent-reliabilist virtue epistemologies? Not at all. As we noted earlier, any robust, full account of intellectual virtue will have to account for *both* faculty virtues and character virtues; so while the agent-reliabilist's chief interest—especially when it comes to acquiring epistemic goods like knowledge—might be *faculty* virtues, intellectual humility might, nevertheless, play an ancillary role.[25] Accurately tracking the positive epistemic status one's beliefs—drawing from the doxastic account of intellectual humility—might be a character virtue that has a significant effect on wide range of cognitive faculties (from vision to self-reflection) and their ability to function properly And in some cases, perhaps intellectual humility might actually help increase the reliability of some individual faculty virtues. In other words, perhaps our faculty virtues can affect our ability to be intellectually humble, *and* perhaps our ability to be intellectually humble can affect the functioning and reliability of our cognitive faculties. For example, someone who is intellectually humble might use faculties of vision, say, more discerningly—accurately tracking the positive epistemic status of visual beliefs and when vision might mislead—leading to fewer false beliefs based off of visual perception.

So, assuming that intellectual humility is an intellectual virtue, then it looks like it will be *best* understood as a character virtue—the sort of virtue at the heart of agent-responsibilism (but also of interest to agent-reliabilism). Following Zagzebski's framework, then, we could explicate intellectual humility in the following way: a given act is an act of intellectual humility if and only if (i) such an act expresses intellectually humble motives, (ii) it is the sort of act that intellectually humble people perform, and (iii) if, in performing the act, the given *telos* of intellectual humility is reached. For example, perhaps the act of reducing one's credence on a given belief when faced with peer disagreement is an act of intellectual humility if (i) such an act expresses intellectually humble motives, (ii) it is the sort of act that an intellectually humble person would do, and (iii) if, in performing the act, the given telos of intellectual humility (in this case, perhaps a greater sensitivity to the truth) is reached. And insofar as Zagzebski's account is aimed at knowledge, if a given act of intellectual humility gives rise to a true belief, then that true belief could be knowledge.

But, of course, that is assuming that intellectual humility is indeed an intellectual virtue. And to be sure, that's probably a fairly safe assumption. If anything, the onus is presumably on anyone who wants to convince us otherwise; in other words, unless we have good reason to think otherwise, we're probably safe to assume that intellectual humility is indeed an intellectual virtue.

That said, however, good reason to think otherwise might be forthcoming—specifically from empirical research. What if we discovered, for example, that intellectual humility was an evolutionary or biological vice? What if we discovered that people who are intellectually humble are less likely to be happy, are less ambitious, less successful, and are less likely to reproduce? Disturbingly, recent empirical research seems to suggest that intellectual arrogance is deeply rooted in human psychology. As we said in Chapter 1, human beings are notoriously (and apparently naturally) disposed to overestimating their intellectual strengths and underestimating their weaknesses; indeed, the evidence is clear that there is a strong tendency to underestimate even our liability to such biases! Do these biases show a natural tendency away from intellectual humility? Furthermore, we are susceptible to all sorts of biases that make intellectual humility difficult. For example, we tend to favor evidence or data received early in our inquiries (primacy bias) and we tend to discount the weight of evidence that counts against hypotheses we endorse (confirmation bias). Second, evolutionary psychologists have offered some intriguing arguments that these dispositions are embedded within our cognitive architecture in ways that can systematically lead us to biased thinking, in some cases for adaptive reasons. Third, some clinicians have argued that intellectual arrogance is necessary for maintaining mental health. The intellectual humble, who see themselves and their condition with unmitigated clarity, are more susceptible to forms of depression, for example. But if all of this is right, then it begins to look like intellectual humility is a biological *vice*! And we might seriously wonder: Can something be a biological vice and still be considered an intellectual virtue?

If intellectual humility is indeed a biological vice, and if we generally want intellectual virtues to be good for people in some significant way—a way that is sensitive to our biological needs and our evolutionary design—then there is a serious worry here that intellectual humility cannot be an intellectual virtue. To be sure, intellectual virtues qua intellectual virtues are typically taken to aim at truth, and moral virtues qua moral virtues are typically taken to be aimed at some form of the good. As such, perhaps the worry that intellectual humility is a biological vice—such that it leads to a *decrease* in the overall well-being of an agent—isn't really a worry that intellectual humility isn't an *intellectual* virtue. So long as intellectual humility really does help agents reach the truth, then perhaps it can still be an intellectual virtue even if it is a biological vice.[26] But insofar as intellectual humility is best understood as a *character* virtue in light of neo-Aristotelian agent-responsibilism, this response may not be available to us. After all, by Zagzebski's lights, intellectual virtues are meant to be a subset of moral virtues.

Thankfully, however, the worry that intellectual humility might be a biological vice—and subsequently *not* an intellectual virtue—can be assuaged in other ways. First of all, having a view of intellectual humility as a virtuous mean—as the virtue between the vices of intellectual arrogance and intellectual diffidence—seems to dissolve the worry. For example, ease of measurement in empirical research might drive a view of intellectual humility as simply the opposite of intellectual arrogance. But such a measure struggles to pull apart the distinction between being intellectually humble and being intellectually diffident. So just because people who *lack intellectual arrogance* are more likely to suffer from depression, that doesn't mean that *intellectually humble* people are more likely to suffer from depression. Perhaps those who lack intellectual arrogance aren't intellectually humble, perhaps they are intellectually self-deprecating, diffident, or servile. Second, there is a growing body of research that suggests that intellectual humility is a tremendous biological virtue. Psychologists have discovered traits and behaviors associated with intellectual humility that facilitate learning, personal growth, and social interaction. Being an arrogant prig, unsurprisingly, generally causes social ostracization. While we might be able to think of arrogant prigs who have achieved success seemingly by being arrogant prigs—usually television personalities, political pundits, etc.—being an arrogant prig does not generally lend itself to personal, holistic thriving. For the time being, at least, we think we can put the worry that intellectual humility might be a biological vice on the shelf; the research doesn't ultimately seem to support such a conclusion at this time. And as such, following our intuitions and lacking significant reason to think otherwise, let's continue to assume that intellectual humility is, indeed, an intellectual virtue.

Conclusion

In Chapter 1, we established that intellectual humility is a critically important subject with tremendous significance in the real world. And we proposed a plausible account of what intellectual humility might be—the doxastic account of intellectual humility. And in all of this, we assumed, naturally enough, that intellectual humility is an *intellectual virtue*. But what is an intellectual virtue anyway? In this chapter, we considered some of the seminal accounts of intellectual virtue found in virtue epistemology. First, in §1, we sketched the broad contours of the two dominant approaches to understanding intellectual virtue: agent-reliabilism and agent-responsibilism. Then in §2, §3, and §4, we explored specific examples of these virtue epistemologies in greater detail. Starting with Ernest Sosa's agent-reliabilism, we considered the *faculty* virtues at the heart of his account of knowledge as belief that is true because it is competent. Then, in §3, we turned to Linda Zagzebski's seminal agent-responsibilism; we considered the character virtues at the heart of her account of knowledge as true belief arising out of an act of intellectual virtue. And, in §4, we considered the unique *proper functionalist* agent-reliabilism of Alvin Plantinga, where intellectual virtues are understood in terms of properly functioning cognitive faculties. With some leading approaches to intellectual virtue on the table, we finally returned, in §5, to intellectual humility and considered how it might fit within that literature. And we decided that, of the proposals under consideration, Linda Zagzebski's agent-responsibilism—with its approach to intellectual virtues as *character* virtues—yielded the easiest (and most intuitive) framework for making sense of intellectual humility as an intellectual virtue. That said, we also made the case that agent-reliabilist accounts of intellectual virtue should, nevertheless, be extremely interested in intellectual humility; intellectual humility, even as a character virtue, can deeply affect and be affected by the reliability of our cognitive faculties.

PART TWO

SCIENCE

3

How do we know who is intellectually humble?

Many psychologists adopt the dictum of Thorndike that whatever exists at all exists in some amount and they also adopt the corollary that whatever exists in some amount can be measured: the quality of handwriting, the appreciation of a sunset, the attitude of an individual toward Communism, the strength of desire in a hungry rat.

GUILFORD, 1954, AS QUOTED IN SAVAGE AND EHRLICH, 1992, P. 3

Any scientific study of a phenomenon will require that it can be measured. If the desire is simply to discover the existence of a phenomenon, some kind of measure is required. If we want to know the relative strength of a phenomenon, a measure is needed. If we want to assess the occurrence of a phenomenon in one case and compare it to the occurrence in another case, we need a standard of comparison, a measure. If we want to devise an intervention that will increase the presence of the desired phenomenon, we need a measure to know if the intervention worked, if an increase can be detected. And so it is with intellectual humility. In order to discover it in people, assess its relative strength, compare one person to another in it, and help promote and increase it in people, we need good measures.

Measurement is a natural place for philosophy and science to meet. When we say, scientifically speaking, a person has more (or less) intellectual humility, what exactly do we mean? Any claim of a scientific investigation to have found, increased, manipulated, mitigated, augmented, inhibited, or obfuscated intellectual humility means that somehow, in some way, intellectual humility was first defined and then measured. It is in the definition of intellectual humility that science turns to philosophy. Measurement is the process of "operationalizing" a theoretical construct so that it can be observed in others (behavioral observation) and/or rated within oneself (self-report). What is "operationalized" is derived from theory, and philosophy provides that theoretical basis for measurement.

§1: The problems and promise of measurement

Philosophical accounts

But there can be tensions here, too. On the one hand, the philosophical accounts of intellectual humility—like those we considered in Chapter 1—are aimed at elucidating the virtue in all of its complexities and intricacies. That's one of the reasons why counterexamples (like STRANDED, MOTHER, etc.) are taken so seriously; if an account of intellectual humility falls victim to a counterexample, then there is a strong onus on the account to either explain away the counterexample (why it's not really a counterexample) or modify the view so as to account for the counterexample. On the other hand, when psychologists set out to measure a virtue like intellectual humility, a premium is placed on ease of measurement. They need an account of intellectual humility that can be operationalized and easily used in the lab.

As such, psychologists might worry that philosophical accounts of intellectual humility—with their aim of capturing the full complexities of the virtue—are too complex to be measured. Consider, for example, Don Davis and Joshua Hook's criticism of the doxastic account of intellectual humility (or IH):

Our main reaction to [the doxastic] model of IH was we struggled to understand how this model would work "in the trenches." As researchers, we are interested in definitions and models of IH that lead to clear strategies for measuring the construct and developing an empirical research program. As clinicians, we are interested in how IH is perceived and judged in actual relationships and communities, such as religious discussions and interfaith dialogue. . . . [The doxastic] definition of IH is complex. We call it a "goldilocks definition": IH is not a unitary construct but rather the "just right" combination of several constructs interacting with each other (e.g., whether or not someone was misled by false evidence). Complex definitions that include many moderators (i.e., qualifications) are difficult to measure, so we tend to prefer to simplify definitions and treat qualifiers as different constructs that may moderate the relationship between IH and other outcomes. As psychologists, we fear it may be impossible to define and measure this aspect of [doxastic] model in a psychologically meaningful way. (Davis and Hook, in press)

Contrary to what Davis and Hook say, we would like to suggest that the complexities and limitations of the doxastic account actually enjoy an *admirable* fit with the real world—and that demanding *less* from an account of intellectual humility actually doesn't account for what we find in the trenches. Life in the trenches, in the real world, is messy. It's complex. Properly understood, virtues are often going to be *extremely* difficult to viably measure across personality types, social dynamics, cultural contexts, etc. In giving an abstract and complex view of the virtue of intellectual humility, it seems to us that *we are actually tracking the complexity we find in the trenches, in the real world.*

When Davis and Hook complain that the doxastic account of intellectual humility is too complex to be easily measured, one response is, "That's life in the trenches!" We shouldn't always expect virtues to yield easy measurements. Sure, we can give a simple definition of intellectual humility so that it yields easy measurements, but *if ease of measurement is what's driving our definitions, then there is a real chance our definitions won't fully capture the virtue.*

But even if intellectual humility—as a complex virtue that might look different for different beliefs, in different environments, and in different people—cannot be straightforwardly measured, that doesn't mean that there isn't tremendously valuable measurement work to be done on intellectual humility. For example, we might think that intellectual humility largely corresponds with the absence of dogmatism; as such, developing a straightforward measure along these lines would be extremely valuable and relevant. But, we'd simply be remiss if we tried to straightforwardly conflate intellectual humility with the absence of dogmatism. If we are going to try to develop an account of intellectual humility that applies across contexts, cultures, personalities, and belief types—from the belief that 2 + 2 = 4 to beliefs about metaphysics—then we are simply going to *need* an open-ended and sufficiently abstract account to work with. In the end, we consider it a *virtue* of the doxastic account that it provides a broad enough framework of intellectual humility that it can apply across a full range of cases and track the complexities and stalemates of life "in the trenches."

So, as we consider some of the recent work that has been done on the measurement of intellectual humility, it's important that we frame this discussion by appreciating what such measurements are and what they are not. *Such measurements are, we propose, valuable tools for tracking important aspects of intellectual humility.* The absence of dogmatism, a willingness to engage with disagreement, and an openness to others' points of view are all going to be deeply relevant to intellectual humility, and measurements along these lines might even accurately track intellectual humility across a wide range of cases. *But such measurements are not, we suggest, full definitions of intellectual humility.* If that were the goal, then these measurements would fail. A number of theorists, for example, have given us valuable measures for tracking the absence of dogmatism. If, however, we conflated such a measure with intellectual humility, then we would be left with a deeply impoverished definition. By such lights, intellectual humility would be impossible for beliefs that might *warrant* dogmatism—for example, the belief that 2 + 2 = 4. And what is more, such a view is completely unable to distinguish intellectual humility from the most self-deprecating intellectual servility and diffidence.

Folk theories

In addition to philosophical accounts, everyday or "folk" conceptions of a concept can inform ways to measure the concept. These might be best used as "augments" to more robust philosophical accounts, helping to give shape to the way those concepts are operationalized. In the introduction, we shared a study we conducted on the "implicit" or folk theory of intellectual humility. That study revealed that the concept of an intellectually humble person, in the folk mind, is a complex combination of epistemic, self-oriented, and other-oriented dimensions. We described the epistemic dimension as the "Intelligence/ Love of Learning cluster," which included descriptors like smart, bright, and intelligent, combined with elements such as curiosity, inquisitiveness, and love of learning. The social aspects of intellectual humility in the folk mind had two different dimensions. The first was a self-oriented/intrapersonal dimension that describes a person's quality of being before others that we called the "Humility/Modest cluster." It contained words and phrases like "modest," "not-a-showoff," and "doesn't brag." The second social aspect was more other-oriented and had interpersonal descriptors that indicate how a person interacts with others, such as "polite," "honest," "reliable," and "unselfish." We called this the Respectful/Considerate cluster.

Intellectual humility in the folk mind has a clear and robust social status dimension that describes a person's stance as knowledgeable before others (self-oriented/intrapersonal) along with additional social descriptors that indicate a preference for civility (other-oriented, interpersonal), but it also has a unique epistemic dimension having to do with curiosity and love of learning. Importantly, in the folk mind, an intellectually arrogant person links pride with intellect, while intellect drives curiosity and love of learning in an intellectually humble person. These ideas could be used in fashioning items for self-report measures, and guide the settings and circumstances in which intellectual humility is best measured. It is important to note that, while folk theories alone cannot account for a full understanding of intellectual humility, neither should a philosophical account contradict what is in the folk mind. As we suggested in the first chapter, because intellectual humility is a multifaceted and multilayered virtue with many dimensions, such facets as the interpersonal and intrapersonal—in addition to the epistemic—can be built upon or understood within the doxastic account.

§2: Issues of scientific measurement

Reliability

When devising measures of psychological constructs, researchers use various criteria to determine the efficacy and validity of those measures. The first is called "reliability" and refers to the consistency of the measure. There are three basic questions involved here (Huck, 2000): Does a subject respond to the measure consistently when retaking the test (test-retest reliability)? Do the items and procedures consistently measure the same underlying characteristic (internal consistency)? Are a group of raters observing a phenomenon (in the case of behavioral observation or textual analysis) consistent (inter-rater reliability)?

Validity

The other issue involved in measurement is validity. Validity is not the same as reliability. Just because a test measures something consistently and reliably does not mean it is measuring the intended construct. For example, you could have an instrument designed to measure intellectual humility, but which consistently measures intellectual courage. It is reliable in that it measures intellectual courage consistently, but it is not a valid measure for intellectual humility. Validity refers to the accuracy of the measure. Reliability is necessary for a valid measure, but does not guarantee validity, for in order for a measure to be valid (accurate), it must be reliable (consistent, Huck, 2000). While there are many forms of validity that come into play in measurement, we limit this discussion to those we consider most important.

Content validity

Content validity is the degree to which the content of the measure tracks and reflects the concept that is under investigation (Huck, 2000). This is where philosophy and science best meet. When psychologists are trying to operationalize a concept by devising test items that can measure a given construct, they have some construct or theory in mind. Items or procedures for the measure are generated on the basis of a theory of the construct. In the case of intellectual humility, if you hold to the doxastic account, items or procedures that measure the accuracy of tracking positive epistemic status would be the focus. If you take the Roberts and Wood account, measuring ego investment in epistemic beliefs would be the focus. Again, there is no requirement to pick one philosophical perspective in generating content validity. Folk theories of intellectual humility may also inform the content, as well as theories from cognitive science and other realms. In fact, most researchers sample broadly across theories, especially when attempting to devise a general or global measure of intellectual humility (see discussion of individual measures below).

Construct validity

Another type of validity that is important in devising measurements of psychological phenomena is construct validity. The classic definition of a construct is "some postulated attribute of people, assumed to be reflected in test performance" (Cronbach and Meehl, 1955). With construct validity, both the study of the construct as an attribute of a person (internal), and the relationship of the person's performance on the particular construct to performance on other constructs (external, Lissitz and Samuelsen, 2007) are studied. Construct validity, then, is how a measurement hangs together internally and how it is similar to (but different enough from) related constructs.

Both the internal and external aspects of construct validation are informed by theory. Factor analysis is often used to confirm the internal validity of a construct to see if the measure does, indeed, reflect all the aspects of the construct that were expected from the theoretical accounts (Huck, 2000). We will see some examples of internal construct validity through factor analysis below. External construct validity is proved by testing subjects on other constructs both related to (convergent validity) and different from (discriminant validity) the construct in question.

Divergent validity

One real worry in the measurement of any virtue, especially intellectual humility, is the high potential for what is called social desirability. This is the tendency to respond to items in a measure that would be viewed positively by others. Since intellectual humility is a socially desirable trait, people may not report honestly about their capacity for it. Moreover, there is a paradoxical effect in measuring humility and intellectual humility. That is, if a person rates themselves high in humility, are they really being humble? One way to control for social desirability is to test for it and compare those scores with a test of intellectual humility. A test in which subjects score high on intellectual humility but low on social desirability would be said to have divergent validity, that is, intellectual humility would prove to be very different from social desirability, and, therefore, it would be valid as a stand-alone concept. There may be other concepts that intellectual humility might be measured against to prove divergent validity such as narcissism and self-righteousness.

Another worry is that people will not honestly or accurately give a self-report on virtue, calling into question that method. There is some confidence that intellectual humility can be measured by self-report from the experience of the development of humility measures. For example, Landrum (2011) found that social desirability did not correlate with self-report measures of humility. Researchers have examined this issue in relation to creation of measures of intellectual humility as well, which we will examine later in this chapter.

Convergent validity

Convergent validity refers to how well a construct correlates with theoretically similar, but distinct, psychological constructs that already are being measured. In our own theorizing on what constructs might be related to intellectual humility, we have identified a number that might be related to, but distinct from, intellectual humility. This is by no means an exhaustive list of possible correlates with a measure of intellectual humility, but gives a suggestion for some direction in this regard. Some of these have been tested against existing measures of intellectual humility, which we will discuss below:

Accuracy

Since the doxastic account involves accurate tracking of the positive status of one's own belief, accuracy in reasoning is one area of convergence with intellectual humility. Kunda (1990), in an analysis of the work on accuracy-driven reasoning, concluded that when "people are motivated to be accurate, they expend more cognitive effort on issue-related reasoning, attend to relevant information more carefully, and process it more deeply, often using more complex rules" (p. 481). Kruglanski and Mayseless (1987) report that a high need for accuracy (what they call a heightened fear of invalidity) motivates people to seek comparison with those who disagree with them. The focus on accuracy, then, invites the thinking agent into a posture of intellectual humility because (a) that agent may realize that he or she has a less than complete understanding and needs to seek more information, (b) it helps the agent to focus on what others might think of the same phenomenon, and (c) it will focus the agent on objective criteria for the phenomenon.

Actively Open-minded Thinking

"Actively Open-minded Thinking" (AOT) is a measure of openness to belief change and cognitive flexibility. Stanovich and West (1997) believe that these thinking dispositions can provide information about an individual's epistemic goals and values. Those who showed a high reliance on argument quality by relying less on prior beliefs scored significantly higher on the AOT composite scale. This open and flexible thinking disposition held even when they controlled for cognitive ability. For example, a disposition such as the willingness to change beliefs reflects the goal of getting as close to the truth as possible, and the disposition to carefully evaluate arguments indicates a value for accuracy. It might be fair to infer that those with a high reliance on argument quality would have a better chance of accurately tracking the positive epistemic status of their beliefs.

Rule-based thinking

Directing one's attention to processes, objective criteria, and rules of analysis can also aid in reducing systematic bias thereby increasing accuracy. For example, when personal traits are ambiguous (e.g., whether or not one is intelligent, or a good driver), people draw on idiosyncratic definitions of traits and abilities to assess themselves as better than average at a certain task or trait. Once given criteria of judgment, however, they are more accurate in their assessment relative to their peers (Dunning, Meyerowitz, and Holzberg, 2002). Evans (2007) demonstrates that when questions are asked in a way that engages analytic reasoning processes, biases are reduced. Intellectual humility may correlate highly with those situations where objective processes, criteria, and rules of analysis are in play.

Perspective taking

One aspect of an open and flexible thinking disposition that marks intellectual humility is the capacity to weigh evidence for and against a strongly held belief, including the opinions and beliefs of others who hold a position different from one's own. This requires a certain capacity for perspective taking: a movement from the focus on one's own thoughts to include the perceptions, thoughts, and ideas of others. This adjustment can be as simple as considering alternative points of view and as complex as trying to assess another person's thoughts. Studies have found that asking people to consider the possibility that competing hypotheses are true is sufficient to undo the bias of one-sided thinking (Sedikides, Horton, and Gregg, 2007; Wilson, Centerbar, and Brekke, 2002).

Need for cognition

An individual difference that lends itself to the kind of epistemic activity characteristic of intellectual humility is the "need for cognition," defined as "a stable individual difference in people's tendency to engage in and enjoy effortful cognitive activity" (Cacioppo et al., 1996, p. 198). People high in need for cognition expend more effort analyzing content and quality of arguments (Haugtvedt, Petty, and Cacioppo, 1992), consider arguments central to the issue rather than peripheral features (Petty, Cacioppo, and Goldman, 1981), enjoy complex cognitive tasks (Cacioppo and Petty, 1982), and are attracted to messages that appeal more to rational argument than emotion (Haddock et al., 2008).

Need for closure

Another extensively studied motivational characteristic that could have a bearing on the science of intellectual humility is the need for closure—that is, the need to make a decision, to have an issue *closed* (Kruglanski, 1990; Kruglanski et al., 2009; Webster and Kruglanski, 1994). Lay epistemic theory, formed as part of a general framework for the development of all kinds of knowledge (Kruglanski et al., 2009), operates from fundamental assumption that knowledge is derived from evidence. Evidence can come from all sources, but a special category of evidence in lay epistemic theory comes from the opinions of other people (testimony). There are individual differences in the process of hypothesis testing and evidence gathering according to lay epistemic theory. Individuals who take in and process less information before making a judgment, and give preference to information met early in the decision-making process, are said to be high in need for closure. Because of the early closure in the epistemic process, they also have higher confidence in their judgments than those with a high need to avoid or postpone closure. They tend to be influenced by preexisting stereotypes and prejudices in their judgment of people and their actions, and do not pay much attention to circumstances or information specific to the individual. People high in need for closure will, for the most part, look to compare their thoughts to those of similar mind and to reject or devalue others who do not share their perspectives and judgments (Kruglanski, 1990).

Personality measures

It seems intuitive enough that intellectual humility could map well onto certain personality traits described by models of personality such as the Five-Factor Model (The Big Five, McCrae and Costa, 1987, 1997) and the HEXACO (Lee and Ashton, 2004), and that comparison with these models might lead us to constructs that are similar, but different enough to aid in testing convergent validity. For example, high levels of the Openness to Experience factor might correlate with high intellectual humility, especially when we look at specific facets of the Openness construct. The facet "openness to ideas," for example, seems to capture an element of curiosity we would expect to find in the intellectually humble and the "values" facet might figure into whether someone is willing to really consider an opposing political or religious view with charity. Similar corollaries of intellectual humility might exist within some facets of Agreeableness, Conscientiousness, and even Emotional Stability.

Along these lines, special attention might be given to the HEXACO model of personality, which adds the dimension of Honesty-Humility (H) to the factors mentioned above (Ashton and Lee, 2005). A connection between the H dimension and socially important criteria has already been demonstrated (Ashton and Lee, 2008). Additionally, the H factor has been negatively correlated with particularly vicious personality traits (e.g., narcissism, psychopathy, Machiavellianism, materialism, and power-seeking), traits we would expect to find somewhere opposite to intellectual humility (Ashton and Lee, 2005, 2007).[1] Not surprisingly, the H factor has also been used to show that trait humility is linked to higher social relationship quality (Peters, Rowatt, and Johnson, 2011).

Other virtues

There are related virtues that have been studied in the past in psychology that could inform the convergent validity of measures of intellectual humility, like wisdom (Grossmann et al., 2010; Sternberg, 1985), humility (Tangney, 2000), and modesty (Gregg et al., 2008). Research into folk conceptions of wisdom reveals components such as open-mindedness, not being afraid to admit and correct a mistake, and listening to all sides of an issue (what Sternberg [1985] calls *sagacity*). These traits—which are related to, but not specifically labeled as, intellectual humility—coalesce to form a consistent factor in studies of the folk concept of wisdom (Clayton and Birren, 1980; Sternberg, 1985). Meacham (1990) defines wisdom exclusively in terms that reflect intellectual humility (knowing that one does not know and that knowledge is fallible). Grossmann et al. (2010) have devised a wise reasoning measure that codes for intellectual humility (defined as recognizing the limits of one's knowledge).

General humility, as it has been defined and studied, also has epistemic dimensions. In a seminal theoretical piece in the psychology of humility, Tangney (2000) grounds the definition of humility in two dimensions: a social dimension, understood as a proper understanding of the self (accurate assessment, keeping one's abilities/accomplishments in proper perspective, low self-focus); and an epistemic dimension, understood as a certain intellectual disposition (acknowledging mistakes, intellectual openness). Measures of humility have reflected these dimensions (e.g., Davis et al., 2011). We might expect intellectual humility to be similar to, but distinct from, these measures of humility.

Another possible virtue that could inform the convergent validity of intellectually humble is modesty. In a prototype analysis conducted on the "everyday" conception of modesty, Gregg et al. (2008) uncovered four central categories of terms used to describe the modest person (humble, shy, not boastful, and solicitous) and six peripheral categories (honest, likable, not arrogant, attention-avoiding, plain, and gracious). From their study, they conclude that modesty has both a public (solicitous) and a private (humble, shy) character, and, further, that the public character of modesty has pro-social elements. The category "solicitous" was modified by descriptors that indicate an external, other-centered orientation that was intrinsic to modesty (caring, considerate, empathic, helpful, kind, thoughtful, and understanding).

§3: Existing measures of intellectual humility

While the study of the science of intellectual humility is still in its early stages, several instruments have been devised and tested that attempt to measure intellectual humility. Some are global measurements that are intended to measure this virtue in a comprehensive way either through self-report (Krumrei-Mancuso and Rouse, 2016; Leary et al., 2016; Porter, 2015), or through informant report (McElroy et al., 2014). Others intend to measure aspects of intellectual humility, (like open-mindedness, or willingness to revise arguments) and are often aimed at responses to specific situations or contexts, such as learning, or disagreement.

When reviewing these measures, it is good to keep in mind a folk proverb: the devil is in the details. In order to understand how a researcher is operationalizing a concept, it is good to look at the specific items generated to cover that concept. When trying to understand the convergent and discriminate validity of a concept, it is good to look at the specific measures against which the new measure is being compared and what the specific correlations are. If the researcher has done an analysis that shows what value the measure might add in measuring a certain concept—that is, what the measure might explain about the concept over and above existing measures (incremental validity)—that is also good to know. We will examine three new global self-report measures of intellectual humility in such detail below. Then we will look at some measures of intellectual humility that use informant report as a method. We will also foreshadow some of the other ways researchers who are doing studies in developmental and social psychology operationalize intellectual humility to see the breadth of measures being used to capture and quantify this intellectual virtue.

It appears that the first use of the label of "intellectual humility" in the psychological literature was in a measure that was devised as a subset of a larger construct measuring wise reasoning (Grossmann et al., 2010). Subjects were asked to reason about issues that were personally meaningful to them (career prospects in a recession, social changes as a consequence of politics), which were then coded along two dimensions, "dialectical thinking" (recognition of the likelihood of change) and "intellectual humility" (recognition of uncertainty and the limits of knowledge). The results show that when the subjects were able to distance themselves from the topics at hand, they showed more capacity for wise reasoning, including intellectual humility (Kross and Grossman, 2012).

While the "recognition of the uncertainty and limits of knowledge" is an important aspect of intellectual humility, it is too narrowly focused to provide a full assessment. Moreover, it was devised as a part of an investigation into wisdom, and not the result of direct theoretical work on intellectual humility. Recent work in psychology and philosophy has afforded richer conceptions for measurement and the possibility of a more comprehensive and inclusive scale.

Comprehensive Humility Scale

Krumrei-Mancuso and Rouse (2016) devised the Comprehensive Intellectual Humility Scale, in part in response to these richer, emerging definitions and in part to provide a scale that could be used in many settings and was easy to administer. Drawing on diverse conceptions of intellectual humility in both philosophy and psychology, Krumrei-Mancuso and Rouse (2016) settled on the definition of intellectual humility as "a non-threatening awareness of one's intellectual fallibility" (p. 5). This was informed by the Roberts and Wood (2007) conception of intellectual humility: the absence of intellectual arrogance that is coupled with a motiving concern for epistemic goods such as knowledge and truth. They also considered the perspective of Aristotelean virtue epistemology, which recognizes intellectual humility as a "virtuous mean" between too much confidence in beliefs (intellectual grandiosity) and too little (intellectual diffidence). Examples of such behaviors found in the psychological literature include being open to others' ideas, being open to belief revision, not dogmatically rejecting others' viewpoints and not giving up beliefs too easily when challenged. The idea reflected in the literature that intellectual humility involves an appreciation of the limits of one's knowledge also played into their conception. Finally, their conception of intellectual humility involved both interpersonal and intrapersonal aspects.

In order to construct a self-report instrument that used natural language for how people might speak about intellectual humility, the researchers generated items from focus groups of students and the general public, which yielded 187 potential items. Eighteen experts rated these on face validity, construct validity, and clarity of wording, and from this process retained 118 items. Through three iterations of pilot testing with both college students and the general public, they reduced the number to seventy-three items. These items were administered to 380 participants found through MTurk. Two sets of factor analysis of their responses yielded a four-factor model. The researchers selected up to six of the best items per factor, resulting in a twenty-two-item scale. The self-report scale showed strong psychometric properties, with a coefficient alpha of 0.87 for the full scale, and one ranging from 0.74 to 0.89 for the subscales (study 2), and a decent test-retest reliability for the full scale (0.75 after one month and 0.70 after three-months). The subscales proved less reliable in retest, which gives support for the use of the full scale.

To get a feel for how Krumrei-Mancuso and Rouse (2016) operationalized their definition of intellectual humility, here are the four subscales with an example from each:

1 *Independence of Intellect and Ego* (e.g., "When someone contradicts my most important beliefs, it feels like a personal attack." This item is scored in reverse.)

2 *Openness to Revising One's Viewpoint* (e.g., "I am open to revising my important beliefs in the face of new information.")

3 *Respect for Others' Viewpoints* (e.g., "Even when I disagree with others, I can recognize that they have sound points.")

4 *Lack of Intellectual Overcompetence* (e.g., "My ideas are usually better than other people's ideas." This item is scored in reverse.)

The subjects were asked to rate themselves on these and other items on a five-point Likert-type scale ranging from *Strongly Disagree* to *Strongly Agree*.

To demonstrate convergent, divergent, and incremental validity, Krumrei-Mancuso and Rouse (2016) tested their new measure against a number of extant measures for humility (Ashton and Lee, 2008; Goldberg et al., 2006; Landrum, 2011), open-minded thinking (Stanovitch and West, 2007), intellectual humility (McElroy et al., 2014), narcissism (Gentile et al., 2013), psychological entitlement (Campbell et al., 2004), social desirability (Crowne and Marlow, 1960), and openness to experience, tolerance, conformity, and social confidence (Goldberg et al., 2006). Their measure has a small but significant correlation with age ($r = 0.09$) and with social desirability ($r = 0.22$). These were controlled for in subsequent analyses. Factors one and two of the measure (independence of intellect and ego, openness to revising one's viewpoint) were the main drivers of the correlation with social desirability. There was a moderate correlation with intellectual humility ($r = 0.52$) and open-minded thinking ($r = 0.56$), and small to moderate correlations with humility (range: $r = 0.21–0.42$) proving adequate convergent validity with these measures.

Incremental validity, the capacity of a new measure to explain variability beyond an existing measure, was shown through a series of hierarchical regressions. When measured against open-minded thinking, the CIHS showed better predictive ability than another measure of intellectual humility (12.4 percent of the variance after entering age, social desirability, and scores on the Intellectual Humility Scale, McElroy et al., 2014). The CIHS also predicted open-mindedness above what the general humility measures accounted for (26.2 percent of the variance beyond age, social desirability, and the three humility measures). Moreover, the humility scales predicted variance beyond what the CIHS accounted for when measured against narcissism and psychological entitlement (34.6 percent of the variance in narcissism and 30.8 percent of the variability in psychological entitlement beyond age, social desirability, and the CIHS). Humility is a better predictor of these two constructs than is intellectual humility, demonstrating the discriminate validity of the new measure.

Krumrei-Mancuso and Rouse (2016) also wanted to test what the CIHS would predict about open-minded thinking, tolerance, and openness to experience beyond what they called cognitive complexity (e.g., desire to understand many areas of knowledge, synthesize ideas, and engage in logical thinking). First, they established that their measure is positively related to open-minded thinking ($r = 0.57$), tolerance ($r = 0.28$) and openness to experience ($r = 0.40$). Then they showed that the CIHS predicted more of the variance in open-minded thinking (28.6 percent), tolerance (5.1 percent), and openness to experience (15.8 percent) after controlling for select traits of cognitive complexity (plus age and social desirability). The desire to know, engage with ideas, and practice logical thinking, while related to intellectual humility, do not tell the complete story of a person's capacity to engage in open-minded thinking, practice tolerance, and be open to experience. Intellectual humility, as measured by the CIHS, gives a more complete picture by adding information to what goes into these traits.

This measure admirably attempts to be as comprehensive as possible in assessing intellectual humility. The four factors cover much of the philosophical ground that has been gone over thus far. The measure proves to be adept at predicting open-minded thinking, tolerance, and openness to experience, at least insofar as these were measured by the instruments used in this study. The correlation between the social desirability scale and the two subscales of the measure (independence of intellect and ego, openness to revising one's viewpoint), though small, raises an interesting question. If social desirability is tapping into some kind of tendency toward diffidence, then showing some correlation might actually be a strength of the scale, for it can reveal something about the "diffident" end of the intellectual humility spectrum. Still, the CIHS predicted variance beyond social desirability when the researchers controlled for it. As we stated at the outset of this chapter, no instrument can be "comprehensive" in assessing intellectual humility, but the use of this measure will certainly further our understanding of the relationship of intellectual humility to other aspects of human life.

Intellectual Humility Scale (General)

Leary et al. (2016) took a team approach, forging a definition of intellectual humility in collaboration with a group of social scientists and the philosophers. The philosophers in the group (Dennis Whitcomb, Heather Battaly, Jason Baehr, and Daniel Howard-Snyder) have proposed the philosophical definition of intellectual humility as "*proper attentiveness to, and owning of, one's intellectual limitations*" (see Chapter 1 for a discussion). This team approach to devising a measure of intellectual humility is unique. A scientist might read broadly in philosophy to develop a theory and to define a construct, and even consult with philosophers on their theory, but ultimately it is the scientist (or team of scientists) who constructs the definition.[2] While both depend on a deep interaction between philosophy and science, the approach to a definition in Leary et al. (2016) is more direct. In this approach, philosophers and scientists collaborate on both theory building and definitions, both philosophical and psychological constructs. The psychological definition agreed upon by this group is that intellectual humility involves "recognizing that a particular personal belief may be fallible, accompanied by an appropriate attentiveness to limitations in the evidentiary basis of that belief and to one's own limitations in obtaining and evaluating relevant information" (p. 3). This definition holds whether the beliefs in question are matters of fact or matters of opinion.

In addition to the philosophical considerations, Leary et al. (2016) looked to some existing constructs in psychology to inform their approach. Although they consider intellectual humility to be fundamentally a private assessment of a person's beliefs, they recognize that it is exhibited and expressed through interactions with others (either through an openness to the beliefs of others, a lack of self-importance or pride in one's beliefs, an unwillingness to negotiate ideas with others, or asserting a misplaced confidence in wrong information). However, in their view, intellectual humility must be distinct from other psychological constructs that tap into some of the same tendencies. For example, although dogmatism would be negatively related to intellectual humility because of a lack of recognition of the limitations to the belief, it is different because dogmatism is often tied to a specific set of beliefs whereas intellectual humility is more global. Likewise, the concept of belief superiority—a notion that my beliefs are better or more correct than others' beliefs—would not constitute intellectual humility in its absence because a person with belief superiority can grant that there are other, equally valid ideas, and/or still be open to belief revision as new evidence comes on board. Leary et al. 2016 also consider the personality trait of Openness in the Five-Factor Model (McCrea and Costa, 1987, 1997) to be a related, but broader concept that will still tap into some of the aspects of intellectual humility. Finally, Leary et al. (2016) express a worry that intellectual humility might be conflated with lack of confidence in ideas, and correlate with an unfavorable view of a person's intellectual ability. This could stem from lack of access to complete information, lack of expertise, lack of experience, or other factors.

Leary et al. (2016) set out to create a short, general assessment of intellectual humility based on the consensus definition arrived at through their collaborative work with philosophers and other social scientists. It is general in the sense that it is not domain-specific, but it can be applied across, and to, many different domains of knowledge and experience. To assess the discriminant validity of the measure, they compared it to other psychological constructs around open-mindedness, openness to experience, and closed-mindedness.[3]

They began by generating twenty-three items that aligned with the three components of their definition: (1) recognition that one's beliefs may be fallible, (2) attentiveness to the quality of the evidence in support of one's beliefs, and (3) awareness of one's limitations in obtaining and evaluating relevant information. They tested these items with 300 participants online through MTurk. They subjected the results to a factor analysis and chose those items that "demonstrated high communalities in a factor analysis of the items and represented the breadth of the definition" (p. 7). The six-item scale loaded on a single factor, making it best used as a single construct. Some examples of the items are: "I recognize the value in opinions that are different from my own"; "In the face of conflicting evidence, I am open to changing my opinions"; and "I accept that my beliefs and attitudes may be wrong" (p. 36). The Cronbach's alpha—a statistical test for the reliability of the scale—was 0.82.

To demonstrate convergent, divergent, and incremental validity, Leary et al. (2016) tested their new measure against a number of extant measures for the Big Five personality traits (BFI; John, Donahue, and Kentle, 1991), facets of openness to experience (Costa and McCrae, 1992), epistemic curiosity (Litman and Spielberger, 2003), existential quest (van Pachterbeke, Keller, and Saroglou, 2012), need for cognition (Cacioppo and Petty, 1982), dogmatism (Altemeyer, 2002; Rokeach, 1960), intolerance of ambiguity (Martin and Westie, 1959), self-righteousness (Falbo and Belk, 1985), narcissism (Raskin and Terry, 1988), social vigilantism (Saucier and Webster, 2009), and social desirability (Reynolds, 1982). As they were also interested in the relationship between intellectual humility and other epistemic virtues, they listed nine virtues (along with descriptions of them, adapted from Baehr, 2014), and asked participants to rate (on a scale of one to five) the extent to which these virtues described them. The virtues were curiosity, intellectual autonomy, attentiveness, intellectual thoroughness, open-mindedness, intellectual courage, intellectual tenacity, and intellectual humility.

As the researchers expected, there were significant, positive correlations between their measure of intellectual humility and openness (in a range from $r = 0.24$ to $r = 0.40$), agreeableness ($r = 0.15$), epistemic curiosity (subscales range: $r = 0.27$–0.35), existential quest ($r = 0.35$), and need for cognition ($r = 0.34$). The measure correlated negatively with dogmatism (Altemeyer's [2002] measure: $r = 0.20$; Rokeach's [1960] measure: $r = -0.45$), intolerance of ambiguity ($r = -0.32$), and self-righteousness ($r = -0.35$). Narcissism and social vigilantism did not correlate with intellectual humility. Regarding correlations between the participants' ratings on the scale and their ratings of themselves on other virtues, the strongest were with intellectual humility ($r = 0.37$) and open-mindedness ($r = 0.43$), but the measure also correlated significantly with all the other intellectual virtues, though less strongly (ranging from $r = 0.23$ to $r = 0.31$).

These results show that, while this measure of intellectual humility taps into some of the same processes as are represented by openness to experience and open-mindedness, these processes are only a part of what is involved in being intellectually humble. In a similar way, those high in need for cognition show some of the same impulses as the intellectually humble. Because they enjoy seeking out information to consider it in greater detail than most others, they may think more deeply about what kind of evidence supports the information and see that not all positions should be strongly held. The significant correlation with self-righteousness, but not with narcissism, shows that this measure may do well to distinguish between pride in one's ideas (self-righteousness) and pride in oneself in general (narcissism).

Intellectual Humility Scale

As part of her dissertation work, Tennelle Porter (2015) devised an intellectual humility scale. She drew broadly from psychology and philosophy in constructing the theoretical basis for her measure. From psychology, Porter was informed by work on humility that recognizes that humility is defined both interpersonally (as a recognition of the value of others in any given endeavor) and intrapersonally (as an accurate view of one's own abilities, Tangney, 2000). From the philosophical literature in intellectual humility, she considered the Roberts and Wood (2003) account that defines intellectual humility in terms of a low concern for status; an account from Hopkins, Hoyle, and Toner (2014) that intellectual humility is understanding that one's own beliefs and opinions are fallible and, in the discovery of better information, being open to changing beliefs and opinions; and the view, from Samuelson et al. (2014), that intellectual humility is a virtuous mean between diffidence and arrogance. All these views, Porter claims, recognize that an awareness of cognitive fallibility is a hallmark of intellectual humility. To this she adds the insight from the psychological literature on humility— that intellectual humility also involves valuing the intellect of others—to arrive at a definition of intellectual humility as "recognizing the partial nature of one's knowledge and valuing others' intelligence" (p. 5).

Porter (2015) began with a twenty-three-item scale and reduced the items to six through a two-step process of factor analysis along with eliminating items that did not reflect the two factors she had identified as central to intellectual humility (recognizing the partial nature of one's knowledge and valuing other's intelligence). The alpha-level that indicated the internal consistency of the measure was 0.63. Examples of items that reflect an awareness of cognitive fallibility were: "I am willing to admit it if I don't know something" and "I don't like it when someone points out an intellectual mistake I made" (reverse coded). Examples that reflect valuing other's intelligence were: "I actively seek feedback on my ideas, even if it is critical" and "I acknowledge when someone knows more than me about a certain subject."

In two studies, Porter (2015) tested her measure against constructs that were theoretically related to intellectual humility. The first sample comprised

176 students from a community college (mean age = 23.61); the second was a sample of adults recruited online through MTurk (mean age = 32.84). The results from these two studies were that intellectual humility was positively associated with Need for Cognition (r = 0.28/0.41, Cacioppo and Petty, 1982), Openness to Experience (r = 0.26/0.40), Agreeableness(r = 0.37/0.41), Conscientiousness (r = 0.36/0.25, Big 5, John, Donahue, and Kentle, 1991), General Humility (Study 1, r = 0.26, Bollinger, 2010, as cited in Porter, 2015), and Epistemic Curiosity (Study 1, r = 0.46, Litman and Spielberger, 2003), and modesty (Study 2, r = 0.31, Park, Peterson, and Seligman, 2004), as Porter had expected. Need for Cognitive Closure (Webster and Kruglanski, 1994) and Narcissism (Emmons, 1987) showed mixed results across the two studies, demonstrating a significant correlation in study 2 (r = -0.18 and r = -0.20, respectively) but no significant correlation in study 1. Porter also tested her measure against how subjects performed in an imagined disagreement. Those who reported more respectful attributions and more open-minded responses were significantly more likely to score high in intellectual humility.

It may seem (and even be!) tedious to report all of the different measures against which intellectual humility was assessed along with all the respective correlations, but there is something to be learned from providing such detail. Remember, the devil is in the details. When claiming that a construct has validity vis-à-vis other related constructs, it is important to know what intellectual humility is being measured against. It is interesting to note that there is no measure common to all three studies we have examined thus far. While all assessed intellectual humility against "openness to experience," they did not use the same measure of that construct. Two of the three shared some measures (e.g., need for cognition, the Big 5, social desirability, and narcissism), but they did not always have similar results with these measures. Granted, each measure may be tapping into different forms of intellectual humility, but it seems to prove the point made at the outset of this chapter:

measurements are useful for tracking certain aspects of intellectual humility, but no one measure can capture it all.

Informant reporting measures

Another approach to measuring intellectual humility is informant report. Instead of reporting on the presence of the construct within yourself, as in self-report methods, informant reports have you looking for and rating this trait in others. McElroy et al. (2014) took this approach, in part, because of their view of intellectual humility as a relational concept—that is, because intellectual humility "helps people predict how they will be treated by a target person" (p. 20). By their definition, intellectual humility is marked by an understanding of the limits of one's knowledge and an openness to ideas as well as a capacity to control arrogance and exchange ideas in a manner that does not give offense, by both presenting and receiving ideas respectfully. This measure was constructed much like the self-report measures we have described. Items were generated and tested by factor analysis yielding a sixteen-item scale that had two factors that aligned with their definition: one reflecting intellectual openness (items like: "Is good at considering the limitations of their perspective; Is open to competing ideas") and the other (reverse coded) that reflects intellectual arrogance (items like: "Often become angry when their ideas are not implemented; Become angry when their advice is not taken"). The internal consistency scores of the subscales were good (0.92–0.94 for Intellectual Openness and 0.93 for Intellectual Arrogance).

McElroy et al. (2014) tested how well their measure could distinguish between people of intellectual humility, modesty, and drive. They randomly assigned participants to imagine people either low or high in one of those traits, and then participants rated them using the Intellectual Humility Scale, a trust scale (DHT, Larzelere and Huston, 1980), and the Big 5 (John et al., 1991). There were no significant differences in the ratings of an intellectually humble person and a modest person, but ratings of the intellectually humble person versus the driven person were significantly different, demonstrating some discriminate validity of the measure (versus drive at least). Also, intellectual humility was positively related to trust ($r = 0.74$), and, as we have seen in other studies, to agreeableness ($r = 0.78$), openness ($r = 0.54$), conscientiousness ($r = 0.58$), and negatively related to neuroticism ($r = -0.58$). Finally, McElroy et al. (2014) used the measure to assess religious leaders who had betrayed the participants in some way. They found that participants were more readily able to repair the relationship with those leaders who were perceived as more intellectually humble through forgiveness and a willingness to work on conciliation. Intellectual humility ratings were also related to positive attitudes toward God and not being angry at God.

In an intriguing study contrasting informant measures with self-report, Meagher et al. (in press) noted that there are potentialities and problems with each when measuring intellectual virtues and vices. In their study, they assembled a group of strangers, had them engage in several tasks together, and then had them rate themselves and others on intellectual humility, intellectual arrogance, interpersonal dominance, competence, the Big 5, and some exploratory items related to self-enhancement (positive self-attributes). They analyzed the data in a way that could produce consensus among the members on the informant ratings. On the informant report, there was no consensus on the intellectual humility or arrogance of fellow participants, but the participants reached consensus on interpersonal dominance, extraversion, and being funny. Regarding self-report, those that rated themselves high on intellectual humility also rated themselves high on positive self-attributes, those who rated themselves high on intellectual arrogance tended to rate themselves low on those attributes (especially emotional stability and conscientiousness).

The procedure was repeated in a second study with a group that had worked together for several months and were fairly well acquainted with one another. Similar results were obtained for the correlations between self-reports and self-enhancement. However, this time there was consensus on the ratings of one another in the group. Those people rated highly by the group on one trait were also likely to be rated highly on other traits. There was a significant correlation between how participants viewed themselves on intellectual arrogance and how the group viewed them on this construct ($r = 0.39$). From this study, we get a fuller picture of how complicated it can be to measure virtues. By using items to indicate self-enhancement (beyond the usual measures of social desirability), the study showed that people who view themselves as virtuous also see themselves as better leaders, funnier, and more competent than others. Results indicate that rating strangers on virtues is problematic, but that when people know one another, the accuracy between self-ratings and informant ratings increases. This finding might give us pause about the efficacy of judging the epistemic virtue of strangers and gives good evidence to support the value of getting to know those with whom you might disagree as a key strategy for civil discourse.

§4: Measuring intellectual humility in context

Among the measures of intellectual humility we have reviewed thus far, two essential elements have been shared across the constructs: an appreciation of the limits of one's knowledge (an awareness, an appropriation, or owning of one's own epistemic fallibility), and an openness to the beliefs, ideas, and opinions of others (including valuing other's opinions and a willingness to revise beliefs when encountering other ideas). While matters of ownership of one's own fallibility (Leary et al., 2016) or concern for status (Krumrei-Mancuso and Rouse, 2016) may be additional elements of the constructs, these two prove central to most operational definitions of intellectual humility. In the pages ahead, you will see these two elements worked out in different ways as researchers explore the development of intellectual humility across the lifespan (Chapter 4), and test the capacity for intellectual humility across situations (Chapter 6). For example, a number of developmental researchers used a child's willingness to seek more information and advice as a measure of intellectual humility (Busch and Legare, 2015; Danovitch and Moser, 2015) or asked children to assess their own knowledge in specific domains (Lockhart, Goddu, and Keil, in press; Danovitch and Moser, 2015). Similarly, when assessing adult behavior, researchers used participants' willingness to continue to receive information with which they might disagree (Jarvinen et al., 2015) or had adults assess their own knowledge (Fisher, Goddu, and Keil, 2015). In some cases, new measures were devised that focused on one aspect of intellectual humility or the other (e.g., Open-Minded Cognition, Price et al., 2015). In addition, intellectual humility might be assessed as the ability to overcome intellectual arrogance, defined as the tendency to overestimate one's knowledge and cognitive abilities and/or a general ignorance of the heuristics and biases that govern much of our cognition (e.g., Dunning [2015], Chapter 5).

As we conclude this chapter on measurement, we return to some points we made early in the chapter, namely, that while measurements are valuable tools for tracking important aspects of intellectual humility, they are not, especially in isolation, full definitions of intellectual humility. While self-reports can give us some information about people's tendency to be open to new information, or to understand the limits of their knowledge, we cannot be certain they will be intellectually humble, even in most situations. As with any complex human behavior, having a number of measures that use different methods (such as informant reports, behavioral checklists, simulations of disagreement, observation in actual disagreement) taken together might approach a more complete picture of intellectual humility. We have just begun to explore, not only how to construct, but also how to measure this vital intellectual virtue and, as such, we are off to a good start.

4

How do we become intellectually humble?

Investigating the ontogenesis—the development through the lifespan—of a virtue or trait can take two forms. One is to discover the mature form of the trait in question and then look to childhood to find its early, immature form. In this way, an existing trait or virtue found in most adults is explained in terms of how it might have been formed in childhood. The other is to start with childhood itself, looking for natural tendencies related to the trait or virtue to see if they change by either diminishing or growing. This method seeks to describe how traits form and develop in order to discover the processes by which traits come into being. Our examination of the development of intellectual humility will be informed by both approaches. Take, as an example of the first approach, a well-known cognitive bias in the psychological literature known as the "better-than-average" effect (sometimes called the Lake Wobegon effect, Kruger, 1999). This is the phenomenon that, in any given sample, a majority of the adults will rate themselves above the 50th percentile in most dimensions of personality and behavior. A well-known example of this effect is a survey conducted at a large university system in which 95 percent of the professors rated themselves above average as teachers (Alicke and Govorun, 2005). This bias may be as good a definition of intellectual arrogance as any (thinking you are smarter than average), and as such would at least inhibit intellectual humility. How does this cognitive bias show up in children? Hagá and Olson (in press) demonstrate that five- to eleven-year-olds also show the better-than-average effect (e.g., they think they run faster, draw better, are nicer, less lazy than their peers), and are a lot like adults in that they don't think they are susceptible to this and other biases (i.e., they think that they rated their own abilities and traits objectively and that they wouldn't show favoritism toward an in-group member). Where children differ from adults is in their beliefs that others would or would not be susceptible to these biases. Adults and older children (aged 10–12) think their peers would be susceptible to these biases while they themselves would be unbiased (called the bias blind spot in the adult literature), yet five-year-olds think their peers would be as unbiased as themselves. We learn something about the development of a trait (in this case, the better-than-average bias) by comparing adult forms with those in childhood. We might wonder, for example, what changed between five and twelve that made the older children look more like adults in their cognitive bias. As an example of the second approach, that is, looking for natural tendencies related to the trait or virtue to see if they change by either diminishing or growing, we might look at how children explore the causes of things and how those processes might change through time as their cognitive capacity grows. Children seem to be more open to possibilities for alternative explanations for causal events. Is this openness something that diminishes over time (we become less humble, less open to alternative explanations)? If so, why? What might explain this change over time?

§1: Nature versus nurture

When investigating the development of intellectual humility, the proverbial "nature" versus "nurture" debate emerges as a legitimate point of inquiry. Nature refers to heritable traits from genetic coding handed down from parents, and nurture refers to the life experiences and socialization processes that form individuals. Is intellectual humility an innate "trait" with predominantly heritable qualities passed through the genetic code from parent to offspring? Or is it more a learned habit or "virtue" that is amenable to environmental influences such as teaching, exposure to exemplary models, rewards, and punishments, and thus can be learned and exercised through force of will? We will not attempt to resolve the issue, but, instead, accept that the expression of intellectual humility in any given individual—like many virtues of both the intellectual and other kinds—are some combination of nature and nurture, comprising both heritable traits and environmental influences.

Since the investigation into the development of intellectual humility is still in its infancy and, from what we know so far, is likely composed of several heritable traits about which there is no strong consensus, the focus of the scientific investigation into the development of intellectual humility has been on the nurture side, that is, the processes of socialization such as teaching, parenting, and learning that might impact the formation of intellectual humility. Nevertheless, a word can be said about the "nature" of intellectual humility by examining those basic traits thought to have some genetic basis that are a part of the constellation of traits that might form intellectual humility. Considering intellectual humility within the framework of conceptions of personality such as the Five-Factor Model (The Big Five, McCrae and Costa, 1987, 1997) and the HEXACO (Lee and Ashton, 2004) leads in a promising direction since work has been done on the relative proportion of heritability in the expression of these traits. It seems intuitive enough that intellectual humility could map well onto certain personality traits described by these models. We can imagine that high levels of the Openness to Experience factor might correlate with high intellectual humility, especially when we look at specific facets of the Openness construct. The facet "openness to ideas," for example, seems to capture an element of curiosity we would expect to find in the intellectually humble; the "values" facet might figure into whether someone is willing to really consider an opposing political or religious view with charity. Similar corollaries of intellectual humility might exist within some facets of Agreeableness and Conscientiousness such as the "trust" and "modesty" facets of Agreeableness, and the "deliberation" facet of Conscientiousness.

All of the Big Five traits have some element of heritability. Openness to Experience tends to garner the highest estimates of genetic influence. Jang, Livesley, and Vernon (1996), in a study comparing monozygotic and dizygotic twins, estimate that 61 percent of the variance of this trait can be accounted for by genetic influences. Agreeableness and Conscientiousness had lower estimates of 41 percent and 44 percent, respectively. Other studies of twins place the heritability estimates for Openness much lower. Bergman et al. (1993) places the estimate of the variability due to genetic influences at 40 percent for Openness, 12 percent for Agreeableness, and 29 percent for Concientioussess. Loehlin et al. (1998) estimate that the heritability of these particular personality traits falls closer to Jang, Livesley, and Vernon (1996), at least for Agreeableness (35 percent) and Conscientiousness (38 percent), but closer to Bergman et al. (1993) for Openness to Experience (45 percent). In a study that assessed the influence of heritability in situations, Lensvelt-Mulders and Hettema (2001) estimate genetic factors account for 0.48, 0.48, and 0.49 of the variance for Openness to Experience, Agreeableness, and Conscientiousness, respectively. Whatever the precise estimates are, it is clear that heritability plays some role in the presence and expression of the personality traits that might contribute to a person's being intellectually humble.

At the facet level, the heritability picture is a bit more mixed. A cross-cultural twins study by Jang et al. (1998) shows that the heritability of some of the specific facets of the Big Five that may have a more direct impact on intellectual humility is not as strongly influenced by genetics. While the "ideas" and "values" facets of Openness to Experience and the "trust" facet of Agreeableness showed very similar heritability estimates (0.48, 0.49, and 0.50, respectively), the heritability estimates for the "modesty" facet of Agreeableness and the "deliberation" facet of Conscientiousness did not rise to the level of significance. This suggests that certain facets of intellectual humility such as modesty and deliberation may be more malleable to environmental influences and, thus, more responsive to training. This is not to say that other facets from the Big Five related to intellectual humility are not responsive to learning and environment. What is clear is that the variability in the expression of intellectual humility, being comprised of a complex set of traits and facets of those traits from the Big Five, will be accounted for, in part, by genetic and heritable factors but will still be amenable to environmental influences such as role models, rewards for behavior, experiences, and direct teaching. Any given trait in an individual, even under the strong influence of heritability, can nonetheless be suppressed or encouraged through environmental influences. The scientific investigation into the development of intellectual humility in children has been to both describe what seems to be innate structures of children's thinking as they relate to intellectual humility and explore those environmental influences that might enhance the development of this intellectual virtue.

§2: Learning and knowledge acquisition in children

A natural domain in which to search for the development of intellectual humility would be the development of thinking in children. How do children seek to know the unknown? What are the cognitive processes children use to know the world? What kind of thinking goes into learning new things? How might intellectual humility fit into these processes? There are different models, frameworks, and theories that have been developed to answer these questions. One that is both widely accepted and particularly well suited to examining the growth and inhibition of intellectual humility in children is called "theory theory" (Gopnik, 2003). Theory theory posits that children think like little scientists by continually constructing and then revising theories about the structure of the world and the way the world works, including the social world. Children, like scientists, observe the world and begin to form theories about how the world is structured, what might cause what, how this or that might work. Then, through experience, they gather more data that either reinforces the theory or revises it.

The origin of this approach to cognitive development has its roots in Piaget's concepts of assimilation and accommodation. Piaget's claim was that thinking had different structures at certain stages in human development, and information was either assimilated into those structures, or the structures needed to be accommodated to fit new information that did not fit previous thought structures. In the same way, as a child receives new information and has new experiences, information can either be assimilated into the theories the child has formed about the world or the theories can be changed, augmented, or modified to accommodate the new information and make sense of it. In this way, children, like little "scientists," form theories about the world's causal structures, including the social world, and test those theories. As new data comes through new experiences, those theories are either reinforced (assimilation) or modified (accommodation) to make the best possible sense of the world. Children can also use these theories about the world's causal structure to make predictions, and possibly even test them out. Children form theories about human intention and motivation (theory of mind), theories of life and growth (naïve biology), theories of physical causation and laws (naïve physics), to name a few.

Alison Gopnik (2003), one of the originators of the "theory theory," explains the process in more detail:

The basic idea is that children develop their everyday knowledge of the world by using the same cognitive devices that adults use in science. In particular, children develop abstract, coherent systems of entities and rules, particularly causal entities and rules. That is, they develop theories. These theories enable children to make predictions about new evidence, to interpret evidence, and to explain evidence. Children actively experiment with and explore the world, testing the predictions of the theory and gathering relevant evidence. Some counter evidence to the theory is simply reinterpreted in terms of the theory. Eventually, however, when many predictions of the theory are falsified, the child begins to seek alternative theories. If the alternative theory does a better job of predicting and explaining the evidence, it replaces the existing theory. (p. 6)

At the heart of learning, according to "theory theory," is theory revision. We hold theories of the world—the physical, the biological, and the social world—and we test those theories against experience to see if they are true. As evidence confirms the theory, we hold those theories tightly. For example, we hold a theory of gravity from a very early age. That theory is continually reinforced by experience. Things tend to fall down. Children love to test this theory when they discover that they can cause things to fall down and, because every time the cup is knocked off the table it falls to the floor, a firm theory of gravity is formed. However, children might also be testing the theory that adults around them will pick up the things they have caused to fall and give them back (a hypothesis that seems to require continual testing as anyone who has spent some time around toddlers can well attest). This theory (that adults will pick up something they have caused to fall and give it back) children might hold less firmly because some adults do conform to this theory (mom or dad), and some do not (strangers in a restaurant) and those who do conform, do so intermittently (mom or dad eventually tire of the game). To use the language of the doxastic account articulated in Chapter 1, children ought to be dogmatic about a theory of gravity (that things fall down when you let them go, or knock them off, from a high position) and would be virtuous in holding fast to it. Children ought to be more humble about the theory that people will pick up and give back to them things that they have let go (or knocked off) from a high place and would be virtuous to hold that theory more lightly. Children ought to hold the theory that things fall up very lightly, indeed, because that experience is very rare and could be better explained by an alternative hypothesis or theory (a hidden causal agent, for example). Thus learning, like intellectual humility, might be described as the process of testing theories about the world in order to learn how firmly, or lightly, one ought to hold them. The goal of learning (and intellectual humility) is to hold a theory with "proper" firmness, one that conforms to the truth about the world, insofar as that truth can be apprehended.

This idea, that learning is a process of discovering just how firmly one ought to hold theories about the world, has been further refined by the "theory theorists," through incorporating ideas from Bayesian statistics into their views of how children learn. Learning, in this view, is not the process of holding a single theory about the world and then proving or disproving it before forming another theory that can then be tested. It is, rather, a process of holding many hypotheses that might explain the evidence or the observed phenomena and learning through experience and testing which is more probable. Bayesian learning is the process of assigning "weights" to any given hypothesis about the world according to how probable that hypothesis is compared to other, alternative hypotheses. Gopnik and Wellman (2012) explain theory change, which is at the heart of learning, this way:

> In the course of theory change, children gradually change the probability of multiple hypotheses rather than simply rejecting or accepting a single hypothesis. Moreover, this process of revision can yield many intermediate steps. Evidence leads children to gradually revise their initial hypotheses and slowly replace them with more probable hypotheses. This results in a characteristic series of related conceptions that forms a bridge from one broad theory to the next. (p. 1,086)

Gopnik and Wellman (2012) point out that this view actually allows children to learn something new. Rather than acquiring learning at the end of a process of an accumulation of associations, they can actually think anew (form alternative hypotheses) based on patterns of evidence. This also accounts for the "gradual and piecemeal" way children's thinking develops. It can account for how new information can be brought to bear on prior knowledge in such a way that learning can occur and new knowledge is generated. The drawbacks of this view have to do with the vast number of possible hypotheses that might explain any given phenomenon. With so many possible explanations, choosing which hypotheses to test and what evidence is relevant become problematic.

One distinctive feature of children's learning, compared to that of adults, is that children spend a greater portion of time in "exploratory learning" (learning about the world in order to know the world for its own sake) than they do in "exploitation learning" (learning about the world for a particular purpose or goal, Buchsbaum et al., 2012). Exploration learning allows for wide-ranging discovery and for a capacity to adapt to many different kinds of environments and situations, but it also means that the particular demands of the environment cannot be addressed until after learning has occurred. Survival would demand extensive exploitative learning in order to best know what to avoid and what to exploit in any particular environment. Human development allows for a "protected" period of exploration learning when children depend on the exploitative learning of their adult caretakers to insure their survival. Exploration learning employs particular kinds of learning mechanisms that afford the discovery of causal relationships and which allows humans to not only know the world, but also make predictions based on theories of causal structures of the world. In exploration learning, networks of causal relationships become causal models that allow new inferences to be drawn, different predictions to be entertained, and counterfactual possibilities to be tested. In the search for the best model—the one that fits the evidence from experience—Bayesian learning mechanisms are employed. This model aims for the "virtuous mean" of holding a belief (a hypothesis) with appropriate firmness (stability) while being open to counterevidence (flexibility). This combination of stability and flexibility is characteristic of Bayesian reasoning (Gopnik and Wellman, 2012).

Part of exploratory learning in childhood is simply trying things out through free play and testing how things work in the world by manipulating causal effects. Gopnik and Welman (2012) report on research that demonstrates that children's exploratory play involves what they call a kind of "intuitive experimentation"—that is, it is sufficiently structured so as to help children discover causal relationships. In this way, children seem to be actively seeking out evidence to help them discover the "truth" about the world. Children also use observation and imitation to discover causal structures and show variability in their approach to discovering evidence. They might employ two or three strategies and test multiple hypotheses in their exploratory play.

Children not only act like "little scientists" through exploration, they also learn through explanation, another part of the scientific process. Christine Legare (2014) proposes that explanation and exploration operate in tandem in learning—in a "synergistic" fashion—with explanation as the way children generate, limit, and evaluate hypotheses, and exploration as the means for testing them. In her research, she has discovered that children learn most effectively when they encounter evidence that is inconsistent with their prior experience and expectations because it promotes theory revision through the generation and testing of new hypotheses to explain the anomaly. Children explore more, and do so more systematically, when seeking an explanation for inconsistencies in the form of unusual or unexpected events. Seeking explanation also guides their exploration and can influence the kinds of exploration children engage in. In this way, exploration and explanation motivate children to learn. Legare (2014) notes that inconsistency alone is not enough to motivate learning, since both children and adults can and do ignore inconsistent evidence or reject it by holding to prior theories and hypotheses (confirmation bias). However, explanation in tandem with exploration opens up the possibility for generating alternative hypotheses and beginning the process of weighing which hypothesis might best account for all the evidence (Legare, 2012).

Explanation may offer other benefits for learning. It may also promote intellectual humility—that is, the capacity to revise beliefs in response to new information. As Legare, Schult, Impola, and Souza (in press) aver:

> If explanation plays a role in acquiring new information and constructing new understanding, then learners should explain the observations that have the greatest potential to teach them something new; namely, those that are *inconsistent* with respect to their current knowledge and thus motivate further information seeking. (p. 4)

The process of explaining inconsistent evidence opens up the "hypothesis space"—the capacity to consider alternative explanations—and allows for children to consider other possibilities as to why something might be happening and what the cause might be. Being open to alternative hypotheses and to exploring evidence that would help one check the veracity of those hypotheses are at the very heart of learning. They are also at the very heart of intellectual humility. The question that Legare and colleagues explore is the role of explanation in the generation of hypotheses and its influence on the kinds of exploration children engage in to test those hypotheses. They wonder how exposure to information that is inconsistent with prior expectations might open children to formulate and revise existing theories of how the world works and thus promote learning. Of special interest was how children might use information that crossed domains in this process. For example, would children be able to use information from the biological domain to inform the causal explanation for an action that had been considered primarily from a psychological (intentional) domain? Research indicates that, while children reason along domain-specific lines, they are also capable of differentiating between domain-specific explanations (Legare et al., in press).

To test these questions, Legare and colleagues (Legare et al., in press) showed a video of two actors, each stating a different preference for a fruit (apple/banana). Researchers then asked children to explain the behavior of video-taped actors in two conditions: a consistent condition (each reaching for their favorite fruit), and a test condition in which one actor behaved in a manner that confirmed expectations (reached for an apple) and the other in a manner that was inconsistent with stated preferences (reached for an apple when the banana was their favorite). Ninety-one percent of the children in the test condition explained the unexpected behavior of actor 2 as a new preference. The children were then shown new evidence (actor 2 was actually reaching for a cookie that was obscured by the apple in the initial test condition) and then asked to give a further explanation. Upon receiving this new evidence, 85 percent of children revised their previous explanation of actor 2's motives from a new preference (likes apples) to a new goal (likes cookies). The researchers, using a similar procedure, tested whether or not children would revise their explanation with evidence from a different domain of knowledge (biological evidence). In this case, the second actor did not choose a preferred food because it was contaminated (by a bug). Similar to the first study, 92 percent of the children explained the unexpected behavior in terms of a new preference (psychological domain) before the new evidence was revealed. Upon seeing the bug on the fruit, 78 percent of the children switched to an explanation from the biological domain (contamination, e.g., "it's yucky") while 22 percent retained the psychological explanation they had given before (e.g., "doesn't like it"). This demonstrates that most children can flexibly shift between domains as they consider new evidence in the process of explaining unexpected results.

Using a different research paradigm, Busch and Legare (2015) sought to test how children (aged 5–9) use evidence to discover an actor's preference when the preference is actually unknown. The children were given a task to discover which fruit was the actor's favorite: an apple, a banana, or an orange. A video was shown that established that the actor preferred a banana to an apple. A subsequent video was shown to establish four different conditions. In the consistent condition, the actor once again selected a banana over the apple. In the inconsistent condition, the actor selected an apple over a banana. In the ambiguous condition, the children saw the actor select an orange over an apple. Finally, in the deductive condition, they saw the actor select an orange over a banana. The correct answer in every case was that the actor's favorite was the orange.

After the confirmation trial, the researchers asked the children, "Do you think you need more information to figure out the actor's favorite fruit, or do you think you know which one, between the apple, the orange and the banana, is the actor's favorite?" If the children answered that they knew the actor's favorite, they were asked: "Which one do you think is the actor's favorite, and how do you know?" If the children guessed the favorite was orange, then they were correct regardless of the condition they were in, and they completed the study. If their guess was incorrect or they said they needed more information, they then got to select whether they wanted to view novel information (e.g., seeing the actor choose between the fruit selected in the trial and another fruit) or to watch repeat information, which would be the video they had just watched. The process was repeated, until the children said they knew the actor's favorite, and they guessed that it was the orange. Results show that inconsistent and ambiguous evidence motivated information seeking and increased the accuracy of children's guesses, whereas the consistent condition discouraged information-seeking behavior and led to less hypothesis revision, thereby leading to less accuracy when children guessed the actor's favorite. Moreover, there is a developmental trend in which older children are more likely to request more information in the face of inconsistent or ambiguous information. Results also show that older children are significantly better at figuring out the correct preference in the deduction condition than younger children. This experiment also indicates that the confirmation bias has as strong a pull in children as it does in adults, since in the confirmation trial, children showed high rates of guessing with low rates of accuracy regardless of age. However, consistent with other research by Legare (2012), this study shows that ambiguous and inconsistent information effectively opens children up to consider alternative hypotheses and to consider theories that seem to have been ignored by participants in the consistent condition.

Children have the marks of traits that are central to intellectual humility including belief revision in the face of new evidence and a willingness to be open to, and to seek out, new information in order to form the most accurate and vertical conception of the world. Yet, they are also curiously intellectually arrogant, overconfident about what they know (Lockhart, Goddu, and Keil, in press), and susceptible to the same biases as adults that tilt toward intellectual arrogance such as a confirmation bias (Legare, 2014). Kristi Lockhart and her colleagues (Lockhart et al., in press) have demonstrated that this overoptimism about current and future abilities, which children have about certain malleable skills and attributes (such as neatness and kindness), also extends to knowledge acquisition. In a series of studies, they asked three groups (children aged 5–7, 8–10, and adults aged 18–22) how much a five-year-old person would know about ten different knowledge items (e.g., how things work, moral knowledge, something a child would know, something an adult would know) and how much a thirty-five-year-old person would know about the same items. The 5- to 7-year-old children were more overoptimistic about knowledge for the protagonist at both ages compared to the other groups, while the 8- to 10-year-old group was more optimistic about the 35-year-old's potential knowledge compared to the adult group. The same results were obtained in a follow-up study in which the researchers asked the participants to rate their own knowledge when they were five and when they will be thirty-five. In a third study, researchers tested whether children had different assessments of knowledge depending on the valence (negative versus positive outcomes). In this case, valence affected the 8- to 10-year-old group alone, showing an emerging realization that people will not like to learn negative things.

While an overoptimistic assessment of one's current and future knowledge may be characteristic of intellectual arrogance, it need not be an impediment to the development of intellectual humility. Lockhart et al. (in press) aver that overoptimism, especially in reference to future knowledge, may be a form of deference to older adults as more knowledgeable and an acknowledgment that, as a child, one has a lot to learn. Their research also shows that children are not only optimistic about their own knowledge potential, but also have the same rosy view of the knowledge of others, both their own age and older. This "nonjudgmental optimism" may, in fact, be a motivating factor in learning as it allows for trusting others as truthful sources of knowledge, a key element in intellectual humility.

Part of learning is an awareness of your thought processes, especially an awareness of when you make mistakes so that you can learn from them. This awareness of cognitive thought processes is known as metacognition. Metacognition is also a crucial element in the development of intellectual humility. The more one is aware of one's thought processes—especially one's capacity for knowledge and one's ability to make mistakes—the more one is positioned for intellectual humility. Danovitch and Moser (2015) studied 6- to 8-year-olds and examined their capacity for intellectual humility as operationalized on two dimensions: an assessment of their own knowledge and their willingness to seek out advice from others. To measure knowledge self-assessment, children were asked to rate on a five-point scale their ability to answer twelve difficult questions in the domains of biology and mechanics (e.g., why are some people born with red hair?). The children were then asked, on those same questions, whether they, a doctor, or a mechanic would be best to answer the question (assessing their willingness to seek advice). The children who rated themselves as knowledgeable were less likely to seek advice. These children also tended to have lower IQ scores than those who were more humble about their knowledge. On these knowledge assessment dimensions, there is evidence that intellectual humility increases during childhood.

Danovitch and Moser (2015) also measured the children's capacity to monitor their performance and to detect errors as well as their ability to bounce back after making mistakes and make corrections. They gave the children simple computer tasks that required them to make simple decisions while monitoring the electrical activity of their brains (EEG). For example, in a go/no go task, the children had to hit the space bar when a wild animal appeared on the screen to "capture" it for the zoo, and withhold hitting the space bar when an orangutan appeared who would help "capture" the animals. Those with better error detection show a specific brain pattern (called an error response positivity or Pe) and, because of better error detection, they are more rapidly able to correct mistakes and become better at the task faster. Results from their study show that children who sought advice in the intellectual humility tasks were more aware of their mistakes in the go/no go tasks (had a higher Pe). Moreover, those who had a more "humble" assessment of their knowledge recovered more quickly from mistakes and began more readily to correct them. While this held true for all boys, for the girls it was more complicated. There was an interaction between knowledge assessment and advice seeking such that only the girls who had a "humble" knowledge self-assessment showed a significant relationship between advice seeking and error detection and only those who sought advice had a significant relationship between knowledge self-assessment and a capacity to learn quickly from mistakes in the go/no go task. This direct connection between error detection and advice seeking, and knowledge assessment and mistake correction, is very informative for the development of intellectual humility. It seems clear that a path to developing this virtue runs through metacognition, that is, through developing better awareness of one's thought processes, one's capacity for making mistakes, and a realistic assessment of one's knowledge.

§3: Epistemic trust and the development of intellectual humility

One key issue in learning and knowledge acquisition in both adults and children is epistemic trust (Harris, 2012). From a child's point of view, it is easy to see why this is so crucial. If a child must rely only on his or her own experience to gain knowledge, that child's knowledge of the world is severely impoverished compared to that of the child who can learn from others' experience. Indeed, this is our evolutionary advantage over other species. We can gain knowledge from others' experience and learn from them, provided the knowledge they transmit is reliable and trustworthy. So how do we determine whether an informant is trustworthy? It seems as if the default position is to trust others as informants (Gilbert, 1991), though we approach informants with new information by what Paul Harris and his colleagues characterize as "skeptical trust" (Harris, 2012). Regarding the veracity and trustworthiness of informants, adults and children seem to pay attention to three variables: the size of the difference between an initial belief and the new information (accuracy), the confidence with which an informant holds a belief about the new information, and an evaluation of the credibility of the informant (Jaswal and Malone, 2007). Evaluating the discrepancy between an initial belief and the new information is straightforward enough and can be assessed through a direct comparison of what you know and what you are told. However, the other two factors involve some kind of assessment of the character of the informant, gleaned through an analysis of that person's confidence and credibility. Studies show, for example, that young children may favor the person who appears more confident in their knowledge over one who appears uncertain. (Birch, Akmal, and Frampton, 2010).

In an effort to better understand the relationship between virtue and trustworthiness, we conducted a study looking at the kinds of people children will trust for new information (Samuelson et al., 2015). We showed children informants who the children knew were guilty of different kinds of moral/ conventional violations and asked the children who they trusted to provide them with good information about a particular unfamiliar object—that is, who the children thought had the right name for an object they had never encountered. We hypothesized that the children's decisions to trust information from an informant would be influenced by the moral/conventional violation that was committed by the informants in question. Specifically, we hypothesized that the level of violation severity would correspond to the judged trustworthiness of the informant (i.e., greater judged severity of violation would result in lower trustworthiness).

In a separate pilot study, we showed children aged 4–7 scenes depicting five moral violations according to moral intuition theory (Haidt, 2001): Harm/ Care, Justice/Fairness, Purity/Sanctity, Authority/Obedience, and In-group/ Loyalty along with three conventional violations (eating food with unclean hands, wearing pajamas to school, not thanking someone for a gift) and had them rate the moral severity of each scene. The results showed that children aged 4–7 considered the violations of harm/care and fairness/justice the most severe moral violations; the conventional violation were the least severe; and Purity/Sanctity, Authority/Obedience, and In-group/Loyalty fell between the two. "Moral" here is defined as wrong at all times and places (Smetana and Braeges, 1990). In the epistemic trust study, we showed the children pairs of scenes and asked which of the two protagonists they would trust to provide the right name for an object they had never seen before. The findings suggest that purity violations erode the trustworthiness of informants the most. This is not entirely in line with our predictions from the pilot study, in as much as these findings suggested harm/care violations would be most problematic. However, when we looked at differences based on gender, we found that females were less likely to trust harm/care violators than any other kind of violator. This could be expected according to some moral theory (Gilligan, 1982). We also found some evidence of alternative processes for determining trust when we asked children why they chose a particular informant over another. While many respondents said things confirming our hypotheses (e.g., "because Joey is nasty"), some provided answers that suggested other values (e.g., "because Tyler got away with it") or gave responses that appeared somewhat arbitrary and did not reference the violation at all (e.g., "because Kwoozy [the name for the object according to the chosen informant] sounds like the right name"). The findings lend support to Haidt's (2012) argument that rational explanations seemed to follow gut-level intuitions though the evidence is not strong and further testing is needed. What is clear is that children are making judgments about whom to trust as an informant based on intuitions about their moral character.

If both children and adults assess the character of an informant, is intellectual humility a character trait that will inform trust? To investigate this possibility, Sara Hagá and Kristina Olson (in press) presented children with a picture of an ambiguous object, a candle in the shape of a very real-looking light bulb. Children then heard from three informants, one intellectually humble, one intellectually arrogant, and one intellectually diffident operationalized in this way: the intellectually humble person stated that the object appeared to be a light bulb, and, when another person suggested it might be a candle, seriously considered that the object actually could be something else in reality; the intellectually arrogant person claimed that the object surely was a light bulb and readily dismissed the other person's suggestion; the intellectually diffident person said that the object appeared to be a light bulb, without fully committing to that answer, and then accepted the other person's suggestion without actually scrutinizing it. They then tested children's reactions to these different characters in two pair-wise comparisons (the intellectually humble person vs. the intellectually arrogant; and the intellectually humble person vs. the intellectually diffident) on two dimensions: a social dimension, asking children how likable each informant was, and on an epistemic dimension, asking children whom they would trust for information regarding the names of other unfamiliar objects.

Hagá and Olson (in press) chose to measure children's perceptions of these informants along social and epistemic lines in part because these two dimensions were also found to be salient parts of the implicit theory of an intellectually humble person held in the "folk" mind (Samuelson et al., 2014). As it turns out, they are also salient dimensions of epistemic trust in children. They report on a study by Landrum, Mills, and Johnston (2013) that found that children prefer to learn from a nice nonexpert rather than a mean expert, demonstrating that social graces (niceness, politeness) are a factor in children's estimations of whom to trust for information. On the other hand, children also trust confident informants and prefer to receive information from those who appear to be certain about their knowledge, even if the confidence is not well calibrated to the truth (Tenney et al., 2011). So in the first pair-wise comparison, Hagá and Olson (in press) contrasted two confident informants, an intellectually arrogant person confident in her belief but dismissive of an alternative possibility, and an intellectually humble person, also confident of her belief but "nicer" due to her willingness to consider an alternative possibility to her original belief. They wondered: Will children prefer the intellectually arrogant person because of her supreme confidence (but who is not nice) or the intellectually humble person who is both confident and nice. It turns out that the very young (4- to 5-year-olds) show no preference for one person over the other. One possible explanation Hagá and Olson offer for this finding is that young children are particularly susceptible to two tendencies, namely, favoring the person who sounds the most confident (Jaswal and Malone, 2007) and favoring the nicest person (Landrum et al., 2013). In the case under study, these two tendencies were working in opposite directions, since the intellectually arrogant person sounded more confident but the humble person sounded friendlier. On the other hand, children in the middle group (aged 7–8) favored the intellectually humble person on almost every measure. These results suggest that once children become more sensitized to arrogance and humility, they attach a negative valence to being arrogant and a positive valence to being humble. The older children (10–11) still favored the intellectually humble person, but showed a more nuanced perception that viewed intellectually arrogant people less positively in the social domain (i.e., as less nice), but not in the intellectual domain. By adulthood, "niceness" and "knowledgeability" seem to be completely disassociated, with the arrogant person seen as being as intelligent and knowledgeable as the intellectually humble person, but a lot less nice.

What preferences do children and adults show in a comparison between two "nice" people, when one is more confident than the other? To answer this question, Hagá and Olson (in press) compared an intellectually humble person, who was pretty sure of her initial belief, but willing to consider alternatives, and an intellectually diffident person who was unsure of her initial belief and quickly changed it when an alternative was suggested. Young children (4–5) showed a similar pattern to the comparison of the intellectually humble and the intellectually arrogant person. They showed no preference. However, this lack of preference for either the intellectually humble person or the intellectually diffident person persists into ages 7–8, which suggests that the social dimension is the first to emerge when judging intellectual humility in an informant, and only later (age 10–11) does the epistemic dimension become equally salient. This fits other developmental patterns such as children's growth in moral judgment and reasoning (Kohberg, 1981). In middle childhood, the social dimension has the most weight in moral reasoning (Stage 3), and only later, in adolescence, does more epistemic, principle-oriented reasoning hold sway (Stage 4). This study shows that children show an emerging capacity to judge whom to trust along dimensions defined by intellectual humility. By young adulthood an interesting pattern emerged by which an intellectually humble person was perceived as nicer than an arrogant one and as smarter than a diffident one.

§4: Mindsets and the development
of intellectual humility

Adults and children alike have beliefs about intelligence—implicit theories about how intelligence is acquired and held. They fall along two lines: an essentialist belief about intelligence, that intelligence is a stable, fixed trait that cannot be changed (a fixed mindset); and an incrementalist belief about intelligence, that intelligence is malleable and can grow (a growth mindset). Research has shown that these beliefs have a substantial effect on learning—especially the motivation to learn—and ultimately affect academic achievement. Those who have an incremental belief in intelligence—who believe intelligence can grow incrementally through effort and persistence—tend to be able to form realistic goals (mastery goals), to persist after failure, and to have greater academic success (Dweck, 1999). Moreover, there is a clear relationship between the motivation to learn and implicit theories of intelligence. Those with an incrementalist view are more motivated to persevere after failure and learn from their mistakes (Dweck, Chiu, and Hong, 1995). We might expect that these implicit theories of intelligence would at least be related to intellectual humility and that promoting a growth mindset might also promote aspects of intellectual humility.

The two "mindsets" predict other attitudes and outcomes that are related to intellectual humility. For example, a growth mindset predicts an eagerness to learn (Hong et al., 1999; Mueller and Dweck, 1998), and less defensiveness about mistakes and an interest in learning from them (Nussbaum and Dweck, 2008). When intelligence is considered a fixed quality, it engenders what might be called "intellectually arrogant" attitudes in which some people consider themselves intellectually superior to others, especially when intellectual success reinforces the idea that their fixed intelligence is better than other people's, while, on the other hand, intellectual failure threatens their intellectual status. Having a fixed mindset and an entity view of intelligence can cause people to

inflate the image of their intellectual abilities both in their own self-assessment
and in their presentation of themselves to others. For example, those with a
fixed mindset will inflate their reported test scores (Mueller and Dweck, 1998)
and seek to compare themselves to people who performed worse than they did
(Nussbaum and Dweck, 2008). Having a fixed view of intelligence engenders
these and other defensive strategies that make intellectual humility—which
involves an acknowledgment of the limits of one's knowledge, among other
things—difficult.

In a series of studies, Tenelle Porter (2015) tested some of these
relationships between implicit theories of intelligence and intellectual
humility. Using her own intellectual humility scale (see Chapter 3 for details
and discussion), she found a significant correlation between intellectual
humility and an incrementalist view of intelligence (a growth mindset).
Moreover, she found positive correlations between intellectual humility
and a willingness to listen to opposing viewpoints and to actually choose
to read opposing views when given a choice. She conducted a study with a
group of community college students ($n = 104$) who participated in an online
session in which they were randomly assigned to read fabricated articles that
presented purported scientific evidence for either a growth mindset ("each
person's intelligence can grow and develop over time") or a fixed mindset
("each person has a certain amount of intelligence, and that amount remains
pretty stable over time"). After testing for comprehension, the students were
told to complete, as quickly and as accurately as possible, seven difficult
spatial reasoning problems from a practice dental school admissions test.
Then, regardless of their actual performance, they received predetermined
feedback that they had scored either above or below average. They were
then tested on intellectual humility, confidence in their intelligence, and on
respectful attributions and open-minded responses to opponents in the face
of disagreement. Results showed that those in the growth mindset condition
demonstrated significantly more intellectual humility when controlling for

gender, self-esteem, and confidence in intelligence than those with a fixed mindset. They also made more respectful attributions to their opponents and were more open-minded in their responses in the disagreement exercise. Intellectual humility, when entered into a regression model as a predictor along with the mindset condition, was significantly and positively related to both respectful attributions and open-minded responses, though the mindset condition was not. Intellectual humility proved to play a mediating role between the mindset condition and the respectful and open-minded response to disagreement. Porter's study presents some empirical evidence of a causal link between a growth mindset and intellectual humility and suggests that changing people from an essentialist, or fixed, view of intelligence to an incrementalist, or growth, view may be one way to enhance and develop intellectual humility. This sample comprised college age adults, but a similar link might also be expected in children.

If, as Porter's (2015) work shows, a growth mindset impacts intellectual humility, how might intellectual humility be related to learning? We know that a growth mindset influences learning, especially a motivation to learn (Hong et al., 1999; Mueller and Dweck, 1998). Might we, therefore, also expect that intellectual humility would positively impact learning, especially in such areas as motivation to learn and learning strategies? Samuelson et al. (2014) found that "love of learning" was an attribute that rated highly as descriptive of an intellectually humble person and was nominated exclusively for intellectual humility and not for wisdom (see Chapter 1 for a more detailed description of the study). Other aspects of intellectual humility such as having an awareness of the limits of one's knowledge could also be a motivating factor for learning.

Learning also involves strategies that are dependent on beliefs about knowledge, or epistemic beliefs that are related to intellectual humility (King and Kitchener, 2004). In a review of the literature on the impact of epistemic beliefs on self-regulated learning, Muis (2007) concludes that there is sound evidence that epistemic beliefs are one of the main components involved in self-regulated learning. These beliefs serve as inputs to the metacognitive processes of self-regulated learning by influencing the standards that students use to guide their learning. Thus, if students believe in the certainty of knowledge and that it must come from an authority, they will have the goal of finding only one source of information as the standard that guides them. Further, students will less likely engage in evaluation of the source of knowledge once it is found. By contrast, if students believe that knowledge is tentative and attained through the evaluation of evidence, they will search for multiple sources of information. Moreover, they will engage in comparative analysis, evaluate the trustworthiness of the source, and seek to reconcile the information acquired from experts with their own knowledge and experience. We can conclude that beliefs about knowledge have a strong influence on the motivation to learn from mistakes, on curiosity, on the search for true evidence, and on a love for learning: all aspects of intellectual humility.

Porter (2015) investigated the relationships between epistemic beliefs, intellectual humility, and learning. She began her investigation with a sample of sixty-six college students and assessed them on her nine-item intellectual humility scale. This measure taps participants' willingness to acknowledge the partial nature of their knowledge and to seek feedback, even when negative, which are attitudes related to learning (Samuelson et al., 2012). She also tested for achievement learning goals that assess whether goals are motivated by a growth or fixed mindset (Achievement Goal Inventory, [Grant and Dweck, 2003], cited in Porter, 2015) and for intrinsic goal orientation, metacognitive self-regulation, and effort regulation (as part of the Motivated Strategies for Learning Questionnaire, [Duncan and McKeachie, 2010], cited in Porter, 2015). She also assessed self-esteem and confidence in intelligence and asked some questions assessing attitudes and behavior related to working in groups. Results show that participants who were higher in intellectual humility had learning goals motivated by a growth mindset and were motivated less by wanting to look smarter than their peers. Intellectual humility was also significantly and positively associated with intrinsic goal orientation, metacognitive self-regulation, and effort regulation which means that students high in intellectual humility used the knowledge they had about their own knowledge (metacognition) to help them with their studying and they reported exerting more effort in school than their counterparts with low intellectual humility. Although those high in intellectual humility reported being more collaborative in group work, they did not value group work any more than those who measured low in intellectual humility. Porter (2015) replicated this study with eighty-eight high school students adding a measure of effort beliefs because of its importance to adolescent academic achievement (Blackwell, Trzesniewski, and Dweck, 2007, cited in Porter, 2015). She also added peer and teacher nominations of intellectual humility that were directly related to her nine-item intellectual humility scale and correlated intellectual humility with achievement scores (grades) over time. The associations between intellectual humility and learning goals based on a growth mindset and low status seeking were found in the high school sample as well, as were positive associations with metacognitive strategies and effort regulation. However, high school students high in intellectual humility were more likely to seek help, an association not found in the college sample, and those high in intellectual humility also had positive views about effort (effort beliefs). The peer and teacher nominations did not predict scores on the intellectual humility measure. Intellectual humility in the high school sample, as in the college sample, predicted willingness to collaborate in groups, but not valuing of group work. Intellectual humility did not predict growth in achievement (grades) over time.

Porter's (2015) work shows a robust association between a growth mindset and intellectual humility, and points toward the power that cultivating the virtue of intellectual humility can have on learning, specifically the motivation to learn and using effective learning strategies involving metacognition and effort regulation. More studies on the relationship between intellectual humility and learning will certainly be forthcoming. One grand experiment on the impact of intellectual virtues on learning is being conducted in a charter school in Long Beach, California, called the Intellectual Virtues Academy. Founded by Jason Baehr, the director of the Intellectual Virtues and Education Project at Loyola Marymount University, Los Angeles, their mission is "to foster meaningful growth in intellectual character virtues in a thoughtful, challenging, and supportive academic environment," and their vision is "to equip students to engage the world with curiosity and thoughtfulness, to know themselves, and to live well." They cite fostering a "growth mindset" as one of their core values along with a sense of purpose, culture of thinking, self-knowledge, and openness and respect (from http://www.ivalongbeach.org/about/mission-and-vision). We look forward to learning more from them about the impact that fostering intellectual virtues, especially the virtue of intellectual humility, can have on student outcomes— academic, social, and emotional.

Conclusion

In this chapter, we have explored various issues surrounding the development of intellectual humility over the lifespan, the ontogenesis of intellectual humility. While elements of intellectual humility might be deemed heritable traits, and those we can identify and measure (such as some of the traits of the Big 5, for example, open-mindedness and agreeableness) might inform us of the possibility of the influence of heredity on the expression of this virtue, the complexity of the expression of intellectual humility and our lack of knowledge of all its constituent parts make us hold any claims on the heritability of intellectual humility very lightly. We can make stronger claims about how intellectual humility might be nurtured and developed, however. Theories about how children learn through probability testing fit nicely with an understanding of intellectual humility as giving proper epistemic status to a belief. Children act like "little scientists" and approach the world with hypotheses (beliefs) about how the world might work that they then weigh with experience, holding a belief as lightly or as firmly as experience allows. While children seem to be somewhat arrogant in the assessment of their own knowledge, chronically overestimating their knowledge, they still remain open to the possibility that their hypotheses may be wrong, or at least they seem to remain open to testing the hypotheses and learning from others (Lockhart et al., in press). Inconsistent and contradictory evidence motivates them to learn more (Legare, 2012). Holding this motivation well into adulthood might be one key to developing intellectual humility. There is some intriguing evidence that metacogntition, specifically error detection, might play a role in this openness to learning (Danovitch and Moser, 2015).

Children are not just "little scientists" but "little anthropologists" as well (Harris, 2012). They are sensitive to the social elements of knowledge acquisition, especially the trustworthiness of informants. Studies into this element of how children learn supports our understanding of intellectual humility as having both epistemic and social dimensions (Samuelson et al., 2014). Children make judgments about whom to trust as an informant based on intuitions about their moral character (Samuelson et al., 2015) and their virtue, even the virtue of intellectual humility (Hagá and Olsen, in press). Porter's (2015) work shows a robust association between a growth mindset and intellectual humility, and, together with the other studies reviewed in this chapter, points toward the power that cultivating the virtue of intellectual humility can have on learning, specifically the motivation to learn, and using effective learning strategies involving metacognition and effort regulation.

5

What can human cognition tell us about intellectual humility?[1]

Any account of knowing has as its starting point the capacity and desire to know the "truth," through whatever normative criteria the "truth" can be established. Yet, human beings are notoriously (and apparently naturally) disposed to overestimate their capacity to know the truth and to underestimate their weaknesses (Chaiken, Wood, and Eagly, 1996; Dunning, Leuenberger, and Sherman, 1995; Evans, 2007; Gilovich, Griffin, and Kahneman, 2002; Kunda, 1990; Pronin, Berger, and Molouki, 2007; Stanovich and West, 1997; Wegener and Petty, 1997). Indeed, the evidence is clear that there is a strong tendency to underestimate even our liability to such biases (Pronin and Kugler, 2007)! Furthermore, we are susceptible to all sorts of biases that make knowing difficult. For example, we tend to favor evidence or data received early in our inquiries (Kruglanski et al., 2009) and we tend to discount the weight of evidence that counts against hypotheses we endorse (Nickerson, 1998). Second, evolutionary psychologists have offered some intriguing arguments that these dispositions are embedded within our cognitive architecture—in ways that can systematically lead us to biased thinking, in some cases for adaptive reasons (Mercier and Sperber, 2011). We have developed what are known as cognitive "heuristics," which are mental shortcuts that allow us to quickly process information that can lead to more efficient decision making (Evans and Stanovich, 2013). The downside to this efficiency—these heuristics—is that they don't always help us track the truth, that is, they can lead to biased thinking.

Cognitive science has come a long way toward understanding the roots of these biases, how our cognitive system utilizes biases as a way to efficiently store and sort knowledge—knowledge on which we base our actions. One clear discovery in cognitive science is that these biases that govern our decisions and actions are not always consciously held or analyzed—in fact, most of the time they are not. For example, a few years after the terrorists' attacks on the World Trade Center in New York City on September 11, 2001, Emily Pronin and her colleagues (Pronin, Kennedy, and Butsch, 2006) approached people with a questionnaire that gave a brief description of terrorism and its causes. Some were given a description in the form of an article from the *New York Times* that described the mind of the terrorists as governed by "thorough, rational analysis of their circumstances," while others got a description in the form of the *New York Times* article that stated the terrorist was "motivated by strictly-held ideology and deeply-felt anger." Those who read that terrorists were largely motivated by irrational means were more likely to endorse violent action including air strikes, ground war, and even assassination, and those who read that terrorists were mostly rational were more likely to endorse diplomacy, negotiation, and mediation. This study shows that unconscious biases govern our decision making and actions. How we perceive the attitudes and motivations of others has an impact on how we interact with them. Moreover, we have a "bias against being biased" and believe our perceptions to be objectively true—what scholars have labeled as "native realism"—that is, the belief that we see the world as it really is in objective reality (Kennedy and Pronin, 2008).

§1: Virtue epistemology revisited

Where do these biases come from? Are they a result of our cognitive faculties, the way our brains work? Or is it a matter of habit and training, something that can be mitigated through our effortful practice? Virtue epistemology gives us a way to sort this out, and helps us to better understand our cognitive systems—how we think, and how we might become better at it, specifically how becoming less sure of ourselves through the practice of intellectual humility might help us overcome bias. In this chapter, we will apply some principles and distinctions from virtue epistemology to the literature on cognitive heuristics and biases to gain a better understanding of the promise and perils of our cognitive systems. We will examine questions of how and under what circumstances these heuristics and biases can be characterized as epistemic vices and how the specific epistemic virtue of intellectual humility may help mitigate these vices and steer us toward the fundamental epistemic goal of "truth tracking."[2]

You will remember from Chapter 2 that virtue epistemology, so defined, has developed by and large into two distinct schools: agent-reliabilism and agent-responsibilism or neo-Aristotelianism. The primary difference between the schools is their application of "virtue" terminology. Agent-reliabilism, being modeled along reliabilist lines, applies virtue terminology in regard to faculties, in the same way we might talk about a virtuous knife. In other words, just as we might call a knife virtuous if it does what it is supposed to do (cut things, be sharp, etc.), agent-reliabilism calls various cognitive faculties such as memory, perception, etc., virtuous insofar as they are reliably functioning the way they are supposed to. That is, agent-reliabilism focuses on the reliable functioning (virtuous functioning) of a given agent's cognitive faculties.

Neo-Aristotelian virtue epistemologies, in contrast, are not modeled after reliabilism. Instead of focusing on whether or not a given agent's epistemic faculties are functioning properly and reliable, neo-Aristotelian virtue epistemologists tend to focus more on the agent's epistemic character and epistemic responsibilities. The primary objects of interest for the neo-Aristotelian virtue epistemologist are not cognitive faculties (as it was with the agent-reliabilist) but, rather, intellectual character traits (e.g., intellectual courageousness, open-mindedness, etc.), whether or not a given agent is of the right sort of epistemic character. And being of the right sort of epistemic character often means (at the very least) not only reliably reaching virtuous ends (e.g., truth tracking) but also being virtuously motivated. In other words, in order to be of the right sort of epistemic character, you need not only to be the sort of person who regularly hits upon the truth, but also someone who hits upon the truth for the right reasons (e.g., because you were intellectually courageous as opposed to simply lucky). Not only is neo-Aristotelianism interested in your veritic reliability, it is also interested in what sort of person—what sort of epistemic character—you should be.

The primary difference between agent-reliabilism's virtue epistemology and neo-Aristotelian virtue epistemology that we want to focus on in this chapter is their divergent accounts of intellectual virtue: agent-reliabilists roughly explicating intellectual virtue in terms of cognitive faculties or cognitive competencies (faculty virtues) and neo-Aristotelians roughly explicating intellectual virtues in terms of character traits and motivation (character virtues). The distinction helps us to both take an account of the reliability of our cognitive systems (given the apparent structural features of bias) and determine how that system can help us pursue intellectually virtuous ends.

The psychological literature on heuristics and biases can be usefully divided into studies focused on agent-reliabilism and those focused on agent-responsibilism (or neo-Aristotelianism). On the one hand, we see a concern for the reliability (or lack thereof) of our cognitive systems in the literature that deals with dual-process theories of cognition, heuristics, and biases (Epstein et al., 1992; Evans, 2007; Gilovich, 1991; Gilovich, Griffin, and Kahneman, 2002; Kahneman, 2011; Sloman, 2002; Stanovich, 1999). On the other hand, there is a concern for responsibilism reflected in a focus on the role of motivation in cognition and cognitive bias (Chaiken, Wood, and Eagly, 1996; Dunning, Leuenberger, and Sherman, 1995; Kunda, 1990; Pronin et al., 2007; Wegener and Petty, 1997). It is not as if those concerned with heuristics and biases ignore the role of motivation (Evans, 2007; Stanovich and West, 1997); nor do those primarily interested in the role of motivation ignore cognitive mechanisms and capacity (Chaiken, Wood, and Eagly, 1996). It is, rather, a matter of emphasis. Nevertheless, these distinctions can serve to provide a better understanding of how to best reach the epistemic goal of "truth tracking" in light of the heuristics and biases of our cognitive system.

§2: Reliabilism: Heuristics and biases

There has been a great deal of interest in psychology, economics, and other social sciences in the reliability of our cognitive systems. This has included extensive research into how chronic and systematic biases can result from certain cognitive heuristics that speed processing (see Kahneman, 2011, for one of the latest summaries). Out of research into heuristics and biases has grown a number of what are called "dual-process" theories of human cognition.[3] While each theory has different names for, and different categories assigned to, each process, these theories broadly share a distinction between fast, automatic, and intuitive processes, called Type 1 (also known as System 1) processes, and slow, deliberative, and analytic processes known as Type 2 (also known as System 2) processes (Kahneman, 2011; Kahneman and Frederick, 2002; Stanovich, 1999; Evans and Stanovich, 2013).[4]

The central characteristic of Type 1 processing is its automaticity—processes that do not make much demand on working memory and are not governed by what Evans and Stanovich (2013) call "controlled attention" (p. 236). Because of this, Type 1 processing has many correlated (but not necessarily defining) features, such as rapid processing that sometimes does not reach consciousness, associative processing that reacts to stimuli with minimal cognitive load, and processing that relies on thoughts that are most readily available and dependent on personal experience. Many of the heuristics (mental shortcuts that speed processing) and resulting biases are therefore also correlates of Type 1 processing, though Type 2 processing can also result in systematic biases.[5]

Type 2 processing is characterized by hypothetical thinking: thinking that is "decoupled" from an individual's representation of reality. This "cognitive decoupling" is defined as "the ability to distinguish supposition from belief and to aid rational choices by running thought experiments" (Evans and Stanovich, 2013, p. 236). Stanovich posits two "modes" of thinking within Type 2 processing: "algorithmic" and "reflective" (Evans and Stanovich, 2013; Stanovich, 2009). Although Type 2 processing is more effortful and requires more working memory than Type 1 processing, the individual's capacity for engaging these modes of thinking that are constitutive of Type 2 processing exists on a continuum such that some individuals may execute them with alacrity while others will take more time and deliberation. The algorithmic mode of processing suppresses the automatic responses of Type 1 processing, decoupling from the current representation of the world, in order to compare it to some kind (or kinds) of secondary representation(s). The source of these other representations could come from rule-based thinking, from simulations and hypotheticals based on experiences (or other knowledge sources), and/or from alternative models that are learned, among others. Because the current representation must be held in mind while being compared to other possible representations to find the best one (requiring effort and a load on working memory), algorithmic processing is highly correlated with fluid intelligence, a key factor in intelligence testing (Stanovich, 2009). The "reflective" mode of Type 2 processing is characterized by higher forms of cognitive regulation and reflects the goals and epistemic values of an individual. Labeled as "thinking dispositions" (Stanovich and West, 1997, p. 343), they correlate with such traits and tendencies as open-mindedness, thinking through problems and weighing consequences before taking action, and gathering sufficient evidence before making conclusions, among others (Evans and Stanovich, 2013).

From a virtue reliabilist point of view, epistemic vice cannot reside alone in either Type 1 or Type 2 processing, though most biases are attributed to an overreliance on Type 1 processing (Evans, 2007; Kahneman and Frederick, 2002; Evans and Stanovich, 2013). Type 1 processing can be, and is, quite reliable, and often hits on the truth. The epistemic vice is found in the breakdown of the relationship between the two types of processing and virtue is attained when each plays its appropriate function in the pursuit of epistemic goods such as truth, accurate representation of reality, etc. The relationship has been described as "default/interventionist" (Kahneman, 2011; Evans and Stanovich, 2013), that is, Type 1 processing, because of its efficiency, is the default type of processing until and unless Type 2 thinking, which monitors all thought processes, determines that deeper processing is needed and intervenes to decouple the Type 1 representation to hypothetically entertain other possible representations in order to find the epistemic good (truth, accuracy, knowledge, etc.) (Stanovich, 1999, 2009; Evans and Stanovich, 2013). If Type 2 processing is lazy, negligent, distracted, or overly focused on the self, biases will go unnoticed (Kahneman, 2011). Indeed, there is ample demonstration that biases are effectively reduced through effortful, deliberate, analytic Type 2 processes (Evans, 2007; Kahneman, 2011; Sloman, 2002; Stanovich and West, 1997) though even within those processes, biases can occur along the way (Wilson, Centerbar, and Brekke, 2002; Stanovich, 2009). That the automatic Type 1 processing does not hit upon the truth is not epistemically vicious in and of itself, but it would be if Type 2 processing, for whatever reason, fails to correct or amend the Type 1 representation when it is distorted. Both need to fail in their proper function for an epistemically vicious result.[6]

Stanovich (2009) has built a basic taxonomy that lays out thinking errors and biases along virtue reliabilist lines. First, there are the "cognitive miser" errors (pp. 74–75), which means, as the name implies, that the cognitive system (specifically Type 2 thinking) did not expend enough resources by (1) failing to decouple and therefore going with Type 1 processing even though biased, (2) decoupling but failing to override Type 1 processing when it should have been, or (3) decoupling but perseverating on only one alternative representation when more comparisons are needed. In each case, Type 2 thinking did not perform its proper function in the pursuit of epistemic goods. Then there are "mindware" problems, which can be manifested as a "mindware gap" (p. 75), that is, a gap in the learning necessary for Type 2 processing to recognize the need for decoupling and further reflection. This can include gaps in the knowledge of rules, of procedures and strategies for thinking, of probability, of specific domain knowledge, among others. Then there is "mindware contamination" (p. 76), which includes learned rewards and punishments for not engaging in decoupled thinking, using representations of the world from a egocentric perspective in decoupling, and using knowledge structures that are wrong or misguided in decoupling. As the labels "cognitive miser" and "mindware" imply, the cognitive system is not working virtuously and is prone to epistemic vice due to improper functioning such as failing to engage in Type 2 processing when necessary, gaps in knowledge, and contamination of mental representations used in Type 2 processing.

The heuristics of Type 1 thinking evaluate ideas from within one's own perspective and, therefore, favor ideas that are readily accessible and easily discerned, and conform to prior experience (Dunning, Meyerowitz, and Holzberg, 2002; Sanna, Schwarz, and Stocker, 2002; Pronin et al., 2007; Stanovich and West, 2007). Type 2 processing can also favor what one already believes, knows, and intuits even as it decouples from Type 1 representations (Stanovich, 2009, calls this "egocentric processing," p. 78). While in many instances this self-reliant thinking is adequate, problems and biases arise when reliance on what one knows and intuits does not provide enough information (or the right kind of information) for the task, which, in turn, produces biased judgments. Many of these biases are well known and well documented. There are (among others):

- *The confirmation bias.* The tendency to seek confirmation for opinions and beliefs already held and to ignore disconfirming evidence (Nickerson, 1998). Even academic psychologists are not immune. They rate studies with findings consistent with their prior beliefs more favorably than studies with conclusions inconsistent with their beliefs (Hergovich, Schott, and Burger, 2010).

- *The hindsight bias.* People's predictions of events are remembered as more accurate after the fact than they really were. In predicting the outcome of the German Bundestag elections of 1998, subjects remembered—after the election—their predictions four months earlier as 25 percent closer to the actual results than they had originally predicted (Blank, Fischer, and Erdfelder, 2003).

- *The anchoring and adjustment heuristic.* Cognitive anchors affect people's judgments under conditions of uncertainty. When asked to estimate when George Washington was elected president, participants began with a known date (the Declaration of Independence, 1776) and adjusted from there to the unknown date (Epley and Gilovich, 2002).

- *Overclaiming.* People overestimate their knowledge, at times claiming knowledge of concepts, events, and people that do not exist. In a test of financial literacy, 93 percent of participants claimed knowledge of concepts that do not exist. Moreover, those who view their knowledge ability favorably tend to overclaim more. This holds true even when they are warned about false items in the test (Atir, Rosenzweig, and Dunning, 2015).

- *The my-side bias.* People are biased toward their own opinions and point of view when evaluating evidence, generating evidence, and testing hypotheses, regardless of their level of intelligence. They also have trouble assessing conclusions that conflict with their knowledge of the world. However, when explicitly instructed to consider other points of view, people high in general intelligence and possessing certain thinking dispositions (e.g., AOT) exhibited less biased thinking (Stanovich and West, 2007).

David Dunning (2015) has turned to the literature on psychopathology, specifically schizophrenia, to better understand some of the mechanisms behind our cognitive biases. The difference between schizophrenics who suffer from delusions and those who do not is primarily found in the demonstration of two cognitive habits: jumping to conclusions and a bias against disconfirming evidence. Jumping to Conclusions (JTC) is the habit of making a quick judgment based on insufficient evidence. Bias against Disconfirming Evidence (BADE) is the habit of refusing to change initial judgments when the evidence is pointing away from the adequacy of those judgments. Delusional schizophrenics have a tendency to have a higher incidence of both of these habits. Dunning (2015) tested these habits in the general population to see if they impacted some of the cognitive failures that come from the literature on biases, heuristics, and decision making, namely, the endorsement of implausible beliefs, a lack of correspondence between confidence in knowledge and the accuracy of that knowledge, and common errors in logic, probability, and estimation in decision making.

To test JTC, participants were presented with a scenario in which there was a fisherman on one of two lakes, one with predominantly gray fish (some red), the other with predominantly red fish (some gray). As each fish was caught, participants were told the color. They could state their conclusion about which lake the fisherman was on at any time, up to eight fish. Those who jumped to conclusions guessed after only a few fish were caught and their color revealed. BADE was assessed by a series of stories with four different, yet plausible, conclusions. After each sentence was read, the participants rated the plausibility of each conclusion. By the third sentence, it was clear which was the most plausible. Those who were high in BADE continued to rate their original conclusion highly, even in the face of disconfirming evidence. The results indicate that those high in both JTC and BADE were more likely to endorse implausible beliefs (e.g., large corporations pressure health officials to repress the knowledge that cell phones cause cancer, or Princess Diana's death was an organized assassination of the British royal family, or psychokinesis is real). Both JTC and BADE predicted the participants' demonstration of overconfidence in their knowledge and their inability to assess when they were wrong. Finally, JTC, but not BADE, predicted errors on tasks of logic, probability, and estimation (anchoring and adjustment). From this research, we could conclude that good habits that would cultivate intellectual humility would be to resist JTC and, when evidence points you away from initial impressions, to be willing to revise your beliefs.

§3: Responsibilism: Motivation, goals, and values in cognition

As noted above, responsibilism (neo-Aristotelian virtue epistemology) is not as interested in the reliability of our cognitive mechanism (compared to the reliabilists) as it is in whether or not a given agent has the right sort of epistemic character. A person with the right sort of epistemic character will not only reliably reach virtuous ends but will also be virtuously motivated. Psychologists, too, are interested in epistemic motivation and the goals and values of cognition. Many of them use dual-system theories of cognition as their framework. There is some disagreement, however, about whether these are character traits in the sense that they are an enduring part of one's personality, or whether these traits are largely situational, that is, dependent on the agent's state.

In light of a cognitive system that oftentimes is prone to biases because of a failure of Type 2 processing to decouple from Type 1 representation when necessary, one avenue of exploration into virtuous knowing would be to investigate processes and actions that attenuate biases. From a virtue-responsibilist point of view, the vice of cognitive bias lies in this inability (or perhaps refusal) to decouple from the singular representation of reality that Type 1 processing provides. In this way, the cognitive system, in its insistence to stay with Type 1 representations and to not make algorithmic or hypothetical comparisons to other possible representations, could be characterized as "self-centered." Therefore, reducing or eliminating these biases might involve some kind of engagement with an "other": someone or something that "decenters" the cognitive system, engages decoupling, and entertains different ways of thinking and other points of view. Indeed, a review of the literature reveals several types of "other-centered" thinking as effective techniques for reducing biases: the use of rules of analysis (a process used by many others to arrive at a more consensual judgment), a search for accuracy (representing reality that is shared by others), a need to be accountable for one's judgments (to defend one's thoughts to another), and exposure to differing perspectives (seeing things from another's point of view). The presence or absence of these factors often hinges on motivation and the epistemic goals and values of thinking agents and thus favors the responsibilist or neo-Aristotelian account of virtue epistemology.

Rule-based thinking

Directing one's attention to processes, objective criteria, and rules of analysis can aid in reducing systematic bias. For example, when personal traits are ambiguous (e.g., whether or not one is intelligent or a good driver), people draw on idiosyncratic definitions of traits and abilities to assess themselves as better than average at a certain task or trait. Once given criteria of judgment, however, they are more accurate in their assessment relative to their peers (Dunning, Meyerowitz, and Holzberg, 2002). Evans (2007) demonstrates that when questions are asked in a way that engages analytic reasoning processes, biases are reduced. For example, his research has shown that the usual matching bias evident in the original form of the Wason card selection task is eliminated when the rule is highlighted over the surface features, making the need to falsify in order to rightly complete the task explicit. Stanovich (1999) has noted that many of the tasks involved in heuristics and biases depend on an understanding and mastery of normative rules of thought (logic and statistics), which is within the purview of the algorithmic function of Type 2 processing. Those attuned to rule-based, algorithmic thinking perform better on these tasks. Understanding can come through training (as the research reported in Stanovich [1999] demonstrates), through the framing and presentation of the problem (Evans, 2007), through cognitive ability (high analytic reasoning capability), and through the possession of certain open and flexible thinking dispositions that "serve the ends of epistemic rationality" (Stanovich and West, 1998, p. 180).

Accuracy and accountability

Situations that call for accuracy in judgment promote slower, more deliberative thinking. Kunda (1990), in an analysis of the work on accuracy-driven reasoning, concluded that when "people are motivated to be accurate, they expend more cognitive effort on issue-related reasoning, attend to relevant information more carefully, and process it more deeply, often using more complex rules" (p. 481). For example, when people know they will be judged on accuracy, they are more accurate in evaluating their own abilities (Armor and Taylor, 2002). However, Petty, Wegener, and White (1998) caution that motivation for accuracy may not be enough to attenuate bias, and that bias can also occur in the correction process. Nevertheless, Kruglanski and Mayseless (1987) report that a high need for accuracy (what they call a heightened fear of invalidity) motivates people to seek comparison with those who disagree with them. The focus on accuracy, then, invites the thinking agent into a more "humble" epistemic posture because (a) that agent may realize that he or she has a less than complete understanding and needs to seek more information, (b) it helps the agent to focus on what others might think of the same phenomenon, and (c) it will focus the agent on objective criteria about the phenomenon. The focus on accuracy and accountability emphasizes the situational factors that attenuate a generalized human tendency toward biased thinking.

Having to defend one's thoughts and judgments to others might include the need to be accurate, but also injects the notion of accountability, which promotes a more careful analysis of one's thoughts and arguments. Mercier and Sperber (2011), in a thorough examination of the many abstract reasoning tasks that are used to measure heuristics and biases, demonstrate that when the same reasoning tasks are set in the context of making an argument or defending a position, the reasoning of the participants is less biased and more complete. Moreover, they make the case that the confirmation bias, in the context of producing arguments to convince others of the rightness of one's beliefs, can produce a "division of cognitive labor" (p. 65). Because participants in a disagreement want to bring the best evidence they have found to support their beliefs, the confirmation bias serves them well collectively: together, two disagreeing parties will tend to marshal relevant evidence in favor of their favoring positions. However, in the context of a discussion with others over the best evidence, or the best argument (the *process of evaluating* an argument, not its production), the confirmation bias no longer serves them well. Therefore, this division of cognitive labor works in the context of disagreement, provided (and this is an important caveat) people have "a common interest in the truth" (p. 65) and go through the hard work of evaluating and selecting the best argument with the best evidence. Most people are quite good at the task of evaluating the best argument, both at the individual and group level, when motivated to do so. When held accountable under a time pressure, however, people exhibit the primacy effect, giving more weight to information they received first (Kruglanski et al., 2009).

The key to mitigating bias may be in taking the position of "a common interest in the truth." A study by Stanovich and West (1997) on the capacity of the individual to evaluate an argument fairly in light of previously held beliefs is informative in this regard. Three hundred and forty-nine college students completed a measurement called the Argument Evaluation Test (AET) in which they first indicated the strength of their beliefs regarding certain social and political issues and then (later in the testing process) evaluated the quality of the arguments of a fictitious individual on these same issues. Their analysis resulted in two groups, one with a high reliance on argument quality and a low reliance on prior belief and another with a low reliance on argument quality and a high reliance on prior belief. They compared the mean scores of the two groups on various measures including a composite score that measured AOT (Active Open-minded Thinking), which indicated openness to belief change and cognitive flexibility. Those who showed a high reliance on argument quality by relying less on prior beliefs scored significantly higher on the AOT composite scale. This open and flexible thinking disposition held even when they controlled for cognitive ability.[7] Stanovich and West (1997) assert that these thinking dispositions can provide information about an individual's epistemic goals and values. For example, a disposition such as the willingness to change beliefs reflects the goal of getting as close to the truth as possible, or the disposition to carefully evaluate arguments indicates a value for accuracy. It might be fair to infer that those with a high reliance on argument quality had the epistemic goal of "a common interest in the truth." Thinking dispositions function more like enduring traits that are less influenced by varying circumstances, though they are seen as "malleable" and, therefore, teachable skills (Baron, 1994).

Perspective taking

One aspect of an open and flexible thinking disposition that helps mitigate biases is the capacity to weigh evidence for and against a strongly held belief, including the opinions and beliefs of others who hold a position different from one's own. This requires a certain capacity for perspective taking: a movement from the focus on one's own thoughts to include the perceptions, thoughts, and ideas of others. This adjustment can be as simple as considering alternative points of view and as complex as trying to assess another person's thoughts. Studies have found that asking people to consider the possibility that competing hypotheses are true is sufficient to undo the bias of one-sided thinking (Sedikides, Horton, and Gregg, 2007; Wilson, Centerbar, and Brekke, 2002). The issue can be complicated, however, by the primacy effect. Jonas et al. (2001) demonstrated that the order of the presentation of other points of view can impact debiasing. The confirmation bias was stronger in a situation in which subjects were exposed to other points of view sequentially and lessened when subjects had access to all the points of view simultaneously. The sequential presentation encouraged the subjects to remain focused on their prior commitments, whereas those who had the information presented simultaneously were able to compare their beliefs to many points of view. This might lead to the conclusion that entertaining more alternatives would help attenuate bias, but Sanna, Schwarz, and Stocker (2002) have shown that, in the case of hindsight bias, more is not better. Subjects who were asked to produce twelve reasons why the British-Gurkha war could have come out differently were more susceptible to hindsight bias than those who had to produce only two reasons. They surmise that the difficultly of coming up with twelve counterfactual reasons makes alternative outcomes seem less likely and the actual outcome more so, putting the availability heuristic into play. However, those who came up with only two reasons performed as well as the control group who did not know the outcome of the war. Thus, in moderation, considering a counterfactual perspective helped attenuate hindsight bias.

Often, bias is the result of a lack of perspective taking. Birch and Bernstein (2007) propose that a similar inability to take the perspective of naïve others is at the core of both children who are unable to successfully complete Theory of Mind (ToM) tasks and adults who exhibit hindsight bias. In each case, the "knower" and the naïve other do not share the same information because the knower is biased by the primacy of current knowledge and belief. On the other hand, perspective taking itself is also prone to bias. When assessing the behavior of others, people exhibit what is known as the correspondence bias, which is the tendency to make dispositional inferences from behaviors that can be mostly explained by the situations in which they are found. For example, when observing a girl at a party who does not talk very much, you assume she is shy. Later you find out that she is from another country and is not very confident in her English-speaking ability. A few months later, you meet her again at a party and observe that she is very talkative, even extroverted. It was being in a foreign country without much confidence in speaking the language that had made her look shy at first, when, in fact, she has a disposition toward extroversion. This comes about, in part, because of what Gilbert and Malone (1995) call an "egocentric assumption," which includes an inability to "put (oneself) in someone else's epistemic shoes" (p. 26, i.e., construe the situation as the actor does). However, when one is specifically prompted to see a situation as another sees it, egocentric biases can be attenuated. For example, Todd et al. (2011) found that subjects who performed a perspective-taking task showed less implicit or automatic racial bias (as measured by the personalized evaluative race IAT) than a control group that did not engage in perspective taking. One possible explanation the researchers offered was that since the self is the anchor in evaluating others, lessening the distance between the self and the person of another race through perspective taking allowed for more positive evaluations of the person of another race.

§4: Heuristics and biases as intellectual arrogance

In a limited sense we might say that heuristics and biases exhibit the vice of "intellectual arrogance" because they result, in part, from an inability to "decouple" from Type 1 representations and the thinker remaining unable to leave his or her own perspective. There are also instances when decoupling occurs and Type 2 thinking is engaged, but it remains focused on the self, resulting in egocentric thinking (Stanovich, 2009). In both cases, thought remains "self-centered." We see this exhibited in many of the biases identified in the literature. The self- centeredness is found in the general human tendency to use the self as an anchor against which the other is compared and the world is known (Dunning, Krueger, and Alicke, 2005; Guenther and Alicke, 2010). We are biased toward that which comes fastest and most easily to mind (availability or representative heuristic, Kahneman and Frederick, 2002), which is often thoughts about the self (Dunning, Meyerowitz, and Holzberg, 2002; Kruger, 1999). We overrely on our introspections, considering the more objective, behavioral facts as secondary (Pronin and Kugler, 2007). We are biased toward self-enhancement and justify our beliefs and actions— even altruistic action—in terms of self-interest (Miller, 1999). Even beyond the "better-than-average" effect, our thinking is biased toward the self in comparison to others (Sedikides and Gregg, 2008). This is not mere egoism, for while we tend to think of ourselves as "better than average," we can also think of ourselves as below average in comparison to others (Kruger, 1999). We consider our thoughts as representative of a reality that is shared by others (Gilbert and Malone, 1995; Ross and Ward, 1996). Moreover, we tend to assume too early that our memories, judgments, intuitions, and beliefs are sufficient for the epistemic task at hand (Evans, 2007).

Self-centered thinking is not, in and of itself, intellectual arrogance. Indeed, it is only natural that our own experiences are going to be more readily available to us as evidence. It can only be characterized as arrogance when self-centered thinking is not sufficient to hold a belief in accordance with the evidence, if we count on what we know more than we ought.[8] Normally, Type 1 processing provides the information needed to make the decisions and judgments necessary to successfully navigate life (Evans, 2007; Stanovich, 1999). It does so with great efficiency. The problem comes when Type 1 processes are not sufficient and thinking is not decoupled from Type 1 representations: when it is necessary to move beyond what one immediately knows, believes, and/or remembers to incorporate other information—that is, when Type 2 processes intervene and, in a slower, deliberative, and sequential manner, bring more information to bear until the mind is satisfied that it knows what it needs to know. That information can come from within the self, by accessing memories that broaden the data or evidence at hand, it can come from others who offer a different perspective, and it can also come from the application of rules of analysis that help determine what is sufficient to make a judgment. Type 2 processing, however, is also prone to bias because of the sequential nature of its processing, taking up one mental model at a time until a sufficient one is found (Evans, 2007). Some biases, like those that occur from framing effects, can be the result of a Type 2 processing that has decoupled, but is focused on a singular model from a source outside the self that stimulates all other subsequent thought (serial associative cognition with a focal error, Stanovich, 2009). This might be best characterized as an exhibition of intellectual diffidence—the opposite of intellectual arrogance because it is too "other" focused—yet still missing the mark of holding a belief with the proper firmness that the belief warrants.[9]

The examples of behaviors and techniques noted above that help to reduce biases share the common aspect of "decentering" (decoupling) thought to include and consider the "other" through the use of rules of reasoning, a concern for accuracy, a need for accountability, and taking the perspective of others. One common theme in the literature is the role of motivation in debiasing thought (Chaiken, Wood, and Eagly, 1996; Dunning, Leuenberger, and Sherman, 1995; Kunda, 1990; Wilson, Centerbar, and Brekke, 2002), pointing to the conclusion that correcting biases is an effortful process that requires some kind of motivation to overcome the self-centered tendencies of our cognitive system. In this way, it reflects the neo-Aristotelian (responsibilist) notion of epistemic virtue: that it must be consciously practiced to overcome our more arrogant cognitive tendencies and avoid the possibility of appearing too diffident to others by giving in too easily or not evaluating the other's position rigorously.

§5: Avoiding and mitigating biases with intellectual humility

We propose that the set of traits and dispositions that best avoid the vices of intellectual arrogance and intellectual diffidence as we have defined them, and help mitigate biases (open-mindedness, gathering all available evidence, concern for accuracy and accountability, among others) is best characterized by the epistemic virtue of intellectual humility. We have seen evidence that epistemic characteristics and behaviors that might contribute to intellectual humility are both influenced by situations (inducing intellectual humility as a state, Armor and Taylor, 2002) and are part of an individual's thinking dispositions (which makes intellectual humility look more trait-like, Stanovich and West, 1997; Stanovich, 2009). If intellectual humility requires the effortful control of Type 2 thinking processes, it may be hard to defend intellectual humility as a trait that is held with any stability, making intellectual humility appear more a state than trait. Nevertheless, there are individual differences in the capacity for effortful control and the characteristics that lend themselves to intellectual humility that are more stable and trait-like. Part of the resolution might be found in Stanovich's tripartite mind (Stanovich, 2009; Evans and Stanovich, 2013), which posits an autonomous mind (Type 1 processes), an algorithmic mind, and a reflective mind (two aspects of Type 2 processes). The algorithmic mind, being highly correlated with general intelligence, is more trait-like in its manifestations, while the reflective mind is defined by state-like thinking dispositions (though these can also show trait-like individual differences in certain conditions [see Stanovich and West, 2007]). Either way, responsibilist virtue epistemology would recognize that intellectual humility *can* be developed, enhanced, and trained. On the one hand, those low in the trait could cultivate the habits of intellectual humility through practice (while those high in the trait could grow in expertise through the same means). On the other, creating the right pressures and circumstances (such as accountability) could induce intellectual humility (or attenuate intellectual arrogance and intellectual diffidence).[10] Like the state/trait debate in personality and social psychology, intellectual humility is neither simply state nor trait, but the result of the complex interaction of person and environment that is a part of all personality development (Fleeson, 2004).

From a dual-process point of view, another empirical question worthy of investigation is whether or not "other-centered" thinking could become a part of Type 1 cognition, that is, whether or not it could become a habit of thought that is automatic, effortless, and intuitive. Some indications in the literature suggest that it can. For example, the short intervention in perspective taking outlined above resulted in implicit and unconscious correction of racial bias (Todd et al., 2011).[11] Thinking dispositions and algorithmic thinking can be trained and practiced to automaticity (Stanovich, 2009). The literature on moral expertise could also yield clues about the development of habitual, "other-centered" thinking. Using insights from dual-process theory, Narvaez (2008) sees both systems at work in the development of moral expertise, noting that expertise is developed by immersing novices in environments that build up their intuitions and by giving them explicit guidance on how to solve problems in the given domain. The training of moral intuitions begins even in the early experiences of attachment and continues through novice-to-expert instruction. Drawing on expertise training in other fields, Narvaez notes that in such training, "perceptions are fine-tuned and developed into chronically accessed constructs, applied automatically; action schemas are honed to high levels of automaticity" (p. 313). Like developing any virtuous habit, intentionality on the part of parents, teachers, and mentors to train habits such as open-mindedness, accurate representation of reality, and the search for the best evidence in a systematic and sustained manner would contribute to the "chronic accessibility" of intellectual humility.

Conclusion

While it may seem as though the virtue of intellectual humility might be best explicated in terms of neo-Aristotelian virtue epistemology's character traits, there is no obvious reason why our concepts of intellectual humility cannot be explicated in terms of agent-reliabilism's virtue epistemology as well. Presumably, any robust, full account of intellectual virtue will have to account for both cognitive faculty virtues and character trait virtues; whether one does this along the lines of agent-reliabilism or neo-Aristotelianism could be, to some extent, a matter of emphasis. For a person can hold a belief more strongly (or weakly) than warranted due to biases inherent in our cognitive systems, or because of some lack of character, just as a person can exhibit virtuous knowing via the proper functioning of one's cognitive system or through the exercise of a virtuous character.

Straightforwardly, those of us interested in explicating intellectual humility in light of the function (or malfunction) of our cognitive faculties might take special interest in the model of intellectual virtue afforded by agent-reliabilism. Conversely, those of us interested in explicating intellectual humility as something more like a character trait might take special interest in the model of intellectual virtue afforded by neo-Aristotelianism. Either way, it can be defined as holding a belief as firmly as it is warranted, whether such warrant is derived from the proper functioning of our cognitive systems or whether such warrant is brought about by the exercise of a particular way of knowing (a trait).

Within either framework of virtue epistemology, we argue that the epistemic virtue of intellectual humility is mostly found in the conscious exercise of Type 2 thinking and can come about in a manner consistent with either mode of virtue epistemology: through the proper collaboration of Type 1 and Type 2 processes (agent-reliabilism) or through the conscious practice of applying Type 2 thinking when appropriate (neo-Aristotelianism). The literature investigating ways to attenuate cognitive biases suggests at least four habits that would lend themselves to cultivating intellectual humility and lead away from intellectual arrogance: the use of rules of analysis, a search for accuracy, being accountable for one's judgments, and exposure to differing perspectives. Certain traits appear to create a natural disposition toward intellectual humility and other forms of virtuous knowing (i.e., the need for cognition, [Cacioppo and Petty, 1982], active open-minded thinking [Stanovich and West, 1997], the need for closure [Kruglanski, 1990], and those traits from factor models of personality that relate to intellectual humility such as open-mindedness, conscientiousness, and humility [Ashton and Lee, 2005; McCrae and Costa, 1997]). These traits can be trained, enhanced, and cultivated. Just as habits play a role in cultivating any virtue, habits of the mind can bring about intellectual humility and other epistemic virtues. They serve to curb the vice of intellectual arrogance, even in the face of a cognitive system that can be prone to biased thinking. Perhaps our cognitive system is not in and of itself "vicious," but it may take conscious effort and virtuous habits of the mind not to make it so.

6

Are some people born humble?

Let's say you are very open-minded to different political arguments but very close-minded when it comes to religious convictions. Could you be characterized as an intellectually humble person? Let's say you had strong opinions about the right way to discipline children and were not afraid to tell others your views (even if they were not very receptive), yet you were willing to listen to advice about cooking. Would you understand yourself as an intellectually arrogant person? Intellectual humility has many trait-like qualities, but even traits vary in their expression across situations. In this chapter, we explore intellectual humility as a character trait, and how situations might influence the expression of that trait.

§1: Intellectual humility as a character trait

The recent interest in studying virtues and character, inspired by the positive psychology movement, has been informed largely by the methods and approach of personality psychology. Peterson and Seligman (2004) in their seminal work *Character Strengths and Virtues* declare that "the stance we take toward character is in the spirit of personality psychology and specifically trait theory" (p. 10). In their conception, virtues are core characteristics that are universally valued across cultures (wisdom, courage, humanity, justice, temperance, and transcendence) whereas character strengths (traits) are "the psychological ingredients—processes or mechanisms—that define the virtues" (p. 13). Personality psychology defines a trait as an attribute of a person that is relatively long-lasting and stable (Funder, 2010). Philosophers use a similar language to define character traits, defining them as a "relatively long-term stable disposition to act in distinctive ways" (Harman, 1999). The key to the definition is that these characteristics, traits, and dispositions are expressed over the long term and are relatively stable across situations (Funder, 2010).

Personality psychologists are interested in individual differences between people regarding the relative expression of traits. In this way, the studies are often comparative, measuring how much a given trait influences the thought and behavior of an individual compared to others who share the same trait. For example, when measured on the Big 5 personality traits (extraversion, agreeableness, conscientiousness, neuroticism, and openness), individuals show high or low levels of each trait relative to other people. Each trait is orthogonal, that is, a high or low score on any one trait does not influence the score on the other traits (McCrea and Costa, 1987). Intellectual humility may, or may not, work in the same way. It may also have orthogonal characteristics relative to other character traits such that, for example, being high in intellectual humility may not impact how high or low a person is in courage, or persistence. However, as with the Big 5, some character traits and virtues may show some kind of correlative relationship. For example, just as people who score low on neuroticism often score high on agreeableness and conscientiousness (Funder, 2010), those high in intellectual humility may be high in forgiveness or prudence. Finding those character traits and virtues that correlate with intellectual humility would be a fruitful area of future research.

Another interest in personality psychology is to explore individual differences in personality traits as they relate to life outcomes. Ozer and Benet-

Martínez (2006) published a study that showed how various life outcomes were associated with high levels of the Big 5 personality traits. The outcomes could be on an individual level such as personal happiness, an interpersonal level such as family relations, or what they called institutional level, that is, job performance or criminal behavior. High agreeableness, for example, is associated with better psychological health, more peer acceptance, and higher job attainment. High neuroticism is associated with poor coping, poor family relations, and higher occupational dissatisfaction (Ozer and Benet-Martínez, 2006). We might imagine similar correlational studies with intellectual humility. There may also be mediating factors in the relationship between intellectual humility and life outcomes. Given the clear association between intellectual humility and positive interpersonal relationships (Samuelson and Church, 2014), we might expect that those who are high in intellectual humility would get along better with their coworkers, leading to better job satisfaction or career longevity. Research along these lines, in many and various domains of human interaction (family, friendships, politics, etc.), would not only be interesting but also useful.

Besides correlations between intellectual humility and other virtues, there may also be correlations between intellectual humility and existing traits related to information seeking, curiosity, and other epistemic pursuits. We have already noted some in the chapter on measurement; however, in this section we highlight them in more detail: the need for cognition (Cacioppo and Petty, 1982), the need for closure (Kruglanski, 1990), and those traits from factor models of personality that relate to intellectual humility (Ashton and Lee, 2005; McCrae and Costa, 1997).

Need for cognition

An individual difference that lends itself to the kind of open-minded thinking characteristic of intellectual humility is the "need for cognition," which is defined as "a stable individual difference in people's tendency to engage in and enjoy effortful cognitive activity" (Cacioppo et al., 1996, p. 198). People high in need for cognition expend more effort analyzing content and quality of arguments (Haugtvedt, Petty, and Cacioppo, 1992), consider arguments central to the issue rather than peripheral features (Petty, Cacioppo, and Goldman, 1981), enjoy complex cognitive tasks (Cacioppo and Petty, 1982), and are more attracted to messages that appeal to rational argument than emotion (Haddock et al., 2008). Those with a high need for cognition use what Petty, Cacioppo, and Goldman (1981) call the "central" route of analysis, which employs deliberative, rational processes (Type 2), whereas those with a low need for cognition take the "peripheral" route, which relies on heuristics and attends to surface features (Haugtvedt, Petty, and Cacioppo, 1992). It is important to note that those high in need for cognition are more susceptible to context bias demonstrated in mood priming and primacy-recent effects. Cacioppo et al. (1996) aver that this is because those high in need for cognition form stronger initial attitudes compared to those low in need for cognition. When perceived biases are obvious or detectable, however, individuals high in need for cognition are more likely to make the cognitive effort necessary to correct their judgments and consider all the evidence.

Since those high in need for cognition are more curious, open-minded, and enjoy the search for knowledge, it may be one of the important characteristics that make up intellectual humility (Cacioppo et al., 1996; Stanovich and West, 1997). It reflects an intrinsic motivation for effortful cognition that is more process- than results-oriented, and which can be developed and can change over time (Cacioppo et al., 1996). However, little research has been done on the development of the need for cognition. Although there may be a heritable component, some of the antecedent experiences that would contribute to its development would be those that reinforce a love of learning, experiences of mastery over subjects, a sense of control over one's learning, and experiences of coping with interpersonal problems through reason and verbal competence. Need for cognition is correlated with many important skills for optimal development. For example, Njus and Johnson (2008) found that the college students they surveyed who showed high levels of Eriksonian psychosocial identity achievement were also those high in need for cognition. In a recent study, Leary et al. (2016) found that their measure of intellectual humility correlates significantly with need for cognition, indicating a positive relationship between the two constructs. Exploring the factors that go into the development of the many correlates of the need for cognition such as high self-esteem, problem-solving effectiveness, openness to experience, and intrinsic motivation might also shed light on cultivation of this important trait (Cacioppo et al., 1996) and may be informative in the cultivation of intellectual humility.

Need for closure

Another extensively studied motivational characteristic that could have a bearing on the science of intellectual humility is the need for closure (Kruglanski, 1990; Kruglanski et al., 2009; Webster and Kruglanski, 1994). By "closure" we mean the need to make a decision, to have an issue *closed*. The concept is part of a general framework for the formation of all kinds of knowledge called lay epistemic theory (Kruglanski et al., 2009). This theory has a fundamental assumption that knowledge is derived from evidence. Evidence can come from all sources, but a special category of evidence in lay epistemic theory comes from the testimony of other people (other people's opinions). Lay epistemic theory has noted individual differences in the process of hypothesis testing and evidence gathering. Individuals high in need for closure will take in and process less information before making a judgment and give preference to information met early in the decision-making process. Because of the early closure in the epistemic process, they also have higher confidence in their judgments than those with a high need to avoid or postpone closure. They tend to be influenced in their judgment of people and their actions by preexisting stereotypes and prejudices, paying less attention to situational or individuating information. People high in need for closure will, for the most part, look to compare themselves to those of similar mind and to reject or devalue others who do not share their perspectives and judgments (Kruglanski, 1990). These attributes hold for what lay epistemic theory calls "non-specific" closure, which is a need for a firm answer to any question in order to avoid confusion and ambiguity. Such cognitive behaviors are motivated by a need to "seize and freeze" early in the judgment process on information that is easily accessible and affords closure. A search for "specific" closure, by contrast, means that a person is looking for a particular answer to a specific question. A person high in this need (for specific closure) may actually postpone closure until a desirable answer that might bolster self-esteem or be more positive or optimistic can be found (Kruglanski et al., 2009). By closing off the gathering of evidence too early (non-specific closure) or by searching only for evidence that yields a desirable answer (specific closure), those who are high in need for closure are more susceptible to the numerous cognitive biases outlined above (such as the availability heuristic or the confirmation bias). Using virtue language, they may be more susceptible to intellectual arrogance (and, therefore, be less intellectually humble).

Lay epistemic theory affords a unique look at the issue of the self-centered nature of heuristics and biases. While both the need for closure and the use of heuristic rules that preference easy-to-process evidence favor the self as a source of knowledge, the theory introduces another influence on the judgment process: epistemic authority. Kruglanski et al. (2009) define the concept of epistemic authority as "encompassing a combination of perceived expertise and trustworthiness. . . . It addresses the extent to which an individual is prepared to rely on a source's information and to accept it as evidence for the veracity of the source's pronouncements" (p. 175). The key to the function of epistemic authority is in the comparison of the self to another. The decision to rely on the authority of another may depend in part on the perceived gap in epistemic authority between the other and the self. In combination with a need for closure, this could lead to either an overreliance on the self as epistemic authority (intellectual arrogance) or a denigration of the self as an epistemic authority and an overreliance on others (gullibility or "group think"). The "virtuous mean" of intellectual humility in the context of lay epistemic theory may lie in a proper balance of a need for closure with an openness to new information and a tolerance for ambiguity, along with a capacity to discern when the self is enough of an epistemic authority and when others need to be sought out and relied upon.

In the only investigation to test intellectual humility against need for closure and need for cognition, Porter (2015) found that in two different samples of adults, need for cognition was positively correlated with her measure of intellectual humility (0.28 and 0.40) while need for closure was negatively correlated with intellectual humility in only one sample (−0.17). This finding underscores the importance of the aspects of the need for cognition trait, such as curiosity, open-mindedness, and the search for knowledge, for our understanding of intellectual humility.

Intellectual humility and personality: The Big 5

Considering intellectual humility within the framework of conceptions of personality such as the Five-Factor Model (The Big Five, McCrae and Costa, 1987, 1997) and the HEXACO (Lee and Ashton, 2004) leads in a promising direction. We can imagine that high levels of the Openness to Experience factor might correlate with high intellectual humility, especially when we look at specific facets of the Openness construct. The facet "openness to ideas," for example, seems to capture an element of curiosity we would expect to find in the intellectually humble; the "values" facet might figure into whether someone is willing to really consider an opposing political or religious view with charity.

Similar corollaries of intellectual humility might exist within some facets of Agreeableness, Conscientiousness, and even Emotional Stability.

Along these lines, special attention might be given to the HEXACO model of personality, which adds the dimension of H (honesty-humility) to the factors mentioned above (Ashton and Lee, 2005). A connection between the H dimension and socially important criteria has already been demonstrated (Ashton and Lee, 2008). Additionally, the H factor has been negatively correlated with particularly vicious personality traits (e.g., narcissism, psychopathy, Machiavellianism, materialism, and power-seeking) that we would expect to find somewhere opposite to intellectual humility (Ashton and Lee, 2005, 2007): a finding that lends some support to the understanding of intellectual humility as involving a lack of concern for one's status (see the discussion of intellectual humility and status in Chapter 1). Not surprisingly, the H factor has also been used to show that the humility trait is linked to higher social relationship quality (Peters, Rowatt, and Johnson, 2011).

Despite these helpful leads in the personality literature, it seems important to avoid an oversimplified association of intellectual humility with certain personality traits. Even traits that seem to track with intellectual humility could have their own special hazards. For example, a trait like Openness could easily be an impediment to intellectual virtue if it leads to a kind of non-committal intellectual paralysis. And a person scoring high in Agreeableness might be too compromising, sacrificing intellectual honesty for likability.

As the science of intellectual humility continues to develop, various measures and constructs of intellectual humility are being tested against the Big 5 and the HEXACO in order to assess construct validity. Because of its epistemic dimension, Openness to Experience is often shown to correlate with measures of intellectual humility. Tenelle Porter (2015) tested her measure of intellectual humility with two different samples of adults and found significant correlations ranging from 0.26 to 0.40 with Openness to Experience. She also found significant correlations in both samples between her measure and Agreeableness and Conscientiousness, and in one sample with Extraversion. Krumrei-Mancuso and Rouse (2016), using a slightly different measure for Openness, also found a robust correlation between their measure of general intellectual humility and Openness (0.40). They did not measure other constructs from the Big 5, but did find significant correlations between intellectual humility and general humility, open-mindedness, and tolerance. Price et al. (2015) tested their construct of "Open-Minded Cognition," a key component of intellectual humility, and found significant positive correlations with a variety of personality traits including openness to experience, agreeableness, emotional stability (the obverse of neuroticism), and conscientiousness. One intriguing finding of their work was that Open-Minded Cognition was positively associated with Empathic Concern (Davis, 1983). Leary et al. (2016) also found positive correlations with openness, along with measures of epistemic curiosity, and existential quest.

Intellectual humility and personality: The Big 2

A recent development in personality and social psychology is a growing discernment of the importance of two main dimensions that are useful in guiding the description of personality traits, and how those traits are perceived and judged in individuals, groups, and cultures, namely, agency and communion (Abele and Wojciszke, 2007). Sometimes called the "Big Two" (Abele and Wojciszke, 2013; Bruckmüller and Abele, 2013), they are based on two "fundamental modes of existence" (Bakan, 1966) that reflect two intuitive categories of social information processing: perspectives on the self and perspectives of other people. Thus agency is related to what Able and Wojciszke (2007) call the "goal-pursuit of the self," while communion is related to "consideration of others" (p. 751). Each is identified by its differential focus, that is, agency as individual striving with its dimensions of competence, instrumentality, and power, and communion as social relatedness characterized by warmth, morality, expressiveness, and affiliation (Abele and Wojciszke, 2013). These two categories can also be used as themes to organize the Big 5 traits, with agency reflecting the personal growth dimensions of the traits (Extraversion and Intellect) and communion reflecting the socialization dimensions (Agreeableness, Conscientiousness, and Emotional Stability, [Digman, 1997]).

Since agency is characterized by the pursuit of personal goals and exhibition of skills and accomplishments (traits such as competence, intellectual goodness, or dominance); and communion is related to forming and maintaining social connections (traits such as warmth, morality, social goodness, or nurturance, [Bruckmüller and Abele, 2013]), intellectual humility, with its epistemic and social dimensions might fall in with either dimension of the Big Two. The intellectual dimension, with its focus on the pursuit of truth, might align it more on the agentic side, while the social dimension, with its emphasis on the social skills required for collaborative pursuit of knowledge, might land it more on the communal side (Samuelson and Church, 2014).

Gregg, Mahadevan, and Sedikides (in press) used a cross-sectional design to examine patterns of relations that might occur between agency and communion on the one hand, and measures of intellectual arrogance and intellectual humility, on the other. They operationalized communion (C) and agency (A) on three different levels: socially, as inclusion (C) and status (A); dispositionally, as warmth (C) and competence (A); and behaviorally, as amiability (C) and assertiveness (A) using self-report scales and items developed in previous research. Intellectual humility and intellectual arrogance were measured by novel instruments developed by the researchers. They found that the higher an individual's communal traits (inclusion, warmth, and amiability), the more that person exhibited aspects of intellectual humility (was more rationally objective) while the opposite was true for those with higher agentic traits (they were less rationally objective). In addition, the higher an individual scored on the measures of agency, the more an individual showed a tendency toward intellectual arrogance (higher BIAS scores). Their conclusion is that high agency and low communion predicts high intellectual arrogance.

§2: Situational determinants of intellectual humility

We have been discussing intellectual humility as a trait with a certain expectation that, as a trait, it is fairly stable, that is, it will determine a person's behavior in most situations, except for some kind of reasonable response to changing circumstances. This gives us a basis by which we can describe a person as intellectually humble and so, depending on the efficacy of the measure used to determine whether or not any given person has what it takes to be intellectually humble, once we have made such a determination, we might also have a basis on which to predict their behavior. We may even be able to correlate intellectual humility with some important life outcomes, especially in the interpersonal realm, as has been done with other traits such as the Big 5 (Ozer and Benet-Martínez, 2006).

There is some controversy in the field of social and personality psychology about the power of personality traits to influence behavior. People are not consistent in their behavior across situations (Fleeson, 2004). For example, a person at wedding reception A is observed going from table to table, greeting each guest, laughing, and generally being the life of the party, while that same person, at wedding reception B is observed sitting alone most of the time, talking only to a handful of people. What is the difference? At wedding A, he is the father of the bride and the "host" of the party. At wedding B, he is a guest at the wedding of a distant relative and knows hardly anyone. Is this person an introvert or an extrovert? The answer is: it depends. The situation seems to be the determining factor. What is important to study is not how traits make people behave in a certain way, but how people's perceptions of situations and their reactions to them make people behave in a certain way (Fleeson, 2004; Funder, 2010).

Those who question the capacity of traits to determine behavior across situations point to a number of studies that demonstrate the power of the situation (e.g., Harman, 1999). While there are many, the one that may be most interesting from an intellectual humility point of view is the classic experiment in obedience by Stanley Milgram (1963). In this experiment, a subject, who thinks he is participating in an experiment about learning (all the subjects were male), is required to give electric shocks to a "learner" if he makes a mistake on a memory task. The learner, who was a trained confederate of the experiment, was strapped into a chair in a room separate from the "teacher" or subject. The learner was told in the presence of the subject that "although the shocks can be extremely painful, they cause no permanent tissue damage." In the room with the subject was an "experimenter" dressed in a gray lab coat, who was also a trained confederate.

Beginning at 15 volts, the subject was instructed to increase the voltage by 15 volts after each wrong answer, going all the way up to 450 volts. On the device delivering the shock were labels at various points indicating "15 = Slight Shock," "75 = Moderate Shock," "135 = Strong Shock," "195 = Very Strong Shock," "255 = Intense Shock," "315 = Extreme Intensity Shock," "375 = Danger: Severe Shock," and "435 = XXX." At the 300-volt level, the learner stopped answering, only pounding loudly on the wall of the room at each shock. The subjects were instructed to treat a non-answer as a wrong answer and encouraged to continue. Past the 315-volt level, there was no further response from the learner. Of the forty participants, five quit at 300 volts, nine between 315 and 375, and twenty-six went all the way to 450.

For our purposes, it is interesting to look at the details of the experiment. Milgram (1963) reports that the subjects often showed reluctance to go on and looked to the experimenter for advice or sometimes simply said that they did not want to go on. At this point, the experimenter gave up to four different prods in the following order:

Prod 1: Please continue or Please go on.

Prod 2: The experiment requires that you continue.

Prod 3: It is absolutely essential that you continue.

Prod 4: You have no other choice, you must go on.

Milgram (1963) reports that the experimenter was to use as many prods as necessary to "bring the subject into line" and to begin the sequence again "on each occasion that the subject balked or showed reluctance to follow orders." Two additional prods were offered.

If the subject asked if the learner was liable to suffer permanent physical injury, the experimenter said: Although the shocks may be painful, there is no permanent tissue damage, so please go on. [Followed by Prods 2, 3, and 4 if necessary.]

If the subject said that the learner did not want to go on, the experimenter replied: Whether the learner likes it or not, you must go on until he has learned all the word pairs correctly. So please go on. [Followed by Prods 2, 3, and 4 if necessary.] (Milgram, 1963)

These details seem to indicate that the subjects were experiencing some kind of epistemic struggle regarding the morality and efficacy of this procedure and they looked to the experimenter for advice. Sometimes they even had made up their mind to quit, but the prods from the experimenter changed their minds and they continued. Moreover, a variety of subsequent experiments have shown that when the subject can choose whether or not to give the shock and what level of shock to give, instead of being required to give the next level of shock at each trial, there is a significant drop in the amount of punishment subjects deliver (Blass, 1991). We can infer that, left to their own ideas of proper punishment, the subjects in Milgram's original experiment might have shown a similar restraint. So, while we might attribute the obedience of the subjects to vicious character traits such as lack of courage, or lack of empathy for the victim, among others, the subjects show an alarming level of intellectual diffidence, acquiescing to the idea of what is right given by the "authority in the lab coat." The seemingly intellectually humble thing, whether intellectual humility is understood as accurately tracking positive epistemic status or not, would have been to assert that giving a person extreme shocks to help them learn is wrong and to quit the procedure.

So why did only five quit before the "Extreme Intensity Shock" level (and only just before), nine more before the "Danger: Severe Shock" level, and why were twenty-six willing to go past XXX to the highest level of shock? Presumably, there was a range of intellectual humility present within the forty participants, not all of them intellectually diffident to the extreme. Social psychologists (see Funder, 2010) and some philosophers (Harman, 1999) point to the power of the situation—the prestigious lab at Yale, the experimenter in the lab coat stating firmly, but not impolitely, that the subject must go on—that overwhelms any trait or virtue and dictates behavior. In a different situation, the subjects may be less diffident. Indeed, subsequent experiments by Milgram show that rates of obedience drop when the experiment is conducted in a run-down office building instead of the Yale campus, or when the experimenter is dressed in plain clothes instead of in a lab coat (Blass, 1991).

Many situations might influence the expression of intellectual humility away from the "virtuous mean" and toward either end of the "vicious" spectrum, whether toward intellectual diffidence or toward intellectual arrogance. A number of recent studies with different methodological approaches have investigated the effect of the situation on intellectual humility and its vicious counterpart, intellectual arrogance. The first approach is to focus on situations that affect either the perception or expression of intellectual arrogance across individuals, investigating what kinds of situations might increase intellectual humility in general. The second approach is to measure the trait of intellectual humility in individuals and to then test under which circumstances that trait is either more or less present. This approach is more interested in the person by situation interaction, and asks the question: "Under what circumstances and in which situations do individuals show more or less intellectual humility?"

Milyavsky, Kruglanski and Schori-Eyal (2015) investigated the perception of intellectual arrogance and wondered under what circumstances intellectual arrogance was more or less tolerated. In their study, intellectual arrogance was operationalized by a protagonist's dismissal of unwanted advice. In a series of studies, they asked people to judge a protagonist's dismissive behavior in various situations while manipulating the circumstances (the manner of dismissal and the protagonists' relative expertise) and the outcomes of the situation. In their review of the literature, they posit that there are two criteria by which one judges arrogance: (1) actual superiority, that is, whether or not the person claiming superior knowledge is justified in that claim (c.f. Samuelson et al., 2012), and (2) the interpersonal manner of the claimant, that is, whether or not a person is impolite or disrespectful of others when making certain claims. Regarding actual superiority, they note that in most situations only the reputation of the claimant or the outcome of his or her assertions is the means by which one can judge how justified a person is in any given claim. Dismissive behavior, on the other hand, is more readily assessed in any given situation. Their investigation examines the relative importance of actual superiority and interpersonal manner in the perception of intellectual arrogance.

Milyavsky et al. (2015) found that while relative expertise and outcome are criteria by which people judge the merit of a protagonist's claim, "outcome information trumps expertise information" and "politeness trumps competence information" when judging intellectual arrogance. In their study, they asked people to judge the arrogance of a protagonist in various situations. In the situation testing relative expertise, participants are presented with a protagonist who is either an expert or a novice and has a project (culinary, robotics). He/she then gets advice from either a novice or an expert. The protagonist rejects the advice. Participants viewed the protagonists as more arrogant in situations where they rejected the advice of someone with more expertise. To test the strength of outcomes, participants were presented with a protagonist with medium expertise who rejects the advice from either a novice or an expert and the outcome of the project is either positive or negative. The results show that participants perceived the dismissive behavior as less arrogant depending on the outcome. For example, when the outcome was positive, even rejecting the advice of someone with more expertise is not seen as intellectually arrogant. However, when the protagonists had relatively less expertise than the advice-giver and were dismissive of the advice, they were judged to be more arrogant, unless it was justified by a positive outcome. Thus, "outcome trumps expertise."

Milyavsky et al. (2015) then tested the relative power of polite versus impolite behavior when judging intellectual arrogance. They presented an expert (surgeon, advertising executive) who is describing a procedure to a non-expert/fellow expert who then questions the proposed technique. The expert reacts politely or impolitely. Participants in the study rated how polite and knowledgeable the protagonists (experts) and advice-giver were. The results show that in all cases, the protagonists that demonstrate an impolite response are judged as more arrogant, regardless of relative expertise, or even of successful outcomes. In the final section of their study, Milyavsky et al. (2015) tested "folk theories" about what kind of information is most relevant when judging intellectual arrogance. They presented the situation in which a protagonist of unknown expertise has a project and rejects the advice of a friend of unknown expertise. The participants are asked to rate the extent to which they would like to know more about how polite the protagonist was, his or her relative expertise, and the outcome of the project after his or her rejecting the advice. In the folk theory, expertise is more important than outcomes when judging arrogance, but politeness and expertise are equally important. These findings hold for situations at home (friends) and at work (colleagues). This series of studies shows that circumstances matter when judging the arrogance (or humility) of a person. While we might consider the relative expertise and the manner of rejection as the most important criteria for judging arrogant behavior, the experiments show that, in fact, outcomes matter more than expertise, while the interpersonal manner carries the most weight of all.

This study shows how circumstances and situations alter the perception of arrogance in another person. What about situations that make us more arrogant? Are there contexts that exacerbate our general human tendencies to overestimate our knowledge? Fisher et al. (2015) present a fascinating study of how searching the Internet influences people to think that the information they have access to there is now a part of their own knowledge base and makes them more confident about what they think they know. Their study was motivated by a suspicion that the Internet, with its unique access to vast amounts of knowledge and expertise, and the speed with which that knowledge is accessed, might interfere with our ability to keep track of how we rely on it and could distort our view of our own knowledge and abilities. They base this suspicion on the robust finding in the literature that demonstrates how inept we are at making accurate assessments of our own knowledge. For example, people think they are of above average competence in most things, a phenomenon known as the better-than-average effect. A well-known example is a survey conducted at a large university system in which 95 percent of the professors rated themselves above average as teachers (Alicke and Govorun, 2005). Or people overestimate their ability to explain things even when they are familiar with the domain (Fisher and Keil, 2015). Moreover, Fisher et al. (2015) cite the phenomenon of transactive memory—shared information among a group of people—with each person in the group having specialized knowledge that is then accessible to the group. The literature they review indicates a tendency for people to overestimate what they personally know because they are a part of a shared network of knowledge. They also report on evidence that suggests that the Internet could be understood as a transactive memory network. Given this possibility and the natural tendency to overestimate our own knowledge and ability, Fisher et al. (2015) wonder whether the external source of knowledge available to those who use the Internet is conflated with the knowledge they have in their own head and inflates the confidence they have in their own explanatory knowledge.

To test these ideas, Fisher et al. (2015) asked participants to research questions that were general enough so that they might be able to give some answer without looking up the exact details (e.g., "How does a zipper work?") under two conditions: one group of participants was instructed to use the Internet in their research and another group was instructed not to. After this induction task, the participants were asked to rate their ability to provide detailed answers to a set of four questions in six domains that were not a part of the first phase (weather, science, American history, food, health treatments, and the human body). For example, in the domain of weather, one of the questions was, "How do tornadoes form?" and in the domain of history, "Why were the first labor unions formed?" The researchers expected participants would not have much confidence in answering these questions because they require detailed, domain-specific knowledge. The results showed that the participants that used the Internet in the induction phase had greater confidence in their ability to give detailed answers to the questions in the second phase compared to those instructed not to use the Internet. These results held even when participants rated their ability to answer detailed, domain-specific questions prior to the induction and were constrained to spend the same amount of time researching the questions in the induction phase.

Since the question in the dependent measure was phrased "How well could you explain the answers to questions similar to these about [the topic at hand]?" the researchers worried that participants in the Internet condition might have interpreted "you" to mean knowledge in their heads plus the knowledge accessible to them online. To clarify this, they mounted two additional experiments in which they altered the dependent measure so that participants could literally indicate how much knowledge they thought was "in their head." They gave the participants images of seven different fMRI scans with varying activation levels (from low to high) with the color red as the indicator of high activation. The participants were told: "Scientists have shown that increased activity in certain brain regions corresponds with higher quality explanations" (p. 5). They then asked participants to select the image that would correspond to a picture of their brain activity when answering the questions about their own ability to answer the knowledge questions in the six domains. The results were the same as in the first set of experiments. Those in the Internet condition rated their ability to answer detailed, domain-specific questions higher than those who did not use the Internet in phase one, even when the phrase "without any outside sources" was added to the rating assessment in phase two. That is, they indicated that they had more detailed, domain-specific knowledge "in their head" by indicating higher activation levels.

The results indicate that the act of searching the Internet creates a condition by which people think they possess more knowledge "in their head," independent of outside sources, when compared to those in a "no Internet" condition. But does using the Internet create a "halo effect" by increasing confidence in one's explanatory knowledge ability in general? To answer this question, Fisher et al. (2015) altered the six knowledge topics in their dependent measure to domains of self-knowledge that cannot be answered via an Internet search (personal history, personal future, relationships, local culture, personal habits, and emotions). In this case, there was no difference between the two groups. Using the Internet to research questions in phase one had no impact on the participants' confidence in answering autobiographical questions for which the Internet would be no help. Therefore, using the Internet does not produce a general overconfidence in knowledge and one's ability to use that knowledge to explain detailed, domain-specific phenomena.

So, what might be at work here? What might explain the effect using the Internet had on one's confidence to answer general knowledge questions? Fisher et al. (2015) conclude that there is something in the act of searching the Internet for knowledge that drives overconfidence in explanatory knowledge. In their final set of experiments, they changed the induction phase. Instead of instructing one group to use the Internet and another not to, they created a condition in which one group was free to search the Internet for explanatory information, while the other group was provided a link to an article that contained the answer and thereby restricted from searching. The results showed that those who searched the Internet freely felt they had higher explanatory knowledge on the six domains than those restricted to the link. This finding held regardless of whether the participants used an unfamiliar search engine, were given questions to research that were easily answered by a Google search (e.g., "Why is ancient Egyptian history more peaceful than Mesopotamian history?") versus nearly impossible to answer (e.g., "Why is ancient Kushite history more peaceful than Greek history?"), or conducted a search that returned only irrelevant results or no results at all. The authors conclude: "Searching for answers online leads to an illusion such that externally accessible information is conflated with knowledge 'in the head' [and the effect] is driven by querying Internet search engines." Furthermore, "the results of these experiments suggest that searching the Internet may cause a systematic failure to recognize the extent to which we rely on outsourced knowledge" (p. 10).

§3: Both trait and situation in intellectual humility

The results of the previous study illumine our understanding of the influence a situation, such as surfing the Internet, can have on intellectual humility (defined, in this case, as the appropriate assessment of one's intellectual ability and knowledge base). What they did not measure were the traits of their participants, whether or not some had more intellectual humility than others, and whether or not using the Internet differentially inflated a sense of confidence in knowledge (a form of intellectual arrogance) depending on one's level of intellectual humility. We would describe such an approach as "interactionist," which recognizes that situations do have a great influence in determining behavior, but at the same time that the truth is that both come into play. Taking the Milgram (1963) study as an example, someone who is high in intellectual humility—who has a proper balance between intellectual arrogance and intellectual diffidence—may show less obedience in the situation than someone high in intellectual diffidence. The interactionist approach would study the relative stability of a trait like intellectual humility across situations. For example, in situations in which extreme obedience is demanded, those high in intellectual humility would be less willing to give up on closely held convictions than those high in intellectual diffidence. In a situation where less obedience is demanded, the persons high in intellectual humility would still be less willing to give up closely held convictions relative to those high in intellectual diffidence. Fleeson (2004) provides an apt description of the interactionist approach:

> The same person changes his or her behavior quite rapidly and frequently, presumably in response to changing situation. . . . Although this within-person variance is large and presumably due to individuals adapting to situations, it is possible that individuals adapt such that they nonetheless maintain their relative position compared with others in the same situations. (p. 85)

There have been recent studies that have taken this interactionist approach to intellectual humility and yielded fruitful insight. We highlight a few here.

Since the study of intellectual humility is still in its early stages, the first tasks in these investigations is to create measure of traits that are related to intellectual humility and then test them in different situations. Victor Ottati and his colleagues (Price et al., 2015; Ottati et al., 2016) have developed a trait measure for Open-Minded Cognition, which they describe as a "cognitive style . . . marked by a willingness to consider a variety of intellectual perspectives, values, attitudes, opinions or beliefs; even those that contradict the individual's prior opinion" (Price et al., 2015, p. 3). They take an interactionist approach, conceiving of Open-Minded Cognition as comprising both trait-like (dispositional) and situational components. Therefore, an individual's average level of open-mindedness across situations would be indicative of "an individual's chronic level of open-mindedness" (p. 5). By the same token, situations may merit increased or decreased levels of open-mindedness, depending on the reaction the situation demands. Price et al. (2015) explored open-minded cognition in three conditions: general open-minded cognition (OMC-G), political open-minded cognition (OMC-P), and religious open-minded cognition (OMP-C). They developed a measure to test for each. The six items of the measure are nearly identical. Three assess a person's openness to different or new opinions, arguments, and viewpoints, and three assess a person's resistance or "closedness" to arguments, ideas, or messages, especially those with which they disagree. The difference is that the political measure inserts the word "political" before the words arguments, ideas, opinions, etc., the religious measure inserts the word "religious," while the general measure has no qualifier. (e.g., I try to reserve judgment until I have a chance to hear arguments from both sides of an [political/ religious] issue.)

The evidence for trait expression in different situations in this study comes from the differential correlations of the three measures with other trait measures. For example, the general and political scales show a significant negative correlation with dogmatism, but the religious scale does not, and while the religious scale correlates significantly with humility, the other scales do not. A similar pattern is shown in relation to the Conscientiousness, Neuroticism, and Agreeableness subscales of the Big 5. All three measures correlate with three of the four subscales of Stanovitch and West's (2007) measure of Active Open-Minded Thinking, but only the political measure correlates with the "counter-factual thinking" subscale. From these results, we see that across individuals, different contexts tap different kinds of characteristics and traits. Moreover, the results show that within individuals, a person can have a high level of Open-Minded Cognition in one area, for example politics, while having a low level in another, for example religion.

Ottati and his colleagues (Ottati et al., 2016) further examined the interaction of disposition and situation in Open-Minded Cognition. They constructed a model, called the Flexible Merit Standard Model, that can account for both disposition and situation in the expression of Open-Minded Cognition. They surmised that in any given situation, a person determines how much Open-Minded Cognition is merited, that is, across situations, the standard by which one should be open-minded is flexible. That determination, of course, is influenced by how chronically open-minded that person is across situations. Therefore, the Flexible Merit Standard Model accounts for a trait x situation interaction in the expression of Open-Minded Cognition.

To test this model, they presented participants in their study the following scenario, which they deemed the "open" situation:

> Assume you are listening to a panel discussion regarding voting rights within U.S elections. The panelists provide reasons why all U.S. citizens should be permitted to vote in U.S. elections. The panelists cite the U.S. Constitution, the Bill of Rights, and the letters of several founding fathers to support their position. (Ottati et al., 2016)

In the "closed" situation, the scene began with the same sentence, but ended with the following:

> The panelists argue that U.S. citizens who are ethnic minority group members should be denied the right to vote in U.S. elections. They claim

that such a policy will ensure that better leaders are elected, and will save the United States from frightening social changes. (Ottati et al., 2016)

In a series of studies, participants were asked a set of questions that assessed whether they thought one *should* be open-minded in either of these situations (Open-Minded Cognition Situational Norm Scale) or whether they themselves *would* be open-minded in either of these situations (Situation-Specific Open-Minded Cognition Scale). Results showed that the ratings the participants gave on the "I would" statements were mediated by the ratings they had given to the same situations on the "one should" statements. They then tested these across eighteen different scenario pairs. The results support the Flexible Merit Standard Model by showing that the perceptions of the "one should" ratings (situational norm) mediates the effect of the situation (open or closed) on ratings of the "I would" statements (Situation-Specific Open-Minded Cognition).

To further test the relative influence of disposition versus the situation on the expression of open-minded cognition, Ottati et al. (2016) first gave participants the General Open-Minded Cognition Scale (Price et al., 2015) and then read an article about a situation that was designed to activate either the open- or closed-minded norm. They then completed the Situation-Specific Open-Minded Cognition scale. From the results of this study, Ottati et al. (2016) report:

> Clearly, *both* dispositional and situational forces are at play when individuals adopt a particular level of Open-Mindedness in a specific situation. In many situations, the dispositional and situational forces function as separate and independent sources of norm activation that produce additive effects (*Additive* Postulate). In some situations, however, individuals high in dispositional Open-Mindedness may be more responsive to the situation than individuals low in dispositional Open-Mindedness (*Discerning Open-Mindedness* Postulate). (p. 30)

Ottati et al. (2016) call this the "Joint Influence Hypothesis" and it confirms what Fleeson (2004) and others have asserted that neither dispositional tendencies nor situational forces are adequate in explaining a person's behavior at any given time, but it is the interaction of the two in specific contexts that will determine how a person acts and reacts. This is an especially important insight for intellectual humility. As Price et al. (2015) show, there are differences even within a person depending on whether the situation is politics or religion. Knowing how important the interaction of situation and personality is to human encounters could help us develop more civil ways of discourse, especially in politics and religion.

Mark Leary, Rick Hoyle, and their colleagues (Leary et al., 2016; Hoyle et al., 2016) took a similar interactionist approach in their study of intellectual humility. First, they devised and tested a general measure of intellectual humility (Leary et al., 2016, see Chapter 3 for a detailed discussion) and tested it in a variety of situations. They wondered how intellectually humble people would behave in a situation of disagreement (e.g., religion and politics). In one of their studies (Leary et al., 2016), they sorted the participants into two groups, those scoring low on their general intellectual humility scale and those who scored high on the scale. They then determined how religious individuals were within those two groups. Finally, participants were randomly assigned to read one of three essays on the effects of religion on individuals and society, one pro-religious, one antireligious, and one offering a balanced view. Participants then rated how much they agreed with the essay, the accuracy of the beliefs of the writer, the impression they had of the writer on a number of personal qualities (e.g., warm or cold, moral or immoral), how they felt while reading the essay, and finally, they answered a question on religion's effect on society on a positive to negative scale and how certain they were about their own personal religious views. They found that the higher people scored in the intellectual humility measure, the less they were certain of their views and the less they thought their views were superior to those of others. Moreover, though the majority of participants disagreed with the antireligious essay, only those high in intellectual humility were more open to it. They preferred the balanced view and not those that were one-sided. The other situation they examined was people's reaction to politicians who change their minds. Those high in intellectual humility were more willing to vote for a candidate who changed positions on an issue, than those who were low in intellectual humility.

While the series of studies conducted by Leary et al. (2016) tested their measure of general intellectual humility and how people who score high or low on that measure might react in different situations (politics, religion), the authors wondered if there was a more precise way to get at the interaction of trait and situation by measuring *specific intellectual humility*, that is, how intellectually humble a person is in relation to a particular topic or issue. In a series of studies, Hoyle et al. (2016) tested this possibility. First, they created a flexible measure of intellectual humility that allowed for the insertion of a specific topic or view (e.g., Although I have particular views about _____, I realize that I don't know everything that I need to know about it.). Participants rated whether or not the items in the measure were like them or not at all like them. They tested this measure in increasingly specific subject areas: domains, which are general subject areas (e.g., politics); topics, which are subject areas within a domain (e.g., gun control); and issues, which are specific controversies within a topic (e.g., background checks for gun purchases). The psychometric properties of the measure proved adequately strong across domains, topics, and issues.

Hoyle et al. (2016) hypothesized that the more specific the issue, the less people will be intellectually humble (hold more strongly to a view). Thus, while a person might be intellectually humble about politics in general, they may not be as intellectually humble about gun control, and may show even less intellectual humility about background checks for gun purchases. What they found was that while there was a modest overlap between a person's scores on the general intellectual humility measure and the measures of specific intellectual humility, the correlation did not necessarily weaken as the issues became more specific. However, what they did find was that the more extreme a person's view on a specific issue was (the more they strongly agreed or disagreed with an issue such as "physician-assisted suicide should be legal in all states," for example), the lower their specific intellectual humility. They also found that the method by which people came to their views had an impact on their specific intellectual humility. Those whose opinions were formed by their own exploration and study were less intellectually humble than those who formed opinions by other means (e.g., from experts, anecdotal evidence, non-experts, "gut feelings," common knowledge, common sense, religious teachings, emotions, or evaluation of facts and careful reasoning). There is an interesting convergence here with the Fisher et al. (2015) study in which they found the act of searching the Internet increased intellectual arrogance.

Conclusion

In this chapter, we have explored the situational and dispositional determinants of intellectual humility. We began first by positioning the study of intellectual humility in the tradition of personality psychology and examining those qualities of intellectual humility that appear relatively long-lasting and stable, thereby making intellectual humility look much like a personality trait. We proposed that because intellectual humility is a complex phenomenon with many facets, it is likely composed of many traits and attributes already measured in social and personality psychology, such as some of the Big 5 (Openness to Experience, Agreeableness, Conscientiousness, and even Emotional Stability, McCrae and Costa, 1987, 1997) as well as the Big 2 (agency and communion,

Abele and Wojciszke, 2007). We looked also at epistemic traits such as need for cognition (Cacioppo et al., 1996) and need for closure (Kruglanski, 1990). Scholars have begun to define and measure intellectual humility (e.g., Porter, 2015; Krumrei-Mancuso and Rouse, 2016; Leary et al., 2016) and related traits (Open-Minded Cognition, Price et al., 2015) to examine its stability and expression across time and situations.

It has become clear that intellectual humility is also influenced by situations. Milyavsky et al. (2015) demonstrated how situation affects the perception of intellectual arrogance, and, by extension, intellectual humility. Fisher et al. (2015) showed how searching the Internet can influence how much knowledge people claim as their own, leading people to the vice of overclaiming self-assessed knowledge. Finally, we have seen an interactionist approach to the study of intellectual humility, measuring its expression in general and in specific situations (Ottati et al., 2015; Price et al., 2015; Hoyle et al., 2016; Leary et al., 2016).

So what are we to conclude? Is intellectual humility a stable and long-lasting trait or is it blown about by the winds of the situation? The answer is yes to both. About the trait versus situation debate, Fleeson (2004) concludes:

There is no longer any need for debate because large within-person variability and the sensitivity of behavior to situations are not a threat to the viability of traits, and the power of traits is not a threat to the need to explain the considerable amount of within-person behavioral variability. It is time for the study of personality to go forward with both approaches. (p. 86)

We believe this holds true for intellectual humility as well. Developing measures to assess the relative disposition of intellectual humility in people is a necessary step in furthering our understanding of this important intellectual virtue. Examining the situations that either promote or inhibit the expression of intellectual humility is also a critical line of investigation. Testing the trait of intellectual humility in various situations will yield critical knowledge of how intellectual humility plays out. The later line of research—the trait x situation interaction—may be most informative in promoting conditions for more civil discourse, especially in areas of disagreement. Learning how to exchange ideas in an intellectually humble way, and identifying the situations that might promote such exchange, would make a positive impact on our society, indeed.

7

How do emotions affect our ability to be intellectually humble?

The Platonic vision of the passions being subjected to the authority of reason is difficult to sustain in light of contemporary psychological research on the emotions. Because emotions play an important role in cognition in general, we have good reason to expect that they will play an important role in the intellectual virtues, and in intellectual humility in particular. Emotions help focus attention, interrupting other behavioral and cognitive inputs (Greenberg, 2004). Emotions organize people toward goals, needs, and concerns, and motivate people toward specific adaptive actions designed at addressing them (Oatley and Jenkins, 1992). Emotions can help guide decision making (Damasio, 1995).

§1: Theories of emotion and cognition

The case that emotions affect cognition—and therefore could impact the expression of intellectual humility—might best be made by considering the curious case of Phineas Gage. His story has been used in psychology and psychiatry to illustrate the role of emotion in cognition (Funder, 2010; Damasio, 1995). It is particularly interesting as we consider how emotions might influence intellectual virtues like intellectual humility or vices like intellectual arrogance. In 1848, Gage was a supervisor on a construction crew that was building a railroad through central Vermont in the United States of America. His work involved drilling holes into the rock, filling the rock with explosives, and tamping the explosives down with a rod before setting a fuse into the hole for eventual ignition. While tamping down the explosive powder, something went terribly wrong and the powder ignited, sending the rod through Gage's skull, into his cheekbone just below his left eye and exiting out of the top of his head. Quite remarkably, he survived the accident and lived for another fifteen years (Funder, 2010; Damasio, 1995).

We now know that Gage suffered a traumatic injury to his frontal lobe. Specifically, the left frontal and middle left lobes had been destroyed. This damage was later confirmed by modern 3-D imaging of Gage's actual skull itself (MacMillian, 2008). The descriptions of Gage's behavior offered by his attending physician offer some intriguing hints as to how emotion might play into the exercise of intellectual virtues and vices. After the accident, his physician observed that Gage became "fitful, irreverent, indulging at times in the grossest profanity (which was not previously his custom), manifesting but little deference for his fellows, impatient of restraint or advice . . . at times pertinaciously obstinate, yet capricious and facilllating [sic]" (Harlow, quoted in Funder, 2010). These descriptions sound like classic expressions of intellectual arrogance: little deference for his fellows, impatient of advice, obstinate. While we might have to hold the truth of these observations "lightly" due to the fact that they come from one person and there is a lot of myth surrounding the story of Gage, it is, nevertheless, clear that his brain damage did result in a personality change (MacMillan, 2008). Moreover, it appears the personality change was related to Gage's inability to regulate his emotions, or more specifically, his brain damage may have interrupted the ability of his emotions to inform his decisions (Damasio, 1995).

Somatic marker hypothesis

The story of Phineas Gage is a nice illustration of what can happen when our cognitive system is disrupted and no longer works the way in which it is designed—that is, it is an example from our earlier discussion of the agent-reliabilism brand of virtue epistemology (see Chapters 2 and 5 for a discussion). In the normal function of our cognitive system, emotions inform cognition. Antonio Damasio (1995) and his colleagues (Bechara, Damasio, and Damasio, 2000) have speculated that the damage suffered by Phineas Gage was similar to that in patients they have examined who, for various reasons, had suffered damage to the ventromedial sector of their brain. This is the same area reported by Gage's physician and subsequently confirmed by 3-D imaging of Gage's skull.[1] In their many studies, Damasio and colleagues (Damasio, 1995; Bechara, et al., 2000) have found severe disturbances in the social behavior of their patients with damage in this part of the brain. Besides affecting their ability to observe normal social conventions, it profoundly influences their ability to make good decisions. For the most part, the intellectual abilities of these patients are well preserved (e.g., memory, recall, attention) and they seem to do well on tests of their executive function. However, they show an abnormality in processing emotions and feelings. By studying patients with damage to the ventromedial sector of the brain, Bechara et al. (2000) have gained valuable insights into the role emotion plays in our intellectual functioning, specifically decision making.

According to their hypothesis, the ventromedial sector of the brain provides the place of connection between assessing the situation at hand and the emotional markers (including bodily sensations) usually paired with similar situations in the past experience of an individual. This area of the brain is the place where the "disposition" of the current situation confronting an individual, about which a decision or response must be made, is linked with the "disposition" of similar situations in the past experience of the individual— that is, the type of emotion that has been associated with similar situations in past experience. Linking present construal of the situation with a "previously learned factual-emotional set" (p. 297) informs the decision making in the present situation because of the emotional associations with the rewards or punishments of previous situations. Without the linkage between the facts of the situation as they are presently assessed by an individual and the emotions previously associated with an individual's experience in similar situation, decision making is compromised.

They call this model the "somatic marker hypothesis" (Damasio, 1995; Bechara et al., 2000) because the activation of emotions through this linkage involves responses in the body—that is—felt emotion. An individual may or may not be conscious of these somatic markers, but they are a part of what informs decision making. They demonstrate this by engaging individuals in a gambling task in which there are great rewards and great punishments that result from drawing cards from one set of decks, and moderate rewards and moderate punishments when drawing from another. The key is that over time, choosing cards from the set of decks that provides moderate rewards results in a net gain, while choosing cards from the high risk/high reward set results in a net loss. Those subjects who have no damage to the ventromedial section of the brain learn over time which set of decks will bring the most rewards. Those with damage to the ventromedial section do not "mark" the pain of the punishment from the high risk decks and continue to choose from them, even though experience teaches that the risk is not worth it. Evidence for the "somatic marker hypothesis" comes from measuring the skin conductance response (SCR) of both normal subjects and those with ventromedial damage as they engaged in this task. Normal controls began to have higher SCRs over time when selecting from the high risk decks. These "anticipatory SCRs" were not present in those subjects with damage to the ventromedial section of the brain. Interestingly, those patients with ventromedial damage were able to use emotion to aid memory, but not decision making. Bechara et al. (2000) conclude that "damage to the VM cortex weakens the ability to re-experience an emotion for the recall of an appropriate emotional event" (p. 304). Just as children might remember they will be punished or not receive a reward if they do not do as their parents say, yet children are unable to resist temptation because they do not have enough experience with the consequence of their choice, so are those with damage to their ventromedial section of the brain unable to assess the severity of an outcome because they lack the connection to the emotion of the outcome and thus are unable to make a beneficial decision.

While this research is focused on decision making, it also has a direct connection to intellectual humility. As we have seen in our own research (Samuelson et al., 2015), intellectual humility has both epistemic and social dimensions. Often, the exercise of intellectual humility may involve an assessment of the social aspects of a situation in which emotion comes into play. Also, the work of Damasio and colleagues (Damasio, A., 1995; Damasio, H., 1994; Bechara et al., 2000) brings up the intriguing possibility that the epistemic side of intellectual humility is informed by emotion—a remembrance of when, in the past, a person may have got it wrong—and that emotion informs the present assessment of the epistemic situation such that it allows one to hold a position more lightly, be more open to learning, and entertain alternative ideas.

High and low road of emotion

Emotions impact cognition and, therefore, intellectual humility, in many other ways. Referring to Zajonc's (1980) emotion system, Griffiths (1997) argues that "people often respond with fear or anger to a given stimulus whether they want to or not. The system is largely opaque to our central cognitive processes" (p. 93). It is not that higher cognitive processes cannot exert any influence on emotional processes whatsoever, but that in many cases those cognitive processes are insufficient to alter habitual emotional patterns. For example, if a person is phobic toward snakes, no amount of assurance that a particular snake has had its fangs and venom removed will be sufficient to allow a snake to be placed around his or her shoulders.

Concerning this relation between emotion and cognition, LeDoux (1996) has made a case for a high and low road for the production of emotion. In the low road, the amygdala senses danger and sends a direct emergency response to the brain and body. In the high road, information is sent from the amygdala through the thalamus to the neocortex, allowing for the potential for conscious reflection on the emotional response. The low road is twice as fast as the high road, making it often difficult for the reasoning system to intervene before the experience of emotion. Therefore, people are often moved toward the specific action tendencies of particular emotions without being consciously aware of it. Reflecting on these tendencies, Greenberg and Pascual-Leone (2001) assert, "We thus see that much cognition is in the service of affective goals, and that emotion informs reasoned action" (p. 174).

Appraisal theory of emotion

Those who subscribe to the appraisal theory of emotion emphasize the role of cognition in the experience of emotion. For example, Clore and Ortony (2008) define emotion as "cognitively elaborated affective states" (p. 626) in which the recognition of common elements of situations (both internal and external), informed by the person's motivation in the situation, constitutes the "state" of emotion. Emotions are "felt" through a complex interaction of an evaluation of the situation (cognitive, perceptual), physiological responses (somatic, emotional), motivational influences (action readiness, needs, and wants), motor components (behavioral), and subjective experience (feelings). Each component informs the other in a continuous and recursive manner to comprise emotional appraisal and both the conscious and unconscious experience of the emotion (Moors et al., 2013). In this way, emotional appraisal, like other cognitive processes, functions "virtuously" when both emotion (affective evaluation of a situation) and cognition (cognitive appraisal of the evaluation) play their proper role.

A specific example of the relationship of emotion and cognitive appraisal is social psychology research into "mood as information" (Schwartz and Clore, 2003). This research explores how situations might affect our mood, which in turn, colors our appraisal and assessment of things. For example, Schwartz and Clore (2003) report on findings from a number of their experiments showing that subjects were more satisfied with their lives on sunny days, as opposed to rainy days. This finding held only when the attention of the subjects was not drawn to the weather. If they were aware of the weather, they would draw an inference between that and their answer to the life-satisfaction question. What Schwartz and Clore (2003) conclude from two decades of research is that "subjective experiences are a source of information in their own right" (p. 299) affecting cognitive appraisals. That is, they surmise that people often ask themselves "How do I feel about this?" when making a cognitive appraisal and in that process may miss the fact that their current mood may influence their appraisal. Thus a positive mood results in more positive assessments, while a negative mood results in more negative ones. If the mood (as information) is somehow discredited, then the influence is lost.

What is interesting about the research reported by Schwartz and Clore (2003) is that, when the emotion or mood is noticed, it has less influence. This is consistent with findings from the studies by Bechara et al. (2000) reported above, in which the normal subjects are often shifted away from bad choices before they are aware of the sense of impending punishment associated with the bad choice. The relative accessibility of mood and emotion makes them an influential part of cognitive assessment, though, as Schwarz and Clore (2003) point out, they may be most influential when processing motivation is low—that is, when people have little need to pay attention to their cognitive processes—whereas the content of the issue at hand is more influential when processing motivation is high. Interestingly, they report findings from a number of experiments showing that participants with sad moods appear to be engaging in more systematic cognitive processing than those with happy moods. As we have seen in the chapter on heuristics and biases (Chapter 5), systematic processing helps mitigate the natural propensity toward intellectual arrogance brought on by our biases. Does this mean sad people have more intellectual humility? We might propose that such a question warrants further investigation.

The fact that cognition can be in the service of emotion has implications for intellectual humility. For example, an adamant position asserted on grounds of unbiased, objective, rational claims (e.g., behaviorism is the only true form of psychology) might be constructed in the service of affective goals (e.g., such a position helps one avoid the fear of losing one's academic position and the embarrassment of appearing wishy-washy or unintelligent). Emotional influences may lead one to maintain a default position, closing oneself off to the ideas of another. Perhaps part of intellectual humility is to be aware of how one's emotions can impact cognition, belief formation, and holding on to positions when challenged.

Emotions and cognitive biases

A great deal of research has focused on how emotions factor in cognitive bias. For example, Pyszczynski et al. (1993) review evidence that people bias or distort their perceptions, concepts, and judgments to protect themselves from negative emotional states and conclude that "a number of findings suggest that emotional states do indeed mediate many cognitive distortions and biases" (p. 177). They also find that expressing the emotions toward which the cognitive distortions are presumably directed substantially reduces the need for such distortions and biases. Literature on Terror Management Theory (TMT) provides another interesting avenue of research regarding the way emotion biases cognition. TMT holds that anxiety about one's death is managed, at least in part, by validating one's current cultural worldview, leaving people closed off to alternative worldviews (Greenberg, Solomon, and Pyszczynski, 1997; Mikulincer and Florian, 2000). In addition, a deep well of research exists regarding confirmation bias and its affective components. Westen et al. (2006) outlined the neural bases of motivated reasoning, a form of implicit emotion regulation where people naturally adopt judgments that minimize negative and maximize positive emotion states. These researchers state that "processes of approach and avoidance, motivated by affect or anticipated affect, may apply to motivated reasoning, such that people will implicitly approach and avoid judgments based on their emotional associations" (p. 1947).[2]

Emotional intelligence

Another potential area of research that could inform the study of intellectual humility is emotional intelligence. Mayer et al. (2001) set their concept of emotional intelligence in the context of relationships stating: "When a person's relationship with another person or an object changes, so do their emotions toward that person or object . . . [emotional intelligence is] an ability to recognize the meanings of emotions and their relationships and to use them as a basis in reasoning and problem solving" (p. 234). Within this framework, emotional intelligence might inform intellectual humility because, just as emotional intelligence contains both epistemic and social dimensions, so does intellectual humility (Samuelson et al., 2015).

Emotional intelligence has four branches that correspond to other types of intelligence. The first branch involves accurately perceiving emotions in others and within the self. This might include capacities for recognizing emotions in faces, in voice, or in body language. There are also individual differences in how people can precisely perceive emotions and differentiate emotions within themselves. The second branch involves how emotion is used to facilitate thought and to make decisions. Emotions can help focus attention on relevant details, predict outcomes, guide judgments, and negotiate dilemmas. The third branch is the ability to understand emotions and the workings of emotions. Part of this ability is in naming emotions, analyzing them, and noticing how they trend over time. This capacity grows with age. Finally, the fourth branch is about emotional regulation: the ability to manage emotions in such a way that personal growth and social relations are enhanced. This involves an awareness of the emotions inherent in situations, and an ability to effectively solve emotion-laden problems (Wranick, Barrett, and Salovey, 2007). Mayer et al. (2001) draw a distinction between the second branch (using emotions to facilitate thought) and the other three. This branch is unique in using emotions to enhance reasoning, whereas Branches 1, 3, and 4 involve reasoning about emotions. Moreover, the four branches are viewed as a hierarchy, with emotional perception at the bottom and management at the top. Measuring individual differences in emotional intelligence as they relate to intellectual humility would be a fruitful area of research.

Based on the foregoing review of the research, it seems as though an appropriate interplay of emotion and reason is essential to the virtuous person. Without emotion, our ability to reason is impaired. Without reason, emotion lacks clear direction. The emotional brain is incapable of analytic thought and its promptings can be imprecise, but when it is paired with reason, it affords a person with the greatest adaptive potential.[3] As Greenberg (2008) states, "Emotion moves us and reason guides us" (p. 50). A proper convergence of these two primary human capacities is what some researchers have called emotional intelligence (Mayer and Salovey, 2004), a construct critical for health and relationships. Arguably, this kind of integration of head and heart is the mark of a virtuous person.[4]

§2: Emotional regulation

Emotional regulation, conceived of as an appropriate interaction between emotion and reason (Greenberg and Pascual-Leone, 2006), might also play a role in intellectual humility. As discussed above, embracing the adaptive potential of one's emotional dispositions is certainly an important part of emotional regulation, especially for those who are emotionally overregulated (i.e., those who consistently suppress their emotions). Appropriately harnessing the motivational aspects of emotion, therefore, could aid one's intellectual engagement with another and fuel critical rational processing and reflection in a way that is less distorted and biased. For example, Panfile and Laible (2012) reviewed evidence that establishes emotional regulation as a critical mechanism in the development of empathy. Furthermore, empathy (understood as an affective concern for another) is an important precursor of a number of prosocial and moral behaviors (and an inhibitor of aggressive behaviors). Especially in the context of discussion and learning from another, empathy is presumably a factor involved in intellectual humility. Shortt and Gottman (1997) conducted a study that hints at empathy's role in disagreement. Siblings low in dispositional empathy (both emotional and cognitive) exhibited more belligerent and domineering behaviors in a disagreement setting than did those high in dispositional empathy. They also found that high emotionality (measured by heart rate) was related to belligerence and domination. This evidence further points to the critical role that emotional regulation plays in intellectual humility, particularly in cases of interpersonal interactions and epistemic disagreement. Empathy toward an epistemic peer helps one feel bonded and connected to the other in a way that would encourage understanding and openness. Fosha (2000) describes a number of adaptive *relational* action tendencies that emotion provides, along with the other more specifically self-focused action tendencies. Similarly, Greenberg and Pascual-Leone (2001) state: "Emotions might, for example, tell one that something is wrong in the domain of interpersonal relations, such as an interpersonal bond that has been ruptured or endangered. Thinking then sets to work to create a solution to this problem" (p. 174).

Using a connectionist approach to cognition in their model of emotional regulation, Westen and Blagov (2007) recognize how first impressions, attitude shifts, and emotional processes guide thinking. They propose two kinds of constraints at work in the connectionist framework: cognitive constraints (which are facts and data about the world and the logical consequences of that data) and emotional constraints (which are both current emotional associations and those emotions that are anticipated). Because these constraints have different goals, the brain balances this information to solutions that best fit the data but at the same time result in maximal positive affect with minimal negative affect.

Westen and Blagov (2007) ground this theory in the basic human behavior of approach and avoidance, stating that these processes "motivated by affect or anticipated affect, apply to the judgments people reach, the way they see themselves, and other conscious beliefs and decision [*sic*], such that people will approach and avoid ideas and representations based on their emotional consequences" (p. 284). Thinking is complicated by the fact that while people are trying to make decisions that anticipate optimal emotional results, emotional distortions may compromise the weighing of their options and the decisions they ultimately reach. They tested this theory in a series of studies that presented subjects with situations in which emotions might impact the weight the subjects give the facts, or even distort the perception of the facts. For example, they conducted a series of studies around the time of the impeachment trial of President Bill Clinton and assessed the cognitive and emotional constraints around Clinton's sexual advances toward women, whether he lied to the grand jury, and whether his actions constituted an impeachable offense. They tested for subjects' knowledge of the facts, that is, what they knew about Clinton and the scandal (cognitive constraints). They then asked how they felt at a "gut level" about the two major political parties, about Clinton himself, and about infidelity and feminism in general (emotional constraints). What they found was that subjects' choices were a combination of emotional constraints and cognitive constraints, but "emotional constraints swamped cognition" (p. 385). For example, using their measures of cognitive and emotional constraints taken six to nine months earlier, they could predict with 88 percent accuracy peoples' judgment about whether Clinton's actions constituted an impeachable offense according to the Constitution. More interestingly, when they took cognitive constraints out of the equation, they could predict the same judgments with an accuracy rate of 85 percent. These results inform the findings from situational studies of intellectual humility reported in Chapter 6 that showed a differential level of intellectual humility depending on the situation, especially regarding politics (Ottati et al., 2016; Hoyle et al., 2016). The interplay of emotion and cognition may inform this difference.

There are, of course, individual differences in the expression of emotion and in emotional regulation. Learning how to appropriately temper one's emotional experience is likely a very important aspect of intellectual humility. Roberts (2003) argues that this kind of "emotional self-control," or the ability to alter one's judgment to influence one's emotional states, is a critical aspect of being a rational person. Emotions like disgust, anger, and fear can be disastrous to cognitive openness and rationality (e.g., disgust at another's morality, anger at another's offensiveness, fear of what one's own life would look like if one's strongly held religious belief turned out to be epistemically suspect, sadness over the loss of a previously held idea, etc.). Moors et al. (2013) suggest that, given the complexity of the processes involved in the appraisal of emotions, emotional regulation needs also to be integrated into theories like appraisal theory that integrate emotion and cognition. Emotionally charged topics such as morality, religion, and politics are prime areas of intellectual bias and arrogance. In marriage, disagreements are often emotionally charged; marital success or failure often depends on the couple's ability to handle these discussions. Research on marital conflict could provide useful information on intellectual humility, especially in the context of disagreement, and help illuminate why emotional regulation is so important. For example, Gottman (1995) has found that when one's heartbeat rises to a certain threshold—about 82 beats per minute (BPM) for men (up from an average of 72) and 90 BPM for women (up from an average of 82)—a phenomenon called flooding occurs. Flooding is characterized by the activation of the sympathetic nervous system, which releases adrenaline and cortisol into the nervous system. When one's heart rate increases to 100 BPM, the "flood" of adrenaline results in a "fight or flight" response often accompanied by intense fear or anxiety. While this system has adaptive survival functions, Gottman (1995) argues that emotional flooding severely limits one's ability to "focus on what the other person is saying, which leads to increased defensiveness and hostility" (p. 116). This flooded state takes a toll on one's emotions and cognition, and empathy is very difficult. One is limited in the ability to emotionally connect with another in a way that would provide motivation to remain engaged and attentive. In addition, one is similarly impaired at being able to listen to, and taking, the cognitive position of another. These impairments to essential components of intellectual humility confirm the important role of emotion in disagreement, highlighting the need for emotional regulation. One's ability to appropriately manage emotions (e.g., through breathing, paying attention to emotional states, accepting feelings, and self-soothing) has the potential to play a critical role in the ability to intellectually engage with another, especially in matters of ultimate concern—including religious concerns.

§3: Emotion and cognition in the face of disagreement

Given the foregoing discussion, a natural place to study the role of emotion in intellectual humility is in the arena of disagreement. Of particular interest is the relational dynamics involved in disagreement as the occasion for the introduction of emotion into the thought process. We have seen evidence of this in some of the studies reported above: Gottman's (1995) study showing heightened physiological arousal in the context of marital disagreement and Westen and Blagov's (2007) theory that thinking is guided by emotion through the basic processes of approach and avoidance in the context of political disagreement. The presence of another human being introduces the potential for emotional reactivity that can impact the way thoughts are both processed and presented. These emotional reactions can be unconscious, even based on past experience of relationships, going all the way back to the attachment relationships of caregivers (Mikulincer, Shaver, and Pereg, 2003).

Reddy and Wilson (2015) offer the intriguing suggestion that emotional reactivity can play a role in the exchange of ideas and impact intellectual humility because people consider ideas as "possessions" that are not peripheral but central to the self. Because of this, any threat to an idea or to the knowledge one possesses is a threat to the self. Intellectual humility is difficult in such cases because defending ideas is conflated with self-defense. To acknowledge the limitations of one's knowledge is difficult because it would be an admission of self-limitation. To correct this defensive posture and lower the emotional engagement with the ideas and the potential emotional reactivity in a situation of disagreement, Reddy and Wilson (2015) suggest engaging in the process of "self-distancing" reflected in the work of Ayduk and Kross (2010). In a study in which people were asked to reflect on an emotionally difficult time, those who were able to spontaneously "self-distance," that is, see themselves in a situation from the perspective of an observer, had less emotional reactivity to the memory in the short term. Moreover, those able to spontaneously self-distance showed a greater capacity for problem solving and less reciprocity of negativity (hostility, emotional reactivity) in situations of conflict with someone with whom they were in an ongoing relationship.

Jarvinen et al. (2015), in a study of intellectual humility in the face of disagreement, focus on attachment style (Bolby, 1983) as a critical underlying factor of the relational dynamics involved in disagreement and the subsequent impact of emotion. Their study builds on research by Mikulincer and colleagues (Mikulincer, 1997; Mikulincer and Shaver, 2001; Mikulincer, Shaver, and Pereg, 2003) demonstrating that the dynamics surrounding attachment style and the related strategies of emotional regulation have an effect on cognition and decision making. For example, people with evidence of secure attachment in their relational style have a lower need for cognitive closure and are more likely to depend on new information in making social judgments than those with an avoidant or an anxious-ambivalent style (Mikulincer, 1997).

Jarvinen et al. (2015) wondered about the impact of attachment style on the emotional reactions to disagreement and the subsequent impact on cognitive openness. They based their approach on previous research by Mikulincer, Shaver, and Pereg (2003), showing that the emotional regulation strategies associated with attachment styles had an effect on cognitive openness. Those with an avoidant attachment style employ a strategy that will protect them from painful, negative emotion (they tend to deactivate, or disengage from, the disagreement with another in order to control or avoid the negative emotions), making them less cognitively open. Those with an anxious/ambivalent style, on the other hand, are hyper-vigilant for both real and imagined threats to the relationship. Because of this heightened negative affect, their reflective and cognitive capacities are compromised. They also would be less open to different ideas and thoughts. However, in a situation of disagreement, they might be intellectually diffident, too ready to agree to a counter argument in order to preserve the relationship. Those with a secure attachment style would be the most cognitively open due to the confidence they have in their relationships.

To test these theories, they ran a series of online studies that assessed the cognitive openness of the participants as measured by their willingness to change the strength of a belief after hearing an argument that ran counter to their own belief. Before this assessment, they assigned the participants to be primed in four different conditions: a secure attachment prime, an avoidant attachment prime, an anxious/ambivalent prime, and no prime. The participants then stated their belief (answered yes or no) and rated the strength of that belief on three different questions: (1) Is abortion morally permissible? (2) Does God exist? (3) You can spend 100 dollars either on something fun for yourself (concert, gadget, game, etc.) or on caring for the world's poor. Is it morally permissible to spend the money on yourself? After receiving a counter argument, they were asked again to state their belief and rate its strength. The participants also completed trait measures of attachment and personality (the Big 5).

Results showed that those primed in the secure attachment condition were more open to adjusting their beliefs after hearing counter arguments than those in the ambivalent condition, but only for the God question. The other questions showed no significant differences. However, the researchers also found that those who scored high on secure trait attachment orientation had significantly higher trait openness (the Big 5) than the avoidant group. Jarvinen et al. (2015) conclude:

The safety of secure attachment relationships seems to provide a dispositional capacity to regulate one's emotions and to thus tolerate the threat contained in new experiences and new information, allowing one to maintain a position of cognitive openness. (p. 16)

An additional study found that attachment anxiety, emotional valence, and the rated intelligence of the person presenting the counterarguments significantly predicted participants' openness to hear more counterarguments. While the authors made some adjustments in the second study to simulate a personal give and take in the presentation of the counterarguments, testing a face-to-face exchange of ideas may have produced larger effects than they were able to obtain in an online (and fairly impersonal) exchange. Still, these studies encourage further exploration into the relationship of attachment style and intellectual humility, especially in the context of disagreement. They provide a framework for understanding how, in a situation of disagreement and epistemic threat, intellectual humility can be impacted by unconscious mechanisms of emotional regulation brought about by attachment styles.

§4: Emotional style and intellectual humility

Thus far we have been making the case that emotion will influence the expression of intellectual humility because emotion impacts cognition. Indeed, it may simply be a mistake to separate emotion and cognition in the expression of any human behavior, including intellectual virtues, because emotions inform cognition and vice versa. However, we have seen that emotions can overwhelm cognitive processes just as cognition can suppress emotion. We have been arguing that cognition is affected by emotion—but by this view, emotion is affected, indeed even dependent on, cognition. It may be useful to think of emotion and cognition as two parts of a whole, much the same way that dual-process theories approach cognition (see Chapter 5). The virtuous functioning of our cognitive system is when emotional and cognitive processes work together in a balanced way.

Intellectual humility, then, would be properly expressed when emotion and cognition are brought into proper relation—achieve their proper balance—in decision making and the subsequent behavioral response. Richard Davidson (2005), a leader in the field of the neuroscience of emotion, has developed a way to speak of the interplay of emotion and cognition through a concept he calls "Emotional Style." He contrasts style, which he defines as "a consistent way of responding to the experiences of our lives" (p. xii), with an emotional state, which is the fleeting unit of emotion triggered by an experience but which does not last. It is also contrasted with a mood, which is an emotional feeling that can last and remain consistent over a longer period of time—even days—but which also is relatively short-lived. Finally, a style is also different from an emotional trait, which is understood as an emotion that seems to dominate an individual's stance toward the world (i.e., perpetually angry or annoyed at the world). An emotional trait makes it more likely that you will experience an emotional state because your threshold for experiencing any given emotion (like anger) is lower.

Emotional Style is tied to specific and identifiable brain pathways and circuits. They are the "fundamental building blocks" of our emotional response to the world. Emotional styles, because they are based on brain systems and circuitry, can influence the likelihood of one's experiencing emotional states or particular moods, or expressing certain emotional traits. In addition, because Emotional Style is characterized by specific brain patterns, it underlies personality. Certain traits from the big 5 like Agreeableness or Neuroticism could be understood in terms of the Emotional Style—the brain circuit pattern—that underlies them.

Davidson (2005) posits that Emotional Style has six dimensions:

1   Resilience: how slowly or quickly you recover from adversity.

2   Outlook: how long you are able to sustain positive emotion.

3   Social Intuition: how adept you are at picking up social signals from people around you.

4   Self-Awareness: how well you perceive bodily feelings that reflect emotions.

5   Sensitivity to Context: how good you are at regulation of your emotional response to take into account the context you find yourself in.

6   Attention: how sharp and clear your focus is. (p. xiv)

In the following section, we will take a look at each dimension in turn, examine the brain basis for each, and consider its implication for intellectual humility. By doing this, we can not only learn some more about the emotional basis for intellectual humility but also understand the basis for individual differences in the expression of intellectual humility. Moreover, Davidson (2005) has shown that, while individuals have unique Emotional Style profiles, it is possible to change the expression of Emotional Style through changing the brain circuitry that underlies it.

Resilience

Resilience is the ability to recover from the challenges and setbacks that life brings. A challenge, setback, or confrontation will flood the body and brain with negative emotion and the brain will respond with attempts to dampen the emotion and return to a normal or baseline mood. The same process of emotional flooding and subsequent recovery happens with positive emotions. Moreover, this recovery time can be measured with the strength of our eye blink, a reliable measure of how strongly we react to a stimulus, especially a negative one.

Davidson (2005) reports on an experiment in which subjects were placed into an MRI machine to measure their brain activity. First, they recorded baseline activity for eight minutes, four with eyes open, four with eyes closed. Subjects were then shown fifty-one pictures each lasting six seconds. There were an equal number of three types of images: upsetting images such as a baby with a protruding eye tumor; happier images such as a mother and child in an embrace; and neutral images such as a picture of a nondescript room. During or after the presentation of the picture, the subjects heard a short burst of white noise that caused an involuntary blink, the strength of which was measured. A negative emotional state produced a stronger eyeblink compared to a neutral state, while a positive state produced a weaker eyeblink compared to a neutral state. Measuring the eyeblink twice allowed Davidson to determine how quickly the subjects recovered from the negative emotions elicited by the disturbing pictures.

What Davidson found was that individuals with more activation in the left side of the prefrontal cortex during the baseline period had a quicker recovery (their eyeblinks became weaker more quickly) than those will less activation. The left prefrontal area inhibits activation from the amygdala, the source of the negative emotional reaction, and allows a person to recover from the upsetting experience. A strong capacity for resilience depends on a strong connection between the left prefrontal cortex and the amygdala, which allows for greater control of negative emotions. Perhaps you have told yourself during a scary scene of a film, "It's only a movie, it's only a movie." That is an example of your left prefrontal cortex inhibiting the amygdala activation. Those with weak connections between the two regions have more trouble bouncing back from adversity.

Often, arguments or disagreements can be perceived as a threat by a person due to their adversarial nature. In such a case, those with strong resilience may be able to exhibit more intellectual humility because they can control the negative and upsetting emotions that can arise in the confrontation of ideas. This aspect of Emotional Style may have a strong impact on the expression of intellectual humility and may give us great insight into individual differences with regard to the trait.

Outlook

Understanding the role of the prefrontal cortex—the forward part of our brain—is key to understanding both the role of emotion in cognition and how to promote intellectual humility. This region of the brain is the place where emotions are interpreted and processed, often determining our response to situations. This is the case for the Outlook dimension of Emotional Style. An important finding that Davidson (2005) reports from his earlier research regarding the brain basis for this dimension is that the left side of the prefrontal cortex is engaged and active when experiencing positive emotions, while the right side is active with negative emotions.

In order to better understand this dimension of Emotional Style, Davidson and his colleague Aaron Heller decided to study depressed patients in their lab (Davidson, 2005). Davidson had established, in earlier experiments, that depressed patients were, in fact, able to experience positive emotion by their self-reported responses to scenes from comic films intended to induce positive emotions. What they discovered in their subsequent research was that depressed patients are not able to sustain positive emotion as well as their healthy counterparts. This was determined through an experiment in which depressed and healthy subjects were shown pictures intended to induce positive emotions (e.g., pictures of children playing or adults dancing). Experimenters divided the subjects into two conditions: one group was asked to simply view the pictures as normal; the other group were asked to try to sustain the positive emotion they were feeling as long as they could. They gave some suggestions about how this might be done (e.g., thinking of themselves in the happy situation they were viewing). Altogether, seventy-two images were shown to the subjects over a period of forty-five minutes.

The results of this work show a clear pattern of brain activity. The reward circuits in the brains of the subjects were activated when viewing the pleasant pictures. The activity centered on the ventral striatum, "a region located below the cortical surface in the middle of the brain [that] has been shown in previous studies to become active in people anticipating receiving something rewarding or pleasurable. More specifically, what becomes active . . . is a cluster of neurons within the ventral striatum called the nucleus accumbens, a region critical for motivation and generating a sense of reward" (p. 84). Initially, both depressed and healthy subjects showed similar activity. The difference was that healthy patients could sustain the good feelings for the whole session, while the positive emotions of the depressed patients tailed off within minutes. Davidson (2005) cites the strength of the connection between the left side of the prefrontal cortex and the nucleus accumbens as the critical factor, since signals from the former help sustain the activity of the latter. Davidson (2005) goes so far as to say that we can "will [ourselves] into feeling rewarded" (p. 85). Those who fall on the positive side of the Outlook dimension are able to sustain activity in the reward center (nucleus accumbens) through strong signals from the prefrontal cortex.

How might Outlook impact intellectual humility? As Davidson (2005) says, "No brain region is an island" (p. 152). He cites evidence that the same region involved in a positive outlook is implicated in planning and goal-directed behavior. In situations of disagreement or discourse, increasing activity in the reward region of the brain may also impact the goals of the person involved in the disagreement. If the discussion were held in circumstances that promoted a positive outlook—for example, a shared meal or a shared positive experience—this could impact the epistemic goals of the participants (e.g., whether they needed to "win" the argument vs. whether they were seeking a better understanding of the issue), which could affect intellectual humility.

This is the premise behind an effort led by Jonathan Haidt and his colleagues. On the website civilpolitics.org, there are suggestions for interventions that promote civil discourse in situations of disagreement. Haidt (2015) reports on one such effort in which invited participants (six conservative, six liberal) shared a meal and discussed issues on which they disagreed. Haidt surmises that the format of a meal in a private home made people more open and polite, marks of intellectual humility. He cites some evidence of changes in belief from a brief survey of the participants, though the results are mixed. Despite sharp disagreement over issues, Haidt (2015) saw evidence of openness, trust, and a collaborative approach to solving problems without any "partisan sniping and not a shred of hostility" (Haidt, 2015).

Whether the intellectual humility exhibited in Haidt's (2015) experiment was the result of an increased activity in the nucleus accumbens sustained by increased activity in the prefrontal cortex brought about by the pleasant circumstances or by some other means is an empirical question that is yet to be answered. As for techniques that help increase positive Outlook, Davidson (2005) points to cognitive reappraisal and meditation as ways to strengthen the connection between the prefrontal cortex and the reward region of the brain. While there is good reason to expect a relationship between positive Outlook and intellectual humility, especially in situations of disagreement, future research is needed to establish such a relationship.

Social Intuition and Sensitivity to Context

Regarding their relationship to intellectual humility, Social Intuition and Sensitivity to Context are good to consider together because, in the extremes of each, we can see evidence of the extremes of the intellectual humility continuum spoken of in Chapter 1, namely, intellectual arrogance and intellectual diffidence. We begin with Social Intuition. Those low in Social Intuition have trouble reading social and emotional cues from others communicated through facial expressions, body language, tone of voice, and other social cues. Because many of the cues come through visual perception, the fusiform gyrus—an area of the brain that specializes in reading faces—is less active in those with low Social Intuition. At the same time, their amygdala—the area that is involved with signaling emotions, especially fear—is highly active. The interaction of these two areas makes up the Social Intuition style. Davidson (2005) tells of examining the brain activity of a patient who was low in Social Intuition. When the patient was asked to read the emotions depicted on pictures of various faces, the activity in the amygdala increased, and only when the patient averted his gaze did the activity in the amygdala fall.

Since intellectual humility has a strong social dimension, the capacity to read the social cues of others is a necessary skill in the expression of this intellectual virtue. A person low in Social Intuition who is in a discussion or disagreement may not be sensitive to or even aware of the other person's disagreement and may come off as arrogant by exhibiting such behaviors that accompany lack of Social Intuition like not listening well or not responding to the other's desire to speak. Being well tuned to social cues would at least allow for more intellectual humility because many of the social aspects of intellectual humility require such an ability (e.g., listening, responding to both tone and content of argument, sensitivity to turn-taking in conversation, etc.).

On the other side of the intellectual humility continuum is intellectual diffidence—giving in too easily to another person's ideas and arguments. The Sensitivity to Context style may be implicated in one's being too timid in expressing ideas, opinions, and beliefs, especially in the face of disagreement or argument. Those in the high extreme of Sensitivity to Context may be eager to please or so in tune with the expectations of those around that they may be afraid to make a mistake or say the wrong thing. Both are marks of intellectual diffidence. On the other hand, a person can be so tuned out of social context— for example, they might make an inappropriate comment, or express an emotion that is misplaced—that they might be perceived as arrogant.

Davidson (2005) locates the brain activity involved in the Sensitivity to Context dimension between the prefrontal cortex and the hippocampus, specifically the anterior hippocampus, which is close to the amygdala and responsible for controlling the inhibition of behavior in different contexts. Evidence for the role of these regions in Sensitivity to Context came from studying war veterans suffering from post-traumatic stress disorder (PTSD), who showed a low Sensitivity to Context. An example of this would be the inability to distinguish between the sound of gunfire in a battle signaling danger and the sound of a car backfiring in a safe urban context. These patients have a smaller hippocampus compared to non-PTSD patients. This affects decision making as the hippocampus communicates with the prefrontal cortex and is a part of the brain system involved in memory retrieval. In the case of this style, the ideal for intellectual humility may be found in the middle of the two extremes. Too much sensitivity produces diffidence in a situation of disagreement, while too little may produce an inappropriate response or even arrogance. Again, testing people at the extremes of this style in situations of disagreement would help us understand some more about the emotional basis of intellectual humility, especially on the extreme of intellectual diffidence.

Self-Awareness and Attention

We are seeing a pattern in the interplay between cognition and emotion—not only as it relates to the practice of virtues like intellectual humility, but also in everyday functioning—namely, a proper balance between the two. While emotion can energize and inform cognition, too much emotion can overwhelm decision making or disrupt attention and focus. Too little emotion or too much cognitive control can lead to insensitivity and cut us off from crucial information for decision making and action. What is ideal, especially in relationship to intellectual humility, is a proper balance between cognition and emotion,

While the Self-Awareness dimension of Emotional Style may not have a direct bearing on the mechanisms of intellectual humility, it has an impact insofar as it provides a person with information about their emotional state that can, in turn, inform their approach to the situation at hand. It involves the insula, a region of the brain that receives signals from the visceral organs. Davidson (2005) reports that those who have higher insula activity have a better awareness of their emotions. Too much awareness may be detrimental because it can cause a hyperfocus on one's body (hypochondria, panic disorder) and distract from thinking and reasoning. Too little awareness would run the risk of underestimating the emotional import of the topic or situation and lead to an inappropriate response. Knowing how one is feeling while discussing or investigating a topic is important information when engaging oneself and others in the topic.

Attention, the ability to focus on the salient details of a situation or topic, is more directly related to the practice of intellectual humility. There are two aspects to this dimension: selective attention, which is the ability to focus on relevant details of the situation and ignore those not relevant, and open, non-judgmental awareness, which is the capacity to remain open to all incoming information and not get stuck on one piece or one particular aspect of the situation (including one's own distracting thoughts). Davidson points to studies that show that the prefrontal cortex—the area of the brain that controls much of our conscious thought and cognition—plays the critical role in the Attention dimension of Emotional Style. By having participants pay specific attention to a stimulus (a particular tone sounding in a particular ear or the occurrence of a number in a series of letters) and measuring brain activity, Davidson and his colleagues found two specific brain patterns related to Attention. One involves "phase locking," which is when signals from the prefrontal cortex are synchronized with the stimulus (the sound of the tone), a capacity that can be developed with practice and that some are better at than others. The other involves an electrical signal in the brain that is produced in response to a specific external event. Having the proper strength of this signal allows a person to pay attention to existing events while also staying open to new events. Too weak a signal and a person may miss the event all together. Too strong a signal and the person may overly attend to the first event and miss the second. A "virtuous" mean of attention and openness marks the Attention dimension.

A key component of intellectual humility is this capacity of open, non-judgmental awareness, which allows a person to remain open to new information, entertain alternative ideas while suspending judgment, and focus on relevant details while ignoring distractions. All these are a part of the Attention dimension of Emotional Style. Moreover, this activity is based mainly in the prefrontal cortex, an area of the brain critical to the effortful control required in the exercise of intellectual humility. The examination of the brain basis of these Emotional Styles fits well with the work reported in Chapter 5 on the two systems theory of cognition. Intellectual humility is possible when the two systems work together, with the more conscious and deliberative aspects of our cognitive system (System 2) controlling and selecting those aspects of our quicker and less conscious mind (System 1). Though emotions inform both Systems, the prefrontal cortex is clearly involved in the System 2 process of selection and control of thoughts generated by System 1, just as the prefrontal cortex is involved in the recovery of emotional flooding in Resilience, the sustaining of positive emotion in Outlook, the interpretation of context in Sensitivity to Context, and the development of non-judgmental openness in Attention.

In the same way that intellectual humility can be found on a continuum between the extremes of intellectual diffidence and intellectual arrogance, so may landing in a balanced place on the continuum in each of the Emotional Styles be the key to how these styles relate to the expression of intellectual humility. In theory, being on the higher end of Resilience and Outlook would be better for intellectual humility, as it would allow for the control of negative emotions and the harnessing of positive emotions in situations of disagreement and discussion. Having a balanced Social Intuition, Self-Awareness, and Sensitivity to Context would allow for the right amount of attention to be paid to the situational cues and the interplay of emotions involved in the exchange of ideas between people. Finally, having a strong, focused Attention allows a person to listen non-judgmentally and attend to the relevant details in a discussion. What is especially important about Davidson's (2005) presentation of Emotional Style as it relates to intellectual humility—and any practice of virtue for that matter—is his message that these capacities are malleable and can be trained and strengthened. Like any habit, through practice in self-regulation, meditation, cognitive reappraisal, and other means, a person can work on strengthening those dimensions that contribute to intellectual humility in particular, and to well-being in general.

Conclusion

As we said above, without emotion, our ability to reason is impaired. Without reason, emotion lacks clear direction. Arguably, this kind of integration of head and heart is the mark of a virtuous person. A robust empirical understanding of intellectual humility is impossible without serious attention to emotion, including its motivational and adaptive functions, its influence on cognition, its interpersonal influences, and its regulation. Different strategies for facilitating intellectual humility in epistemic partners (e.g., either accessing and evoking their emotions or attempting to manage and control them) will depend on a number of factors, including the topic of conversation, the context, the emotional history between the partners, various personality factors, their levels of emotional arousal, the emotional content involved, etc. All of these factors may expand and inform a proper understanding of intellectual humility.

In addition, the more we understand about the role of emotion in cognition, the better we will be able to both understand intellectual humility and promote its practice. While emotion is a clear motivating factor in cognition, it can also cloud or distort the pursuit of epistemic goods. To practice an intellectual virtue, there must be enough emotion to motivate the pursuit of truth and enough reason to discern it. Moreover, since intellectual humility has both epistemic and social dimensions, appraising our emotions, regulating them, and having emotional intelligence will help in the social sphere where intellectual humility is practiced. Understanding our own Emotional Style will also help navigate our reactions to epistemic challenge and disagreement.

Understanding the role of emotion in cognition may be especially important for the doxastic view of intellectual humility. Since the central task is to properly *value* beliefs, status, and abilities, emotion will play a central role. Returning to the life of Phinneas Gage with which we started this chapter, he and patients like him who had a brain injury that damaged the connection between emotion and cognition had trouble making decisions because no end or good had any more value than another (Damasio, 1995). Emotions inform value, which reason then discerns. Our understanding of the capacity to value the good will be better informed by understanding the interplay of emotion and cognition.

PART THREE

APPLICATION

8

Can you believe
what you hear?

We rely on testimony. Whether it's a friend, a witness to a crime, or an expert in a given field, we depend on what other people tell us. But there are times when we clearly shouldn't believe what we hear (or at the very least take what we hear with a significant grain of salt). There are times when people lie or mislead. Sometimes, being trusting—perhaps when we're listening to politicians, car salesmen, etc.—is a mistake (perhaps indicative of the vice of gullibility). But, of course, there are also times when a shrewd and untrusting disposition does both ourselves, as hearers, and our interlocutors, as speakers, a serious disservice. As such, several pressing questions arise: When can we trust what we hear? When, if ever, does testimony give us knowledge? When are we obliged to listen to testimony with a discerning ear? And when, if ever, are we obliged to trust without qualification?

In this chapter, we will explore some of the philosophical questions surrounding testimony. But what is the relevance to intellectual humility? We will consider this question a good deal later in the chapter, but for now we will consider the following powerful case from Miranda Fricker's (2007) *Epistemic Injustice: Power and the Ethics of Knowing*:

It is the Fifties, and we are in Venice. Herbert Greenleaf, a rich American industrialist, is visiting, accompanied by a private detective whom he has hired to help solve the mystery of the whereabouts of his renegade son, Dickie. Dickie Greenleaf recently got engaged to his girlfriend, Marge Sherwood, but subsequently spent a great deal of time travelling with their "friend" Tom Ripley—until Dickie mysteriously disappeared. Marge is increasingly distrustful of Ripley because he seems to be obsessed with Dickie and suspiciously bound up with his strange disappearance. She also knows very well that it is unlike Dickie—unreliable philanderer though he undoubtedly was—simply to do a bunk, let alone to commit suicide, which is the hypothesis that Ripley is at pains to encourage. Ripley, however, has all along done a successful job of sucking up to Greenleaf senior, so Marge is entirely alone in her suspicion—her correct suspicion—that Dickie has been murdered, and that Ripley is his killer. . . . Greenleaf is only too aware of how little he himself knows of his son—pathetically enthusiastic as he is at the prospect that the private detective might help make good this ignorance—and yet he fails to see Marge as the source of knowledge about Dickie that she manifestly is. This attitude leads Greenleaf to ignore one of Marge's key reasons for her correct hypothesis that Dickie has died at the hands of Ripley: she finds Dickie's rings at Ripley's place, one of which had been a gift from her and which he had sworn never to remove. Greenleaf ignores it, partly because he underestimates Dickie's commitment to Marge, so that in his eyes any promise to Marge on Dickie's part is virtually worthless; but mostly because Ripley successfully constructs Marge as "hysterical." Indeed, not only Greenleaf but also Marge's friend, Peter Smith-Kingsley, comes to perceive her that way, so that the net result is a collusion of men against Marge's word being taken seriously. The theme of knowledge ever to the fore in the dialogue, we at one point hear her off-screen, shortly after she finds the rings, her powers of expression seemingly reduced to a self-contradictory mantra, repeating emphatically to the incredulous Greenleaf, "I don't know, I don't know, I just know it"; and it is at this point that Greenleaf replies with the familiar put-down, "Marge, there's female intuition, and then there are facts—" (Minghella, 2000, p. 130). A number of these sorts of exchange build up to the scene in which Marge, being taken back to America, is being ushered on to a boat but breaks away to lunge at Ripley, exclaiming, "I know it was you—I know it was you, Tom. I know it was you. I know you killed Dickie. I know it was you." MacCarron, the private detective, comes out of the waiting boat physically to restrain her, and the stage direction reads: "Ripley looks at him as if to say: What can you do, she's hysterical. MacCarron nods, pulls her onto the boat" (Minghella, 2000, pp. 86–88, 135).

Herbert Greenleaf wants to know what happened to his son, Dickie; after all, that's why he has come to Venice and hired a private detective. Marge knows what happened to Dickie, and she is more than happy to tell Greenleaf; however, he won't listen. Greenleaf doesn't value Marge's testimony, and subsequently fails to recognize valuable information. As Miranda Fricker unpacks this story, Greenleaf is guilty of committing epistemic injustice against Marge. According to Fricker (2007), Greenleaf has wronged Marge "in [her] capacity as a giver of knowledge" (p. 7).

This seems exactly right, but we wonder if there is another vice at work here, lurking in the conceptual neighborhood. Perhaps we could also easily think of Greenleaf as guilty of *intellectual arrogance*. In snubbing Marge's testimony, Greenleaf is unjustifiably assuming that his cognitive faculties are better positioned or equipped than Marge's. And he attributes far more positive epistemic status to his beliefs regarding his son than is actually merited. But, then again, maybe we could also easily think of Greenleaf as guilty of *intellectual diffidence*. Despite Dickie's treasured rings being found at Ripley's place, Greenleaf doesn't attribute nearly the positive epistemic status to the belief that Ripley could be the killer that he should. And, again and again,

Greenleaf simply does not track the positive epistemic status of the valuable information that Marge offers him.

In this chapter, we will first, in §1, consider the basic anatomy of testimonial exchanges, and then, in §2, unpack some ways that testimonial exchanges might fail, with special interest in ways failures of intellectual humility might cause such failures of testimony. And finally, in §3, we will turn to some recent work by John Greco—"Recent Work on Testimonial Knowledge" (2012) and "Testimonial Knowledge and the Flow of Information" (2015)—to explore how theoretical work in testimony might further highlight the importance of intellectual humility.

§1: The anatomy of testimony

There is a lot going on in our typical, everyday testimonial exchanges. Cultural contexts, relationships, personal histories, etc., can all color and inform the ordinary exchange of beliefs, facts, and ideas. For example, John might look like a very shady character—someone whom very few people, when first seeing him, would trust even for basic information like directions (let's say he has the misfortune of perpetually looking like he is stoned out of his mind). But John is Sara's brother, and she has known him all her life. She knows that John has always been incredibly trustworthy and reliable. As such, when John tells Sara that p, she believes him and, intuitively, it seems like she can now *know* that p. But her knowledge does not seem to primarily *rest* merely on John's testimony; instead, it is Sara's extensive and long-running relationship with John that is facilitating the acquisition of knowledge. After all, if John were to tell someone on the street—someone with no prior history with John—that p, then they probably wouldn't believe him. (After all, I imagine very few of us would believe the testimony of strangers who look stoned out of their minds!). And even if such a person *did* believe John's testimony that p, we would be hesitant to say that such a hearer now *knows* that *p*. Why? Because someone's looking like they are stoned out of their mind is typically an undermining defeater for almost anything they might tell us.

So if we're going to talk about testimony, we need to try to clear the air, so to speak. We need to try to isolate and focus on simple acts of testimony, acts of testimony that are (as much as possible) devoid of anything that might otherwise distract from the act of testimony *itself*. Jonathan Adler (2012) has helpfully provided several conditions to help identify "a class of core cases [of testimony] that isolate our dependence on the word of the speaker and whatever epistemic resources are available in ordinary conversational contexts" (sec. 1). Let's consider six of these now.

We have already hinted at one of Adler's conditions when we discussed the shady-looking character John and his sister Sara. As he explains, in an isolated testimonial exchange between a hearer and a speaker, "the hearer" should have "no special knowledge about the speaker. For the purposes of the present discussion, the ideal speaker should be a *stranger* to the hearer, since personal knowledge of a speaker will affect a hearer's justification for accepting the speaker's testimony" (Adler, 2012, sec. 1). As we've already noted, when John tells Sara that *p*, we might very well grant that she can now know that *p*. That said, however, it is not John's *testimony* that is facilitating the acquisition of knowledge; it is Sara's history with John as a reliable and trustworthy person (despite his appearance) that makes the knowledge acquisition possible. As such, if we're going to focus on the act of testimony itself, we should try to consider cases where a hearer has no prior relationship with the given speaker.

Another feature of typical, everyday testimonial exchanges that can distract us from simple acts of testimony is testimony that contains more than one assertion. Consider the following case:

GOOD CONVERSATION: Mary is visiting Chicago, and she is trying to find the Willis Tower (formerly known as the Sears Tower). While walking down the street, she sees Martha, a normal-looking stranger, and asks for directions. Martha gives Mary what sound like plausible directions. But what is more, Martha goes on to tell Mary the history of the tower (some of which Mary is already familiar with) and gives Mary advice regarding additional places to visit in the City (some of which Mary already has on her itinerary). Bolstered by Martha's seeming knowledgeability, Mary continues on her journey to the Willis Tower.

Like what we see in GOOD CONVERSATION, exchanges often take place in the context of broader conversations. From her conversation with Martha, it looks like Mary now knows how to get to the Willis Tower. But because of her extended conversation with Martha, her knowledge of where to find the Willis Tower rests not only on Martha's testimony but also on the extended conversation that demonstrated Martha's familiarity with the city. If we want to focus solely on the philosophical import of Martha's testimony, then we need to limit the testimonial exchange to no more than one assertion. To quote Adler (2012) again, "This eliminates any justification an assertion might receive by being part of a group of cohering, mutually-supportive assertions" (sec. 1).[1]

Testimonial exchanges often take place within groups of people, and how the group reacts to a given assertion can deeply affect how the assertion is received (be it positively or negatively). Consider another case:

GROUP TALK: Bill is visiting Chicago, and he is trying to find the Willis Tower. Bill needs directions, so he decides to stop by a busy coffee shop to ask for directions. He asks Frank, the first barista he sees, how to get to the Tower. Frank tells Bill what sound like plausible directions. Overhearing what Frank is saying, the other baristas and several of the customers nod in agreement, and Bill sees this.

In this example, Bill presumably now knows how to get to the Willis Tower. However, this knowledge rests not only on Frank's testimony, but also on the unspoken agreement of the other baristas and customers. So again, if we're interested in isolating testimony as a possible source of knowledge, we should try to eliminate any "justification the testimony might receive by corroboration from other speakers" (Adler, 2012, sec. 1).

Testimony can often be validated by other, sometimes non-testimonial, sources. However, whenever someone believes that *p* on the basis of testimony, then, if we're focused on testimony itself, such a person should sustain that belief on the basis of that testimony. Consider another case:

TACO: Tracy is visiting Chicago, and she is trying to find the Willis Tower. While walking down the street, she sees Tim, a normal-looking stranger, and asks for directions. Tim gives Tracy what sound like plausible directions, and Tracy goes on her way. Shortly thereafter, Tracy smells the unmistakable smell of her favorite Chicago taco truck, which she knows is almost always parked by the Willis Tower at that time of day. Following the smell of delicious tacos, Tracy quickly finds her way to the Tower.

While Tracy presumably knew how to get to the Tower *originally* from Tim's testimony, the powerful smell of tacos and the knowledge of their whereabouts (i.e., near the Willis Tower) quickly usurped Tracy's need for Tim's testimony, allowing her to follow her nose instead of Tim's directions. So, for our purposes, we are primarily interested in cases of testimony where the "testimony sustains the corresponding belief in the hearer" (Adler, 2012, sec. 1).

Sometimes, as Adler (2012) points out, "institutional or professional demands for accuracy" (sec. 1) can affect how (and to what extent) we rely on the testimony of others. Consider another case:

INTERVIEW: Matthew has applied for a job as a widget salesman. Karen is interviewing Matthew for the job, and asks him about his previous experience selling widgets. Matthew tells her that he was the top widget salesman in a large competing company for 5 years running.

If Matthew were to tell Karen about his widget-selling accomplishments at an informal meet and greet, then perhaps Karen could simply believe what she is told and move on. In a highly institutionally and professionally demanding context like a job interview, however, just being told about an accomplishment by an interviewee might not be enough. There might be a professional and institutional expectation that Karen will do some fact checking on all of the people interviewing for the job, fact checking that could confirm Matthew's claim. But since most testimonial contexts are not nearly so demanding, we'll just limit ourselves to cases where such demands are absent.

And finally, it's worth stressing that, in the core cases of testimonial exchange that we are most interested in, we are assuming that a "norm of truthfulness holds" (Adler, 2012, sec. 1). There are times and places where norms of truth-telling are not operational, and those are places where testimony takes on a very different character. There are places in the world, for example, where a premium is placed on not disappointing people—places where if someone is asked a question, they would make up an answer rather than disappoint with an "I don't know." Imagine S was in such a place, and S was trying to find her hotel. If she were to ask a random stranger on the street for directions, they'd give her an answer, but it'd be anyone's guess as to whether the directions were good (since directions would be given even if they had no earthly clue where the hotel was). Such a context seems very a-typical. And testimony in such a-typical contexts is not our current aim.

So, in sum, our core cases of testimonial exchange will involve two strangers—a person giving the testimony (let's call this person SPEAKER) and a person receiving the testimony (let's call this person HEARER). SPEAKER's testimony involves a single assertion, and SPEAKER's testimony is solely responsible for sustaining HEARER's belief. And finally, the context of the testimony is one where there is a shared norm of truth-telling and where there are no unusual professional or institutional demands for accuracy.

In other words, for any two given strangers, HEARER and SPEAKER, in a context where there is a shared norm of truth-telling and where there are no unusual professional or institutional demands for accuracy, something like the following diagram is emerging:

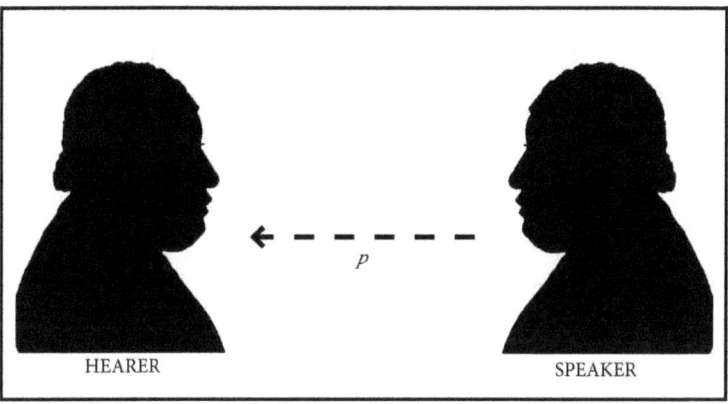

FIGURE 8.1 *A Core Case of Testimony.*

In Figure 8.1, we have one speaker making a single assertion, *p*, to a single hearer. This all leaves us with a relatively simple mold, which all of our core cases of testimonial exchange must fit within.

§2: Intellectual humility and how testimony can go wrong

Now that we have a model for basic cases of testimony, we can begin to see specific areas where testimony can go wrong. Assuming that the goal of testimony is for a given HEARER to acquire knowledge through the utterance of a given SPEAKER, testimonial exchanges go *wrong* whenever the HEARER does *not* acquire knowledge from the SPEAKER's utterance—and looking at Figure 8.1, we can highlight four general areas where testimony can go wrong: (i) the HEARER, (ii) the SPEAKER, (iii) the utterance *p*, and (iv) the general environment. Let's now consider an example of each.

Obviously enough, if there are significant problems with a given HEARER—if, for example, HEARER is severely inebriated—then the HEARER won't be able to acquire knowledge from SPEAKER's utterance that *p*. Consider the following case:

> BAD HEARER: HEARER is visiting Chicago. While walking down the street, he sees SPEAKER, an ostensibly normal-looking stranger, and asks for directions to the Willis Tower. SPEAKER gives HEARER what sound like plausible directions. However, given that HEARER is deeply confused about the major skyscrapers in Chicago—for example, regularly confusing the Willis tower with the Trump tower—it is not clear that HEARER knows how to get to the Willis Tower, since it is unclear whether or not HEARER actually knows what building "Willis Tower" refers to.

Given HEARER's deep confusion about Chicago skyscrapers, when he asks for directions to the Willis Tower, we might wonder whether or not he is really looking for the Willis Tower. And even if SPEAKER gives HEARER flawless, clear, and precise directions, it's not clear that he can acquire knowledge from these directions because he is so very confused about what buildings are what in downtown Chicago.

Additionally, if there are significant problems with a given SPEAKER—if, for example, a given speaker is severely intoxicated or otherwise rendered sufficiently unreliable—then anyone who hears SPEAKER's testimony will be unable to acquire knowledge from it. Consider another case:

> BAD SPEAKER: HEARER is visiting Chicago, and wants to visit the Willis Tower. While walking down the street, he sees SPEAKER, an ostensibly normal-looking stranger, and asks for directions. SPEAKER gives HEARER what sound like plausible directions; however, SPEAKER is deeply confused about the names of Chicago skyscrapers—regularly, for example, confusing the Willis Tower for the Trump Tower. As such, it is not at all clear that

HEARER can know how to get to the Willis Tower from SPEAKER's testimony, because there is a real chance that SPEAKER is confusing the Willis Tower with the Trump Tower.

Given SPEAKER's deep confusion about Chicago skyscrapers in BAD SPEAKER, any testimony about those skyscrapers—including testimony regarding how to get to them—seems undermined. SPEAKER, in this case, is not a reliable source of testimonial knowledge about Chicago skyscrapers.

Naturally enough, another way that a given testimonial exchange can go wrong is if the testimony, the assertion itself, is bad. Consider another case:

BAD ASSERTION: HEARER is visiting Chicago, and wants to visit the Willis Tower. While walking down the street, he sees SPEAKER, an ostensibly normal-looking stranger, and asks for directions. SPEAKER gives HEARER what sound like plausible directions. On this occasion, however, SPEAKER—who is normally a very reliable and helpful giver of directions—decides to sow some chaos in the world and gives HEARER directions to the town dump instead of directions to the Willis Tower.

Given that SPEAKER lies to HEARER regarding the location of the Willis Tower, HEARER simply cannot acquire knowledge as to how to find the Willis Tower from SPEAKER's testimony. Lying regarding p, obviously enough, undermines the transferal of knowledge regarding p.

How can an environment inhibit the acquisition of knowledge in a standard case of testimonial exchange? Consider the following case:

BAD ENVIRONMENT: HEARER is visiting Chicago, and wants to visit the Willis Tower. While walking down the street, he sees SPEAKER, an ostensibly normal-looking stranger, and asks for directions. Unbeknownst to HEARER, however, nine out of ten Chicagoans are deeply put off by the Sears Tower's name being changed to the Willis Tower. So much so, in fact, that if asked for directions to the "Willis Tower," nine out of ten Chicagoans would actually give directions to the town dump in protest. SPEAKER, as it happens, is not one of those Chicagoans who is put off by the name change; so when SPEAKER is asked for directions to the Willis Tower, he reliably gives directions to the Willis Tower.

There's nothing wrong with HEARER or SPEAKER in BAD ENVIRONMENT— and SPEAKER gives good testimony, he gives HEARER good directions to the Willis Tower. Why should we be hesitant to grant HEARER knowledge in this case? Because, like the protagonist's belief in FAKE BARN cases, his correct belief (regarding the location of the Willis Tower) is extremely lucky. He could have very easily asked any of the other Chicagoans on the street, the majority of whom would have given him directions to the town dump instead of the Tower.

It might be worth noting that many (if not most) instances of testimony have another feature that is not accounted for in Figure 8.1: namely, the *question* that prompted a given assertion. See the following figure:

In Figure 8.2, we see HEARER asking a question, which prompts SPEAKER's assertion. While, strictly speaking, testimony does not require the asking of a question—someone could simply spout an assertion unprompted—testimony is, nevertheless, often prompted by a question.

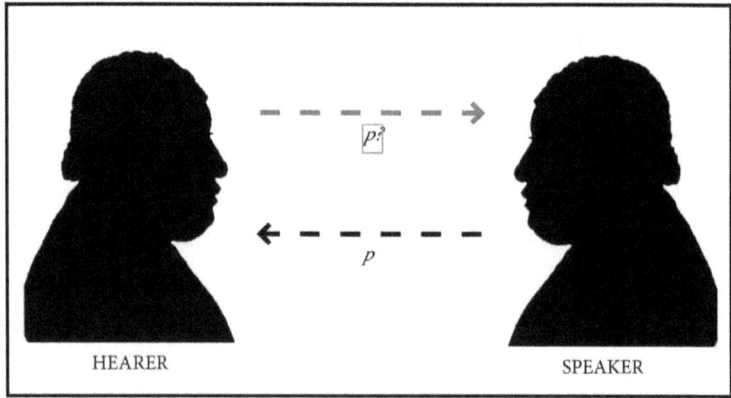

FIGURE 8.2 *Testimony Prompted by a Question.*

This is worth noting because questions are such a common feature in testimonial exchanges. And as such, they are also a common feature that can go wrong in such a way that precludes the acquisition of knowledge. Consider the following case:

BAD QUESTION: HEARER is visiting Chicago, and wants to visit the Willis Tower. While walking down the street, he sees SPEAKER, an ostensibly normal-looking stranger, and asks for directions. While asking, however, HEARER misspeaks, and accidentally asks for directions to the Trump Tower instead. SPEAKER gives HEARER ostensibly good directions to the Trump Tower; however, since HEARER wasn't really interested in going to the Trump Tower, he didn't really listen. And being too embarrassed to admit his error, HEARER simply nods politely to SPEAKER's directions and moves on.

In BAD QUESTION, HEARER does not gain knowledge as to how to get to the Willis Tower, because HEARER asked the wrong sort of question. To be sure, HEARER in BAD QUESTION is not confused regarding the difference between Willis Tower and Trump Tower (as HEARER was in BAD HEARER), but simply asked a confused question.

We want to now propose a weak thesis, a thesis that should be relatively easy to defend: that failures in intellectual humility can produce failures in testimonial exchange. Of course, intellectual humility doesn't guarantee that testimony will work as it should. For example, someone can be perfectly intellectually humble and still be lied to (as in BAD ASSERTION). Or someone can be perfectly intellectually humble and still find themselves in environments hostile to knowledge acquisition via testimony (as in BAD ENVIRONMENT). But what is more, intellectual vices—namely, intellectual arrogance or intellectual diffidence—are not any guarantee that testimony will *fail*. Someone can be a complete arrogant jerk and still acquire knowledge via testimony. Someone can be intellectually servile and self-deprecating and still acquire knowledge via testimony. But in any case, someone who fails to be intellectually humble is more susceptible to failures in testimonial exchange than, everything else being the same, someone who *doesn't*, someone who *is* intellectually humble.

Recall Miranda Fricker's (2007) example in *Epistemic Injustice*, which draws from Anthony Minghella's (2000) screenplay *The Talented Mr Ripley— Based on Patricia Highsmith's Novel*. In that example, we saw Herbert Greenleaf commit acts of epistemic injustice by systematically and unjustly undervaluing Marge's testimony regarding the fate of Dickie (Greenleaf's son and Marge's fiancé) simply because she is a woman. And all the while, Greenleaf systematically and unjustly overvalued the testimony of Ricky, who turns out to be Dickie's killer, all because Ricky is a man. As Fricker (2007) explains:

> This example . . . presents us with a case of a hearer's testimonial sensibility delivering a prejudiced perception of the speaker. Thus we are presented with a fault in judgment occurring at the spontaneous, unreflective level. The spontaneous operation of Greenleaf's testimonial sensibility is flawed, for it is trained in part by the gender prejudices of the day. Sometimes there can be a fault at the reflective level too, however, depending on how far the context places the onus on the hearer to shift intellectual gear and engage in active, self-critical reflection concerning the deliverances of his testimonial sensibility . . . our [example] illustrate[s] a hearer . . . failing to correct for identity prejudice in [his] testimonial sensibility. . . . [The hearer] fail[s] to exercise any critical awareness regarding the prejudice that is distorting [his] perception of the speaker, so that the distorted spontaneous deliverance of [his] testimonial sensibility is left unchecked. (p. 89)

What we would like to suggest now is that Greenleaf's "gender prejudices," which led to the epistemic injustice committed against Marge, can be seen as tied to a lack of intellectual humility.

The first place we noted where testimonial exchanges could fail is with the HEARER—with the person receiving the testimony. And we think we can easily see the failure of testimony in Fricker's example as a failure in Greenleaf, who, in this instance, is playing the role of the HEARER. It is Greenleaf, the HEARER, who fails to listen to the excellent testimony of Marge. And it is Greenleaf, the HEARER, who listens unreflectively to the lies and deceptions of Ricky. Like HEARER in the case of BAD HEARER, Greenleaf is unable to competently process the information he's given. But if we draw from the doxastic account of intellectual humility—where intellectual humility is the virtue of accurately tracking what one could non-culpably take to be the positive epistemic status of one's own beliefs—we can easily think of the failure in Greenleaf as a failure *in intellectual humility*. After all, Greenleaf is simply not accurately tracking what he could non-culpably take to be the positive epistemic status of his belief regarding his son—the belief which is of central importance to the case. Greenleaf is intellectually arrogant in holding his belief regarding the lack of value of Marge's testimony and the value of Ricky's testimony as strongly as he does. And, ultimately, Greenleaf is intellectually arrogant in holding his belief regarding his son's fate as strongly as he does, because he has systematically (and out of prejudice) failed to track defeaters of his belief (presented by Marge).

Of course, the testimony in the case of Greenleaf's search for his son fails for *lots* of reasons. Like the BAD ASSERTION case, Ricky's lie helps preclude viable testimonial exchange. And perhaps we could make the case that there was something wrong with the environment Greenleaf found himself in (like the BAD ENVIRONMENT case), an environment with a critical mass of liars and co-conspirators in spreading gender prejudice. But it is worth stressing that had Greenleaf been more intellectually humble—had he done a better job at accurately tracking the positive epistemic status of his beliefs (specifically his belief regarding the fate of his son and his belief regarding the value of Marge's testimony), these other threats to testimonial exchange might have been mitigated or otherwise assuaged. If Greenleaf had been a better, more intellectually humble HEARER, then maybe he could have recognized Ricky's bad assertion (or later recognized he had defeaters for Ricky's assertion that he needed to address). And maybe if Greenleaf had been a better, more intellectually humble HEARER, he could have recognized the poor quality of his environment and taken extra precautions. Greenleaf's failure, I propose, to accurately track the epistemic value of women's testimony (including the testimony of Marge) fed his prejudice and led to epistemic injustice.

And to be sure, this result doesn't rest on the doxastic account of intellectual humility; other accounts of intellectual humility could come to a similar verdict. Take Roberts and Wood's (2007) account of intellectual humility again, where intellectual humility is "a striking or unusual unconcern for social importance, and thus a kind of emotional insensitivity to the issues of status" when it comes to acquiring epistemic goods (p. 239). Greenleaf, I think we can agree, is simply not sufficiently insensitive to issues of status when it comes to pursuing epistemic resources regarding his son's fate. In particular, Greenleaf seems *hypersensitive* to his and Ripley's status as men over and against Marge's status as a woman. So again, it looks like we could say that Greenleaf's failure at intellectual humility fed his prejudice and ultimately led to epistemic injustice.[2]

To drive home the connection between intellectual humility and testimony—along with failures of intellectual humility and failures in testimony—let's consider another example. We look again at an example from Miranda Fricker (2007), this time drawing from Harper Lee's (1960) *To Kill a Mockingbird*:

> The year is 1935, and the scene a courtroom in Maycomb County, Alabama. The defendant is a young black man named Tom Robinson. He is charged

with raping a white girl, Mayella Ewell, whose family's rundown house he passes every day on his way to work, situated as it is on the outskirts of town in the borderlands that divide where whites and blacks live. It is obvious to the reader, and to any relatively unprejudiced person in the courtroom, that Tom Robinson is entirely innocent. For Atticus Finch, our politely spoken counsel for the defense, has proved beyond doubt that Robinson could not have beaten the Ewell girl so as to cause the sort of cuts and bruises she sustained that day, since whoever gave her the beating led with his left fist, whereas Tom Robinson's left arm is disabled, having been injured in a machinery accident when he was a boy. . . . As it turns out, the members of the jury stick with their prejudiced perception of the defendant, formed principally by the racial stereotypes of the day. Atticus Finch challenges them to dispense with these prejudicial stereotypes; to dispense, as he puts it, with the "assumption—the evil assumption—that all Negroes lie, that all Negroes are basically immoral beings, that all Negro men are not to be trusted around our women" (Lee, 1960, p. 208). But when it comes to the verdict, the jurors go along with the automatic distrust delivered by the prejudices that structure their perception of the speaker. They find him guilty. And it is important that we are to interpret the novel so that the jurors really do find him guilty. That is to say, they do not privately find him innocent yet cynically convict him anyway. (pp. 23, 25)

What caused this failure of testimony? Why did the jury fail to acquire knowledge regarding Tom's innocence? As we saw with Greenleaf, we see that the jury's failure to acquire knowledge regarding Tom's innocence—the failure of Tom's and others' testimony to produce knowledge—is because they fail in their role as HEARERs. It is the jurors, as HEARERs, who fail to listen to the testimony of Tom and Atticus (especially when he challenges their prejudices). And it is the jurors, the HEARERs, who listen unreflectively to the lies and deceptions of their own prejudices and those of the prosecuting attorney. Like HEARER in the case of BAD HEARER, the jurors are unable to competently process the information they are given.

And here again, we think we can see the jury's failure as HEARERs and the subsequent unjust conviction of Tom *as driven by and tied to their failures in intellectual humility*. Again, if we draw from the doxastic account of intellectual humility—where intellectual humility is the virtue of accurately tracking what one could non-culpably take to be the positive epistemic status of one's own beliefs—we can easily think of the failure in the jurors as HEARERs as a failure *in intellectual humility*. If the jurors had been accurately tracking the positive epistemic status of their belief regarding Tom's guilt, then they would have taken into account Tom's disabled arm and his testimony. But their prejudices and assumptions kept them from accurately tracking the positive epistemic status of their belief regarding Tom's guilt, which only reinforced their prejudices and racism.

And again, some other accounts of intellectual humility seem to give us the same diagnosis of the case. Recall Roberts and Wood's (2007) seminal account of intellectual humility again, where intellectual humility is "a striking or unusual unconcern for social importance, and thus a kind of emotional insensitivity to the issues of status" when it comes to acquiring epistemic goods (p. 239). The jurors are simply not sufficiently insensitive to issues of status when it comes to pursuing epistemic resources regarding Tom's innocence. In particular, the jurors seem *hypersensitive* to their status as white over and against Tom's status as a black man. So again, it looks like we could say that the jury's failure at intellectual humility fed their prejudice and ultimately led to epistemic injustice.[3]

And as we saw in the case of *The Talented Mr Ripley*, there are a number of factors that are contributing to the failure of testimony, the failure of the jury to acquire knowledge regarding Tom's innocence. Perhaps we could say that there was a failure in the SPEAKER, in this case Tom. Tom cannot be too up front with his testimony, because he walks a proverbial minefield of bias and prejudice. As Fricker (2007) explains:

> In a showdown between the word of a black man and that of a poor white girl, the courtroom air is thick with the 'do's and 'don't's of racial politics. Telling the truth here is a minefield for Tom Robinson, since if he casts aspersions on the white girl, he will be perceived as a presumptuous, lying Negro; yet, if he does not publicize Mayella Ewell's attempt to kiss him (which is what really happened), then a guilty verdict is even more nearly assured. This discursive predicament mirrors his practical predicament at the Ewell's house on that fateful day when Mayella grabbed him. If he pushes her away, then he will be found to have assaulted her; yet if he is passive, he will equally be found to have assaulted her. So he does the most neutral thing he can, which is to run, though knowing all the while that this action too will be taken as a sign of guilt. [The prosecuting attorney's] interrogation of Tom is suffused with the idea that his running away implies culpability. . . . Running away, it seems, is something a black man in Maycomb County cannot do without incriminating himself. Similarly, there are many things he cannot say in court and stand a chance of being heard as truthful. (pp. 23–24)

Through no fault of his own, Tom cannot be as entirely candid and forthright as the SPEAKER in this case. As a SPEAKER, he simply *can't* tell the truth without it being misinterpreted by the HEARERs, the jury, as powerful reason to form false beliefs. And while we might also point to the ENVIRONMENT as a part of the problem that is forcing TOM into such a predicament—after all, Alabama in the early twentieth century is hardly an ideal environment for racially charged testimony of African Americans—we think the driving force behind the failure of testimonial exchange lies in the HEARERs, the jury. It is their inability to accurately track the positive epistemic status of Tom's testimony—their failure in intellectual humility—that is driving Tom's guarded testimony as a SPEAKER and the problems in the environment. Here again, we think we can see the jury's failure as HEARERs, the failure of testimonial exchange, and the subsequent unjust conviction of Tom *as driven by and tied to their failures in intellectual humility.*

We've outlined what core cases of testimony look like—one HEARER with one SPEAKER, with no previous history, one assertion, etc.—and we've sketched various ways in which these core cases of testimony might fail to produce knowledge. And now, we think it is sufficiently clear that *failures in intellectual humility can lead to failures in testimonial exchange, to the failure of testimony to lead to knowledge.* Again, that's not to say that failures in intellectual humility *always* lead to failures in testimony (sometimes arrogant jerks are perfectly apt at giving and receiving assertions). And that's not to say that failures in testimony are *always* caused by failures in intellectual humility (sometimes testimony just goes wrong, and no one is at fault). The weak thesis that we hope we can now agree on, however, is that failures in intellectual humility *can* lead to failures in testimony.

But our strategy has, thus far, been somewhat piecemeal. We've seen how intellectual *arrogance* can lead to a failure in testimony when a HEARER is too suspicious of a SPEAKER's testimony—as when Greenleaf doesn't take Marge's testimony seriously—essentially making the acceptance of testimony too *difficult.* And we've seen how intellectual *diffidence* can lead to a failure in testimony when a HEARER is all too accepting of a SPEAKER's testimony—as when Greenleaf all too readily accepts the testimony of Ripley, even when he should have been a prime suspect—essentially making the acceptance of testimony too *easy.* The big question we're considering in this chapter is: "Can we believe what we hear?" And while I think a broad and general picture is emerging—we should trust people like Marge and Tom, and we should not trust people like Ripley—it would be helpful if we could sketch a systematic approach that might fill in some of the details here. In the next section, we are going to do just that. And, once again, we will see how our understanding of intellectual humility can fit within a systematic approach to testimony.

§3: Is testimonial knowledge epistemically distinct?

Almost everyone agrees that, in standard cases, receiving testimony that *p* gives someone justification for believing that *p*. And many of us would want to say that such justification is, in at least the standard cases, good enough to allow someone to *know* that *p*. But where does this justification come from? Is testimony a unique source of epistemic goods? Or is testimony simply a species of a more general source of epistemic goods, say, induction? (After all, maybe you can know that *p* from the testimony that p simply because, more often than not, in standard cases of testimony, when people testify that *p*, you've found *p* to be true.) What, if anything, is special about testimony? Or, as John Greco (2015) aptly put it, "Can testimonial knowledge be 'reduced' to knowledge of another kind, for example inductive knowledge, or is testimonial knowledge its own kind of animal, irreducible to any other kind?" (p. 275). These are some of the guiding questions that have most shaped the epistemology of testimony, and, as we'll see, formulating a systematic response to them can give us new ways to understand intellectual humility's relationship to testimony.

In this section, we will first explore some of the problems surrounding possible answers to the above question, and highlight what looks like a serious dilemma: Roughly, if we take testimony to offer a special source of justification or knowledge—a source that is irreducible to any other, such as induction—then there is a worry that testimonial justification is *too easy* to come by. Alternatively, if we take testimonial justification to simply be a species of induction, say, then it looks like testimonial justification and testimonial knowledge might be *too difficult* to come by. Drawing from John

Greco's seminal work in "Recent Work on Testimonial Knowledge" (2012) and "Testimonial Knowledge and the Flow of Information" (2015), the second part of this section will explore a plausible, systematic approach to overcome this dilemma—an approach that can help us further highlight intellectual humility's relationship to testimony.

As you might expect, when theorists consider a question like "Is testimony a unique source of epistemic goods?" they largely fall into two unsurprising categories: those who say "yes" and those who say "no." Those who say "yes"—that the knowledge acquired via testimony is irreducible to any other source—are usually called "anti-reductionists." And those who say "no"— that knowledge acquired via testimony can be reduced to other sources (like induction)—are usually called reductionists. And as John Greco (2012) points out, "[It] is now customary to see David Hume as the archetypal reductionist about testimony" (p. 16). To quote from Coady's (1992) pioneering work "Testimony: A Philosophical Study":

> Here it is accepted that we may know in cases where we rely upon testimony but our dependence upon testimony is itself justified in terms of other supposedly more fundamental forms of evidence, namely, the individual's own observations and his inferences from them. (p. 22)
>
> Essentially, [Hume's] theory constitutes a reduction of testimony as a form of evidence or support to the status of a species . . . of inductive inference. (p. 79)

And standing in contrast to Hume, Greco (2012) notes that "Thomas Reid is commonly cited as the archetypal antireductionist or fundamentalist about testimony" (p. 16). Again, quoting Coady (1992):

> The fundamentalists refuse to accept that our reliance on testimony can be "justified" in terms of some other supposedly more fundamental sources of knowledge. . . . our reliance on testimony should be regarded as fundamental

to the justification of belief in the same sort of way as perception, memory, and inference are. Thomas Reid is the only philosopher, as far as I know, who has explicitly adopted a position like this. (p. 23)

Following this stage setting by Coady, Greco, and many others, a significant portion of the literature on the epistemology of testimony has seen scholars filing in behind either Hume or Reid.[4] Either testimony is seen as special—offering a *sui generis* source of epistemic goods—or it is seen as reducible to other epistemic sources.

But we should be careful here. As Greco (2012) helpfully points out, there are three related, though distinct, questions that seem to often get woven together in the literature: First, there is the question we are centrally interested in here: "Is testimonial knowledge epistemically distinct or *sui generis*?" Let's call this the *distinctive* question. The distinctive question is often conflated or combined with two others: "Is testimonial knowledge reason-dependent?" and "Does testimonial knowledge involve default justification?" (p. 17). Call these the *reason-dependent* question and the *default justification* question respectively. To see how these questions have been blended together, consider the following passage from Elizabeth Fricker's (1994) excellent work, "Against Gullibility":

> The epistemological "problem of justifying belief through testimony" is the problem of showing how it can be the case that a hearer on a particular occasion has the epistemic right to believe what she is told—to believe a particular speaker's assertion. . . . The solution can take either of two routes. It may be shown that the required step—from "S asserted that P" to "P"—can be made as a piece of inference involving only familiar deductive and inductive principles, applied to empirically established premises. Alternatively, it may be argued that the step is legitimized as the exercise of a special presumptive epistemic right to trust, not dependent on evidence. (p. 128; also referenced in Greco, 2012, p. 18)

Here we see Fricker assuming that reductionism (the first route) entails the non-distinctiveness of testimony *and* the reason dependence of testimonial justification. And she assumes that anti-reductionism (the second route) entails a distinctiveness thesis regarding testimony *and* the thesis that testimonial knowledge need not be reason dependent. And consider how Fricker (1994) later understands the "presumptive right" thesis, which "she takes to be a defining characteristic of anti-reductionism" (Greco, 2012, p. 18):

> It is a normative epistemic principle, amounting to the thesis that a hearer has the epistemic right to believe what she observes an arbitrary speaker to assert, just on the ground that it has been asserted; she need not attempt any assessment of the likelihood that this speaker's assertions about their subject matter will be true, nor modify her disposition to believe according to such an assessment. (p. 127; also referenced in Greco, 2012, p. 18)
>
> [The key element of a presumptive right thesis is] the dispensation from the requirement to monitor or assess the speaker for trustworthiness, before believing in it. Thus, it may be called a [presumptive right] to believe blindly, or uncritically, since the hearer's critical faculties are not required to be engaged. (p. 144; also referenced in Greco, 2012, p. 18)

Here again Fricker seems to think that anti-reductionism rejects reason-dependence and she seems to think that this goes hand in hand with testimony enjoying default justification. As John Greco (2012) explains, Fricker seems to be thinking that "the anti-reductionist rejects reason-dependence, and so does not require that the hearer base her testimonial beliefs on reasons. . . . [If this is the case, however, then] there is nothing left to require of [the hearer]—she is free to believe blindly or uncritically" (pp. 18–19).[5] Here Fricker seems to be running together the *reason-dependence* question with the *default justification* question.

But, of course, Elizabeth Fricker isn't the only one to blur the distinctions between these questions. In "It Takes Two to Tango: Beyond Reductionism and Non-Reductionism in the Epistemology of Testimony," Jennifer Lackey (2006a) seems to blur these questions as well. Consider the following passage:

> There are two central components to reductionism. The first is what we may call the Positive-Reasons Component: justification is conferred on testimonial beliefs by the presence of appropriate positive reasons on the part of hearers. . . . This gives rise to the second component—what we may call the Reduction Component. Because the justification of testimonial beliefs is provided by these non-testimonially grounded positive reasons, testimonial justification is said to reduce to the justification of sense perception, memory and inductive inference. (pp. 160–61)

Here Lackey seems to assume that reductionism includes a commitment to the thesis that testimony must be reason-dependent *and* the thesis that testimony provides distinctive, *sui generis* knowledge. For reductionists and anti-reductionists regarding testimonial knowledge, the *reason-dependent* question is, at least according to Lackey, tied to the *distinctive* question.[6]

While we might easily think that these things go together—for example, if you think that testimonial knowledge is sui generis, then you probably think that testimonial knowledge isn't reason-dependent and enjoys default justification—they *can* come apart. As Greco (2012) so aptly explains:

> Consider first that testimonial knowledge might be both distinctive and reason-dependent. This will be the case if testimonial knowledge requires nontestimonial reasons for its evidence, but also requires something else that is distinctive to testimonial knowledge. Likewise, testimonial knowledge might be reason-independent but not involve default justification. This will be the case if testimonial belief does not depend on reasons for its evidence, but does depend on certain other kinds of cognitive functioning on behalf of the hearer. For example, it is possible that testimonial knowledge depends on some noninferential (nonreasoning) capacity for discriminating reliable

from unreliable testifiers. Such a faculty might be perceptual, for example, operating on facial expressions, body language, and/or speech patterns that serve as perceptual cues for competence and sincerity. More generally, a number of psychologists and philosophers have suggested that we employ powers of discrimination for evaluating testimony and testimonial sources, and that these cannot be assimilated to some reasoning process, or to some faculty for inferring conclusions from evidence. Accordingly, we should draw a clear distinction between the reason-independence thesis and the default justification thesis: testimonial knowledge may be reason-independent, in the sense of not requiring inference or reasoning from evidence, and yet not involve default justification, because it requires the exercise of noninferential critical capacities. (pp. 17–18)

Finally, the considerations above also show that testimonial knowledge might be distinctive and yet not involve default justification. For suppose either (a) that testimonial justification requires nontestimonial reasons, but also something else distinctive, or (b) that testimonial justification is reason independent, but requires distinctive noninferential capacities for discriminating reliable from unreliable testimony. Either way, testimonial knowledge will be distinctive, but will not involve default justification. (p. 18)

These are, then, *distinctive* questions; someone can think, for example, that testimonial knowledge is *sui generis* without thinking that testimony enjoys default justification, say. These are distinctive questions. So we need to try to keep them apart.

The question at the heart of the reductionist versus anti-reductionist debate—the question that we are centrally interested in in this section—is the distinct question: "Is testimonial knowledge epistemically distinct or *sui generis*?" Reductionists, again, answer in the negative—claiming that knowledge acquired via testimony can be *reduced* to other epistemic sources (like induction). Anti-reductionists, again, answer in the affirmative—claiming that knowledge acquired via testimony is irreducible (at least in some cases) to any other epistemic source. But as you might expect, both sides of this debate—both the reductionists and the anti-reductionists—face some serious and related worries. And given that reductionism and anti-reductionism account for all of the logical space—that is, either you're a reductionist or an anti-reductionist, there is no third option—then these worries can easily lead to what looks like a dilemma. Consider John Greco's (2012) excellent description of the worry facing reductionism:

> The major criticism raised against reductionism is that it entails overly skeptical results. Specifically, it is charged that the sort of inductive evidence that reductionism requires is typically unavailable to the hearer. If testimonial knowledge requires such evidence, then this sort of knowledge will be rare. But this is an unacceptable result, the objection continues. Our reliance on testimony is ubiquitous, and so if we lack knowledge here, then the skeptical results cannot be contained. A nearly universal skepticism results. Reductionists respond by trying to show how such evidence is in fact available, despite initial appearances. (pp. 16–17)

Testimonial knowledge, given reductionism, seems far too difficult to come by. The worry is that radical, intractable skepticism seems to be looming on the horizon if we accept reductionism.[7] But lest we jump too quickly toward anti-reductionism, we should be sure to note that worries lie that way as well. Again, Greco (2012) gives us an apt summary:

> The major criticism raised against antireductionism is that it makes testimonial knowledge too easy. If testimonial belief does not require nontestimonial evidence—if it is permissible to believe that p merely on the basis that someone says that p—then this looks like gullibility. More generally, knowledge seems to require some sort of critical appraisal on the

part of the knower, but in the absence of appropriate evidence, this seems to be lacking. Antireductionists often respond along two lines. First, they emphasize the danger of skeptical results if one insists on the reductionist picture. Second, they associate reductionist demands for evidence with an overly individualistic (and insufficiently social) approach in epistemology. The idea is that reductionism is wedded to an inappropriate ideal of the individual, autonomous knower. An adequate theory of knowledge, it is argued, must recognize the social dimensions of knowledge, including the relations of epistemic dependence that are manifested in testimonial knowledge. (p. 17)

So, with reductionism, knowledge seems to be far too difficult to come by, leading to radical skepticism. But with anti-reductionism, knowledge seems to be far too easy to come by, championing gullibility and ascribing "knowledge" to beliefs that are intuitively not knowledge. So, it seems, we are facing a grim dilemma, where neither option is terribly appealing.[8]

Let's try to unpack this dilemma with some cases. On the one hand, reductionism seems to lead to skeptical conclusions. In far too many cases where we would intuitively want to grant a hearer with testimonial knowledge, it seems implausible that the hearer could possibly have the sort of inductive evidence reductionists require. As Greco (2015) elsewhere explains:

A special case involves small children learning from their caretakers. Is it really plausible that small children are good inductive reasoners, in a way that would be required to account for their testimonial knowledge in such terms? There are good reasons for saying no. First, one might think that children lack the requisite reasoning capacities for making complicated inductive inferences. Second, and even if such capacities are granted, it is implausible to think that children have the requisite inductive evidence, that they have made the number and range of observations needed to make a quality inference, assuming they have the capacities to do so. (p. 276)[9]

We intuitively think children can know all sorts of things based on testimony. When young children ask us whether or not, say, there is milk in our refrigerator, it seems like they can gain knowledge from what we tell them. Intuitively, they can have testimonial knowledge even though they do not seem to have the inductive faculties or resources available to them to meet the reductionist's demands. Reductionism, again it seems, puts the bar for testimonial knowledge too high—making testimonial knowledge too difficult to come by.

But on the other hand, there seem to be cases that suggest that anti-reductionism puts the bar too low—making testimonial knowledge too easy to come by. Again, Greco (2015) helpfully gives us an example:

> Consider a seasoned investigator whose task is to question a potentially uncooperative witness. The investigator asks questions and the witness answers them, but clearly the investigator should not just believe whatever the witness says. On the contrary, she will employ skills learned and honed over a career to discern what is and is not believable in what the witness asserts. Moreover, it is plausible to think of these skills in terms of bringing to bear inductive evidence. Plausibly, a seasoned investigator will employ various well-grounded generalizations to determine whether the witness is telling the truth in a particular instance. Some of these generalizations might be well articulated—perhaps they are formulated explicitly in investigator Guides and Handbooks. Others might be less well articulated, but still the result of relevant observations over time. In any case, it looks like nothing special is going on here, epistemically speaking. On the contrary, the effective investigator looks to be a good inductive reasoner. (pp. 277–78)

Here, obviously enough, if a seasoned investigator just believed what he was told—if he or she didn't ground his testimonial knowledge in careful induction—he'd be epistemically remiss, being gullible and easily exploitable. Now, without reductionist constraints, testimonial knowledge seems far too *easy*.

Put the situation in terms of necessary and sufficiency conditions. In some cases—cases involving a seasoned investigator interrogating an uncooperative witness, for example—it looks as though good inductive evidence is necessary for testimonial knowledge. This is in keeping with the reductionist claim that knowledge is reducible to other sources of epistemic goods, specifically induction. In other cases—cases involving small children learning from their caregivers, for example—it looks as though the sufficiency conditions for testimonial knowledge do *not* include having good inductive evidence. Small children, the worry goes, can have testimonial knowledge from their caregivers without having good inductive evidence. And this is in keeping with anti-reductionist claims that the epistemic goods afforded by testimony are *sui generis* and not reducible to other sources.

Framing the debate in this way—in terms of whether having good inductive evidence is necessary for testimonial knowledge—brings the aforementioned dilemma into sharp focus. Consider the following argument:

1   Either testimonial knowledge requires good inductive evidence on the part of the hearer or it does not.

2   If it does not, then testimonial knowledge is too easy. There will be cases counted as knowledge that should not be.

3   If it does, then testimonial knowledge is too hard. There will be cases not counted as knowledge that should be.

Therefore,

4   An adequate account of testimonial knowledge is impossible: a given account must make testimonial knowledge either too easy for some cases or too hard for others. (Greco, 2015, p. 279)

If we don't like the conclusion *that an adequate account of testimonial knowledge is impossible* (4), then we have to deny at least one of the premises (1, 2, or 3). So long as we want a single account of testimonial knowledge that applies to all cases, then the first premise seems undeniable—either testimonial knowledge requires good inductive evidence or it doesn't, there doesn't seem to be any other option. And it looks like we can't deny the *second* premise either. If testimonial knowledge does *not* require having good inductive evidence, then we can easily generate cases that would be counted as knowledge that shouldn't be—cases, for example, where a seasoned investigator believes whatever an uncooperative witness tells her and without good inductive evidence to do so. But what is more, it looks like we can't deny the *third* premise either. If testimonial knowledge *does* require having good inductive evidence, then we can easily generate cases where someone lacks such evidence yet intuitively has knowledge—cases, for example, of small children learning from their caregivers. But if we can't deny any of the premises, we're stuck with the conclusion—*an adequate account of testimonial knowledge is impossible.*

In order to see how to avoid such a conclusion, Greco (2015) suggests that we consider the role the concept of knowledge plays in our "conceptual-linguistic economy" (p. 282). And following Edward Craig, Greco suggests that the role of our concept of knowledge is to highlight good information or good informants. To quote Craig (1999):

> Any community may be presumed to have an interest in evaluating sources of information; and in connection with that interest certain concepts will be in use. The hypothesis I wish to try out is that the concept of knowledge is one of them. To put it briefly and roughly, the concept of knowledge is used to flag approved sources of information. (p. 11)

And that sounds quite plausible. Human beings are social creatures and we are extremely dependent on information; we need a way to flag good information and good informants. And our concept of "knowledge," Craig argues, meets these needs. As Greco (2015) summarizes Craig's idea, "The concept of knowledge serves to govern the production and flow of actionable information, or information that can be used in action and practical reasoning, within a community of information sharers" (p. 283).

Let's say that's approximately right—that the role of knowledge is to flag good information. Building off Craig's idea, Greco (2015) notes that

> we should expect there to be at least two kinds of activity governed by the concept of knowledge. First, there will be activities concerned with *acquiring* or *gathering* information, or getting information into the community of knowers in the first place. . . . Second, there will be activities concerned with *distributing* information throughout the community of knowers; that is, there will be mechanisms for distributing information that is already in the social system. . . . In sum, there will be activities that get information into the system in the first place, and activities that keep the information flowing. Let's call the first *acquisition activities* and the second *distribution activities*. (p. 283)

Let's suppose there is a group of people trapped on a deserted island with flora and fauna that are completely unknown to anyone in the group. Pressed by the need for food, someone might eat some of the berries that are plentiful on the island. This would be an example of the first type of activity governed by the concept of knowledge; in this case, someone is *acquiring* or *gathering* information about the edibility of the given berries. If the berries were discovered to be of good nutritional value (and not poisonous), then the berry-taster might then *distribute* that information among the group, which would be an example of the second type of activity governed by the concept of knowledge.

And there are norms that govern both of these activities. As Greco (2015) goes on to explain:

> The norms governing the acquisition activities play a "gatekeeping" function—they exert quality control so as to admit only high quality

information into the social system. The norms governing distribution activities, on the other hand, answer to a distributing function—they allow high quality information already in the system to be distributed as needed throughout the community of knowers. Insofar as testimony plays this distributing function, it serves to make information already in the system available to those who need it. . . . It is reasonable that the norms governing the acquisition of information should be different from the norms governing the distribution of information. Suppose we were writing the norms, or setting the standards, for these two kinds of activity. We should make it harder to get information into the system than we make it to distribute that information, once in. Again, that is because the dominant concern governing the acquisition function is quality control—we want a strong gatekeeping mechanism here, so as to make sure that only high quality information gets into the community of information sharers. But the dominant concern governing the distributing function will be easy access—we want information that has already passed the quality control test to be easily and efficiently available to those who need it. Different norms or standards are appropriate to these distinct functions. (pp. 283–84)

The norms governing knowledge *acquisition activities* should be relatively rigorous. Continuing with the deserted island example, we wouldn't want someone to claim knowledge simply on the grounds that the given berries *look* edible; norms governing the acquisition of knowledge preclude such a result—looking at berries is not an approved source of information when it comes to judging their edibility. Norms governing knowledge distribution activities, however, are not that rigorous. Once someone has properly judged that a given type of berry is good to eat, the standards for sharing that information should be quite low. Intuitively, someone should be able to know that the mysterious berries are good to eat simply on the basis of someone who's already acquired that knowledge saying so.

Now, let's remember the dilemma facing testimonial knowledge. If we assume reductionism, there are cases where testimonial knowledge seems too difficult to come by—it's not easy to see, for example, how small children learn via testimony since they are plausibly unable to meet the high reductionist standards on testimonial knowledge. If, on the other hand, we assume anti-reductionism, there are cases where testimonial knowledge seems too easy to come by—an uncooperative witness's testimony alone should not amount to knowledge, but it's unclear what resources anti-reductionism could draw from to preclude it. And insofar as there is no third option—reductionism and anti-reductionism account for all of the logical space—then we're left with an unhappy conclusion: *that an adequate account of testimonial knowledge is impossible.*

Building off the work of Edward Craig, however, we are now seeing that there are two kinds of activity governed by the concept of knowledge—each with its own set of norms. The norms governing *acquisition activities* should be quite rigorous. We don't want just any information getting into our information economy, we only want *good* information. And the norms governing distribution activities should be relatively relaxed. Once we have good information, we should be able to share it freely and easily. The "concept" knowledge serves two roles. And plausibly, testimonial knowledge serves these two roles as well. As Greco (2015) explains:

> [Testimonial] knowledge itself comes in two kinds. In other words, it is plausible that testimonial knowledge sometimes serves the distribution function of the concept of knowledge, and sometimes the acquisition function. The distribution function gives us . . . the most plausible treatment of [the case involving small children]. But it is also plausible that testimony sometimes serves an acquisition function, bringing information into a community of knowledge for the first time. This is perhaps the best treatment of [cases like seasoned investigator and uncooperative witness].

This explains why a student or a child, when in appropriate circumstances, can believe straight away what a teacher or a parent tells her, and also explains why an investigator or interviewer cannot. In short, different norms govern the different kinds of testimonial exchange, some of which are at the service of information distribution within a community of knowers, others of which are at the service of information uptake for first use in a community of knowers. (p. 285)

Earlier, when considering the dilemma facing any viable account of testimonial knowledge, we assumed that we wanted a single account of testimonial knowledge that applied to all cases. Perhaps we're now seeing that this is not the case.

But if testimonial knowledge comes in two "kinds," then it looks like we might have the material to viably avoid the dilemma's conclusion: that *an adequate account of testimonial knowledge is impossible.* First of all, it looks like we can now deny the first premise, that "either testimonial knowledge requires good inductive evidence on the part of the hearer or it does not." As Greco (2015) explains:

Suppose we parse premise 1 this way: Either *all* testimonial knowledge requires good inductive evidence on the part of the hearer or *no* testimonial knowledge does. In that case we reject premise 1. That reading of the premise looks innocent so long as we are assuming that all testimonial knowledge should be treated the same way. On the present account, however, there are two kinds of testimonial knowledge, one of which carries the evidential burdens of inductive knowledge and the other of which does not. (p. 287)

If testimonial knowledge comes in two *kinds*, as Greco has suggested, then it looks like in some cases testimonial knowledge requires good inductive evidence, but in other cases it doesn't. In cases where testimonial knowledge is governed by the norms of *acquisition activity*—cases like the one where the seasoned investigator is interrogating an uncooperative witness—then testimonial knowledge will indeed require good inductive evidence. In cases where testimonial knowledge is governed by the norms of a *distribution activity*, however—cases, for example, where small children are learning from their caregivers—testimonial knowledge does not require good inductive evidence. For the former, norms are guided by quality control, trying to flag good information. For the latter, norms are guided by a need to spread good information quickly and efficiently throughout a given epistemic community.

But maybe premise one is best understood as saying that "[Either] all testimonial knowledge requires good inductive evidence on the part of the hearer, or it is not the case that all testimonial knowledge carries that requirement" (Greco, 2015, p. 287). Given this reading, we would no longer want to deny the first premise of the dilemma; but we would then want to deny premise two. As Greco (2015) explains: "In effect, premise 2 now assumes the following: that if not all testimonial knowledge requires good inductive evidence, then no testimonial knowledge does" (p. 287). Given that testimonial knowledge comes in two kinds—one governed by the norms of acquisition, the other governed by the norms of distribution—such an understanding of premise two is false.

In any case, the framework for testimonial knowledge Greco has laid out gives us the resources for avoiding the conclusion of the dilemma; given that knowledge comes in these two kinds—sometimes serving a distribution function of the concept of knowledge, and sometimes an acquisition function— we have a powerful strategy for dissolving what was previously a crippling dilemma. And what is more, Greco has given us what seems to be a convincing answer to the central theoretical question at the heart of the reductionist versus anti-reductionist debate: *Is testimonial knowledge epistemically distinct or sui generis?* As Greco (2015) explains:

In effect, the present account implies that there are two kinds of testimonial knowledge, one of which can be reduced to knowledge of another sort, and the other of which cannot be. Accordingly, we might say that a reductionist account of testimonial knowledge is correct for some cases, whereas an anti-reductionist account is correct for others. However, this is probably too generous to the reductionist. That is because, properly understood, the reductionist claim is that all testimonial knowledge can be reduced to knowledge of another kind. The anti-reductionist claim, properly understood, is to deny this. If that is the right way to understand the dispute, then the present account is anti-reductionist. (p. 286)

Almost everyone agrees that, in standard cases, receiving testimony that *p* gives someone justification for believing that *p*. And many of us would want to say that such justification is, in at least the standard cases, good enough to allow someone to *know* that *p*. But where does this justification come from? Is testimony a unique source of epistemic goods? Or is testimony simply a species of a more general source of epistemic goods, say, induction? These sorts of questions that have most shaped the epistemology of testimony and are often centered on the reductionist versus anti-reductionist debate. Greco has given us a systematic understanding of this debate that provides some possible answers to these questions; but what is more, it gives us some new ways to understand intellectual humility's relationship to testimony.

The framework for testimonial knowledge Greco has laid out can give us another layer of explanation for how testimonial knowledge can fail and how intellectual humility can drive that failure. Consider once again, Herbert Greenleaf's shameful treatment of his son's fiancé, Marge. Greenleaf wants to know what happened to his son, Dickie. Marge knows what happened to him— he was murdered by his friend, Ripley—and Marge repeatedly tries to tell this to Greenleaf. Unfortunately, however, Greenleaf won't listen to Marge's testimony; instead, he disparagingly dismisses her testimony as simply "female intuition."

Previously we noted that one of the places where testimonial exchanges could fail is with the HEARER—with the person receiving the testimony. And we proposed that the failure of testimony in Fricker's (2007) example is largely a failure in Greenleaf, who, in this instant, is playing the role of the HEARER. It is Greenleaf, the HEARER, who fails to listen to the excellent testimony of Marge. And it is Greenleaf, the HEARER, who listens unreflectively to the lies and deceptions of Ricky. And again, drawing from the doxastic account of intellectual humility—where intellectual humility is the virtue of accurately tracking what one could non-culpably take to be the positive epistemic status of one's own beliefs—we can easily think of the failure in Greenleaf as a failure *in intellectual humility*.[10] After all, Greenleaf is simply not accurately tracking what he could non-culpably take to be the positive epistemic status of his belief regarding his son—the belief which is of central importance to the case. Greenleaf is intellectually arrogant in holding his belief regarding the lack of value of Marge's testimony and the value of Ricky's as strongly as he does. And, ultimately, Greenleaf is intellectually arrogant in holding his belief regarding his son's fate as strongly as he does, because he has systematically (and out of prejudice) failed to track defeaters for his belief (presented by Marge).

But now, drawing from Greco's framework, I think we can say a bit more about this case—we can say a bit more about how, specifically, Greenleaf failed as a HEARER. When listening to Marge regarding the fate of Dickie, Greenleaf applies the acquisition norms to her testimony. This is setting the bar too high. Marge, plausibly, has already done the hard work of flagging good information. And now that she has the good information—now that she knows that Ripley is Dickie's murderer—Greenleaf *should* apply the norms of a distribution activity to her testimony. But he doesn't. Additionally, especially given Marge's misgivings, Greenleaf *should* apply the norms of an acquisition activity to Ripley's testimony; Greenleaf should not simply take Ripley at his word. But he does. Marge has done the hard work in flagging good, actionable information regarding the fate of Dickie, so she should be welcomed as an insider within Greenleaf's epistemic community—an insider where distributive norms apply. But instead, Greenleaf treats Marge like an epistemic outsider—taking her testimony with unreasonable degrees of skepticism and doubt. And again, in contrast, as a plausible suspect in Dickie's death, Ripley should have been viewed as an epistemic outsider—as someone whose testimony needs to be scrutinized. Instead, Greenleaf views Ripley as an epistemic *insider*—as someone with whom distributive norms apply—simply because he's a man. In sum, to put it roughly, if Greco is right that there are two kinds of testimonial knowledge—with two different sets of governing norms—then it looks like Greenleaf is mixed-up regarding what norms should apply to Marge's testimony and what norms should apply to Ripley's. To Greenleaf, Marge *qua* a woman is an epistemic outsider and Ripley *qua* a man is an epistemic insider. This mix-up is, no doubt, driven by prejudice and sexism, which, as Fricker (2007) rightly highlighted, leads to epistemic injustice.

What we would like to again suggest is that Greenleaf's prejudice and sexism, that lead to his misapplication of testimonial norms and the epistemic injustice committed against Marge, can be seen as tied to a lack of intellectual humility. Drawing from the doxastic account of intellectual humility, Greenleaf's failure to appreciate and accept the good, actionable information presented by Marge—applying acquisition norms of testimony when distributive norms of testimony were called for—is a failure to accurately track the positive epistemic status of Marge's testimony, a failure of intellectual humility. And Greenleaf's failure in hastily accepting of Ripley's "bad" information—applying distributive norms of testimony where acquisition norms of testimony were called for—is simply a failure to accurately track the positive epistemic status of Ripley's testimony, a failure of intellectual humility. In the end, Greenleaf is intellectually *arrogant*, by the doxastic account's lights, to hold his belief about Dickie's fate as strongly as he does, given that he systematically ignored countervailing evidence while blindly accepted bad information.

The final proposal: The failure of testimony in Fricker's (2007) example is a failure in Greenleaf as a HEARER. How so? Thanks to Greco's framework of the two kinds of testimony, we can point to what looks like Greenleaf's application of acquisition norms when distributive norms were called for, and his application of distributive norms when acquisition norms were called for. But behind all of this, we've seen how a failure of *intellectual humility* can drive such a failure in testimonial exchange. No doubt, we rely on testimony. Whether it's a friend, a witness to a crime, or an expert in a given field, we depend on what other people tell us. But there are times when we clearly shouldn't believe what we hear (or at the very least take what we hear with a significant grain of salt). There are times when people lie or mislead. Sometimes being trusting—for example, when we're listening to politicians, car salesmen, etc.—is a mistake (perhaps indicative of the vice of gullibility). But, of course, there are also times when a shrewd and untrusting attitude does both ourselves, as hearers, and our interlocutors, as speakers, a serious disservice. *Being intellectually humble can help us know when we can believe what we hear. And failures of intellectual humility—be it intellectual arrogance or intellectual diffidence—can lead to failures of testimony.*

9

How should we handle disagreement?

When we think about practical applications of intellectual humility, we often think of how intellectual humility might speak to disagreements—especially disagreements amongst peers. When we think about intellectual arrogance, we often think of someone who is unflinchingly dogmatic and unwilling to compromise on their belief in the face of dissent, disagreement, and defeaters. And when we think about intellectual diffidence, we often think of someone who is far too easily persuaded to give up on (or reduce their credence in) his or her beliefs. *How we handle disagreement seems to be at the heart of intellectual humility.*

And people can disagree on just about any subject—from politics, to religion, to morality, to matters of fact, to matters of taste, etc. And disagreement among epistemic peers—interlocutors who are equally familiar with the relevant data and just as intelligent, clever, rational, etc.—can be found (to at least some degree) in almost every realm of inquiry. As Richard Feldman and Ted A. Warfield (2010) note in the introduction to their seminal collection, *Disagreement*:

Disagreement is common. Two expert weather forecasters disagree about the weekend forecast. Two equally well-informed economists disagree about the most likely movement in interest rates. Two chess players with the same ranking disagree about whether "white" stands better in a given board position. The available examples are limitless and range widely over nearly all aspects of life. (p. 1)

And this raises important epistemic questions. When faced with a disagreement with an epistemic peer, are we obliged to compromise on our beliefs, or otherwise revise them? No doubt, this seems right in some cases, but surely there are also cases where we should stick to our proverbial guns. Surely, if we compromised on *every* belief that is contested (or perhaps merely *potentially* contested) by one of our peers, it seems as though we would be mired in far-reaching, radical skepticism. Besides, aren't there times when we can simply agree to disagree?

Contemporary epistemology is currently enjoying vibrant debate regarding the epistemic import of peer disagreement. Thus far, however, the debate has largely centered on avoiding two epistemic vices, namely, intellectual arrogance and intellectual diffidence. On the one hand, philosophers like Christensen (2007), Feldman (2006), Elga (2007), and Kornblith (2010) have argued that, when disagreeing with an epistemic peer, we should be willing to revise (or perhaps give up on) our relevant beliefs—to do otherwise, to be unwilling to revise our beliefs and to disregard the divergent opinions of our peers, seems profoundly dogmatic and arrogant. On the other, however, philosophers such as Foley (2001), Kelly (2005), Wedgewood (2007), and van Inwagen (2010) have argued that, when faced with peer disagreement, there are times when we should be willing to hold our epistemic ground—to do otherwise, to give up on our carefully formed beliefs in the face of peer disagreement, seems, at least in many cases, irresolute and epistemically ineffectual.

Surprisingly, however, in trying to avoid such epistemic *vices*, very little attention has been given to explicating or understanding the corresponding *virtue*—intellectual humility—the virtuous mean between intellectual arrogance and intellectual diffidence. In this chapter, we argue that an appreciation of intellectual humility can inform the debates surrounding peer disagreement and help us better understand when and why intractable disagreements occur. This is done in two sections. First, in §1, we use three cases of peer disagreement that afford easy solutions—cases of peer disagreement found in the contemporary literature that we can generally agree on how they should be handled—to sketch a rough trajectory of virtuous responses to peer disagreement, a trajectory that mirrors the doxastic account of intellectual humility. Second, in §2, we consider some notoriously difficult instances of peer disagreement—such as disagreements regarding morality, politics, and religion—and use our notion of intellectual humility to help us understand when and why such intractable disagreements occur. But, ideally, we don't just want to know *when and why* intractable disagreements occur—though that's certainly helpful—we also want to know what we should *do* when faced with such disagreements. In §3, we will consider Catherine Elgin's (2010) paper, "Persistent Disagreement," and explore a possible answer.

§1: Easy cases of disagreement and intellectual humility

Naturally enough, most of the literature surrounding the epistemic import of peer disagreement focuses primarily on those cases that prove the most challenging and the most puzzling. That said, however, it is well worth our time to consider cases of peer disagreement that we can generally agree on how they are reasonably handled in order to better understand those cases that are more intractable. In this section, we will consider three "easy" cases of disagreement—cases of peer disagreement that afford relatively easy solutions—in order to sketch a broad outline of reasonable, good, or *virtuous* approaches to peer disagreement. Held together, these virtuous approaches to peer disagreement will help us map a rough trajectory of virtuous responses to disagreement, a trajectory that divides the epistemic vices of intellectual arrogance and intellect diffidence, a trajectory of intellectual humility. And it is this trajectory of intellectual humility that will (in §2) help us understand when and why intractable disagreements occur.

The cases we will consider in this section will outline a broad spectrum of virtuous responses to peer disagreement. First, we will look at a case of peer disagreement that—as evidenced in the philosophical literature—intuitively seems to require belief-revision on the part of the relevant interlocutors, what we might call *virtuous revision*. Similarly, we will then consider a case that intuitively seems to allow for a healthy dose of dogmatism, what we might call *virtuous dogmatism*. Third, and finally, we will consider a case of peer disagreement that intuitively seems to allow for a healthy dose of skepticism, what we might call *virtuous skepticism*. The hope is that in considering a wide range of divergent cases, the broad spectrum and trajectory of the relevant virtue will become clearer.

Virtuous revision

Most of our day-to-day, ordinary beliefs are epistemically innocuous—we may believe we have milk in the refrigerator, we may believe that a given orchid is a *Platanthera tescamnis,* we may believe (based on a foggy memory) that the capital of Maine is Augusta, not Portland. Though we sincerely believe such things, we don't hold them all that dearly or firmly, we don't attribute all that much positive epistemic status to them, and we certainly wouldn't lose sleep if we discovered that we were mistaken, or that an epistemic peer happened to disagree with us. Likewise, most of our day-to-day, run-of-the-mill disagreements with our peers are fairly benign. Many of our ordinary beliefs are such that, if they were challenged, no great epistemic quandary would arise. Most of our ordinary beliefs are such that any disagreements to the contrary can be easily resolved. Consider the following case from Hilary Kornblith's (2010) work, "Belief in the Face of Controversy":

VIRTUOUS REVISION: [Suppose] that you and I go out to a restaurant with a number of friends. After a large meal, the check comes and we agree to split the bill evenly. You and I are each quite good at mental arithmetic. I take a look at the bill and figure out what each person owes, and I put my share in the middle of the table. You look at the bill and figure out what each person owes and put your share in the middle of the table, and then we notice that we have put in different amounts. We are each well aware of the other's mathematical abilities, and we are each convinced of each other's honesty. At least one of us has made a mistake. It would be unreasonable for me to conclude that, since, one of us has made a mistake, it must be you. The reasonable thing to do in this situation, and surely what most people in fact do in this situation, is suspend belief. We each go back to the bill and try to recompute the proper share. (p. 32)

Most of our day-to-day, run-of-the-mill disagreements are like VIRTUOUS REVISION. We may disagree with an epistemic peer about whether we have milk in the refrigerator, whether the capital of Maine is Portland or Augusta,[1] and whether a given orchid is a *Platanthera tescamnis* or a *Platanthera sparsiflora*. And in all of these cases, the disagreement can be easily resolved. We can look in the refrigerator. We can look at a map. We can consult an orchid guidebook or perhaps an expert botanist. The reasonable thing to do in such cases is to revise the belief (withhold belief or at least adjust the positive epistemic status that one attributes to the given belief) until we can look in the refrigerator, check a map, consult an expert botanist, etc.

Virtuous dogmatism

Of course, not all forms of peer disagreement should force revisions onto our beliefs. There are some beliefs that we hold too dearly, beliefs that are too central or too fundamental and indeed too important to afford adjustment, revision, or suspension. Consider the following case:

> VIRTUOUS DOGMATISM: Jill is a philosopher, working away in an office, when one of her colleagues, Jack, stops by to chat. Now, Jill considers Jack to be her epistemic peer—she has no reason to suspect that Jack is in anyway less intelligent, educated, or clever than herself. Nevertheless, this day Jack surprises Jill with a shocking revelation. Jack confides in Jill that he has recently stopped believing that 2 + 2 = 4. Now, if Jill knows anything, she knows that 2 + 2 = 4. Does Jack's disagreement on this force Jill to reconsider her beliefs about basic arithmetic? Seemingly not. To all intents and purposes, Jill simply *cannot* give up on or significantly modify such beliefs. Such beliefs are too important and too consequential.

While legitimate peer disagreement in cases like VIRTUOUS REVISION reasonably force the interlocutors to suspend, modify, or revise their respective beliefs, we can presumably agree that such a result does not seem reasonable in cases like such as VIRTUOUS DOGMATISM, in cases where the disagreement is over beliefs that are too precious, dear, central, foundational, etc. to revise or give up. In "You Can't Trust a Philosopher," Richard Fumerton (2010) addresses a case just like Virtuous Dogmatism:

> If I am justified in believing anything, I am justified in believing that 2 + 2 = 4. My hitherto trusted colleague, a person I always respected, assures me today, however, that 2 + 2 does not equal 4. Does this rather surprising discovery of my colleague's odd assertion defeat my justification for believing that 2 + 2 = 4? Hardly. . . . To convince myself that he really is disagreeing with me, I would have to convince myself that he is crazy. And, as soon as I become convinced that he is crazy, I will not and should not pay any attention to what he believes. My justification for believing that he has lost his mind neutralizes whatever epistemic significance his disagreement with me might otherwise have had. (pp. 95–96)

In cases like VIRTUOUS DOGMATISM, a dogmatic inflexibility seems reasonable. The belief that 2 + 2 = 4 presumably enjoys maximal (or nearly maximal) positive epistemic status. Even though our interlocutor in such cases is, by hypothesis, an epistemic peer, any claim to peerhood is seemingly lost once it becomes clear that they are sincerely and genuinely at odds with beliefs that are so central, so foundational, so consequential.[2] Being sincerely and genuinely at odds with such beliefs is crazy. And when an epistemic peer goes crazy, at least within a certain domain, they are no longer a genuine peer within that domain. In cases like VIRTUOUS DOGMATISM, dogmatism—an uncompromising stance regarding one's beliefs—seems entirely reasonable, and virtuous.

Virtuous skepticism

So, we can seemingly agree that there are recognizable cases of peer disagreement where the reasonable thing to do is modify, revise, suspend, or otherwise compromise on our belief (cases like VIRTUOUS REVISION). What is more, it seems like we can also agree that there are recognizable cases of peer disagreement where the reasonable thing to do is to be dogmatic, stick to your proverbial guns, and be uncompromising in your beliefs (cases like VIRTUOUS DOGMATISM). The final "easy" cases we want to consider before moving on to the more problematic (if not intractable) forms of peer disagreement are those cases concerning beliefs that we hold with a healthy dose of skepticism, genuine beliefs that are recognized as enjoying relatively little positive epistemic status and are held loosely with little firmness. Consider the following case:

VIRTUOUS SKEPTICISM: Susan and Ingrid are both accomplished theologians; however, they disagree about the highly theoretical, abstract, and fairly esoteric issues surrounding lapsarianism. Susan is a talented advocate of supralapsarianism, and Ingrid is an equally talented advocate of infralapsarianism. (It is not important what these views actually amount to; all we need to appreciate at this point is that they are theoretical, abstract, and fairly esoteric.) They both deeply appreciate and respect each other's work, and neither one of them has any reason to question the other's intelligence, competence, or understanding of the relevant literature. And while they have engaged with each other's work in depth and for many years, they both remain committed to their respective views on this issue.

The relevant beliefs in VIRTUOUS SKEPTICISM are presumably held much more loosely and attributed with far less positive epistemic status than, say, the relevant beliefs in VIRTUOUS REVISION or VIRTUOUS DOGMATISM.[3] An advocate of supralapsarianism or infralapsarianism will presumably recognize the highly theoretical, abstract, and complex nature of the lapsarianism debate and hold his/her belief with a healthy dose of skepticism—skepticism that would presumably be unfounded when divvying up bills or doing basic arithmetic.[4] Indeed, the advocate of supralapsarianism or infralapsarianism will presumably hold their belief with enough skepticism so that the disagreement of the peer will be of relatively little significance—just a drop in the metaphorical bucket. And as such, it seems reasonable or virtuous that such peer disagreement does very little to affect the belief of protagonists in cases like VIRTUOUS SKEPTICISM—cases where the belief in question is concerning a topic so abstract, so theoretical, so complex that it is held very loosely and (consciously or subconsciously) taken to enjoy relatively little positive epistemic status.

The virtuous trajectory and intellectual humility

To be sure, even if we can agree on what might be the approximately reasonable response in the above cases, serious and troubling questions are, no doubt, lurking in the neighborhood. Even if we can agree that protagonists in cases like VIRTUOUS REVISION should somehow revise their beliefs, we may yet wonder what precisely that revision should amount to. Even if we can agree that protagonists in cases like VIRTUOUS DOGMATISM should be dogmatic about their basic beliefs, we may yet wonder what constraints ultimately warrant such epistemic rigidity. Even if we can agree that the protagonists' beliefs in cases like VIRTUOUS SKEPTICISM should be relatively unaffected by peer disagreement (since peer disagreement does little to increase the already high levels of skepticism surrounding the given belief), we may yet wonder if even tenuous belief is actually warranted in such scenarios. Add to this the complexities introduced by scenarios where the peerhood of our interlocutors is not obvious or scenarios where the relevant disagreement is either unknown to the interlocutors or merely possible, and the dizzying complexity surrounding the epistemic significance of disagreement comes plainly into focus.

Nevertheless, if we can indeed agree on what might be the approximately reasonable response to cases like VIRTUOUS REVISION, VIRTUOUS DOGMATISM, and VIRTUOUS SKEPTICISM, we can make significant headway toward a systematic understanding of intellectual humility and the virtue at the heart of the disagreement literature. There are two factors worth tracking across such cases: (i) the positive epistemic status with which the (pre-disagreement) belief is (consciously or subconsciously) attributed and (ii) the positive epistemic status which the (pre-disagreement) belief *actually enjoys*. In VIRTUOUS REVISION, the protagonist attributes a moderate amount of positive epistemic status to his belief, and the belief in question, while perhaps generally unlikely to be false, enjoys a moderate amount of positive epistemic status. In VIRTUOUS DOGMATISM, the protagonist holds her belief with absolute firmness (it's difficult to think of anything she might believe more than $2 + 2 = 4$) and the belief in question, let's assume, actually enjoys a tremendous amount of positive epistemic status. In VIRTUOUS SKEPTICISM, the protagonist attributes her belief with very little positive epistemic status, and, given the theoretical complexities surrounding the belief in question, this is exactly the amount of positive epistemic status the belief enjoys. These results allow us to outline and provisionally map reasonable (or *intellectually virtuous*) responses to peer disagreement. Consider the following figure:

Given that it is attributed (consciously or unconsciously) with the high degree of positive epistemic status that it deserves, the protagonist's belief in VIRTUOUS DOGMATISM is in the upper right-hand corner of the graph. Given that it is attributed with the moderate degree of positive epistemic status that it deserves, the protagonist's belief in VIRTUOUS REVISION would presumably be roughly in the center of Figure 9.1. Finally, given that they are held with the low degree of positive epistemic status that they actually enjoy, the protagonists' beliefs in VIRTUOUS SKEPTICISM are in the lower left-hand corner of Figure 9.1. And this pattern of beliefs seemingly maps a trajectory for intellectual virtue, where intellectual virtue is, roughly, *believing as one ought*—call this the *virtuous trajectory*.

This virtuous trajectory is the trajectory of intellectual humility. Again, *prima facie*, humility (*simpliciter*) is presumably the virtuous mean between arrogance and diffidence. The humble person does not think too highly of himself/herself, nor is he/she completely self-deprecating. Likewise, *intellectual* humility is presumably the virtuous mean between intellectual arrogance

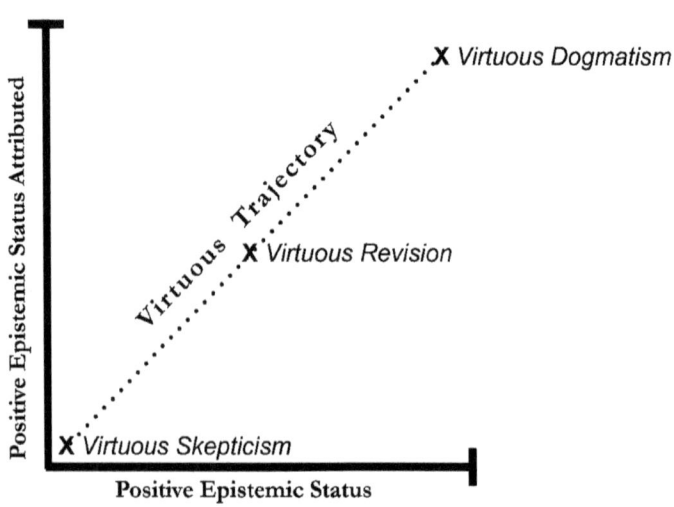

FIGURE 9.1 *The Virtuous Trajectory of Disagreement.*

(*attributing more positive epistemic status to one's beliefs than they actually enjoy*, the upper left-hand corner of the graph) and intellectual diffidence (*attributing less positive epistemic status to one's beliefs than they actually enjoy*, the lower right-hand corner of the graph). Correspondingly, the intellectually humble person is presumably someone who (roughly) does not think too highly of his/her beliefs. What is more, however, the intellectually humble person is also presumably someone who (roughly) does not think too little of his/her beliefs. In short, intellectual humility is arguably something like (or minimally) believing as you ought—accurately tracking the positive epistemic status of one's beliefs.

§2: Problematic disagreement

In the previous section, we considered three cases of peer disagreement that we can generally agree on how they are reasonably handled, and, taken together, these "easy" cases map a trajectory of intellectual virtue, the virtue of intellectual humility. In this section, we use this trajectory of intellectual humility to highlight two classes of peer disagreement in the philosophical literature that are perennial and seemingly intractable. *The first class we will call borderline cases.* While falling on the trajectory of intellectual virtue, borderline cases of peer disagreement are puzzling because, as we will see, they nevertheless fall *between* the reasonable solutions afforded by the "easy" cases in the previous section, pulling our intuitions in two different directions. *The second class we will call vicious disagreements.* Cases of vicious disagreement are intractable *not so much* because we feel pulled in two different directions about them, but because they involve beliefs that are all too prone to being off the trajectory of intellectual virtue, disagreements that involve beliefs that are all too prone to being intellectually *vicious*, disagreements that involve beliefs that are all to prone to being off the trajectory of *intellectual humility*. While this taxonomy of the perennial and seemingly intractable cases of peer disagreement afforded by an understanding of intellectual humility will not immediately resolve such cases, the hope is that it *will* shed light on when and why such disagreements occur.

Borderline cases

Some cases of peer disagreement might be more problematic than any of the cases considered thus far primarily because they are *borderline cases*, cases where the belief in question is on the trajectory of intellectual virtue but not plainly an instance that would require revision, dogmatism, or skepticism in the face of peer disagreement. Consider the following case from "Persistent Disagreement" by Catherine Z. Elgin (2010):

> BORDERLINE: Suppose two paleontologists, Jack and Jill, are epistemic peers who disagree about the fate of the Neanderthals. Jack believes that Neanderthals were an evolutionary dead end. Unable to compete, they simply died out. Jill believes that Neanderthals evolved into later hominids whose descendants are alive today. Because the issue is complex and the evidence is equivocal, they come to different conclusions about it. What should they (and we) make of their disagreement? In particular, should the fact that an epistemic peer disagrees with Jack have any effect on the epistemological status of his belief? Should Jack's knowledge of that fact have any effect? (p. 54)

Allow that, the deliverances of paleontology fairly reliably hit the truth and merit being held with a reasonably high degree of firmness; in any case, let's assume that the deliverances of paleontology are such that they deserve to be attributed with more positive epistemic status than a cursory glance at a restaurant bill (cf. VIRTUOUS REVISION) and less positive epistemic status than the average adult's understanding of basic arithmetic (cf. VIRTUOUS DOGMATISM). And let's assume Jack and Jill are taking their beliefs to enjoy

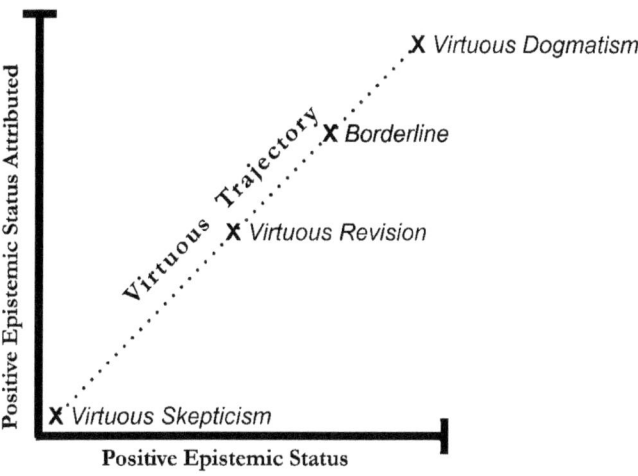

FIGURE 9.2 *The Virtuous Trajectory and Borderline Cases.*

the positive epistemic status due the deliverances of paleontology (i.e., they are on the trajectory of intellectual virtue). This would place their respective beliefs roughly here, as indicated by "Borderline" below:

Should Jack and Jill revise their beliefs? Or can they reasonably hold their epistemic ground? As Elgin (2010) notes, opinions diverge:

> Some philosophers, such as Richard Feldman, Hilary Kornblith, and David Christensen, contend that the existence of peer disagreement undermines one's grounds for belief.[5] If someone with the same evidence, training, background knowledge and reasoning abilities came to the opposite conclusion from Jack's, that is evidence that Jack's grounds are inadequate. Such philosophers think that epistemic agents should moderate their views in light of the disagreement. Others, such as Thomas Kelly and Richard Foley, maintain that it is reasonable for a thinker to retain his opinion in the face of disagreement with an epistemic peer.[6] They think that epistemic agents should be resolute. (p. 54)

And given our diagnosis of BORDERLINE as a borderline case, this makes perfect sense. If (i) the deliverances of paleontology merit being attributed with a fairly high degree of positive epistemic status (more than a cursory glance at a restaurant bill and less than the average adult with basic arithmetic) and (ii) Jack and Jill are attributing their beliefs with the positive epistemic status due the general deliverances paleontology, then we are pulled in two directions. It is unclear whether Jack and Jill should revise their beliefs (as in VIRTUOUS REVISION) or whether they can reasonably hold their epistemic ground (as in VIRTUOUS DOGMATISM). Our outline of intellectual humility does not tell us the right answer in these cases; however, it does give us a systematic framework for understanding why such disagreements are problematic and puzzling in the first place.

Vicious disagreement

However, there are problematic and puzzling cases of peer disagreement that are not borderline cases. There are cases of peer disagreement that are intractable *not* so much because we feel pulled in two different directions about them but because they involve beliefs that are extremely personal, consequential, and intimate, beliefs that are all too prone to being attributed (consciously or unconsciously) with almost unmatched positive epistemic status even when they shouldn't be. In cases like VIRTUOUS REVISION, VIRTUOUS DOGMATISM, and VIRTUOUS SKEPTICISM, the protagonists roughly proportioned the amount of positive epistemic status attributed to their belief to the positive epistemic status actually enjoyed by their belief—they didn't attribute more positive epistemic status to their belief than they ought, they were on the trajectory of intellectual humility. Some beliefs, however, are all too prone to what we might call intellectual vice, where the belief is attributed with positive epistemic status that it does not merit.[7] Consider the following case:

> **Vicious Disagreement**: Conrad is a committed conservative. Most of his friends are conservatives. He frequents conservative blogs and websites. And he is part of a broader conservative community. Libby, however, is

a liberal. Most of her friends are liberals. She frequents liberal blogs and websites. And Libby is part of a broader liberal community. Conrad believes that abortion should be illegal, except perhaps in cases involving rape or cases where pregnancy threatens the life of the mother. In contrast, Libby believes, among other things, that abortion should be *legal* and made easily accessible to women everywhere. Conrad and Libby are equally intelligent, clever, and discerning. Nevertheless, when Conrad and Libby discuss their differences in opinion and review all of the arguments both for and against their respective positions, they both remain unmoved.

For beliefs that are extremely personal, consequential, and intimate—beliefs regarding religion, politics, and morality being archetypal—there can be a lot at stake. The respective political beliefs of Conrad and Libby in VICIOUS DISAGREEMENT, for example, deeply affect how they each view the world, what they read with the most attentiveness, who their closest friends are, and perhaps even whom they trust the most.[8] Indeed, their political beliefs are so near and so dear to them that giving them up could be intellectually cataclysmic.

Conrad and Libby attribute their respective beliefs regarding politics with high levels of positive epistemic status. Of course, Conrad may very well think that his belief merits his firm commitment to conservative politics, but, then again, Libby may very well think that her belief merits *her* firm commitment to liberal politics. Conversely, given the firmness with which Conrad is committed to conservatism, he presumably thinks that Libby's firm commitment to liberalism is unmerited. Likewise, given the firmness with which Libby is committed to liberalism, she presumably thinks that Conrad's firm commitment to conservatism is unmerited.[9] And assuming that incompatible views cannot both merit being attributed with a high degree of positive epistemic status, at least one of the interlocutors in cases like VICIOUS DISAGREEMENT is committing an intellectual vice—attributing more positive epistemic status to his/her belief than he/she ought.[10] The problem, however, is determining who the culprit is. Conrad may, with regret, think Libby is somehow intellectually misguided, perhaps chalking her strong dissent to the noetic effects of like-minded, liberal colleagues at work. Likewise, Libby may, with regret, think that Conrad is actually the intellectually misguided one, perhaps chalking up his strong dissent as a product of his questionable choices in news outlets.

In VIRTUOUS DOGMATISM, the interlocutors are at odds about what they ought to believe regarding basic arithmetic. In VIRTUOUS REVISION, the interlocutors are at odds about what they ought to believe regarding what each owes on a restaurant bill. In VIRTUOUS SKEPTICISM, the interlocutors are at odds about the debate surrounding lapsarianism. In all of these cases, however, we can generally agree on how to handle them. The protagonist in VIRTUOUS DOGMATISM should stick to her proverbial guns and continue to believe that 2 + 2 = 4 with the utmost firmness. The interlocutors in VIRTUOUS REVISION should withhold or otherwise revise their beliefs until they can get a second glance at the bill. And given the theoretical,

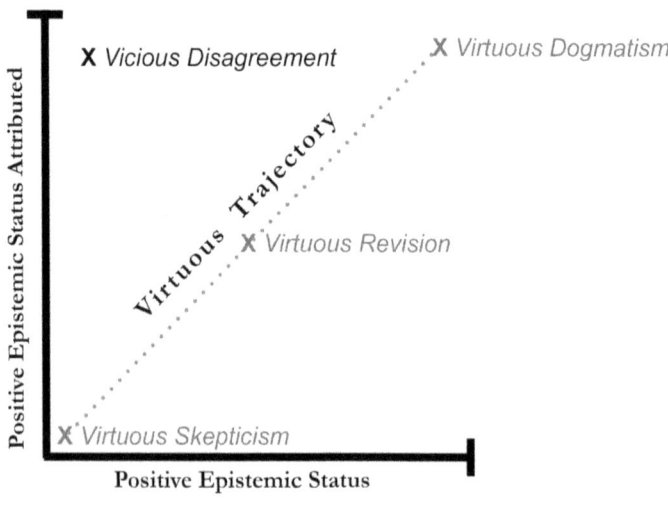

FIGURE 9.3 *The Virtuous Trajectory and Vicious Disagreement.*

abstract, and esoteric nature of their debate, the interlocutors in VIRTUOUS SKEPTICISM should attribute their beliefs with so little positive epistemic status that peer disagreement is relatively inconsequential. Cases like VICIOUS DISAGREEMENT, however, are far more intractable. Cases like VICIOUS DISAGREEMENT involve beliefs that are so personal, so consequential, and so intimate that *they are particularly and notoriously prone to intellectual vice*; in particular, they are prone to being attributed with almost unmatched positive epistemic status even when it is ultimately unmerited—*they are particularly and notoriously prone to being off the trajectory of intellectual humility:*

And this makes our disagreements as to what positive epistemic status religious, political, moral, etc., beliefs merit vast. All too often, we simply cannot agree on what the relevant data, arguments, evidence, intuitions, etc., are, let alone what positive epistemic status they merit; and all too often, we attribute any intellectual vice to our interlocutors rather than ourselves. More so than any of the cases considered so far, we cannot agree on what one ought to believe.

§3: An intellectually humble response to intractable disagreement

Thus far, we've seen how our intuitions regarding how easy cases of peer disagreement should be handled dovetails with intellectual humility; more specifically, we've seen how the proposed "virtuous trajectory" of how easy cases of disagreement should be handled maps onto the doxastic account of intellectual humility. And we've seen how that trajectory can make sense of when and why intractable disagreements occur. *But what should we do when faced with such disagreements?* Insofar as everyone has beliefs about politics, ethics, and religion that aren't shared universally (or even universally amongst our peers), we *are* faced with such disagreements. So, what's the intellectually humble thing to do? In this section, we will consider Catherine Elgin's paper "Persistent Disagreement" and propose a possible solution—an approach to handling persistent, intractable disagreements that is compatible with (if not driven by) intellectual humility.

In the previous section, we warned that some disagreements, disagreements like those in cases like VICIOUS DISAGREEMENT, that involve beliefs so personal and so consequential that they are particularly prone to being attributed with far more positive epistemic status than they actually enjoy.[11] Perhaps the intellectually humble thing to do in such cases is to be vigilant! In other words, perhaps we should recognize that some of our beliefs are particularly prone to intellectual vice, so we should be extra careful and reflective to make sure we are indeed accurately tracking the positive epistemic status of our beliefs. Intellectual humility, unsurprisingly, can be extremely difficult, but, nevertheless, we should do our level best to achieve it. If Conrad and Libby's respective beliefs about abortion are such that they are extremely prone to being attributed with far more positive epistemic status than they actually enjoy, then it looks like the intellectually humble thing for both of them to do is to carefully reflect on the positive epistemic status of their beliefs to guard (as best they can) against intellectual vice.

But what if, after honest and careful reflection, they both find that, by their best reckoning, they *are* accurately tracking the positive epistemic status of their respective beliefs? What if the evidence they are considering is equivocal? What's the intellectually humble thing to do *then*? To quote Catherine Elgin (2010):

> The serious difficulty comes with persistent disagreement, where no easy or obvious resolution is available. The evidence is equivocal. The evidence class contains misleaders, but there is no consensus about which the misleaders are. Should opponents suspend judgment in these cases too? Suppose two paleontologists, Jack and Jill, are epistemic peers who disagree

about the fate of the Neanderthals. Jack believes that Neanderthals were an evolutionary dead end. Unable to compete, they simply died out. Jill believes that Neanderthals evolved into later hominids whose descendants are alive today. Because the issue is complex and the evidence is equivocal, they come to different conclusions about it. What should they (and we) make of their disagreement? In particular, should the fact that an epistemic peer disagrees with Jack have any effect on the epistemological status of his belief? Should Jack's knowledge of that fact have any effect? (pp. 53–54)

Perhaps, looking at the VICIOUS DISAGREEMENT case, Conrad can non-culpably attribute his conservative stance toward abortion with a high degree of positive epistemic status. And perhaps Libby can non-culpably attribute her liberal stance toward abortion with a high degree of positive epistemic status, too. Again, what's the intellectually humble thing to do *then*?

Opinions diverge on an answer—depending, as we've suggested, on what intellectual vice we most want to avoid. On the one hand, some philosophers have argued that, when disagreeing with an epistemic peer, we should be willing to revise (or perhaps give up on) our relevant beliefs—to do otherwise, to be unwilling to revise our beliefs and to disregard the divergent opinions of our peers, seems profoundly dogmatic and arrogant. On the other hand, however, other philosophers have argued that, when faced with peer disagreement, there are times when we should be willing to hold our epistemic ground—to do otherwise, to give up on our carefully formed beliefs in the face of peer disagreement, seems, at least in many cases, irresolute and epistemically ineffectual. As Elgin (2010) puts it:

The choices we have entertained are between moderating one's views and standing firm—roughly, between being spineless and being stubborn. Epistemic agents who moderate their beliefs in the face of disagreement seem spineless, abandoning their convictions as soon as a serious challenge appears on the scene. Resolute epistemic agents seem stubborn, simply insisting that there must be something wrong with their opponent's reasoning, since there is plainly nothing wrong with their own. (pp. 57–58)

But we're not just trying to avoid vices like intellectual arrogance, stubbornness, spinelessness, and intellectual diffidence; we want to find the *virtuous* thing to do! What could that be?

Elgin has us consider a case from Peter van Inwagen's (1999) "It is Wrong Everywhere and Always, for Anyone to Believe Anything upon Insufficient Evidence," which highlights van Inwagen's persistent, intractable disagreement with David Lewis:

DAVID LEWIS PROBLEM: David Lewis believed that infinitely many possible worlds exist, each of them just as real as the actual world. There is no denying that he believed this. Moreover, there is no denying that he was incredibly smart, philosophically gifted, and intellectually responsible. He examined the arguments for and against his position with enormous care. It is no false modesty for me to say that David Lewis was a far better philosopher than I am. Nevertheless, I think he was wrong. I cannot refute his position; it is admirably well defended. But, despite Lewis's intelligence and arguments, I do not believe that there exist real possible worlds, consisting of material objects and inaccessible from the actual world. I believe that the only world is the actual world. I think that my belief is reasonable. But David Lewis thought otherwise. He was not my epistemological peer; he was my epistemological superior. So should I not revise my opinion to agree with him? After all, if a knowledgeable physicist tells me that, despite what I think, electrons are not material particles, but clouds of energy, I revise my belief to accord with hers. So in some cases, at least, it seems epistemically reasonable to defer to my epistemic superiors. Is my disagreement with Lewis different? (Elgin, 2010, p. 58)

What's van Inwagen's response? That Lewis must be, somehow, mistaken. He can't point to any fault in Lewis's argument, but he nevertheless holds that it has to be wrong. To quote van Inwagen (1999):

> I suppose my best guess is that I enjoy some sort of philosophical insight [with respect to these issues] that, for all his merits, is somehow denied to Lewis. And this would have to be an insight that is incommunicable—at least I don't know how to communicate it—for I have done all that I can to communicate it to Lewis, and he has understood perfectly everything I have said, and he has not come to share my conclusions. (p. 274)

But there is a real worry that such a response is deeply unsatisfying. But as we've already noted, it seems like giving up, and following Lewis in his modal realism seems "excessively open-minded" (Elgin, 2010, p. 59). But, to just dig in our heels and declare that Lewis must somehow be wrong about his unusual (albeit extremely well defended) view seems arrogant and shockingly dogmatic.

But Elgin (2010) thinks that the DAVID LEWIS PROBLEM can help us see a possible solution to this dilemma. As she explains:

> [Despite] the fact that Lewis's position is brilliantly constructed, admirably defended, and beautifully argued, I find it incredible. I simply cannot believe it. Since "ought" implies "can," that I cannot believe it entails that it is not the case that I ought to believe it. And that I cannot believe that it might be true entails that it is not the case that I should suspend belief or lower my degree of belief that the only real world is the actual world. It is philosophically interesting and perhaps troubling that a position I find utterly incredible admits of such a strong defense. But my belief in a unique world is not in jeopardy. (pp. 59–60)

Traditionally, the dilemma posed by disagreement has been put in terms of what we should do in light of peer disagreement. Should we revise or otherwise withhold our belief, which might seem spineless? Or should we remain steadfast and assume the irrationality of our interlocutor, which might seem dogmatic and arrogant? According to Elgin (2010), the dilemma is misconceived. "Ought" implies "can" and, according to Elgin, if we can't help but follow the evidence or reason (or other epistemic considerations), then making demands regarding what we should or shouldn't do when faced with disagreement is "wrong-headed" (p. 61). By Elgin's lights, such debates "are like debates about whether I should be less than 6 feet tall. I do not have any choice" (p. 61).

Such an approach to disagreement seems to work in cases like the DAVID LEWIS PROBLEM, because it seems right to say that, no matter the evidence, we simply cannot bring ourselves to be modal realists. But does such an approach generalize more broadly? After all, as Elgin (2010) points out: "That there are infinitely many real possible worlds is incredible; that the Neanderthals were an evolutionary dead end seems not to be" (p. 60). According to Elgin (2010), such an approach *does* generalize. As she explains:

> Belief is responsive to evidence. Given a body of evidence, there is no choice about what to believe. So, even if it is not a priori incredible that the Neanderthals were an evolutionary dead end, when Jill surveys the evidence she finds it incredible, given that evidence, that the Neanderthals were an evolutionary dead end. In light of the evidence, she cannot believe it. Different epistemic agents might assess the evidence differently and so come to different beliefs. But this is not a matter of choice. They come to different beliefs because the evidence affects them differently.

Belief is not voluntary. Belief aims at truth in the sense that a belief is defective if its content is not true. If believing were something we could do or refrain from doing at will, the connection to truth would be severed. If Jack could believe that Neanderthals were an evolutionary dead end just because he wanted to, then his believing that Neanderthals were an evolutionary dead end would not amount to his thinking that "Neanderthals were an evolutionary dead end" is true. For nothing about the fate of the Neanderthals is affected by what he wants. (p. 60)

So the idea that we can't help but follow our evidence (again, broadly construed) applies, according to Elgin, generally to all cases of peer disagreement. Elgin uses the DAVID LEWIS PROBLEM to highlight the fact that sometimes we can't help but believe what we believe in light of the evidence, to construct a general strategy for solving the dilemma posed by peer disagreement.

While it might make a lot of sense to apply Elgin's solution to the DAVID LEWIS PROBLEM to extreme cases—perhaps Libby and Conrad can't help but have their respective beliefs about abortion—we might wonder if such a solution completely generalizes as Elgin suggests. While Elgin's proposal might be extremely useful in understanding the most intractable, persistent disagreements—disagreements about morality, politics, and religion being archetypal—we might wonder if it's really always the case that belief is *always* involuntary. After all, it certainly seems like *sometimes* people purposefully ignore evidence or believe things despite lacking evidence.[12] We can easily imagine cases—and probably even concrete examples—where someone doggedly refuses to change their belief even when presented with excellent evidence to the contrary. Such a person would be an arrogant jerk. And we can easily imagine cases—and probably even concrete examples—where someone changed their belief despite lacking sufficient evidence. Such a person would be spineless and intellectually diffident. Often, beliefs are and should be responsive to truth, reason, and evidence—and this accounts for the connection between belief and truth—but sometimes, as any cursory glance of the empirical literature regarding heuristics and biases can tell you, they simply aren't.

As such, let's grant that in cases like the DAVID LEWIS PROBLEM, we can't help but believe what we believe. And we can even grant that in cases like BORDERLINE CASES and VICIOUS DISAGREEMENT, people often cannot help but believe what they believe. And this is an extremely valuable insight! Some persistent disagreements are not vicious. Sometimes the evidence (broadly construed) is equivocal. And sometimes two people who are doing their level best to understand a complex issue non-culpably come to different conclusions. People can firmly disagree about a given point and be intellectually humble. But if we generalize this point too far, then we seem to be left with an impoverished sense of epistemic responsibility and culpability. If belief is never voluntary, if our beliefs are always beholden to reason, evidence etc., then we're not open to epistemic praise or blame. It seems like the only sort of assessment we can make about our responses to disagreement is the same sort of assessments we make about other things outside of our control. As Elgin (2010) notes: "If belief is not subject to direct voluntary control, then assessing someone's reaction to disagreement is similar to assessing the weather. 'It is (or is not) regrettable that Jack suspended belief' is like 'It is (or is not) regrettable that it rained on the parade'" (p. 61). But that seems to preclude the possibility of anyone being intellectually arrogant or intellectually diffident. For example, assuming that culpability requires control, it's not easy to see how anyone could *culpably* fail to accurately track the positive epistemic status of his or her beliefs. It's not clear how, on Elgin's view, anyone could be intellectually vicious. But insofar as we have good theoretical and empirical reason to think that people do sometimes ignore reason, evidence, etc., and that people do sometimes believe on insufficient evidence, then we shouldn't accept Elgin's assumption that *all* belief is involuntary.

In the previous section, we suggested that some cases of peer disagreement are intractable because they involve beliefs that are so extremely personal, consequential, and intimate that they are all to prone to intellectual vice (cases like VICIOUS DISAGREEMENT). But what Elgin's suggestion helps us see is that sometimes people can't help believing what they believe. And while we might suggest that people can sometimes ignore evidence or believe on insufficient evidence, sometimes—perhaps especially in cases that involve beliefs that are extremely personal, consequential, and intimate—people can follow the evidence and come to different conclusions. Sometimes, "reasons favoring each side of a dispute are sparse or exceedingly delicate, or the evidence is equivocal, or each side can solve important common problems that the other cannot," and so people can sometimes non-culpably land on different sides of a debate (Elgin, 2010, p. 67). Sometimes—perhaps especially with beliefs that are extremely personal, consequential, and intimate—people cannot help but believe what they believe, since they might find the denial of their belief entirely incredible. As such, it seems wrong-headed to ask, "What should we *do* when faced with such disagreement?" since we might not be able to *do* anything. In these cases, our beliefs, it seems, are out of our immediate control.

The most, it seems, that we can do in such cases is influence our belief formation indirectly. As Elgin (2010) explains:

> Since beliefs are not voluntary, an epistemic agent cannot, even through judicious assessment, bring it about that she retains, or lowers her degree of belief, or suspends belief in the face of a disagreement. She may, however, be able to affect her responses indirectly. Pascal recognizes this in his discussion of the wager. He does not think that one could come to believe that God exists simply by appreciating that it would be prudent to believe that God exists. But he thinks that appreciating that it would be prudent to believe that God exists gives a person reason to put himself in a position to improve his prospects of acquiring the belief that God exists. By engaging in religious practices, interacting with religious people, and avoiding irreligious people and situations, Pascal maintains, a person maximizes his prospects of being moved by factors that foster the belief that God exists. Education has a similar effect. By learning about the cognitive force of

evidence, argument, and expertise, students can be put in a position to be
moved by considerations of one sort or another. And, as both Pascal and the
educators recognize, epistemic agents can learn to appreciate why it might
be worthwhile to maximize their prospects of forming, retaining, revising,
and rejecting beliefs of different kinds. (pp. 62–63)

Perhaps, then, being intellectually humble not only means accurately tracking
the positive epistemic status of our beliefs but also trying to "position" ourselves
to do so. Perhaps part of what determines what we can *non-culpably* take to be
the positive epistemic status of our beliefs is our willingness to put ourselves in
positions where we can be the most receptive to the truth. Perhaps, when faced
with peer disagreement, all we can do is reflect on our belief, do our level best
to make sure that it enjoys the positive epistemic status that we think it enjoys,
and try to position ourselves (through education, for example) to make sure
this reflection is of the highest quality we can muster.

The difficult question, now, is how do we know what "positions" will
best allow us to accurately track the positive epistemic status of our beliefs?
How can we position ourselves so as to be receptive to the truth? How can
we improve our ability to accurately reflect on the positive epistemic status
we take our beliefs to merit? This, as Elgin (2010) points out, is a matter of
"cognitive character formation" and, Elgin notes that "the question then is
what sort of character we ought to form. There is, of course, no guarantee
that our beliefs will respond as we hope they will. But by subjecting ourselves
to the right influences, we maximize our prospects" (p. 63). So, what sort of
character ought we form? The answer, we're afraid, lies outside of the purview
of intellectual humility. *Here, we think, intellectual humility needs the help of
wisdom and courage.*

As we noted in the previous section, we suggested that intellectual humility
can give us a framework for understanding when and why vicious, intractable
disagreements occur. Some disagreements—especially disagreements about

religion, morality, and politics—can be extremely intractable because they involve beliefs that are so personal and intimate that we are prone to ascribe to them far more positive epistemic status than they actually enjoy. What we wanted to know in this section, however, is what we *should do* about this. Drawing from Catherine Elgin's work, we're seeing that perhaps sometimes there's nothing we *can do* about it. Some beliefs just seem completely incredible to us. Conrad, from VICIOUS DISAGREEMENT, presumably simply can't help but believe that abortions should be illegal, except in a strict set of cases. Likewise, Libby presumably simply can't help but believe that abortions should be legal and readily available to women everywhere. While we might ask that Conrad and Libby treat each other with mutual respect and decency, we can't say that they "ought" to give up their respective beliefs, since "ought" implies "can" and that's something they simply can't do. The respective cognitive characters of Conrad and Libby have shaped the positive epistemic status they assign to their respective beliefs. So perhaps, all we can hope for in these cases of vicious disagreement is the right sort of cognitive character, which might improve our ability to carefully reflect on our beliefs and the positive epistemic status that they actually enjoy. The question, of course, is what sort of cognitive character is the right one (or the right sort of one). But, again, determining the answer, unfortunately (though understandably), requires more than intellectual humility—it takes, we propose, wisdom and courage (and maybe even some luck).

Such a result may not be entirely satisfying. But persistent, intractable disagreements are persistent and longstanding for a reason: they don't afford easy solutions. We need to accurately track the positive epistemic status of our beliefs and to honestly reflect on our tracking. But what is more, we need wisdom and courage, we've suggested, to judge what sort of cognitive character best affords honest reflection and a responsiveness to the truth. But that doesn't tell us what to do. And clichéd though it may be, perhaps there's not much we can do in such cases but "agree to disagree."

But let's conclude by noting that there is real value in disagreement, even persistent, intractable disagreement. As Elgin (2010) explains:

Consider the disagreement between materialists and dualists in the philosophy of mind. Materialists accept that whatever is is material; dualists accept that there are irreducibly mental entities or processes as well as irreducibly physical entities and processes. Each side can point to some conspicuous explanatory successes. But each side faces serious difficulties. Either there are outstanding problems that it cannot solve, or the solutions it offers seem inelegant, strained, and ad hoc. What is worse, the serious problems that each faces seem straightforwardly handled by the other. The dualist has a problem explaining the causal link between the mental and the material; the materialist can simply maintain that the connection is straightforward physical causality. The materialist has a problem accounting for qualia and what-is-it-like-ishness; the dualist takes these features to be distinctive marks of the mental. This is all familiar.

[As] Philip Kitcher argues, it is not obvious that our cognitive objectives are best achieved by everyone's marching in lock step to the same conclusion. When the reasons favoring each side of a dispute are sparse or exceedingly delicate, or the evidence is equivocal, or each side can solve important common problems that the other cannot, it may be better for the epistemic community as a whole that some of its members continue to accept each position. In that case, materialists can in good conscience continue to accept materialism. Dualists can in good conscience continue to accept dualism. Agnostics can suspend judgment. Each group then can draw on a different range of commitments for premises in their reasoning and as a basis for their actions. By developing their positions, they put them to the test. Arguably, the only way we will ever find out whether materialism can solve the hard problem of consciousness is for materialists wholeheartedly to accept materialism and push it to its limits. (pp. 67–68)

When we think about practical applications of intellectual humility, we think of how intellectual humility might speak to how we handle disagreement—especially disagreement amongst peers. Again, when we think about intellectual arrogance, we often think of someone who is unflinchingly dogmatic and unwilling to compromise on their belief in the face of dissent, disagreement, and defeaters. And when we think about intellectual diffidence, we often think of someone who is far too easily persuaded to give up on (or reduce their credence in) his/her beliefs. *How we handle disagreement seems to be at the heart of intellectual humility.* But sometimes the right way to handle disagreement isn't to revise your belief or simply dig in your heels. Sometimes the right way to handle disagreement is to reflect carefully on your own views and try to put yourself in a position to be receptive to the truth—to be receptive to how accurately you are tracking the positive epistemic status of your beliefs. Sometimes the only thing you can do is dialogue with your disagreeing peers, and challenge each other toward progress.[13]

10

What does intellectual humility tell us about religion?

In the previous chapter, we discussed how intellectual humility might give us a framework for making sense of what we should do in the face of peer disagreement—disagreement with an interlocutor who is just as intelligent, rational, and informed. We suggested that, in some cases, being intellectually humble means being willing to revise one's belief in the face of such disagreement. But we also suggested that, in other cases, intellectual humility can be compatible with an unwillingness to revise one's belief; indeed, it can be compatible with dogmatism. But this framework also helped us understand *why* some disagreements are extremely intractable—those involving beliefs that are so personal, so consequential, and so intimate that *they are particularly and notoriously prone to intellectual vice*. In particular, they are prone to being attributed (whether consciously or subconsciously) with almost unmatched positive epistemic status even when it is ultimately unmerited. There are some cases of disagreement that are so intractable, it seems almost impossible to agree on how much positive epistemic status the given belief actually enjoys.

And, arguably, no disagreements are as prone to intellectual vice as religious disagreements. The need for intellectual humility is perhaps most pressing when it comes to debates and disagreements surrounding religious commitments. All too often, when faced with difficult religious questions, people are prone to dismissing and marginalizing dissent. As we said at the beginning of this book, around the world, religious debates are incredibly polarizing, and, in many parts of the world, extremely dangerous. And whether it's Christian fundamentalism, Islamic jihadism, or militant atheism, religious dialogue often remains tinted by a terrifying and dehumanizing arrogance, dogma, and ignorance.[1]

So, let's agree; we need intellectual humility when it comes to religious beliefs and commitments. But what does this mean? Does intellectual humility preclude the possibility of firm religious commitments? Does intellectual humility require religious beliefs to be held only loosely? In the first section of this chapter, we want to apply some of the lessons we learned in the previous chapter on the philosophical import of disagreement to the specific case of religious disagreements. We want to explore what intellectual humility can tell us with regard to religion and religious beliefs.[2] And while it initially seems quite plausible that a commitment to intellectual humility will lead to being more circumspect about one's religious beliefs in the face of religious diversity and pluralism, we will argue for a claim that might seem initially counterintuitive: that it is at least *possible* for intellectual humility to be compatible with religious dogmatism; that intellectual humility does not *necessarily* preclude extremely firm religious commitments, even in the face of widespread disagreement.

But such a conclusion might be deeply unsettling. After all, in the opening paragraphs of this book, we highlighted some of the dangers of dogmatism; as such, we might worry that allowing for even the conceptual possibility of virtuous religious dogmatism is an open door to the worst kinds of arrogance. Even allowing for the possibility of religious dogmatism, so the worry goes, allows for Christian fundamentalists, Islamic jihadists, and militant atheists to claim that they're the actualization of that possibility, that their close-mindedness and militancy are somehow not only permissible but virtuous. Call this the *blank check to evil worry*. In the final section, we will review some of the lessons we've learned in the previous chapters of this book to try to assuage this worry, and perhaps give a fuller account of intellectual humility by way of addressing the complex case of religious belief.

§1: Intellectually humble religious dogmatism?

One of the biggest problems facing religious disagreement and debate is the prevalence of intellectual vice—specifically intellectual arrogance. All too often, the most vocal advocates of a given religious (or anti-religious) perspective are also the most viciously dogmatic, close-minded, and unflinchingly adamant in their views—attributing far more positive epistemic status to their beliefs than they usually merit. And such widespread vice all too often causes religious debates and disagreements to be completely intractable. In contrast, if *intellectual humility* were more widespread, then advocates of various religious (and anti-religious) perspectives would better track the positive epistemic status of their religious beliefs—when a given belief enjoys a lot of positive epistemic status and when a belief doesn't.

But when faced with a religious disagreement—especially disagreements with interlocutors who are equally familiar with the relevant data and just as intelligent, clever, rational, etc.—does intellectual humility oblige us to compromise on our religious beliefs, or otherwise revise them? We might easily think so. Given the tremendous religious diversity in the world—with an abundance of informed, intelligent, clever, rational people espousing almost every position—how could anyone be sure that *their* religious (or anti-religious) beliefs are right when so many able people disagree with them?[3] Consider once again the case from Hilary Kornblith's (2010) work, "Belief in the Face of Controversy":

VIRTUOUS REVISION: [Suppose] that you and I go out to a restaurant with a number of friends. After a large meal, the check comes and we agree to split the bill evenly. You and I are each quite good at mental arithmetic. I take a look at the bill and figure out what each person owes, and I put my share in the middle of the table. You look at the bill and figure out what each person owes and put your share in the middle of the table, and then we notice that we have put in different amounts. We are each well aware of the other's mathematical abilities, and we are each convinced of each other's honesty. At least one of us has made a mistake. It would be unreasonable for me to conclude that, since, one of us has made a mistake, it must be you. The reasonable thing to do in this situation, and surely what most people in fact do in this situation, is suspend belief. We each go back to the bill and try to recompute the proper share. (p. 32)

We might think that religious beliefs are relevantly like VIRTUOUS REVISION. We might think that the intellectually humble thing to do when faced with religious disagreement—given that it would be unreasonable and vicious of us to think that our dissenting interlocutors somehow made a mistake and not ourselves—is to suspend belief. And since it's not obvious that we can just recompute (as in VIRTUOUS REVISION) *religious* beliefs, perhaps suspended belief is all we can reasonably hope for. There are an almost unparalleled array of religious beliefs—indeed, religious beliefs that are mutually incompatible—so we might easily assume that the virtuous stance when it comes to religion is *agnosticism*.

That said, as we saw in the previous chapter, there are cases of disagreement—even disagreement with our intellectual peers—where it seems as though we should stick to our proverbial guns, stand our epistemic ground, be dogmatically inflexible. Consider again the following case:

VIRTUOUS DOGMATISM: Jill is a philosopher, working away in an office, when one of her colleagues, Jack, stops by to chat. Now, Jill considers Jack to be her epistemic peer—she has no reason to suspect that Jack is in anyway less intelligent, educated, or clever than herself.

Nevertheless, this day Jack surprises Jill with a shocking revelation. Jack confides in Jill that he has recently stopped believing that 2 + 2 = 4. Now, if Jill knows anything, she knows that 2 + 2 = 4. Does Jack's disagreement on this force Jill to reconsider her beliefs about basic arithmetic? Seemingly not. To all intents and purposes, Jill simply *cannot* give up on or significantly modify such beliefs. Such beliefs are too important and too consequential.

While legitimate peer disagreement in cases like VIRTUOUS REVISION reasonably force the interlocutors to suspend, modify, or revise their respective beliefs, we can presumably agree that such a result does not seem virtuous in cases like VIRTUOUS DOGMATISM, in cases where the disagreement is over beliefs that are too precious, dear, central, foundational, etc., to revise or give up (see Fumerton, 2010, pp. 95–96). In cases like VIRTUOUS DOGMATISM, a dogmatic inflexibility seems virtuous. Even though our interlocutor in such cases is, by hypothesis, an epistemic peer, any claim to peerhood is seemingly lost once it becomes clear that they are sincerely and genuinely at odds with beliefs that are so central, so foundational, so consequential. As we noted earlier, being sincerely and genuinely at odds with such beliefs is crazy. And when an epistemic peer goes crazy, at least within a certain domain, they are no longer a genuine peer within that domain. In cases like VIRTUOUS DOGMATISM, dogmatism—an uncompromising stance regarding one's beliefs—seems entirely reasonable, seems virtuous.

In both cases, VIRTUOUS REVISION and VIRTUOUS DOGMATISM, the protagonists could easily be intellectually humble, at least according to the doxastic account of intellectual humility. In both cases, the protagonists could be (and let's assume are) reliably tracking the positive epistemic status of their respective beliefs. This is an important realization to come to, because it shows us that being intellectually humble doesn't necessarily mean being conciliatory. *Someone can be intellectually virtuous, intellectually humble, without suspending belief in the face of peer disagreement; someone can be intellectually humble while being dogmatic and uncompromising in one's beliefs.* The question is this: Are *religious* disagreements more like VIRTUOUS REVISION, such that the given religious beliefs should be suspended, or are religious disagreements more like VIRTUOUS DOGMATISM, such that religious beliefs can be held with a virtuous dogmatism?

While there is no easy or universal answer to this question—belief in supralapsarianism, say, is presumably in no way on par with the belief that God exists—I think we can make the case that some religious beliefs *could be* more akin to a belief that 2 + 2 = 4 (as in VIRTUOUS DOGMATISM) than to a belief in one's share of a restaurant bill (as in VIRTUOUS REVISION). I think we can make the case that some firm, unwavering religious commitment could be compatible with intellectual humility.[4] What's the salient difference between the relevant, respective beliefs in VIRTUOUS REVISION and VIRTUOUS DOGMATISM? We suggested that it is the positive epistemic status each belief enjoys. The belief that 2 + 2 = 4 (in VIRTUOUS DOGMATISM) presumably enjoys nearly as much positive epistemic status as any belief possibly can. As such, whatever the epistemic import of peer disagreement, such disagreement cannot and should not shift one' confidence in a belief like 2 + 2 = 4. In contrast, the belief based on a casual glance at a restaurant bill (as in VIRTUOUS REVISION) surely does not enjoy anywhere near the same level of positive epistemic status; surely such a belief could and should be upset by peer disagreement.

Some religious beliefs—for example, beliefs like "God exists"—arguably enjoy a substantial amount of positive epistemic status. And, importantly, this positive epistemic status arguably doesn't need to come from theistic proofs or arguments. Just as we can "see" that 2 + 2 = 4, many philosophers of religion (reformed epistemologists, in particular) would want to claim that we can just "see" that God exists. Most of us don't believe 2 + 2 = 4 because of any arguments (though presumably we could produce some if need be); instead, however, we believe $2 + 2 = 4$ just because we see that it's true. In the same way, perhaps theists can claim to believe that God exists because they just see that it's true; no doubt, arguments could be given, if need be, but for at least some theists, that's not what the belief's positive epistemic status rests on. *And if all this is right, then the religious belief that God exists might just be the sort of thing that someone could believe with some virtuous dogmatism, with unwavering epistemic commitment, while remaining intellectually humble.*

But wait. *Surely, all this depends on just how much positive epistemic status religious beliefs really do enjoy!* The value of various religious and anti-religious arguments is *highly* contested. And, of course, atheists and agnostics are going to be *very* pessimistic regarding anyone's claim to just "see" that God exists. While intellectual humility can highlight that it is theoretically possible to be in a position where one could be virtuously dogmatic in one's religious (or anti-religious) beliefs, it is a tricky business knowing who is actually in such a position! And as we saw in the previous chapter, intellectual humility can also help us understand *why* this is so tricky, why religious debates are often so intractable.

Intellectual humility, according to DA‴, was assessed along two axes: how much positive epistemic status a given belief enjoys, and how much positive epistemic status a given agent *thinks* it enjoys. Recall Figure 10.1 from the first chapter:

As such, if a belief enjoys only a very marginal amount of positive epistemic status (perhaps as in VIRTUOUS REVISION), then intellectual humility requires that a given agent reliably track that modest positive epistemic status accordingly. In contrast, if a given belief enjoys a tremendous amount of positive epistemic status (as in VIRTUOUS DOGMATISM), then the intellectually humble agent will value such a belief—tracking its positive epistemic status—accordingly. Attributing (whether consciously or subconsciously) too much

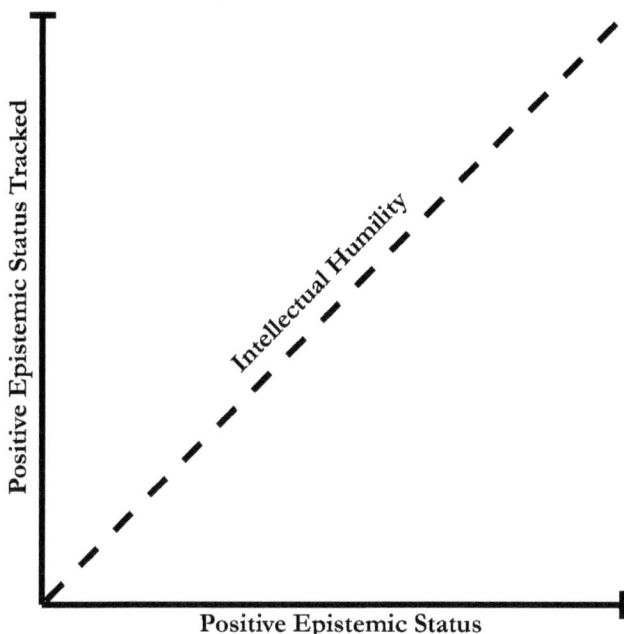

FIGURE 10.1 *The Doxastic Account of Intellectual Humility.*

positive epistemic status to a given belief would be vicious (intellectually arrogant, upper left-hand corner of Figure 10.1), and attributing too little would be vicious as well (intellectual diffidence, lower right-hand corner of Figure 10.1).

As we suggested earlier, part of what makes religious disagreements so intractable is that they involve beliefs that are extremely personal, consequential, and intimate, beliefs that are all too prone to being attributed with a tremendous amount of positive epistemic status even when they shouldn't be. In cases like VIRTUOUS REVISION and VIRTUOUS DOGMATISM, the protagonists roughly attribute the positive epistemic status that their respective beliefs merit—they were on the trajectory of intellectual humility. Some beliefs, however, are all too prone to intellectual vice, where the belief is taken to enjoy far more positive epistemic status than it actually does. Consider again the case of VICIOUS DISAGREEMENT:

> VICIOUS DISAGREEMENT: Christy is a committed Christian. Most of her friends are Christians. She frequents Christian blogs and websites. And she is part of a broader Christian community. Abbey, however, is an atheist. Most of her friends are atheists. She frequents pro-atheist blogs and websites. And Abbey is part of a broader atheist community. Christy is a theist and believes in the authority of the Bible on moral topics. Abbey does not; she is quite convinced that there is no god, and she believes the Bible has no special moral authority whatsoever. Christy and Abbey are equally intelligent, clever, and discerning. Nevertheless, when Christy and Abbey discuss their differences in opinion and review all of the arguments both for and against their respective positions, they both remain unmoved.

Again, for beliefs that are extremely personal, consequential, and intimate—beliefs regarding religion being archetypal—there can be a lot at stake.[5] The respective religious (and anti-religious) beliefs of Christy and Abbey in RELIGIOUS DISAGREEMENT, for example, deeply affect how they each view the world, what they read with the most attentiveness, who their closest friends are, and perhaps even whom they trust the most.[6] Indeed, their religious beliefs are so near and so dear to them that giving them up could be almost as intellectually cataclysmic as giving up the belief that $2 + 2 = 4$.

Christy and Abbey take their respective religious beliefs to have a lot of positive epistemic status. Christy may very well think that her belief merits her strong commitment to Christianity, but, then again, Abbey may very well think that her belief merits *her* strong commitment to atheism. Additionally, given the positive epistemic status Christy attributes to Christianity, she presumably thinks that Abby's commitment to atheism is unmerited. Likewise, given the positive epistemic status Abbey attributes to atheism, she presumably thinks that Christy's firm commitment to Christianity is unmerited.[7] Presumably, at least one of the interlocutors in cases like RELIGIOUS DISAGREEMENT is not intellectually humble—attributing more positive epistemic status to their religious beliefs than they merit. *The problem, of course, is determining who the culprit is.* Christy may, with regret, think that Abbey is somehow intellectually misguided, perhaps chalking her strong dissent to the noetic effects of sin in the world. Likewise, Abbey may, with regret, think that Christy is actually the intellectually misguided one, perhaps chalking up her strong dissent as indicative of an intellectual crutch or reality-distorting indoctrination.

In VIRTUOUS DOGMATISM, the interlocutors are at odds about what they ought to believe regarding basic arithmetic. In VICTUOUS REVISION, the interlocutors are at odds about what they ought to believe regarding what each one owes on a restaurant bill. In both of these cases, however, we can generally agree on how to handle them. The protagonist in VIRTUOUS DOGMATISM should stick to her proverbial guns and continue to believe that 2 + 2 = 4. The interlocutors in VICTUOUS REVISION should withhold their beliefs until they can get a second glance at the bill. Cases like VICIOUS DISAGREEMENT, however, are far more intractable. Such cases involve beliefs that are so personal, so consequential, and so intimate that *they are particularly and notoriously prone to intellectual vice*; in particular, they are prone to being attributed with almost unmatched positive epistemic status even when it is ultimately unmerited—*they are particularly and notoriously prone to being off the trajectory of intellectual humility.*

And this makes our disagreements as to what positive epistemic status religious beliefs merit vast. All too often, we simply cannot agree on what the relevant data, arguments, evidence, intuitions, merit; and all too often, we attribute any intellectual vice to our interlocutors rather than ourselves. More so than any of the cases considered previously, we cannot agree on what one ought to believe.[8] As we've suggested, it's theoretically possible to be in a position where dogmatism regarding one's religious beliefs (particularly with potentially basic beliefs like "God exists") is virtuous; however, the proposed model of intellectual humility helps us see that it is difficult to discern when anyone is actually in such a position.

To be sure, in their forthcoming essay, "Intellectual Humility and Religion: A Psychological Perspective," Joshua Hook and Don Davis (in press) come to a different conclusion. Quite helpfully, they give us three empirically informed reasons why religious beliefs and convictions can be so prone to dogmatism: First, religious beliefs are often epistemically foundational and "load-bearing" for large swaths of people's beliefs about themselves and the world around them (call this the *load-bearing reason*). Second, religious beliefs often serve as signals of group loyalty and membership—signals that regulate whom we listen to, whom we trust (call this the *group-loyalty reason*). And third, religious beliefs are often taken to be most valuable when held with certainty (call this the *assumed certainty reason*). That said, however, Hook and Davis (in press) seem to think that this propensity toward religious dogmatism is incompatible with intellectual humility. While we would agree that religious dogmatism *often* leads to intellectual arrogance (assuming, of course, that most religious views are mutually exclusive), we want to stress that this isn't *necessarily* the case.[9] As we argued above, there is theoretical space for virtuous religious dogmatism.

Consider the belief that 2 + 2 = 4 and the belief that the holocaust really did happen. Both of these beliefs seem to bear the same hallmarks of dogmatism as those identified by Hook and Davis in religious beliefs. Both of these beliefs are going to play an important role within the belief structure we use when trying to understand ourselves and the world (load-bearing reason). If $2 + 2 \neq 4$, then my entire understanding of mathematics, science, logic, and rationality (and everything I apply it to, including my understanding of self) would seem to be drastically undermined. Likewise, if the holocaust really didn't happen, then my entire understanding of history, my trust of others, and the role of authority would be drastically undermined. Additionally, we're guessing most of us would be inclined to alienate anyone who seriously denied that 2 + 2 = 4 or that the holocaust happened (group-loyalty reason). And I suspect most of us would agree that these sorts of beliefs really should be held with an extremely high degree of confidence (the assumed certainty reason). Does this mean that my extremely high confidence that 2 + 2 = 4 and that the holocaust really happened is somehow intellectually vicious? Absolutely not. These sorts of beliefs *should* be held dogmatically, and, we'd like to suggest, that such dogmatism is perfectly compatible with intellectual virtue, with intellectual humility.

And as we noted earlier, it may very well be the case that some religious beliefs are also compatible with virtuous dogmatism. Just as we can "see" that 2 + 2 = 4, say, many philosophers of religion would want to claim that we can just "see" that God exists. And if all this is right, then some religious beliefs might just be the sort of things—like the belief that 2 + 2 = 4—that we can believe with a virtuous dogmatism, with unwavering epistemic commitment, while remaining intellectually humble.

But someone who wants to resist the claim that intellectual humility is conceptually compatible with religious dogmatism might very well point out some salient differences between beliefs like 2 + 2 = 4, the holocaust occurred, and religious beliefs. In particular, such a person could highlight the fact that almost every rational and sufficiently informed person believes that 2 + 2 = 4 and that the holocaust occurred, while, in contrast, there is very little agreement when it comes to religious matters.[10] Rational and sufficiently informed people *can* and *do* disagree wildly regarding the vast majority of religious claims and beliefs. So perhaps it is not so much the fact that religious beliefs are taken to be load-bearing, group-loyalty identifiers that are prone to enjoy assumed certainty that makes them incompatible with intellectual humility. Perhaps it's those features *in conjunction with widespread disagreement*—a phenomenon that Hook and Davis (in press) seem rightly concerned about—that forces such religious dogmatism away from intellectual humility.

But then again, perhaps there are cases where dogmatism is permissible even in the face of widespread disagreement. Consider the following case from Alvin Plantinga's (2000) *Warranted Christian Belief*:

> FRISIAN FLAG: The police haul me in, accusing me of a serious crime: stealing your Frisian flag again. At the police station, I learn that the mayor claims to have seen me lurking around your back door at the time (yesterday midafternoon) the crime occurred; I am known to resent you. I had means, motive, and opportunity; furthermore there have been other such sordid episodes in my past. However, I recall very clearly spending the entire afternoon on a solitary hike near Mount Baker. (p. 450)

The protagonist's belief in FRISIAN FLAG that he is not a thief is presumably fairly foundational and epistemically "load-bearing." After all, it would be quite the epistemic blow if it were the case that his distinct memory of hiking near Mount Baker and his distinct lack of memory of stealing a Frisian flag were somehow deceptive. And such a belief could easily be imagined to be central to the protagonist's group identification. Presumably, the protagonist would expect his friends and family to believe him when he said he didn't steal the flag, and presumably he would feel extremely alienated if they didn't, despite his pleading. Finally, the protagonist's clear and distinct memory of hiking near Mount Baker presumably affords him something close to certainty, and such conviction seems perfectly warranted and expected. As such, the protagonist's belief that he didn't steal the flag seems to be a load-bearing, group-loyalty identifier that is assumed to enjoy something close to certainty. And, importantly for our current purposes, this is a belief that most people disagree with him about. Most people, let's assume, who are aware of the information surrounding the protagonist's "means, motive, and opportunity" for purportedly stealing the flag believe that he actually stole it, believe that he is the thief. Does this mean that if the protagonist were to remain steadfast and dogmatic in his insistence that he didn't steal the flag, that he would be guilty of intellectual vice? Surely not! Because he didn't steal the flag, and he *knows* he didn't steal the flag. And so it looks like even a belief that is a load-bearing, group-loyalty identifier that is assumed to enjoy a level of certainty and faces widespread disagreement *can nevertheless be dogmatically held while remaining intellectually virtuous.*

And, again, it's possible that some religious beliefs are like this. Suppose a group of people truly do "see" that God exists and that the convictions of their specific religious tradition are true. Such people, it seems, could be just like the protagonist in FRISIAN FLAG. Their religious beliefs would be load-bearing, group-loyalty identifiers that are assumed to enjoy a level of certainty, even in the face of widespread disagreement; even so, if they really see that God exists, if they *know* that God exists, then it seems as though they can remain dogmatic regarding their religious beliefs and remain intellectually virtuous, even intellectually humble.

So we want to suggest that there is nothing *necessarily* incompatible with intellectual humility and holding to firm religious beliefs that are load-bearing, group-loyalty identifiers that are assumed to enjoy a level of certainty while facing extensive and widespread disagreement. But it is important to note just how *weak* this conclusion is. *We're not suggesting that all instances (or, indeed, any actual instance) of religious dogmatism are compatible with intellectual humility.* Far from it! We are happy to agree that most (if not all) people end up attributing their religious beliefs (including anti-religious beliefs) with far more positive epistemic status than they really deserve; we're happy to agree that most people end up holding their religious beliefs with a degree of intellectual arrogance. Nevertheless, what we want to suggest is that it is at least *possible* to be in a situation where one can be dogmatic about one's religious beliefs while being intellectually humble.

But how can we know if someone is *in* such a situation? Someone might claim to just "see" that a god of a certain sort exists. And someone else might claim to "see" that a very different god exists. How can we tell who's in the right sort of relationship with the truth? That's the trick. That's the rub.[11] And we're notoriously bad at judging these sorts of things. As Wittgenstein (1980) said, "Nothing is so difficult as not deceiving oneself" (p. 34e). So while I think an understanding of intellectual humility can help us appreciate just what is going wrong in cases of intractable, religious disagreements, perhaps it cannot ultimately resolve such disagreements. Personally, we're okay with that. It leaves room for *other* virtues to play their role—virtues like kindness, honesty, and plain old humility.

In the previous chapter, we argued that intellectual humility can give us a framework for understanding both when and why intractable disagreements occur. And we concluded by noting that when faced with such disagreements, sometimes all we can do is try to put ourselves in a position to be receptive to the truth—to develop the right sort of cognitive character that might best allow us to accurately (and honestly) track the positive epistemic status of our beliefs. What's the right sort of cognitive character? That's a key question, and that's where we arguably reach the limits of what intellectual humility can tell us. Knowing what kind of cognitive character we should develop will require more than intellectual humility, it will require wisdom, courage, and maybe even some luck. For the time being, we suggested, the only thing we can do is dialogue with our disagreeing peers, and challenge each other toward mutual edification and progress.

And to be sure, religious disagreements are notoriously intractable, so the conclusions of the previous chapter seem to apply here as well. Following Elgin, sometimes we simply can't change our beliefs; and since "ought" implies "can," sometimes not even the full force of religious pluralism and overwhelming peer disagreement can establish norms that would force us to change our dearly held religious convictions, because the alternative beliefs seem incredible to us. No doubt, and as a matter of fact, sometimes people do completely change their religious beliefs. But there are two things to note in such cases: First, that this often happens precisely in ways that Elgin's account would predict.

A familiar example would be that of the someone who grew up in a Christian home, failed to connect with a Christian community in college, surrounded themselves with non-Christian friends and influences, and slowly walked away from their faith. Arguably, such a change in belief only came about via a slow change in cognitive character—a change that was brought about by changing influences, friendships, and connections. And second, even if/when we can, by sheer dint of effort, give up on our religious beliefs, we've now seen that it's nevertheless conceptually possible to be dogmatic about religious beliefs and remain intellectually humble. Just as we'd want to say that there is nothing wrong with being dogmatic about 2 + 2 = 4 even in the face of disagreement, we've argued that it's at least possible for someone to remain dogmatic about their religious beliefs in the face of disagreement. At first blush, we might think that a commitment to intellectual humility would require agnosticism about religious beliefs; we might think that intellectual humility is incompatible with firm religious commitment. But we've now seen two ways someone might be firmly committed to some specific religious beliefs and yet remain within the bounds of intellectual humility.

§2: The blank check to evil worry

While it might very well seem as if dogmatism is permissible and compatible with intellectual humility when it comes to beliefs regarding basic mathematics—the belief that 2 + 2 = 4, say—it might be deeply troubling to suggest that it's possible to hold a religious belief (or an anti-religious belief) in the same way and not be guilty of intellectual arrogance. After all, almost everyone agrees that 2 + 2 = 4, but there is a significant amount of disagreement when it comes to religion. To be sure, it's worth underscoring again just how weak our thesis has been; all we've claimed is that it is *conceptually possible* to hold firm religious beliefs and yet be intellectually humble. For all that we've said, it could be the case that no one was ever in such a position, that *in practice* firm religious belief *does* preclude intellectual humility.

Nevertheless, we might worry that even allowing for the conceptual possibility of religious dogmatism that isn't guilty of intellectual arrogance might give a blank check to the worst kinds of fundamentalism and pugnacious close-mindedness. Recall the quote we considered at the start of the book by Dr. Jacob Bronowski (1973):

> There are two parts to the human dilemma. One is the belief that the end justifies the means. That push-button philosophy, that deliberate deafness to suffering, has become the monster in the war machine. The other is the betrayal of the human spirit: the assertion of dogma that closes the mind, and turns a nation, a civilization, into a regiment of ghosts—obedient ghosts, or tortured ghosts.
>
> It is said that science will dehumanize people and turn them into numbers. That is false, tragically false. Look for yourself. This is the concentration camp and crematorium at Auschwitz. This is where people were turned into numbers. Into this pond were flushed the ashes of some four million people. And that was not done by gas. It was done by arrogance. It was done by dogma. It was done by ignorance. When people believe that they have absolute knowledge, with no test in reality, this is how they behave. This is what men do when they aspire to the knowledge of gods.
>
> Science is a very human form of knowledge. We are always at the brink of the known, we always feel forward for what is to be hoped. Every judgment in science stands on the edge of error, and is personal. Science is a tribute to what we can know although we are fallible. In the end the words were said by Oliver Cromwell: "I beseech you, in the bowels of Christ, think it possible you may be mistaken."
>
> I owe it as a scientist to my friend Leo Szilard, I owe it as a human being to the many members of my family who died at Auschwitz, to stand here by

the pond as a survivor and a witness. We have to cure ourselves of the itch for absolute knowledge and power. We have to close the distance between the push-button order and the human act. We have to touch people.

We used this quote to spur our study of intellectual humility, and to highlight the world's great need for such a virtue. But now, we might worry that allowing for even the conceptual possibility of virtuous religious dogmatism is allowing for a "deafness to suffering" and "dogma that closes the mind." Even allowing for the possibility of religious dogmatism, so the worry goes, allows for Christian fundamentalists, Islamic jihadists, and militant atheists to claim that they're the actualization of that possibility, that their close-mindedness and militancy are somehow not only permissible but virtuous. Call this the *blank check to evil worry*. In this final section, we will review some of the lessons we've learned in the previous chapters to try to assuage this worry, and perhaps give a fuller account of intellectual humility by way of addressing the complex case of religious belief.

In Chapter 1, after motivating and highlighting our need for intellectual humility, our central aim was to explore what intellectual humility might be. We started by noting that, *prima facie*, humility is the virtuous mean between something like arrogance, on the one hand, and self-deprecation or diffidence, on the other—that the humble person, to put it roughly, doesn't value herself too much (arrogance) nor does she value herself too little (diffidence or self-deprecation). Instead, she thinks of herself as she should—valuing herself, her status amongst her peers, her abilities as she ought. Building off of this extremely simple and basic view of humility, we noted that an intuitive account of intellectual humility seems to follow. We imagined that *intellectual* humility is the virtuous mean between *intellectual* arrogance and *intellectual* diffidence. We imagined that an intellectually humble person, to put it roughly, doesn't overly value her beliefs (intellectual arrogance), nor does she undervalue them (intellectual diffidence). Instead, she values her beliefs as she ought—valuing her beliefs, their epistemic status, her intellectual abilities as she ought. This roughly led to what we called *the doxastic account of intellectual humility*. And in the first chapter, we unpacked and defended this simple, intuitive account of intellectual humility.

To be clear, our aim in the first chapter was *not* to provide anything like a reductive analysis of intellectual humility—we explicitly did not want to try to provide the necessary and jointly sufficient conditions for intellectual humility.[12] As we noted, recent empirical research suggests that intellectual humility might be a multifaceted and multilayered virtue—with moral dimensions, interpersonal dimensions, intrapersonal dimensions, etc. And as such, we conceded that whatever social or moral dimensions the virtue of intellectual humility might have, we will suggest that it needs to be built upon or understood within this basic, doxastic account. We left the door open to further dimensions of intellectual humility that our *doxastic* account might not capture.

A facet of intellectual humility that is perhaps underrepresented in the doxastic account of intellectual humility is a *social* dimension of the virtue. Folk conceptions of intellectual humility certainly track such a dimension in their understanding of intellectual humility, and a number of theorists have rightly, we think, built in social aspects into their accounts of intellectual humility.[13] And there are a couple of ways social components could be highlighted or otherwise incorporated within the doxastic account, which would help assuage the *blank check to evil worry*.

First of all, as we noted, the doxastic account of intellectual humility is arguably already suited to incorporate interpersonal or intrapersonal elements within it. After all, the concept of *positive epistemic status* is an extremely open-ended concept. If intellectual character virtues or social epistemic virtues are included as at least a part of the positive epistemic status at issue (which we think they should be) and if interpersonal and intrapersonal considerations can be incorporated within such virtues (which they often are), then there is a straightforward way for the doxastic account of intellectual humility to account for such dimensions. And if that's right, then the idea that it's conceptually possible for someone to hold strong religious views does not lead to the *blank check to evil worry*. The dangerous, militant religious (and anti-religious) fundamentalisms would presumably fail to track the positive epistemic status of a whole host of social epistemic and character virtues, and as such would fail at intellectual humility. And insofar as having firm religious (or anti-religious) views does not necessarily lead to such a failure, there is nothing about firm religious (or anti-religious) views that necessarily leads to writing a blank check to evil.

But maybe that's not entirely satisfying. Maybe the social failings of religious fundamentalism that are relevant to intellectual humility go beyond what could plausibly fall within the broad category of *positive epistemic status*. That certainly sounds plausible! In that case, another strategy for assuaging the *blank check to evil worry* becomes available. We could satisfy ourselves with the claim that the doxastic account of intellectual humility is merely a necessary condition on intellectual humility. And maybe something else— another condition—needs to be added to it in order to account for these other, social dimensions. And insofar as the militant, religious fundamentalists would fail to meet any plausible social condition on intellectual humility, then they would fail to have intellectual humility. And (i) if, as we've suggested, intellectual humility is compatible with firm religious commitments and (ii) there is nothing about having firm religious commitments that would necessarily violate any plausible social condition on intellectual humility, then we need no longer worry about the *blank check to evil worry*.

And it's worth noting that such a solution is general, and could be applied even if you think an alternative account of intellectual humility is more plausible than the doxastic account. Just so long as (i) that alternative account includes (or can be modified to include) a social condition on intellectual humility that precludes the actions of militant, religious fundamentalism and (ii) firm religious commitments do not necessarily lead to religious

fundamentalism (which they obviously don't), then we can avoid the worry
that allowing for the possibility of someone being intellectually humble with
firm religious commitments leads to a free pass, at least when it comes to
intellectual humility, to religious (or anti-religious) extremism.

In Chapter 1, we established that intellectual humility is a critically important
subject with tremendous significance in the real world. And we proposed a
plausible account of what intellectual humility might be—the doxastic account
of intellectual humility. And in all of this we assumed, naturally enough, that
intellectual humility is an *intellectual virtue*. That said, it wasn't yet entirely
clear what intellectual virtues actually were. So, in Chapter 2, we turned to
explore the nature of intellectual virtues in general via exploring seminal
accounts of virtue epistemology. First, in §1 of Chapter 2, we sketched the
broad contours of the two dominant approaches to understanding intellectual
virtue: agent-reliabilism and agent-responsibilism. Then in §2, §3, and §4 of
Chapter 2, we explored specific examples of these virtue epistemologies in
greater detail. Starting with Ernest Sosa's agent-reliabilism, we considered the
faculty virtues at the heart of his account of knowledge as belief that is true
because competent. Then, in §3, we turned to Linda Zagzebski's seminal agent-
responsibilism, where we considered the character virtues at the heart of her
account of knowledge as true belief arising out of an act of intellectual virtue.
And, in §4, we considered the unique, *proper functionalist* agent-reliabilism of
Alvin Plantinga, where intellectual virtues are understood in terms of properly
functioning cognitive faculties. With leading approaches to intellectual virtue
on the table, in §5 of Chapter 2, we finally returned to intellectual humility and
considered how it might fit within that literature. And we decided that, of the
proposals under consideration, Linda Zagzebski's agent-responsibilism—with
its approach to intellectual virtues as *character* virtues—yielded the easiest
(and most intuitive) framework for making sense of intellectual humility as an
intellectual virtue.[14]

Drawing from Michael Levin's helpful notation, Linda Zagzebski's understanding of virtue can be understood in terms of the following three conditions:

> Let $T(V)$ be the end or telos of virtue V. Then, for Zagzebski, act A is an "act of V" iff (i) A expresses V-ish motives, (ii) A is the sort of thing V-ish people do, and (iii) A brings about $T(V)$ because of (i) and (ii). (Levin, 2004, p. 399)

For example, the action of saving a child from drowning is an act of courage, say, if and only if (i) such an action expresses courageous motives, (ii) it is the sort of action that courageous people do, and (iii) if, in so doing, the child is actually saved. To be sure, according to Zagzebski, if I try so to save a child yet fail, I may very well have acted courageously but I did not *perform an act of courage*. To use an epistemic case or a case involving an intellectual virtue, the action of thinking carefully about a given inquiry is an act of scrupulousness, say, if and only if such an action (i) expresses scrupulous motives, (ii) is the sort of thing that scrupulous people would do, and (iii) if, in so doing, the given telos (which would include the truth) is reached. Again, if I am so cognizing and yet nevertheless form a false belief, I may very well have cognized scrupulously without performing an act of "cognitive scrupulousness" (Levin, 2004, pp. 399–400). As such, a given act, A, is an act of intellectual virtue if A (i) expresses *intellectually* V-ish motives, (ii) is the sort of thing that *intellectually* V-ish people do, and (iii) the given intellectual telos (which usually includes epistemic good such as truth), is met.

And it's worth remembering these three conditions for Zagzebski's account of intellectual virtue—which, again, we took to be the best framework for making sense of intellectual humility as an intellectual virtue—because it highlights a component that is often overlooked: the motivational component. And while our main objective is to explore what intellectual humility might tell us about religious beliefs, this is a place where religion might speak into our understanding of intellectual humility. In his Tyndale New Testament Lecture, Grant Macaskill (2015) aptly points out that

> the interest in intellectual humility can be traced to what is often referred to as "the (re)turn to virtue" in contemporary philosophy and theology and, particularly, to the growing significance of virtue epistemology. . . . That discipline recognizes that the successful attainment of epistemic goods is inseparable from the intellectual characteristics of the inquirer and, indeed, of the community. The character traits of *all* involved in the pursuit of truth (intellectual courage, tenacity, honesty, etc.) bear on the attainment of epistemic goods, as do other social factors, such as bias and fear. As such, the discipline of virtue epistemology has reaffirmed the importance of personal formation—not, perhaps, without controversy—to the intellectual life of the modern thinker, with an eye upon the great texts of virtue, those of Aristotle and Aquinas.

But, as he turns to explore how intellectual humility might be understood within the New Testament, Macaskill (2015) expresses a worry about the contemporary discussions on intellectual humility: that "what has been discussed in abstraction has generally concerned the epistemic dimension of the intellect, with other dimensions (such as volition) neglected." For Macaskill, a critically important component of intellectual humility within the New Testament is the change that comes from God's work in someone's life.

And it's this focus on the importance of volition for intellectual humility that can give us another solution to the *blank check to evil worry*. While Macaskill is certainly right that theoretical work on intellectual humility has primarily focused on epistemic dimensions while neglecting the importance of volition—and that's the case in this book—that doesn't mean that the latter is completely missing or not represented. We can perhaps most easily see where this comes into play in Zagzebski's three-fold account of intellectual virtues, where in order for an act to be an act of intellectual virtue, it needs to be driven by virtuous motives. And here, again, insofar as (i) firm religious beliefs can be driven by virtuous motives and (ii) the motives of militant, religious (and anti-religious) fundamentalists, let's agree, do not have virtuous motivations, then we don't need to worry about allowing for the possibility of firm religious beliefs leading to the idea that militant, religious (and anti-religious) fundamentalism is somehow permissible. For example, while a virtuous person might very well strongly believe that God exists, that's a far cry from treating people as means to an end or being blind to suffering. Those are things that a virtuous person would not do.

In Chapter 3 we explored some issues surrounding measuring something as complex and multifaceted as intellectual humility. The process of operationalizing such a construct is necessarily reductionist. Even the task of boiling the expression of a virtue down to a 6-item, Likert-type questionnaire might on the face of it seem absurd, especially when trying to assess how a person might approach the question of God's existence. By the same token, keeping in mind the proper and limited role of what a measure might tell us, we can, nonetheless, learn a great deal from measuring intellectual humility. Indeed, the advancement of the virtue depends on it. Two critical dimensions have emerged from the work on measurement thus far: an appreciation of the limits of one's knowledge (an awareness, an appropriation, or owning of one's own epistemic fallibility), and an openness to the beliefs, ideas, and opinions of others (including valuing others' opinions and a willingness to revise beliefs when encountering other ideas). As with any complex human behavior, a number of measures that use different methods, such as informant reports, behavioral checklists, simulations of disagreement, observation in actual disagreement, taken together, might approach a more complete picture of intellectual humility. Measures will not tell you if a person is intellectually humble. They can only tell you that they show aspects of those behaviors we associate with intellectual humility. The true measure will come in the moment a person is faced with the pursuit of epistemic goods. Will you virtuously value your epistemic status such that the epistemic good can be realized? In the face of religious disagreement, will you allow the other his or her beliefs and respect them? The true measure of any virtue is in its practice.

And here, again, we might see material for another response to the *blank check to evil worry*. Seemingly, a large part of what makes the worst kinds of religious (and anti-religious) fundamentalism so horrible is the way in which it is *practiced*. And insofar as someone can have firm religious beliefs without horrendous religious practices (which they obviously can), then allowing for the possibility of firm religious beliefs that are intellectually humble does not open the door to religious (or anti-religious) extremism.

In Chapter 4 we explored the question of the development of intellectual humility across the lifespan, with a special focus on how this virtue might develop in childhood. Children, it seems, are a curious mixture of intellectual humility and arrogance. On the one hand, they seem perfectly willing to revise beliefs because they hold competing hypotheses about the way the world works, hypotheses that gain strength as more experience either confirms or denies their plausibility. On the other, children, especially younger children, are overconfident about what they know and seem to exhibit intellectual arrogance. This confidence, however, does not preclude their learning, nor does it seem to inhibit their curiosity. In fact, they are equally confident that others, especially adults, know as much as they do and that they can learn from others. In this way, we might "become as a child" in our practice of intellectual humility, being confident of what we know, but always willing to learn more. This seems an especially apt stance in the face of religious disagreement. How much can anyone know about something as vast and ineffable as the divine, for example? There is always more to learn, including from someone who might believe there is no God (or gods), or from someone who might worship a different God (or gods). Though it has not yet been studied, there may be something to be learned about intellectual humility from the child like capacity for wonder.

And insofar as a willingness to learn from others *does* highlight an important aspect of intellectual humility—at least when it comes to religious debates—then we can further distinguish firm religious convictions from militant religious (and anti-religious) fundamentalism. Religious extremists, let's agree, don't enjoy much in the way of a childlike wonder when it comes to their religious beliefs. They're not interested in learning from others who might bring another point of view. And seemingly there is nothing about firm religious beliefs that necessarily precludes an interest in learning from others.

From the information presented in Chapter 5, we might despair about our capacity for any intellectual virtue, given the structure of our cognitive system, and our propensity for biases due to the shortcuts and heuristics that operate in our thinking. What we learn from cognitive science about any intellectual virtue, but especially intellectual humility, is that it takes effort and practice to get it right. Our natural habits of mind tilt us toward intellectual arrogance and only by practicing habits such as rule-based thinking, accuracy and accountability, perspective taking, Active Open-minded Thinking, and seeking a common interest in the truth, among others, can we have a hope of mitigating those biases that plague us. Habits can train our cognitive system to operate in proper sequence, coordinating System 1 and System 2 processes in such a way that we can land closer to the truth. Simply having such knowledge of how our cognitive system works, and of the heuristics and biases that can interfere with virtuous practice, is a start. These habits would serve us well, especially in the face of religious disagreement.

And here, again, we might find material for further distinguishing firm religious belief from religious extremism. Perhaps religious (and anti-religious) extremist are less likely to practice habits such as rule-based thinking, accuracy and accountability, and perspective taking, which might offset our natural bent toward intellectual arrogance.

The research reviewed in Chapter 6 reminds us of the power of the situation to determine behavior even, and especially, in the expression of intellectual humility. While there may be some trait-like aspects to intellectual humility such as openness to experience and agreeableness (Big 5), a high need for cognition, a low need for closure, and a proper balance of agency and communion (Big 2), yet even the expression of those traits depends on the circumstances and situation. We see evidence that, especially on the topics of politics and religion, the expression of intellectual humility can vary by situation. The research in Chapter 6, notably those who take an interactionist (person x situation) approach, seems to confirm the conception of intellectual humility as described by DA‴: that it is best assessed along two axes, how much positive epistemic status a given belief enjoys (situation), and how much positive epistemic status a given agent *thinks* it enjoys (person). Again, having knowledge about how both personal traits and convictions interact with situations to determine behavior helps us to better understand, and to better practice, virtues like intellectual humility. Discovering and building up those traits that promote intellectual humility, and understanding and creating the situations that might promote a respectful exchange of ideas, are part of what science can teach us. It can also help us to better negotiate those more intractable disagreements like those related to religion and politics and put further distance between firm religious beliefs and the *blank check to evil* worry.

In Chapter 7 we learned about the interplay of emotion and cognition, and contemplated the implications for the practice of intellectual humility. No topic may be more emotionally charged than the topic of religion, for the reasons cited above, as it is often core to people's identity. The more we understand about the role of emotion in cognition, the better we will be able to both understand intellectual humility and promote its practice. While emotion is a clear motivating factor in cognition, it can also cloud or distort the pursuit of epistemic goods. To practice an intellectual virtue, there must be enough emotion to motivate the pursuit of truth and enough reason to discern it. A key component of intellectual humility is a capacity for open, non-judgmental awareness, which allows a person to remain open to new information, entertain alternative ideas while suspending judgment, and focus on relevant details while ignoring distractions. Moreover, since intellectual humility arguably has both epistemic and social dimensions, appraising our emotions, regulating them, and having emotional intelligence will help in the social sphere where intellectual humility is practiced. Understanding our own emotional style will also help navigate our reactions to epistemic challenge and disagreement. Without emotion, our ability to reason is impaired. Without reason, emotion lacks clear direction. A robust empirical understanding of intellectual humility is impossible without serious attention to emotion, including its motivational and adaptive functions, its influence on cognition, its interpersonal influences, and its regulation. Arguably, this kind of integration of head and heart is the mark of a virtuous person and, again, might be used to further distinguish firm religious commitments from religious extremism.

In Chapter 8, we turned to consider the epistemology of testimony. Testimony, as we noted, is critically important. Whether it's a friend, a witness to a crime, or an expert in a given field, we depend on what other people tell us. But there are times when we clearly shouldn't believe what we hear (or at the very least take what we hear with a significant grain of salt). There are times when people lie or mislead. Sometimes being trusting—for example, when we're listening to politicians, car salesmen, etc.—is a mistake (perhaps indicative of the vice of gullibility). But, of course, there are also times when being shrewd and untrusting does both ourselves, as hearers, and our interlocutors, as speakers, a serious disservice. As such, several pressing questions arise: When can we trust what we hear? When does testimony give us knowledge? And when doesn't it? When are we obliged to listen to testimony with a discerning ear? And when, if ever, are we obliged to trust without qualification or immediately?

And as we explained, if being intellectually humble means accurately tracking the positive epistemic status of one's beliefs, then part of intellectual humility means accurately tracking the epistemic input of our interlocutors.

Failures in testimony, we argued, can be caused by failures of intellectual humility. Recall Miranda Fricker's (2007) example from *The Talented Mr Ripley* (Minghella, 2000). Herbert Greenleaf wants to know what happened to his son, Dickie. Marge knows what happened to Dickie, and she is more than happy to tell Greenleaf; however, he won't listen. Greenleaf doesn't value Marge's testimony simply because she is a woman, and subsequently fails to recognize valuable information. As Miranda Fricker (2007) masterfully unpacks this story, Greenleaf is guilty of committing epistemic injustice against Marge. According to Fricker, Greenleaf has wronged Marge "in [her] capacity as a giver of knowledge" (p. 7).

That seems right; however, as we argued, we could also easily think of Greenleaf as guilty of *intellectual arrogance*. In snubbing Marge's testimony, Greenleaf is unjustifiably assuming that his cognitive faculties are better positioned or equipped than Marge's. And he attributes far more positive epistemic status to his beliefs regarding his son than is actually merited. We also argued that, in other ways, Greenleaf can be considered guilty of *intellectual diffidence*. Despite Dickie's treasured rings being found at Ripley's place, Greenleaf doesn't attribute nearly the positive epistemic status to the belief that Ripley could be the killer that he should. And Greenleaf simply does not track the positive epistemic status of the valuable information Marge offers him again and again. The testimonial failures that surround Greenleaf, we proposed, were caused by failures of intellectual humility.

And if intellectual humility is so tied to testimony—such that part of being intellectually humble requires you to accurately track the epistemic import of what your interlocutors tell you—then it's easy to see how the *blank check to evil worry* might be dispelled. There is nothing inherent to holding firm religious (or anti-religious) beliefs that precludes appropriately accounting for the epistemic import of our interlocutors. And insofar as the worst kinds of militant religious (or anti-religious) fundamentalism *don't* appropriately account for the epistemic import of interlocutors, then they will fall short of intellectual humility. As such, allowing for the possibility of firm religious beliefs being conceptually compatible with intellectual humility simply does not lead to *the blank check to evil worry*.

And, finally, our work in Chapter 9 on the epistemic import of disagreement gave us further material for avoiding the blank check to evil objection. When we think about practical applications of intellectual humility, we think of how intellectual humility might speak to how we handle disagreement—especially disagreement amongst peers. When we think about intellectual arrogance, we often think of someone who is unflinchingly dogmatic and unwilling to compromise on their belief in the face of dissent, disagreement, and defeaters. And when we think about intellectual diffidence, we often think of someone who is far too easily persuaded to give up on (or reduce their credence in) their beliefs. *How we handle disagreement seems to be at the heart of intellectual humility.* And, presumably, militant religious (or anti-religious) zealots handle disagreement in ways that are not compatible with intellectual humility.

As we argued in the first part of Chapter 9, intellectual humility can give us a framework for understanding when and why vicious, intractable disagreements occur. Some disagreements—especially disagreements about religion, morality, and politics—can be extremely intractable because they involve beliefs that are so personal and intimate that we are prone to ascribe them with far more positive epistemic status than they actually enjoy. What we wanted to know later in that chapter, however, is: What *should* we *do* about this? Drawing from Catherine Elgin's work, we're seeing that perhaps there's nothing we *can do* about it. Some beliefs just seem completely incredible to us. Conrad, from VICIOUS DISAGREEMENT, presumably simply can't help but believe that abortions should be illegal, except in a strict set of cases. Likewise, Libby presumably simply can't help but believe that abortions should be legal and readily available to women everywhere. While we might ask that Conrad and Libby treat each other with mutual respect and decency, we can't say that they "ought" to give up their respective beliefs, since "ought" implies "can" and that's something they simply can't do. The respective cognitive characters of Conrad and Libby have shaped the positive epistemic status they assign to their respective beliefs. So perhaps, all we can hope for in these cases of vicious disagreement is the right sort of cognitive character, which might improve our ability to carefully reflect on our beliefs and the positive epistemic status that they actually enjoy.[15]

And here again, we see a reason why the *blank check to evil worry* does not follow from the idea that intellectual humility does not necessarily preclude firm religious (or anti-religious) commitments. Militant, fundamentalist, religious (or anti-religious) zealots do not, we can agree, have the right sort of cognitive character. In Chapter 9, we noted how Elgin (2010) posited that education is something that could be critically important to forming the right sort of cognitive character, to help people learn "about the cognitive force of evidence, argument, and expertise . . . to appreciate why it might be worthwhile to maximize their prospects of forming, retaining, revising, and rejecting beliefs of different kinds" (pp. 62–63). And insofar as religious (and even anti-religious) zealots are often opposed to broad, liberal education, we might easily conclude that their cognitive character is not ideally suited to non-culpably and accurately track the positive epistemic status of their beliefs—that their cognitive characters are not suited for intellectual humility. And insofar as there is nothing inherent to having firm religious (or anti-religious) beliefs that precludes having a good cognitive character—a claim that seems extremely difficult to deny—then allowing for firm, intellectually humble religious beliefs does not lead to the blank check to evil worry.

Conclusion

The first goal of this book, was to explore some of the philosophy and theory behind intellectual humility—to explore what intellectual humility might be (Chapter 1) and how it might fit with accounts of intellectual virtues in general (Chapter 2). And with some theorizing in hand, we turned, in the second part of the book, to survey some of the relevant *empirical* literature surrounding such a virtue and concept. Starting with proposed measures (Chapter 3), we surveyed the growing body of literature on developmental psychology (Chapter 4), human cognition (Chapter 5), traits, dispositions, situations (Chapter 6), and emotions (Chapter 7) that seemed relevant to a more scientifically robust understanding of intellectual humility. And in the final part of the book, we returned to philosophy to consider three plausible applications of intellectual humility: in the philosophy of testimony (Chapter 8), in the philosophy of disagreement (Chapter 9), and finally, in the philosophy of religion (Chapter 10, this chapter).

And, arguably, there is no greater application, no greater challenge for intellectual humility than its relevance to religious debate, dialogue, and disagreement. Few other debates seem so intractable, so polarizing, and so universal, which makes it an excellent arena for exploring the applications of intellectual humility. And in this chapter, in §1, we argued for a relatively weak thesis: that a commitment to intellectual humility does not necessarily mean giving up all firm religious (or anti-religious) commitments, that it is conceptually possible to be intellectually humble and enjoy strong religious (or anti-religious) convictions. But even weak theses can lead to serious objections. Part of what makes religious disagreements so intractable, we suggested earlier, was that we are all too prone to radically overestimate the positive epistemic status our religious (or anti-religious) beliefs enjoy. When it comes to religious debates, we are all too inclined to dismiss and marginalize dissent. As such, when we suggest that it's possible to be intellectually humble and at the same time hold strong religious beliefs, there is a real worry that *everyone* with firm religious beliefs will just assume that *their* strong convictions (or the convictions of their tradition) are the actualization of that possibility, that their strong religious beliefs are compatible with intellectual humility. And because of this, there is a real worry that we are opening the door (at least when it comes to intellectual humility) to the worst kinds of militant fundamentalism, what we called the *blank check to evil worry*. As such, in §2, we drew from all of the previous chapters to put distance between firm religious (or anti-religious) commitments and militant fundamentalism, to show how intellectual humility might be compatible with the former but certainly not compatible with the latter.

And in all of this, as we drew from our work in the previous chapters, we began to see (we hope) a glimmer of a unified picture of the philosophy and science of intellectual humility. Of course, we're not too proud to admit that there is still a lot of work that needs to be done. As an *introduction*, this book only scratches at the surface of some of the relevant philosophical issues (Chapters 1, 2, 8, 9, and 10) and proposes only brief surveys of the growing empirical research (Chapters 3, 4, 5, 6, and 7). We don't pretend to offer the final word on the issue, far from it. *There needs to be further philosophical investigation, and there needs to be further empirical research.* And, thankfully, with the growing amount of work emerging along these lines, it looks like we're going to get it! Our hope is that this introductory work might be useful not only to everyone with an interest in this extremely relevant and timely subject but also to this emerging body of research.

NOTES

Chapter 1

1 To be sure, the epistemic import of peer disagreement will also be of central importance to various theological debates surrounding "religious pluralism" (the view that all religions approximate the ultimate truth) and the problem of divine hiddenness.

2 Similar factor-analytic studies find these traits coalesce to form a consistent factor in folk concepts of wisdom (Clayton and Birren, 1980; Holliday and Chandler, 1986). Meacham (1990) defines wisdom exclusively in terms that reflect intellectual humility (knowing what one does not know and that knowledge is fallible). Grossmann et al. (2010) have devised a wise reasoning measure that codes for intellectual humility (defined as recognizing the limits of one's knowledge).

3 There is, of course, a lot more that can be and has been said about the nature of humility. That said, while such an account is, no doubt, rough and ready, we think it is intuitive and basic enough for the purposes of this Chapter, wherein humility *simpliciter* is not a primary focus.

4 To be sure, it is not obvious that intellectual humility is really a subset of humility. No doubt, this is a reasonable assumption to make (i.e., it is easy to assume that if we are talking about *intellectual* humility, we are talking about a specific type of *humility*). However, it could easily be the case that humility is a subset of intellectual humility: perhaps humility is just being intellectually humble about how one conceives of himself/herself. And if this is correct, then perhaps the most parsimonious way to understand humility is by way of intellectual humility. Indeed, in a seminal theoretical piece in the psychology literature, Tangney (2000) grounds the definition of humility in two realms: a proper *understanding* of the self (accurate assessment, keeping one's abilities/accomplishments in proper perspective, low self-focus) and a certain intellectual disposition (acknowledging mistakes, intellectual openness). Various measures of humility have also reflected these dimensions (Davis et al., 2011; Landrum, 2011; Rowatt et al., 2006). The honesty-humility dimension in the HEXACO assesses only accurate self-understanding (modesty, Ashton and Lee, 2008). Perhaps some of the problems that have been encountered in the measurement of humility could find resolution if humility was seen as a component of intellectual humility.

5 One area in the psychological literature that could address these issues is research into narcissism. Citing Wallace and Baumeister (2002), Peterson and Seligman

(2004) have pointed out that a key tendency of persons with subclinical narcissistic personality traits (which happen to be generally distributed in the population) is to "seek esteem by . . . publicly outperforming others and winning admiration" (p. 467). That is, people who score high in measures of subclinical narcissism work harder to achieve when they know people will notice. Meanwhile, those who score low in subclinical narcissistic personality traits perform just as well in situations where they are likely not to gain recognition. Thus, intellectual humility might be a virtue that holds special promise in an age when vanity in the form of narcissism seems to be an ever-increasing phenomenon (Twenge et al., 2008).

6 To be sure, we might wonder if such a response ultimately undermines the limitations-owning view. If intellectual limitations and intellectual strengths are that interrelated, then we might wonder why we should pull them apart to begin with.

7 Originally printed in P. L. Samuelson, M. J. Jarvinen, T. B. Paulus, I. M. Church, S. A. Hardy, and J. B. Barrett (2015). Implicit theories of intellectual virtues and vices: A focus on intellectual humility, *The Journal of Positive Psychology*, 10:5, 389–406. Reprinted by permission of the publisher (Taylor & Francis Ltd, http://www. tandfonline.com).

8 This was actually once our view.

9 Terms like "justification" or "warrant" sometimes have epistemological baggage attached to them. Justification, for example, often seems attached to internalism. Warrant, for another, is often used as an umbrella term for *whatever bridges the gap between true belief and knowledge*. In this paper, we don't want to make any such commitments. We want to develop a doxastic account of intellectual humility that can apply whether or not you are an internalist or whether or not you're explicitly interested in knowledge. "Positive epistemic status" helps leave those doors open.

10 See Chapter 5 for a detailed discussion of System 1 and System 2 cognitive processes.

11 Later in the book we sometimes still talk about an agent "attributing" positive epistemic status to a belief. But the point here still stands: we don't intend to use "attributing" in such a way that would preclude System 1 cognition.

12 An earlier version of this graph can be found in Ian Church's article "Is Intellectual Humility Compatible with Dogmatism?" (forthcoming), which was produced for Biola University's Center for Christian Thought and generously funded by the John Templeton Foundation.

13 We think this is a really important issue! The science of intellectual humility is currently a very hot topic, and the measurement of intellectual humility is a central area of research. And, it seems, how we think of intellectual humility—be it in terms of a virtuous mean or simply as the opposite of intellectual arrogance—will radically affect how we develop a scale for measuring this virtue. And as we have conversed with some of the scientists who see intellectual humility as the opposite of intellectual arrogance, we worry that their measurements are going to give a misleading assessment; we worry that if someone is extremely self-deprecating, extremely

undervaluing their intellectual abilities and accomplishments, that they are going to be flagged as virtuous, as intellectually humble.

14 Besides, there are a lot of ways to slice the virtue pie. So maybe we shouldn't be too worried if our account of intellectual humility is someone else's meta-virtue (we're actually attracted to the idea of intellectual humility as a meta-virtue) or intellectual honesty. So long as we're not entirely developing an account from the void, it seems like maybe the diversity of opinion surrounding intellectual humility shouldn't concern us too much. And, as it turns out, we don't think our account is coming from the void.

15 Of course, sometimes chapters will aim to explore terrain that overlaps with other chapters—how we handle disagreement in the face of disagreement (Chapter 9), for example, will overlap quite a bit with what intellectual humility might tell us about religious beliefs (Chapter 10).

Chapter 2

1 While it is not without dissent, it is extremely common for people working in this literature to use terms like "intellectual" and "epistemic" synonymously (see, for example, Greco and Turri, 2011). In any case, we will take these terms to be indeed synonymous.

2 To be sure, one need not be committed to virtue epistemology *per se* to account for intellectual virtues—one can account for intellectual virtues without any special loyalty to virtue epistemology—nevertheless, virtue epistemology, naturally enough, offers the most robust and flourishing accounts of intellectual virtue in the philosophical literature.

3 For more on virtue ethics and its distinctiveness, see Anscombe (1958).

4 As Earl Conee and Richard Feldman noted in "The Generality Problem for Reliabilism": "A fully articulated [process] reliabilist theory must identify with sufficient clarity the nature of the processes it invokes. In doing so, the theory confronts what has come to be known as 'the generality problem'" (1998, p. 1).

5 And to be sure, we don't need anything so fanciful as demon helpers to create such a case. Say that Philip is playing a game with his son, where his son needs to try to guess what number Philip is thinking of, anywhere from one to hundred. To do this, Philip's son closes his eyes and waits for the first number that pops into his head, and he subsequently assumes that such a number is a premonition regarding the number in Philip's head. While such a process would normally be incredibly unreliable, whenever Philip's son hazards a guess Philip is sure to think about that number so that his son's guesses are always true. In such a case, even though the son's beliefs are seemingly based on a reliable process, he intuitively lacks knowledge. The truth and reliability of the son's belief has nothing to do with the epistemic efforts of the son.

6   The primary difference between agent-reliabilism virtue epistemology and neo-Aristotelian virtue epistemology that we want to focus on is their divergent accounts of intellectual virtue: agent-reliabilists roughly explicating intellectual virtue in terms of cognitive faculties or cognitive competencies (faculty virtues) and neo-Aristotelians roughly explicating intellectual virtues in terms of character traits and motivation (character virtues). Most often, neo-Aristotelianism can be seen as requiring something more than the agent-reliabilist: a given agent should, according to neo-Aristotelianism, not only have reliable cognitive faculties (like Naïve in CHICKEN SEXER), but also be of the right sort of epistemic character. However, this isn't necessarily the case. Neo-Aristotelianism (as we are currently conceiving of it) could be seen as simply requiring something else, not something more. For example, a neo-Aristotelian could conceivably understand an intellectual virtue—character virtues such as intellectual courage, intellectual steadfastness, etc.—in such a way that it did not necessarily require reliability. Such a neo-Aristotelian might ascribe knowledge to an agent who manifests such a virtue even when the faculties or competencies at play are unreliable.

7   This general point, that character virtues might be developed out of a robust account of agent-reliabilist faculty virtues, is developed in greater detail in Sosa's (2015) work, *Judgment & Agency*, especially Chapter 2, "Virtue Epistemology: Character vs. Competence."

8   Building off of his earlier work, Ernest Sosa has recently developed his virtue epistemology in some new and interesting directions—see, for example, Sosa's (2015) book *Judgment and Agency*. That said, we will be primarily interested in Sosa's earlier work in this chapter as we try to sketch the basic view.

9   For a big picture of how Sosa sees his account in light of the Gettier Problem, see Sosa (2009a, 2: 185–89).

10   For Sosa, (i) and (ii) are seemingly necessary and jointly sufficient conditions on knowledge. What is more, Sosa presumably takes *belief* and *aptness* to be conceptually prior to *knowledge—knowledge*, after all, is understood in terms of *belief* and *aptness* and not vice versa. While Sosa's simple analysis looks substantially different from more classic and more complex reductive analyses like Plantinga's, Sosa's virtue epistemology is, nevertheless, a reductive analysis. See Sosa (2009b); Williamson (2009b). To see Williamson's critique of Sosa's earlier work, see Williamson (2004) in John Greco's (2004) edited volume, *Sosa and His Critics*; unfortunately, Sosa's (2004) "Replies" contains no response.

11   We should note that it is confusing at this point what exactly aptness requires. On the one hand, Sosa seems to say that the protagonist's higher-order belief fails to be apt because its truth is somehow not appropriately contingent on the relevant epistemic competence. On the other hand, Sosa seems to be saying that the higher-order belief fails to be apt because the relevant competence could have very easily led to a false conclusion.

12 To be sure, there are other important agent-responsibilism theories in the literature that we could have drawn from—for example, Jason Baehr's (2012) *The Inquiring Mind*. But Zagzebski's work will receive the bulk of our attention here, because Zagzebski's virtue epistemology (unlike the virtue epistemologies of other agent-responsibilist theorists, including Baehr) is interested in addressing the traditional projects of epistemology. As such, Zagzebski's agent-responsibilism will not only be more "mainstream" but also a better interlocutor with the agent-responsibilist virtue epistemologies we are considering in this chapter. For more on the different kinds of agent-responsibilist accounts of virtue epistemology, see Heather Battaly's (2012) truly excellent piece, "Virtue Epistemology."

13 To be sure, Zagzebski, unlike Sosa, does not seem to have the conceptual resources for defusing (or purportedly defusing) Fake Barn-type cases—that is, the animal knowledge/reflective knowledge distinction.

14 It is worth noting that even if we are skeptical as to whether this is the definition of knowledge that Zagzebski intends, it is, nevertheless, very similar to Sosa's definition—apt belief, that is belief whose attainment of truth is because of or due to a cognitive competence. As such, even if Levin is wrong about how we should read Zagzebski, his reading will, nevertheless, inform our understanding of Sosa.

15 When Sosa defines knowledge as apt belief where aptness is understood as "true *because* competent," a casual reader may think that Sosa is saying that knowledge literally requires truth to be contingent on cognitive competencies—a view that seems overtly mistaken. Surely, for example, we can know that the earth orbits the sun even though such a fact has nothing to do with our epistemic competencies—even though the earth's movement around the sun is in no way contingent on our faculties. Sosa, it seems, needs a different understanding of *because*, but it's not always clear what it could be.

16 In my estimation, Levin is indeed highlighting a *serious* worry for analyses of knowledge like Zagzebski's and Sosa's—a worry that has arguably been underappreciated in the literature. While Levin very helpfully unpacks Zagzebski's virtue epistemology, the full extent of his *critique* is beyond the scope of this chapter and this book.

17 And for anyone who might be worried that a sufficient understanding of the "because" relation that's at the heart of Sosa and Zagzebski's respective epistemologies (drawing from Michael Levin's worry), Plantinga's virtue epistemology helpfully avoids relying on such a relation.

18 Or more accurately, *sufficiently* warranted true belief.

19 For other tabulations of Plantinga's account of warrant (what later iterations refer to as the "nutshell" or "central core" of warrant), see Chignell (2003, p. 445); Plantinga (2000, p. 156).

20   The same would be true if, say, the radiation from the elephant didn't produce the belief that "a trumpet is sounding nearby," but, instead, that "a big gray object is nearby" (Plantinga, 1993b, pp. 6–7).

21   So, in order for a given belief to have warrant, it needs to be produced by cognitive faculties that are functioning properly within a congenial environment— but just how congenial? What if someone is knowingly in an uncongenial environment and know how they might be misled—would relevant beliefs still be barred from warrant? Such issues, Plantinga admits, highlight a vagueness in the theory. There may not be an answer to such questions. See Plantinga (1993, p. 11).

22   See Plantinga's (1993b) description of what he meant by environment (pp. 6–7). Also see Plantinga (2000, pp. 156–58).

23   How high must the statistical objective probability of the beliefs being true be? Here again, Plantinga concedes that there is vagueness. For Plantinga, the amount of warrant a given belief enjoys is relative to how firmly it is believed by the given agent. However high the statistical objective probability of the belief's truth needs to be, Plantinga presumes that "the degree of reliability varies as a function of degrees of belief" (Plantinga, 1993b, p. 18).

24   Of course, if the telos of these character virtues is knowledge—truth from an act of intellectual virtue—it might be the case that someone like Brian, while a brain in a vat, will be unable to enjoy actualized intellectual virtues. (Though, of course, he could still be virtuously motivated and even commit acts of virtue without being virtuous.)

25   Ernest Sosa (2015) does a great job of making this point in his book, *Judgment and Agency*. Specifically, see Chapter 2, "Virtue Epistemology: Character versus Competence."

26   Our focus, here, is whether or not intellectual humility can be conceived of as an intellectual virtue. There is, to be sure, a much broader worry in the literature: whether, given our natural proclivity toward heuristics and biases, intellectual virtues are possible for creatures like us (see Alfano, 2012). This is a serious worry, but it is not our focus here. For an explanation as to how virtue epistemology can account for and make sense of our proclivity toward heuristics and biases, please see our article, "When Cognition Turns Vicious: Heuristics and Biases in Light of Virtue Epistemology" (Samuelson and Church, 2014).

Chapter 3

1   This finding lends some support to the understanding of intellectual humility as involving a lack of concern for one's status (see the discussion of intellectual humility and status in the introduction).

2 Krumrei-Mancuso and Rouse (2016) exemplify this process.

3 They also adapted the measure to specific contexts (e.g., politics, religion), which is discussed in detail in Chapter 6.

Chapter 5

1 The bulk of this chapter first appeared in P. L. Samuelson and I. M. Church (2015). When Cognition Turns Vicious: Heuristics and Biases in Light of Virtue Epistemology, *Philosophical Psychology*, 28:8, 1095–113. Reprinted by permission of the publisher (Taylor & Francis Ltd, http://www.tandfonline.com).

2 Some philosophers worry that psychological theory threatens the viability of virtue epistemology (Olin and Doris, 2014; Alfano, 2012). While we do not aim at engaging with that literature, we see a surprising harmony between the philosophical and psychological research—a harmony that can, if anything, help dissolve such worries.

3 See Chapter 7 of Evans (2007) for a comparative analysis.

4 Recently the language of "systems" has been abandoned by some cognitive scientists in favor of using Type 1 and Type 2 to distinguish these cognitive processes because they do not represent a single system, but the many cognitive systems and neural networks that support each type of thinking (Evans and Stanovich, 2013).

5 Included in Type 1 processing are implicit learning and conditioning, decision-making rules and principles that are so well practiced as to be automatic, and the regulation of behavior by emotions. Stanovich (2009) has given the name TASS (The Autonomous Set of Systems) to these processes because they "respond automatically to triggered stimuli [and are not] under the control of the analytic processing system (System 2)" (p. 57).

6 And this means that according to the credit theory of knowledge espoused by some reliabilist virtue epistemologists (see Greco, 2009, 2010, 2012), Type 1 cognition can produce credit-worthy beliefs—beliefs we would deem knowledge—so long as it is employed in a context where it is generally adequate to its task. Also see Axtell (in press).

7 As measured by SAT scores and a test of verbal ability, though cognitive ability was also a unique and independent predictor of argument evaluation performance.

8 Since much of Type 1 processes is unconscious, we are not accusing the agent of being willfully arrogant. Instead, arrogance means to preference the self as a source of information, when what the self knows, by itself, does not provide enough

for believing in accordance with the facts, whether the agent is conscious of this preference or not.

9   Elsewhere we have defined intellectual humility as a virtuous mean between "holding a belief with the firmness warranted," which avoids the vice of intellectual arrogance (holding your belief too firmly when it is not warranted) on the one hand, and intellectual diffidence (holding a belief too loosely or giving in to another's belief too soon) on the other (Samuelson et al., 2012).

10   Insofar as research into heuristics and biases helps us understand intellectual humility, it is useful to think of intellectual humility as the absence, or the opposite, of intellectual arrogance. As we stated above in the introduction, we hold the view that intellectual humility is not simply the opposite, or absence of something (like intellectual arrogance) and that a robust definition should include positive attributes.

11   There is some intriguing new research into what is called implicit theory of mind in young children that gives evidence for a type of perspective taking that is akin to Type 1 cognition (i.e., autonomous, fast, and cognitively efficient, though somewhat inflexible, Apperly and Butterfill, 2009). What is less known and more controversial is the relationship between implicit and explicit perspective taking, that is, whether the explicit form is of a different type (akin to Type 2 cognition, Apperly and Butterfill, 2009) or if they both tap into the same cognitive processes in conscious and unconscious ways (Schneider et al., 2011). In either case, perspective taking could be enhanced through experience and practice by making explicit perspective taking so habitual as to make it become automatic, on the one hand, or by building the capacity of existing implicit forms, on the other, or both.

Chapter 7

1   There is some controversy whether the damage to his brain and his behavior can be as precisely compared to patients with damage to the ventromedial sector of the brain (MacMillan, 2008).

2   Another potentially illuminating area of research regarding intellectual humility can be found in Forgas's (2002) *affect infusion model* (AIM) where affect "infuses" judgments differentially based on the levels of openness and effort involved in a particular thinking process. Haidt's (2002) commentary on this article is also insightful with regard to moral judgments.

3   Roberts (2003) also argues for the adaptive benefit of emotion with regard to reason, proposing that emotion offers a kind of experiential acquaintance that aids understanding and perception, resulting in an "improved epistemic condition" (p. 326).

4 Some researchers separate the mental world into cognition and affect, whereas others, like Haidt (2002), draw from dual-process theories (Chaiken and Trope, 1999), which differentiate based on two kinds of cognition: reasoning (slow) and intuition (fast). This position includes emotion as one part of the intuitive processes.

Chapter 8

1 To be sure, extended conversations can also provide justification *against* someone's testimony. Consider another case:

BAD CONVERSATION: Jim is visiting Chicago, and he is trying to find the Willis Tower. While walking down the street, he sees Mark, an ostensibly normal-looking stranger, and asks for directions. Mark gives Jim what sound like plausible directions. But what is more, Mark goes on to warn Jim that the Tower is run by alien illuminati who are directing human history and gearing up for world domination-—and Mark stresses to Jim that unless he wears a tinfoil hat, they'll be able to read his thoughts. Distressed by Mark's crazy talk, Jim politely thanks Mark for his time and tries to find someone else to ask for directions.

Here, instead of bolstering the testimony as to where to find the Willis Tower, Mark's extended conversation with Jim actually undermines his testimony. Given Mark's apparent craziness, Jim presumably can no longer know where the Willis Tower is based on his testimony.

2 Interestingly, Whitcomb et al.'s (2015) account of intellectual humility—where intellectual humility is understood as owning one's limitations—does not obviously get us this result. It does not obviously attribute Greenleaf with intellectual arrogance (or some failure of intellectual humility), because it's not clear how Greenleaf is failing to own his limitations. He is failing to own other people's limitations (namely, Ripley's) and he's failing to own other people's strengths (namely, Marge's), but it's not as clear that he's failing to own his *own* limitation. In this way, Whitcomb's et al.'s (2015) account of intellectual humility fails to be sufficiently social. The fact that it cannot see the arrogance at play in Greenleaf is, we think, a strike against it.

3 And again, Whitcomb et al.'s (2015) account of intellectual humility—where intellectual humility is understood as owning one's limitations—does not obviously get us this result.

4 Another key work in setting the stage for the epistemological debates over the last twenty-five years is Bimal Krishna Matilal and Arindam Chakrabarti (1994), *Knowing with Words*.

5 And to be sure, Fricker seems mistaken on this score. As Greco (2012) notes, "[There] might be epistemic work to do that does not involve basing one's belief on

nontestimonial reasons. . . . [Testimonial] justification might require other things on behalf of the hearer. And, therefore, reason-independence does not imply default justification—it does not imply that testimonial justification comes for free" (p. 19).

6   And this leaves room for Lackey to explore a third option between reductionism and anti-reductionism, which might avoid the dilemma facing testimony we sketched earlier. If Lackey can give reductionist answers to some questions and anti-reductionist answers to others, then Lackey thinks she might have a distinct third view on her hands. However, as Greco (2012) points out, "But should there be logical space between reductionism and nonreductionism (or antireductionism)? A preferable way to frame the issues is to take a more fine-grained approach, clearly separating what are distinct questions, and then defining rival positions accordingly" (p. 19).

7   If testimonial knowledge is too difficult to come by, if we were to deprive ourselves of testimonial knowledge, the resulting skepticism would be terrible indeed! As Jennifer Lackey (2006b) put it: "Were we to refrain from accepting the testimony of others, our lives would be impoverished in startling and debilitating ways" (p. 432).

8   Interestingly, the debate between reductionists and anti-reductionists regarding the epistemology of testimony sometimes seems to mirror the debate between conservatives versus dogmatists regarding Moore's proof of an external world (see Wright, 2004, 2007; Pryor, 2000, 2004). Just as dogmatism about Moore's proof allows for the belief in the external world to enjoy positive epistemic status by default (without any antecedent justification), so too do anti-reductionists allow for testimony to enjoy positive epistemic status for a given belief without antecedent justification to think that the testimony is trustworthy. And just as conservatives about Moore's proof require belief in the external world to have antecedent justification, so too do reductionists require belief in an instance of testimony to be supported by antecedent reasons to think that the testimony and/or testifier are reliable.

9   Greco (2015) goes on to elaborate on this point: "a reductionist account of testimonial knowledge, in the sense of 'reductionist' that we are considering here, will have to bottom out in non-testimonial knowledge only. But whether we attribute testimonial knowledge to children early or late, it is implausible that an adequate evidence base, itself devoid of testimonial knowledge, will be in place. What is plausible about attributing testimonial knowledge late is that, as children grow up, their knowledge does increase and so they have more to work with to use in their inductive inferences. What is not plausible, however, is that their knowledge increases in a way that makes it independent of the testimonial knowledge that the reductionist means to explain. Specifically, children learn about who they can trust and when largely by being told as much. Again, the prospects for a reductionist account look dim here" (p. 277).

10 And, as we noted earlier, similar explanations could be given using the Roberts and Wood account of intellectual humility.

Chapter 9

1 As Hilary Kornblith points out, lots of people mistakenly believe the capital of Maine is Portland since that is the largest city in the state. See Kornblith (2010, p. 29).

2 The tenets of basic arithmetic are presumably hinge propositions, "presupposed in the game of giving and asking for reasons" (Philie, 2009, p. 461), *methodological necessities* "whose truth is required, in a given context of inquiry, for the pertinent project of inquiry to proceed" (Brueckner, 2007, p. 285). To compromise on the basic arithmetic could be to compromise on the very framework of reason and to call into question the rationality.

3 While this seems like a reasonable assumption to make, it is worth noting that sometimes even highly theoretical, abstract, and esoteric topics can be the subject of intractable debates. For example, see Peter van Inwagen's (2010) description of his disagreement with David Lewis regarding the compatibilism versus incompatibilism debate in "We're Right, They're Wrong" (pp. 23–24).

4 The radical skeptics among us may think that such skepticism *is* founded across the board; however, we think we can couch the threat of radical skepticism for the time being and assume, like we naturally do, that we are pretty good at knowing quite a few things.

5 See Christensen (2007); Feldman (2006); Kornblith (2010). Note, we are assuming here that peer disagreement does not *always* "undermine one's ground for belief." For example, we noted above that Jill, in the case of Virtuous Dogmatism, can reasonably be dogmatic about the fact that 2 + 2 = 4 even in the face of peer disagreement.

6 See Foley (2001); Kelly (2005).

7 If we understand intellectual arrogance as those beliefs that are held with greater firmness than the evidence warrants, this point suggests that there are some beliefs with which we are particularly prone to intellectual arrogance.

8 Of course, a belief does not necessarily need to be political, religious, or moral in order to deeply affect us. Presumably, given the right circumstances, almost any belief (e.g., a belief in the superiority of Apple computers, a belief in the perils of inorganic food, etc.) can be made surprisingly important for one's view of the world.

9 And because of this they are likely to perceive each other as intellectually arrogant.

10 This assumption does not preclude the possibility of evidence reasonably leading in two different directions. Rather, this assumption merely precludes the possibility of a given set of evidence reasonably leading to two different beliefs that (i) are incompatible and (ii) enjoy a tremendous amount of positive epistemic status.

11 Or, if we're assuming something like the Roberts and Wood account of humility, perhaps we could say such cases of intractable disagreement are so intractable because they are so closely tied to people's status.

12   And this is a point that seems to be backed up by empirical research. See, for example, von Hippel and Trivers (2011).

13   And this is in keeping with the thought that our epistemic goal should be to only believe what is true. As Elgin (2010) explains: "[Where] there is a significant chance that my opponent's view is true, if I want to believe only what is true, I would be well served by not foreclosing inquiry prematurely. If I can recognize that my opponent is rational and might (although I strongly doubt it) be right, then I have reason to hope that she retains her position, develops it, and either comes (as I believe she will) to see the error of her ways or (however unlikely) develops an argument that will demonstrate to me the error of mine. A convinced materialist then has sound epistemic reasons to tolerate dualism" (p. 68).

Chapter 10

1   Indeed, this seems exactly like the sort of dogmatism that Jacob Bronowski warned against in the first chapter of this book.

2   In this chapter, we're primarily interested in how intellectual humility might speak to religious beliefs. But it's worth noting that there is a small but growing body of research on how *various religious perspectives might speak to intellectual humility*. See, for example, Firestone and Safi (2011).

3   Of course, the amount of religious disagreement that we find in the world can be overstated. There is, after all, substantial religious agreement. The vast majority of people, for example, believe in the existence of at least one god. There is substantial consensus on this score. As such, we might wonder that if we take a blanket conciliatory approach to disagreement seriously, this might actually give us some reason to believe in some form of basic theism.

4   To be sure, just because a given belief could be non-culpably attributed with a high degree of positive epistemic status does not mean that that belief is true. As such, we're not arguing for the truth of any given religious belief. Our aim is to show that it's possible for a religious belief to be non-culpably attributed with a high degree of positive status, not that some specific religious (or anti-religious) belief is true.

5   For example, in the fifteenth chapter of his letter to the Corinthians, the Apostle Paul poignantly stresses that if Jesus Christ was not raised from the dead (i.e., if an essential pillar of the Christian faith is false), "[Christians] are of all people most to be pitied" (1 Cor. 15:19, *English Standard Version*). In other words, Paul seems to be suggesting that Christians should be so affected by their Christianity that their lives should be supremely pitiable if Christianity is not true.

6   Of course, a belief does not necessarily need to be political, religious, or moral in order to deeply affect us. Presumably, given the right circumstances, almost any belief

(e.g., a belief in the superiority of Apple computers, a belief in the perils of inorganic food, etc.) can be made surprisingly important for one's view of the world.

7   And because of this they are likely to perceive each other as intellectually arrogant.

8   *And presumably, what one ought to believe depends on what is ultimately true.* Consider the RELIGIOUS DISAGREEMENT case. If Christianity is true, then perhaps Christy is perceiving God via her *sensus divinitatis*, and Abbey is being intellectually blind as a result of original sin. Conversely, if atheism is true, then Abbey via her enlightened faculties is able to escape the folk appeal of religious beliefs; Christy, however, is being intellectually blinded by her defunct commitments to superstition and myth. As such, it seems as though we cannot agree on what one ought to believe in cases like Religious Disagreement, because, in part, we cannot agree on what is true.

9   If the diversity of religious perspectives are largely mutually exclusive (such that, for example, Hinduism can't be true if Judaism is true and vice versa), then that seems to mean that most people are drastically misinformed regarding their religious beliefs and convictions. And seemingly that will mean that such people will be attributing far more positive epistemic status to their religious beliefs than such beliefs actually enjoy, which matches our definition of intellectual arrogance.

10 Though, arguably there are some areas of widespread agreement. The belief that at least one god exists, for example, is one belief that the vast majority of people around the world happen to agree on.

11 And this might actually be the case for disagreements in general. See Hawthorne and Srinivasan (2013).

12 Given the sordid history of trying to provide a reductive analysis of knowledge within epistemology (see Zagzebski, 1994; Church, 2013), we considered the project of trying to provide such an analysis of intellectual humility a Sisyphean endeavor.

13 See Roberts and Wood (2003, 2007); Kallestrup and Pritchard (in press).

14 That said, we also made the case that agent-reliabilist accounts of intellectual virtue should, nevertheless, be extremely interested in intellectual humility; intellectual humility, even as a character virtue, can deeply affect and be affected by the reliability of our cognitive faculties.

15 And, again, the question, of course, is what sort of cognitive character is the right one (or the right sort of one). As we said before, determining the answer, unfortunately though understandably, requires more than intellectual humility—it takes, we propose, wisdom and courage (and maybe even some luck).

BIBLIOGRAPHY

Abele, A. E., and Wojciszke, B. (2007). Agency and communion from the perspective of self versus others. *Journal of Personality and Social Psychology, 93*(5), pp. 751–63. doi: 10.1037/0022-3514.93.5.751.

Abele, A. E., and Wojciszke, B. (2013). The Big Two in social judgment and behavior. *Social Psychology, 44*(2), pp. 61–62. doi: 10.1027/1864-9335/a000137.

Adler, J. (2012). Epistemological problems of testimony. *The Stanford Encyclopedia of Philosophy.* http://plato.stanford.edu/archives/sum2015/entriesestimony-episprob/.

Alfano, M. (2012). Expanding the situationist challenge to responsibilist virtue epistemology. *Philosophical Quarterly, 62*(247), pp. 223–49.

Alicke, M. D., and Govorun, O. (2005). The better-than-average effect. In M. D. Alicke, D. A. Dunning, and J. I. Krueger (Eds.), *The Self in Social Judgment* (pp. 85–106). New York, NY: Psychology Press.

Altemeyer, B. (1998). The other "authoritarian personality." In M. P. Zanna (Ed.), *Advances in Experimental Social Psychology* (Vol. 30, pp. 47–91). New York: Academic Press.

Anscombe, G. E. M. (1958). Modern moral philosophy. *Philosophy, 33*(124), pp. 1–19.

Apperly, I. A., and Butterfill, S. A. (2009). Do humans have two systems to track beliefs and belief-like states? *Psychological Review, 116*(4), pp. 953–70. doi: 10.1037/a0016923.

Armor, D. A., and Taylor, S. E. (2002). When predictions fail: The dilemma of unrealistic optimism. In T. Gilovich, D. Griffin, and D. Kahneman (Eds.), *Heuristics and Biases: The Psychology of Intuitive Judgment* (pp. 334–47). New York, NY: Cambridge University Press.

Ashton, M. C., and Lee, K. (2005). Honesty-Humility, the Big Five, and the Five-Factor Model. *Journal of Personality, 73*(5), pp. 1321–53. doi: 10.1111/j.1467-6494.2005.00351.x.

Ashton, M. C., and Lee, K. (2007). Empirical, theoretical, and practical advantages of the HEXACO model of personality structure. *Personality and Social Psychology Review, 11*(2), pp. 150–66. doi: 10.1177/1088868306294907.

Ashton, M. C., and Lee, K. (2008). The HEXACO model of personality structure and the importance of the H factor. *Social and Personality Psychology Compass, 2*(5), pp. 1952–62. doi: 10.1111/j.1751-9004.2008.00134.x.

Atir, S., Rosenzweig, E., and Dunning, D. (2015). When knowledge knows no bounds: Self-perceived expertise predicts claims of impossible knowledge. *Psychological Science, 26*(8), pp. 1295–1303. doi: 10.1177/0956797615588195.

Axtell, G. (in press). Thinking twice about virtue and vice: From epistemic situationism to dual process theories. In M. Alfano and A. Fairweather (Eds.), *Epistemic Situationism.* Oxford: Oxford University Press.

Ayduk, Ö., and Kross, E. (2010). From a distance: Implications of spontaneous self-distancing for adaptive self-reflection. *Journal of Personality and Social Psychology, 98*(5), pp. 809–29. doi: 10.1037/a0019205.

Baehr, J. (2012). *The Inquiring Mind: On Intellectual Virtues and Virtue Epistemology.* Oxford: Oxford University Press.

Baehr, J. (2015). Virtue epistemology. *Internet Encyclopedia of Philosophy.* http://www.iep. utm.edu/virtueep/.

Bakan, D. (1966). *The Duality of Human Existence. An Essay on Psychology and Religion.* Chicago, IL: Rand McNally.

Baron, J. (1994). *Thinking and Deciding* (2nd ed.). New York, NY: Cambridge University Press.

Battaly, H. (2012). Virtue epistemology. In J. Greco and J. Turri (Eds.), *Virtue Epistemology: Contemporary Readings* (pp. 3–32). Cambridge, MA: MIT Press.

Bechara, A., Damasio, H., and Damasio, A. R. (2000). Emotion, decision making and the orbitofrontal cortex. *Cerebral Cortex, 10*(3), pp. 295–307. doi: 10.1093/cercor/10.3.295.

Bergeman, C. S., Chipuer, H. M., Plomin, R., Pedersen, N. L., McClearn, G. E., Nesselroade, J. R., Costa, P. T., Jr. and McCrae, R. (1993). Genetic and environmental effects on openness to experience, agree-ableness, and conscientiousness: An adoption/ twin study. *Journal of Personality, 67*, pp. 159–79.

Birch, S. A. J., and Bernstein, D. M. (2007). What can children tell us about hindsight bias: A fundamental constraint on perspective-taking? *Social Cognition, 25*(1), pp. 98–113. doi: 10.1521/soco.2007.25.1.98.

Birch, S. J., Akmal, N., and Frampton, K. L. (2010). Two-year-olds are vigilant of others non verbal cues to credibility. *Developmental Science, 13*(2), pp. 363–69. doi: 10.1111/j.1467-7687.2009.00906.x.

Blank, H., Fischer, V., and Erdfelder, E. (2003). Hindsight bias in political elections. *Memory, 11*(4–5), pp. 491–504. doi: 10.1080/09658210244000513.

Blass, T. (1991). Understanding behavior in the Milgram obedience experiment: The role of personality, situations, and their interactions. *Journal of Personality and Social Psychology, 60*(3), pp. 398–413.

Bowlby, J. (1982). *Attachment and loss: Vol. 1. Attachment* (2nd ed.). New York, NY: Basic Books.

Bronowski, J. (1973). *The Ascent of Man.* Documentary.

Bruckmüller, S., and Abele, A. E. (2013). The density of the Big Two: How are agency and communion structurally represented? *Social Psychology, 44*(2), pp. 63–74. doi: 10.1027/1864-9335/a000145.

Brueckner, A. (2007). Hinge propositions and epistemic justification. *Pacific Philosophical Quarterly 88* (3), pp. 285–87. doi: 10.1111/j.1468-0114.2007.00292.x.

Buchsbaum, D., Bridgers, S., Weisberg, D. S. and Gopnik, A. (2012). The power of possibility: causal learning, counterfactual reasoning, and pretend play. *Philosophical Transactions of the Royal Society B, 367*, pp. 2202–12. doi: 10.1098/rstb.2012.0122.

Busch, J., and Legare, C. (2015, May 13). *The development of belief revision in response to evidence.* Paper presented at the Intellectual Humility: Scientific, Philosophical, & Theological Perspectives Conference, Catalina Island, CA.

Cacioppo, J. T., and Petty, R. E. (1982). The need for cognition. *Journal of Personality and Social Psychology, 42*(1), pp. 116–31. doi: 10.1037/0022-3514.42.1.116.

Cacioppo, J. T., Petty, R. E., Feinstein, J. A., and Jarvis, W. B. G. (1996). Dispositional differences in cognitive motivation: The life and times of individuals varying in need for cognition. *Psychological Bulletin, 119*(2), pp. 197–253. doi: 10.1037/0033-2909.119.2.197.

Campbell, W. K., Bonacci, A. M., Shelton, J., Exline, J. J., and Bushman, B. J. (2004). Psychological entitlement: Interpersonal consequences and validation of a self-report measure. *Journal of Personality Assessment, 83*, pp. 29–45.

Chaiken, S., Wood, W., and Eagly, A. (1996). Principles of persuasion. In E. T. Higgins and A. W. Kruglanski (Eds.), *Social Psychology: Handbook of Basic Principles.* (pp. 702–42) New York: The Guilford Press.

Chignell, A. (2003). Accidentally true belief and warrant. *Synthese, 137*(3), pp. 445–58.

Church, I. M. (2013). Getting "lucky" with Gettier. *European Journal of Philosophy, 21*(1), pp. 37–49.

Clayton, V. P., and Birren, J. E. (1980). The development of wisdom across the life span: a reexamination of an ancient topic. In P. B. Baltes and O. G. Brim (Eds.), *Life-span Development and Behavior* (Vol. 3, pp. 104–35). New York: Academic Press.

Clore, G. L., and Ortony, A. (2008). Appraisal theories: How cognition shapes affect into emotion. In M. Lewis, J. M. Havilan-Jones, and L. F. Barrett (Eds.), *Handbook of Emotions* (pp. 628–44). New York, NY: Guiliford Press.

Coady, C. A. J. (1992). *Testimony: A Philosophical Study* (1st ed.). Oxford and New York: Clarendon Press.

Conee, E., and Feldman, R. (1998). The generality problem for reliabilism. *Philosophical Studies: An International Journal for Philosophy in the Analytic Tradition, 89*(1), pp. 1–29.

Costa, P. T., and MacRae, R. R. (1985). *The NEO Personality Inventory Manual.* Odessa, FL: Psychological Assessment Resources.

Craig, E. (1999). *Knowledge and the State of Nature.* Oxford: Oxford University Press. http://www.oxfordscholarship.com/view/10.1093/0198238797.001.0001/acprof-9780198238799.

Cronbach, L. J., and Meehl, P. E. (1955). Construct validity in psychological tests. *Psychological Bulletin 52*(4), pp. 281–302. doi:10.1037/h0040957, retrieved online 11/15 at http://psychclassics.yorku.ca/Cronbach/construct.htm.

Crowne, D. P., and Marlowe, D. (1960). A new scale of social desirability independent of psychopathology. *Journal of Consulting Psychology, 24*, pp. 349–54. doi: 10.1037/h0047358.

Damasio, A. R. (1995). *Descartes' Error: Emotion, Reason, and the Human Brain.* New York, NY: Avon Books.

Danovitch, J., and Moser, J. (2015, May 12). *Neural, cognitive and social contributions to children's intellectual humility.* Paper presented at the Intellectual Humility: Scientific, Philosophical, & Theological Perspectives Conference, Catalina Island, CA.

Davidson, R. J. (2005). *The Emotional Life of your Brain: How its Unique Patterns Affect the Way you Think, Feel, and Live–and How You Can Change Them.* New York, NY: Penguin.

Davis, D. E., and Hook, J. N. (in press). Intellectual humility in the trenches: A reply to Church. Biola University's Center for Christian Thought. http://cct.biola.edu/blog/.

Davis, D. E., and Hook, J. N. (in press). Intellectual humility and religion: A psychological perspective. Biola University's Center for Christian Thought. http://cct.biola.edu/blog/.

Davis, D. E., Hook, J. N., Worthington, E. L., Van Tongeren, D. R., Gartner, A. L., Jennings, D. J., and Emmons, R. A. (2011). Relational humility: Conceptualizing and measuring Humility as a personality judgment. *Journal of Personality Assessment*, *93*(3), pp. 225–34. doi: 10.1080/00223891.2011.558871.

Davis, M. H. (1983). Measuring individual differences in empathy: Evidence for a multidimensional approach. *Social Psychology*, *44*, pp. 113–26.

Digman, J. M. (1997). Higher-order factors of the Big Five. *Journal of Personality and Social Psychology*, *73*(6), pp. 1246–56. doi: 10.1037/0022-3514.73.6.1246.

Dunning, D. (2015, May 13). *Cognitive habits of intellectual arrogance and humility*. Paper presented at the Science of Intellectual Humility Capstone Conference, Catalina Island, CA. May, 2015.

Dunning, D., Krueger, J. I., and Alicke, M. D. (2005). The self in social perception: Looking back, looking ahead. In M. D. Alicke, D. A. Dunning, and J. I. Krueger (Eds.), *The Self in Social Judgment* (pp. 269–80). New York, NY: Psychology Press.

Dunning, D., Leuenberger, A., and Sherman, D. A. (1995). A new look at motivated inference: Are self-serving theories of success a product of motivational forces? *Journal of Personality and Social Psychology*, *69*(1), pp. 58–68. doi: 10.1037/0022-3514.69.1.58.

Dunning, D., Meyerowitz, J. A., and Holzberg, A. D. (2002). Ambiguity and self-evaluation: The role of idiosyncratic trait definition in self-serving assessments of ability. In T. Gilovich, D. Griffin, and D. Kahneman (Eds.), *Heuristics and Biases: The Psychology of Intuitive Judgment* (pp. 324–33). New York, NY: Cambridge University Press.

Dweck, C. S., Chiu, C.-y., and Hong, Y.-y. (1995). Implicit theories and their role in judgments and reactions: A world from two perspectives. *Psychological Inquiry*, *6*(4), pp. 267–85. doi: 10.1207/s15327965pli0604_1.

Elgin, C. (2010). Persistent disagreement. In R. Feldman and T. A. Warfield (Eds.), *Disagreement* (pp. 53–68). Oxford, UK: Oxford University Press.

Emmons, R. (1987). Narcissism: Theory and measurement. *Journal of Personality and Social Psychology*, *52*(1), pp. 11–17.

Epley, N., and Gilovich, T. (2002). Putting adjustment back in the anchoring and adjustment heuristic. In T. Gilovich, D. Griffin, and D. Kahneman (Eds.), *Heuristics and Biases: The Psychology of Intuitive Judgment* (pp. 139–49). New York, NY: Cambridge University Press.

Epstein, S., Lipson, A., Holstein, C., and Huh, E. (1992). Irrational reactions to negative outcomes: Evidence for two conceptual systems. *Journal of Personality and Social Psychology*, *62*(2), pp. 328–39. doi: 10.1037/0022-3514.62.2.328.

Evans, J. S. (2007). *Hypothetical Thinking: Dual Processes in Reasoning and Judgment*. New York: Psychology Press.

Evans, J. T., and Stanovich, K. E. (2013). Dual-process theories of higher cognition: Advancing the debate. *Perspectives on Psychological Science*, *8*(3), pp. 223–41.

Falbo T., and Belk, S. S. (1985). A short scale to measure self-righteousness. *Journal of Personality Assessment, 49,* pp. 172–77.

Firestone, R., and Omid, S. (Eds.) (2011). *Learned Ignorance: Intellectual Humility among Jews, Christians and Muslims.* New York, NY: Oxford University Press.

Fisher, M., Goddu, M. K., and Keil, F. C. (2015). Searching for explanations: How the internet inflates estimates of internal knowledge. *Journal of Experimental Psychology: General.* Advance online publication. http://dx.doi.org/10.1037/xge0000070.

Fisher, M., and C. Keil, F. (2015). The curse of expertise: When more knowledge leads to miscalibrated explanatory insight. *Cognitive Science*, doi: 10.1111/cogs.12280.

Fleeson, W. (2001). Toward a structure- and process-integrated view of personality: Traits as density distributions of states. *Journal of Personality and Social Psychology, 80*(6), pp. 1011–27. doi: 10.1037/0022-3514.80.6.1011.

Fleeson, W. (2004). Moving personality beyond the person-situation debate: The challenge and the opportunity of within-person variability. *Current Directions in Psychological Science, 13*(2), pp. 83–87. doi: 10.1111/j.0963-7214.2004.00280.x.

Fosha, D. (2000). *The Transforming Power of Affect: A Model for Accelerated Change.* New York, NY: Basic Books.

Fricker, E. (1994). Against gullibility. In A. Chakrabarti and B. K. Matilal (Eds.), *Knowing from Words* pp. (125–61). Dordrecht, Netherlands: Kluwer Academic Publishers.

Fricker, M. (2007). *Epistemic Injustice: Power and the Ethics of Knowing.* New York, NY: Oxford University Press.

Fumerton, R. (2010). You can't trust a philosopher. In R. Feldman and T. A. Warfield (Eds.), *Disagreement* (pp. 53–68). Oxford, UK: Oxford University Press.

Funder, D. C. (2010). *The Personality Puzzle* (5th ed.). New York, NY: W. W. Norton and Co.

Gentile, B., Miller, J. D., Hoffman, B. J., Reidy, D. E., Zeichner, A., and Campbell, W. (2013). A test of two brief measures of grandiose narcissism: The Narcissistic Personality Inventory–13 and the Narcissistic Personality Inventory-16. *Psychological Assessment, 25,* pp. 1120–36. doi: 10.1037/a0033192.

Gilbert, D. T. (1991). How mental systems believe. *American Psychologist, 46,* pp. 107–19.

Gilbert, D. T., and Malone, P. S. (1995). The correspondence bias. *Psychological Bulletin, 117*(1), pp. 21–38. doi: 10.1037/0033-2909.117.1.21.

Gilligan, C. (1982). *In a Different Voice: Psychological Theory and Women's Development.* Cambridge, MA: Harvard University Press.

Gilovich, T. (1991). *How We Know What Isn't So: The Fallibility of Human Reason in Everyday Life.* New York, NY: Free Press.

Gilovich, T., Griffin, D., and Kahneman, D. (Eds.) (2002). *Heuristics and Biases: The Psychology of Intuitive Judgment.* New York, NY: Cambridge University Press.

Goldberg, L. R., Johnson, J. A., Eber, H. W., Hogan, R., Ashton, M. C., Cloninger, C., and Gough, H. G. (2006). The international personality item pool and the future of public-domain personality measures. *Journal of Research in Personality, 40,* pp. 84–96. doi: 10.1016/j.jrp.2005.08.007.

Goldman, A. I. (1976). Discrimination and perceptual knowledge. *The Journal of Philosophy, 73*(20), pp. 771–91.

Gopnik, A. (2003). The Theory Theory as an alternative to the innateness hypothesis. In L. Antony and N. Hornsteitn (Eds.), *Chomsky and his Critics*. New York, NY: Basil Blackwell. Retrieved online (11/15) at http://citeseerx.ist.psu.edu/viewdoc/ download?, doi=10.1.1.134.3331&rep=rep1&type=pdf.

Gopnik, A., and Wellman, H. M. (2012). Reconstructing constructivism: Causal models, Bayesian learning mechanisms, and the Theory Theory. *Psychological Bulletin, 138*(6), pp. 1085–1108. doi: 10.1037/a0028044.

Gottman, J. (1995). *Why Marriages Succeed or Fail: And How You Can Make Yours Last.* New York, NY: Simon & Schuster.

Greco, J. (1999). Agent reliabilism. *Philosophical Perspectives, 13*, pp. 273–96.

Greco, J. (2003). Virtue and luck, epistemic and otherwise. *Metaphilosophy, 34*(3), pp. 353–66.

Greco, J. (Ed.) (2004). *Ernest Sosa and His Critics*. Philosophers and their critics. Oxford, UK: Blackwell Publishing.

Greco, J. (2009). Knowledge and success from ability. *Philosophical Studies, 142*(1), pp. 17–26.

Greco, J. (2010). *Achieving Knowledge: A Virtue-Theoretic Account of Epistemic Normativity.* Cambridge: Cambridge University Press.

Greco, J. (2012a). A (different) virtue epistemology. *Philosophy and Phenomenological Research, 85*(1), pp. 1–26.

Greco, J. (2012b). Recent work on testimonial knowledge. *American Philosophical Quarterly, 49*(1), pp. 15–28.

Greco, J. (2015). Testimonial knowledge and the flow of information. In J. Greco and D. Henderson (Eds.), *Epistemic Evaluation: Point and Purpose Epistemology* (pp. 274–90). New York, NY: Oxford University Press.

Greco, J., and Turri, J. (2011). Virtue epistemology. *The Stanford Encyclopedia of Philosophy*. http://plato.stanford.edu/entries/epistemology-virtue/.

Greenberg, J., Solomon, S., and Pyszczynski, T. (1997). Terror management theory of self-esteem and cultural worldviews: Empirical assessments and conceptual refinements. In M. P. Zanna (Ed.), *Advances in Experimental Social Psychology* (Vol. 29, pp. 61–139). San Diego, CA: Academic Press.

Greenberg, L. S. (2004). Evolutionary perspectives on emotion: Making sense of what we feel. In P. Gilbert (Ed.), *Evolutionary Theory and Cognitive Therapy* (pp. 67–88). New York: Springer Publishing Co.

Greenberg, L. S. (2008). Emotion and cognition in psychotherapy: The transforming power of affect. *Canadian Psychology/Psychologie canadienne, 49*(1), pp. 49–59. doi: 10.1037/0708-5591.49.1.49.

Greenberg, L. S., and Pascual-Leone, A. (2006). Emotion in psychotherapy: A practice-friendly research review. *Journal of Clinical Psychology, 62*(5), pp. 611–30. doi: 10.1002/ jclp.20252.

Gregg, A. P., Hart, C. M., Sedikides, C., and Kumashiro, M. (2008). Everyday conceptions of modesty: A prototype analysis. *Personality and Social Psychology Bulletin, 34*(7), pp. 978–92. doi: 10.1177/0146167208316734.

Gregg, A. P., Mahadevan, N., and Sedikides, C. (in press). Intellectual arrogance and intellectual humility: Correlational evidence for an evolutionary-embodied-epistemological account. *Journal of Positive Psychology*.

Griffiths, P. E. (1997). *What Emotions Really Are: The Problem of Psychological Categories.* Chicago, IL: University of Chicago Press.

Grossmann, I., Na, J., Varnuma, M. E. W., Park, D. C., Kitayama, S., and Nisbett, R. E. (2010). Reasoning about social conflicts improves into old age. *PNAS Proceedings of the National Academy of Sciences of the United States of America, 107*(16), pp. 7246–50. doi: 10.1073/pnas.1001715107.

Guenther, C. L., and Alicke, M. D. (2010). Deconstructing the better-than-average effect. *Journal of Personality and Social Psychology, 99*(5), pp. 755–70. doi: 10.1037/a0020959.

Guilford, J. P. (1954). *Psychometric Methods* (rev. ed.). New York, NY: McGraw-Hill. First Edition, 1936.

Haddock, G., Maio, G. R., Arnold, K., and Huskinson, T. (2008). Should persuasion be affective or cognitive? The moderating effects of need for affect and need for cognition. *Personality and Social Psychology Bulletin, 34*(6), pp. 769–78. doi: 10.1177/0146167208314871.

Hagá, S., and Olsen, K. (in press). If I only had a little humility, I would be perfect: Children's and adult's perception of intellectually arrogant, humble and diffident people. *Journal of Positive Psychology.*

Haidt, J. (2001). The emotional dog and its rational tail: A social intuitionist approach to moral judgment. *Psychological Review, 108*(4), pp. 814–34. doi: 10.1037/0033-295X.108.4.814.

Haidt, J. (2015). The first New York City Asteroids Club dinner. http://www.civilpolitics.org/content/the-first-new-york-city-asteroids-club-dinner/. Retrieved online October, 2015.

Harman, G. (1999). Moral philosophy meets social psychology: Virtue ethics and the fundamental attribution error. *Proceedings of the Aristotelian Society, 99*, pp. 315–31. Retrieved online at http://www.filosofia.unimi.it/~zucchi/NuoviFile/harman.pdf.

Harris, P. (2012). *Trusting What You're Told: How Children Learn from Others.* Cambridge, MA: The Belknap Press of Harvard University Press.

Haugtvedt, C. P., Petty, R. E., and Cacioppo, J. T. (1992). Need for cognition and advertising: Understanding the role of personality variables in consumer behavior. *Journal of Consumer Psychology, 1*(3), pp. 239–60. doi: 10.1016/s1057-7408(08)80038-1.

Hawthorne, J., and Srinivasan, A. (2013). Disagreement without transparency: some bleak thoughts. In D. Christensen and J. Lackey (Eds.), *The Epistemology of Disagreement: New Essays* (pp. 9–30). Oxford, UK: Oxford University Press.

Hergovich, A., Schott, R., and Burger, C. (2010). Biased evaluation of abstracts depending on topic and conclusion: Further evidence of a confirmation bias within scientific psychology. *Current Psychology: A Journal for Diverse Perspectives on Diverse Psychological Issues, 29*(3), pp. 188–209. doi: 10.1007/s12144-010-9087-5.

Holliday, S. G., and Chandler, M. J. (1986). *Wisdom: Explorations in Adult Competence.* Basel, Switzerland: Karger.

Hopkin, C. R., Hoyle, R. H., and Toner, K. (2014). Intellectual humility and reactions to opinions about religious beliefs. *Journal of Psychology and Theology, 42*, pp. 50–61.

Hoyle, R. H., Davisson, E. K., Diebels, K. J., and Leary, M. L. (2016). Holding specific views with humility: Conceptualization and measurement of specific intellectual humility. *Personality and Individual Differences, 97*, pp. 165–72.

Huck, S. W. (2000). *Reading Statistics and Research* (3rd ed.). New York, NY: Addison Wesley Longman Inc.

Hume, D. (1948). *Dialogues Concerning Natural Religion* (H. D. Aiken, Ed.). The Hafner Library of Classics. London, UK: Hafner Press.

Jang, K. L., Livesley, W. J., and Vernon, P. A. (1996). Heritability of the big five personality dimensions and their facets: A twin study. *Journal of Personality, 64*(3), pp. 577–91. doi: 10.1111/j.1467-6494.1996.tb00522.x.

Jang, K. L., McCrae, R. R., Angleitner, A., Riemann, R., and Livesley, W. J. (1998). Heritability of facet-level traits in a cross-cultural twin sample: Support for a hierarchical model of personality. *Journal of Personality and Social Psychology, 74*(6), pp. 1556–65. doi: 10.1037/0022-3514.74.6.1556.

Jarvinen, M., and Paulus, T. B., Samuelson, P. L., Reid, A., Church, I. M., and Barrett, J. (2015, May 15). *Attachment and opinion revision: What's the relationship between emotion and cognitive openness?* Paper presented at the Intellectual Humility: Scientific, Philosophical, & Theological Perspectives Conference, Catalina Island, CA.

Jaswal, V. K., and Malone, L. S. (2007). Turning believers into skeptics: 3-year-olds' sensitivity to cues to speaker credibility. *Journal of Cognition and Development, 8*(3), pp. 263–83. doi: 10.1080/15248370701446392.

John, O. P., Donahue, E. M., and Kentle, R. L. (1991). *The Big Five Inventory–Versions 4a and 54.* Berkeley, CA: University of California, Berkeley, Institute of Personality and Social Research.

Jonas, E., Schulz-Hardt, S., Frey, D., and Thelen, N. (2001). Confirmation bias in sequential information search after preliminary decisions: An expansion of dissonance theoretical research on selective exposure to information. *Journal of Personality and Social Psychology, 80*(4), pp. 557–71. doi: 10.1037/0022-3514.80.4.557.

Kahneman, D. (2011). *Thinking, Fast and Slow.* New York: Farrar, Straus and Giroux.

Kahneman, D., and Frederick, S. (2002). Representativeness revisited: Attribute substitution in intuitive judgment. In T. Gilovich, D. Griffin and D. Kahneman (Eds.), *Heuristics and Biases: The Psychology of Intuitive Judgment* (pp. 49–81). New York, NY: Cambridge University Press.

Kallestrup, J., and Pritchard, D. (forthcoming). From epistemic anti-individualism to intellectual humility. *Res Philosophica.*

King, P. M., and Kitchener, K. S. (2004). Reflective judgment: Theory and research on the development of epistemic assumptions through adulthood. *Educational Psychologist, 39*(1), pp. 5–18. doi: 10.1207/s15326985ep3901_2.

Kohlberg, L. (1981). *The Philosophy of Moral Development: Moral Stages and the Idea of Justice: Vol. 1. Essays on Moral Development.* San Francisco: Harper & Row.

Kross, E., and Grossmann, I. (2012). Boosting wisdom: Distance from the self enhances wise reasoning, attitudes, and behavior. *Journal of Experimental Psychology, 141*(1), pp. 43–48.

Kruger, J. (1999). Lake Wobegon be gone! The "below-average effect" and the egocentric nature of comparative ability judgments. *Journal of Personality and Social Psychology, 77*(2), pp. 221–32. doi: 10.1037/0022-3514.77.2.221.

Kruglanski, A. W. (1990). Lay epistemic theory in social-cognitive psychology. *Psychological Inquiry, 1*(3), pp. 181–97. doi: 10.1207/s15327965pli0103_1.

Kruglanski, A. W., Dechesne, M., Orehek, E., and Pierro, A. (2009). Three decades of lay epistemics: The why, how, and who of knowledge formation. *European Review of Social Psychology, 20*(1), pp. 146–91. doi: 10.1080/10463280902860037.

Kruglanski, A. W., and Mayseless, O. (1987). Motivational effects in the social comparison of opinions. *Journal of Personality and Social Psychology, 53*(5), pp. 834–42. doi: 10.1037/0022-3514.53.5.834.

Krumrei-Mancuso, E. J., and Rouse, S. J. (2016). The development and validation of the comprehensive Intellectual Humility Scale. *Journal of Personality Assessment, 98*(2), pp. 209–21, doi: 10.1080/00223891.2015.1068174.

Kunda, Z. (1990). The case for motivated reasoning. *Psychological Bulletin, 108*(3), pp. 480–98. doi: 10.1037/0033-2909.108.3.480.

Lackey, J. (2006a). It takes two to tango: Beyond reductionism and non-reductionism in the epistemology of testimony. In J. Lackey and E. Sosa (Eds.), *The Epistemology of Testimony* (pp. 160–89). Oxford, UK: Oxford University Press.

Lackey, J. (2006b). Knowing from testimony. *Philosophy Compass, 1*(5), pp. 432–48.

Landrum, A. R., Mills, C. M., and Johnston, A. M. (2013). When do children trust the expert? Benevolence information influences children's trust more than expertise. *Developmental Science, 16*(4), pp. 622–38.

Landrum, R. E. (2011). Measuring dispositional humility: A first approximation. *Psychological Reports, 108*(1), pp. 217–28. doi: 10.2466/02.07.09.pr0.108.1.217-228.

Leary, M. R., Diebels, K. J., Davisson, E. K., Isherwood, J. C., Jongman-Sereno, K. P., Raimi, K. T., Deffler, S. A., and Hoyle, R. A. (2016). *Cognitive and interpersonal features of intellectual humility*. Manuscript submitted for publication. Durham, NC: Duke University.

LeDoux, J. E. (1996). *The Emotional Brain: The Mysterious Underpinnings of Emotional Life*. New York, NY: Simon & Schuster.

Lee, H. (1960). *To Kill a Mockingbird*. London, UK: William Heinemann.

Lee, K., and Ashton, M. C. (2004). Psychometric properties of the HEXACO personality inventory. *Multivariate Behavioral Research, 39*(2), pp. 329–58. doi: 10.1207/s15327906mbr3902_8.

Legare, C. H. (2012). Exploring explanation: Explaining inconsistent information guides hypothesis-testing behavior in young children. *Child Development, 83*, pp. 173–85. doi: 10.1111/j.1467-8624.2011.

Legare, C. H. (2014). The Contributions of Explanation and Exploration to Children's Scientific Reasoning. *Child Development Perspectives, 8*(2), pp. 101–6.

Legare, C. H., Schult, C., Impola, M., and Souza, A. L. (in press). Young children revise explanations in response to new information. *Cognitive Development*.

Lensvelt-Mulders, G., and Hettema, J. (2001). Analysis of genetic influences on the consistency and variability of the Big Five across different stressful situations. *European Journal of Personality, 15*(5), pp. 355–71. doi: 10.1002/per.414.

Levin, M. (2004). Virtue epistemology: No new cures. *Philosophy and Phenomenological Research, 69*(2), pp. 397–410. doi: 10.1111/j.1933-1592.2004.tb00401.x.

Levy, S., and Dweck, C. S. (1997). [Revised implicit theories measure.] Unpublished raw data, Columbia University, New York.

Litman, J. A., and Spielberger, C. D. (2003). Measuring epistemic curiosity and its diversive and specific components. *Journal of personality Assessment, 80*(1), pp. 75–86.

Lissitz, R. W., and Samuelsen, K. (2007). A suggested change in terminology and emphasis regarding validity and education. *Educational Researcher, 36*(8), pp. 437–48. doi: 10.3102/0013189X07311286.

Lockhart, K. L., Goddu, M. K., and Keil, F. C. (in press). Overoptimism about future knowledge: Early arrogance? *Journal of Positive Psychology.*

Loehlin, J. C., McCrae, R. R., Costa, P. J., and John, O. P. (1998). Heritabilities of common and measure-specific components of the Big Five personality factors. *Journal of Research in Personality, 32*(4), pp. 431–53. doi: 10.1006/jrpe.1998.2225.

Macaskill, G. (2015, July 8). Jesus, the New Testament and Intellectual Humility. Presented as a Tyndale New Testament Lecture. Tyndale House, Cambridge University.

MacMillian, M. (2008). Phineas Gage: Unravelling the myth. *The Psychologist, 21*, pp. 828–31. https://thepsychologist.bps.org.uk/volume-21/edition-9/phineas-gage-unravelling-myth. Retrieved online September, 2015.

Martin, J. G., and Westie, F. R. (1959). The tolerant personality. *American Sociological Review, 24*, pp. 521–28.

Matilal, B. K., and Chakrabarti, A. (Eds.) (1994). *Knowing from Words.* Dordrecht, Netherlands: Kluwer Academic Publishers.

Mayer, J. D., and Salovey, P. (2004). What is emotional intelligence? In P. Salovey, M. A. Brackett and J. D. Mayer (Eds.), *Emotional Intelligence: Key Readings on the Mayer and Salovey Model* (pp. 29–59). Port Chester, NY: Dude Publishing.

Mayer, J. D., Salovey, P., Caruso, D. R., and Sitarenios, G. (2001). Emotional intelligence as a standard intelligence. *Emotion, 1*(3), pp. 232–42. doi: 10.1037//1528-3542.1.3.232.

McCrae, R. R., and Costa, P. T. (1987). Validation of the five-factor model of personality across instruments and observers. *Journal of Personality and Social Psychology, 52*(1), pp. 81–90. doi: 10.1037/0022-3514.52.1.81.

McCrae, R. R., and Costa, P. T., Jr. (1997). Personality trait structure as a human universal. *American Psychologist, 52*(5), pp. 509–16. doi: 10.1037/0003-066x.52.5.509.

McDowell, J. H. (1994). *Mind and World.* Cambridge, MA: Harvard University Press.

McElroy, S. E., Rice, K. G., Davis, D. E., Hook, J. N., Hill, P. C., Worthington Jr., F. L., and Van Tongeren, D. R. (2014). Intellectual humility: Scale development and theoretical elaborations in the context of religious leadership. *Journal of Psychology & Theology, 42*, pp. 19–30.

Meacham, J. A. (1990). The loss of wisdom. In R. J. Sternberg (Ed.), *Wisdom: Its Nature, Origins, and Development* (pp. 181–211). New York, NY: Cambridge University Press.

Meagher, B. R., Leman, J. C., Bias, J. P., Latendresse, S. J., and Rowatt, W. C. (in press). Contrasting self-report and consensus ratings of intellectual humility and arrogance. *Journal of Research in Personality.*

Mercier, H., and Sperber, D. (2011). Why do humans reason? Arguments for an argumentative theory. *Behavioral and Brain Sciences, 34*(2), pp. 57–74. doi: 10.1017/s0140525x10000968.

Messner, C., and Wänke, M. (2011). Good weather for Schwarz and Clore. *Emotion, 11*(2), pp. 436–37. doi: 10.1037/a0022821.

Mikulincer, M. (1997). Adult attachment style and information processing: Individual differences in curiosity and cognitive closure. *Journal of Personality and Social Psychology, 72*(5), pp. 1217–30. doi: 10.1037/00223514.72.5.1217.

Mikulincer, M., and Florian, V. (2000). Exploring individual differences in reactions to mortality salience: Does attachment style regulate terror management mechanisms? *Journal of Personality and Social Psychology, 79*(2), pp. 260–73. doi: 10.1037/0022-3514.79.2.260.

Mikulincer, M., Shaver, P. R., and Pereg, D. (2003). Attachment theory and affect regulation: The dynamics, development, and cognitive consequences of attachmentrelated strategies. *Motivation and Emotion, 27*(2), pp. 77–102. doi: 10.1023/A:1024515519160.

Miller, D. T. (1999). The norm of self-interest. *American Psychologist, 54*(12), pp. 1053–60. doi: 10.1037/0003-066x.54.12.1053.

Milyavsky, M., Kruglanski, A., and Schori-Eyal, N. (2015). *Evidence for Arrogance: On Relative Importance of Expertise, Outcome, and Politeness Information.* Manuscript submitted for publication. College Park, MD: University of Maryland.

Minghella, A. (2000). *The Talented Mr. Ripley-Based on Patricia Highsmith's Novel.* London, UK: Methuen.

Mischel, W., Ayduk, O., Berman, M. G., Casey, B. J., Gotlib, I. H., Jonides, J., and Shoda, Y. (2011). "Willpower" over the life span: Decomposing self-regulation. *Social Cognitive and Affective Neuroscience, 6*(2), pp. 252–56. doi: 10.1093/scan/nsq081.

Moors, A., Ellsworth, P. C., Scherer, K. R., and Frijda, N. H. (2013). Appraisal theories of emotion: State of the art and future development. *Emotion Review, 5*(2), pp. 119–24. doi: 10.1177/1754073912468165.

Mueller, C. M., and Dweck, C. (1998). Praise for intelligence can undermine children's motivation and performance. *Journal of Personality and Social Psychology, 75*(1), pp. 33–52.

Muis, K. R. (2007). The role of epistemic beliefs in self-regulated learning. *Educational Psychologist, 42*(3), pp. 173–90. doi: 10.1080/00461520701416306.

Narvaez, D. (2008). Human flourishing and moral development: Cognitive and neurobiological perspectives of virtue development. In L. P. Nucci and D. Narvaez (Eds.), *Handbook of Moral Development* (pp. 310–27). New York, NY: Routledge.

New York Times (editorial comment). (1985). "Justice Stewart's Legacy." *The New York Times,* December 9, sec. Opinion. http://www.nytimes.com/1985/12/09/opinion/justice-stewart-s-legacy.html.

Nickerson, R. S. (1998). Confirmation bias: A ubiquitous phenomenon in many guises. *Review of General Psychology, 2*(2), pp. 175–220. doi: 10.1037/1089-2680.2.2.175.

Njus, D., and Johnson, D. R. (2008). Need for cognition as a predictor of psychosocial identity development. *Journal of Psychology: Interdisciplinary and Applied, 142*(6), pp. 645–55. doi: 10.3200/jrlp.142.6.645-655.

Oatley, K., and Jenkins, J. M. (1992). Human emotions: Function and dysfunction. *Annual Review of Psychology, 43*, pp. 55–85. doi: 10.1146/annurev.ps.43.020192.000415.

Olin, L., and Doris, J. M. (2014). Vicious minds. *Philosophical Studies, 168*(3), pp. 665–93. doi: 10.1007/s11098-013-0153-3.

Ottati, V., Wilson, C., and Price, E. (2016). *Open-Minded Cognition in Social Context.* Unpublished manuscript. Loyola University, Chicago, IL.

Ozer, D. J., and Benet-Martínez, V. (2006). Personality and the prediction of consequential outcomes. *Annual Review of Psychology, 57*, pp. 401–21. doi: 10.1146/annurev. psych.57.102904.190127.

Panfile, T. M., and Laible, D. J. (2012). Attachment security and child's empathy: The mediating role of emotion regulation. *Merrill-Palmer Quarterly, 58*(1), pp. 1–21. doi: 10.1353/mpq.2012.0003.

Peters, A., Rowatt, W. C., and Johnson, M. K. (2011). Associations between dispositional humility and social relationship quality. *Psychology, 2*(3), pp. 155–61. doi: 10.4236/ psych.2011.23025.

Peterson, C., and Seligman, M. E. P. (2004). *Character Strengths and Virtues: A Handbook and Classification.* Washington, DC: American Psychological Association, Oxford University Press.

Petty, R. E., Cacioppo, J. T., and Goldman, R. (1981). Personal involvement as a determinant of argument-based persuasion. *Journal of Personality and Social Psychology*, 41(5), pp. 847–55. doi: 10.1037/0022-3514.41.5.847.

Petty, R. E., Wegener, D. T., and White, P. H. (1998). Flexible correction processes in social judgment: Implications for persuasion. *Social Cognition, 16*(1), pp. 93–113. doi: 10.1521/soco.1998.16.1.93.

Philie, P. (2009). Entitlement as a Response to I–II–III Scepticism. *Synthese, 171*(3), pp. 459–66.

Plantinga, A. (1993a). *Warrant: The Current Debate.* New York, NY: Oxford University Press.

Plantinga, A. (1993b). *Warrant and Proper Function.* New York, NY: Oxford University Press.

Plantinga, A. (2000). *Warranted Christian Belief.* New York, NY: Oxford University Press.

Porter, T. (2015). Intellectual humility, mindset, and learning. Unpublished dissertation, Stanford University, Palo Alto, CA.

Price, E. D., Ottati, V., Wilson, C., and Kim, S. (2015). Open-minded cognition. *Personality and Social Psychology Bulletin, 41*(11), pp. 1488–1504.

Pritchard, D. (2005). *Epistemic Luck.* Oxford, UK: Oxford University Press.

Pronin, E., Berger, J., and Molouki, S. (2007). Alone in a crowd of sheep: Asymmetric perceptions of conformity and their roots in an introspection illusion. *Journal of Personality and Social Psychology, 92*(4), pp. 585–95. doi: 10.1037/0022-3514.92.4.585.

Pronin, E., Kennedy, K., and Butsch, S. (2006). Bombing versus negotiating: How preferences for combating terrorism are affected by perceived terrorist rationality. *Basic and Applied Social Psychology, 28*(4), pp. 385–92.

Pronin, E., and Kugler, M. B. (2007). Valuing thoughts, ignoring behavior: The introspection illusion as a source of the bias blind spot. *Journal of Experimental Social Psychology, 43*(4), pp. 565–78. doi: 10.1016/j.jesp.2006.05.011.

Pryor, J. (2000). The skeptic and the dogmatist. *Noûs, 34*(4), pp. 517–49. doi: 10.2307/2671880.

Pryor, J. (2004). What's wrong with Moore's argument? *Philosophical Issues, 14*(1), pp. 349–78. doi: 10.1111/j.1533-6077.2004.00034.x.

Pyszczynski, T., Greenberg, J., Solomon, S., Sideris, J., and Stubing, M. J. (1993). Emotional expression and the reduction of motivated cognitive bias: Evidence from cognitive dissonance and distancing from victims' paradigms. *Journal of Personality and Social Psychology, 64*(2), pp. 177–86. doi: 10.1037/0022-3514.64.2.177.

Quine, W. V. (1969). Epistemology naturalized. *Ontological Relativity and Other Essays* (6th ed.). New York, NY: Columbia University Press.

Raskin, R., and Terry, H. (1988). A principal-components analysis of the Narcissistic Personality Inventory and further evidence of its construct validity. *Journal of Personality and Social Psychology, 54*(5). doi: 10.1037/0022-3514.54.5.890.

Reddy, V., and Wilson, C. (2015, May 13). *Humility and openness to engagement.* Paper presented at the Science of Intellectual Humility Capstone Conference, Catalina Island, CA.

Reynolds, W. M. (1982). Development of reliable and valid short forms of the Marlowe-Crowne Social Desirability Scale. *Journal of Clinical Psychology, 38*, pp. 119–25.

Roberts, R. C. (2003). *Emotions: An Essay in Aid of Moral Psychology* (1st ed.). Cambridge, UK: Cambridge University Press.

Roberts, R. C. (2012). What is it to be intellectual humble: Discussion summary. *The Big Questions Online*. http://www.bigquestionsonline.com/node/135/comment/summary/all.

Roberts, R. C., and Wood, W. J. (2003). Humility and epistemic goods. In M. DePaul and L. Zagzebski (Eds.), *Intellectual Virtue: Perspectives From Ethics and Epistemology* (pp. 257–79). Oxford, UK: Oxford University Press.

Roberts, R. C., and Wood, W. J. (2007). *Intellectual Virtues: An Essay in Regulative Epistemology*. Oxford, UK: Clarendon Press.

Rokeach, M. (1960). *The Open and Closed Mind*. Oxford, UK: Basic Books.

Ross, L., and Ward, A. (1996). Naive realism in everyday life: Implications for social conflict and misunderstanding. In E. S. Reed, E. Turiel and T. Brown (Eds.), *Values and Knowledge* (pp. 103–35). Hillsdale, NJ, England: Lawrence Erlbaum Associates, Inc.

Rowatt, W. C., Powers, C., Targhetta, V., Comer, J., Kennedy, S., and Labouff, J. (2006). Development and initial validation of an implicit measure of humility relative to arrogance. *The Journal of Positive Psychology, 1*(4), pp. 198–211. doi: 10.1080/17439760600885671.

Samuelson, P. L., and Church, I. M. (2014). When cognition turns vicious: Heuristics and biases in light of virtue epistemology. *Philosophical Psychology, 28*(8), pp. 1–19.

Samuelson, P. L., Jarvinen, M. J., Paulus, T. B., Reid, A., Church, I. M., and Barrett, J. (2015, May 14). *Must we trust to be humble?: Character assessment and epistemic trust in children*. Paper presented at the Intellectual Humility: Scientific, Philosophical, & Theological Perspectives Conference, Catalina Island, CA.

Samuelson, P. L., Jarvinen, M. J., Paulus, T. B., Church, I. M., Hardy, S. A., and Barrett, J. L. (2015). Implicit theories of intellectual virtues and vices: A focus on intellectual humility. *Journal of Positive Psychology, 10*(5), pp. 389–406.

Samuelson, P. L., Church, I. M., Jarvinen, M. J., and Paulus, T. B. (2013). The science of intellectual humility white paper. Unpublished manuscript. Retrieved from http://trebuchet.fuller.edu/wp-content/uploads/2013/09/IH-White-Paper.pdf.

Sanna, L. J., Schwarz, N., and Stocker, S. L. (2002). When debiasing backfires: Accessible content and accessibility experiences in debiasing hindsight. *Journal of Experimental Psychology: Learning, Memory, and Cognition, 28*(3), pp. 497–502. doi: 10.1037/0278-7393.28.3.497.

Saucier, D. A., and Webster, R. J. (2010). Social vigilantism: Measuring individual differences in belief superiority and resistance to persuasion. *Personality and Social Psychology Bulletin, 36*, pp. 19–32.

Savage, C. W., and Ehrlich, P. (1992). A brief introduction to measurement theory and the essays. In C. W. Savage and P. Ehrlich (Eds.), *Philosophical and Foundational Issues in Measurement Theory* (pp. 1–14). Hillsdale, NJ: Lawrence Erlbaum Associates.

Schneider, D., Lam, R., Bayliss, A. P., and Dux, P. E. (2012). Cognitive load disrupts implicit theory-of-mind processing. *Psychological Science, 23*(8), pp. 842–47. doi: 10.1177/0956797612439070.

Schwarz, N., and Clore, G. L. (2003). Mood as information: 20 years later. *Psychological Inquiry, 14*(3–4), pp. 296–303. doi: 10.1207/S15327965PLI1403&4_20.

Sedikides, C., and Gregg, A. P. (2008). Self-enhancement: Food for thought. *Perspectives on Psychological Science, 3*(2), pp. 102–16. doi: 10.1111/j.1745-6916.2008.00068.x.

Sedikides, C., Horton, R. S., and Gregg, A. P. (2007). The why's the limit: Curtailing self-enhancement with explanatory introspection. *Journal of Personality, 75*(4), pp. 783–824. doi: 10.1111/j.1467-6494.2007.00457.x.

Shortt, J. W., and Gottman, J. M. (1997). Closeness in young adult sibling relationships: Affective and physiological processes. *Social Development, 6*(2), pp. 142–64. doi: 10.1111/j.1467-9507.1997.tb00099.x.

Siegel, D. J. (2012). *Developing Mind: How Relationships and the Brain Interact to Shape Who We Are.* New York, NY: Guilford Press.

Sloman, S. A. (2002). Two systems of reasoning. In T. Gilovich, D. Griffin and D. Kahneman (Eds.), *Heuristics and Biases: The Psychology of Intuitive Judgment* (pp. 379–96). New York, NY: Cambridge University Press.

Smetana, J. G., and Braeges, J. L. (1990). The development of toddler's moral and conventional judgments. *Merrill-Palmer Quarterly, 36*(3), pp. 329–46.

Sosa, E. (1991). *Knowledge in Perspective: Selected Essays in Epistemology.* Cambridge: Cambridge University Press.

Sosa, E. (2004). Replies. In J. Greco (Ed.), *Ernest Sosa and His Critics* (pp. 275–325). Oxford, UK: Blackwell Publishing.

Sosa, E. (2007). *A Virtue Epistemology: Apt Belief and Reflective Knowledge.* Oxford, UK: Oxford University Press.

Sosa, E. (2009a). *Reflective Knowledge: Apt Belief and Reflective Knowledge.* Oxford, UK: Oxford University Press.

Sosa, E. (2009b). Replies to commentators on a virtue epistemology. *Philosophical Studies, 144*, pp. 137–47.

Sosa, E. (2015). *Judgment and Agency.* New York, NY: Oxford University Press.

Stanovich, K. E. (1999). *Who is Rational?: Studies of Individual Differences in Reasoning.* Mahwah, NJ: Lawrence Erlbaum Associates Publishers.

Stanovich, K. E. (2009). Distinguishing the reflective, algorithmic, and autonomous minds: Is it time for a tri-process theory? In St. B. T. Evans and K. Frankish (Eds.), *In Two Minds: Dual Processes and Beyond* (pp. 55–88). New York, NY: Oxford University Press.

Stanovich, K. E., and West, R. F. (1997). Reasoning independently of prior belief and individual differences in actively open-minded thinking. *Journal of Educational Psychology, 89*(2), pp. 342–57. doi: 10.1037/0022-0663.89.2.342.

Stanovich, K. E., and West, R. F. (1998). Individual differences in rational thought. *Journal of Experimental Psychology: General, 127*(2), pp. 161–88. doi: 10.1037/0096-3445.127.2.161.

Stanovich, K. E., and West, R. F. (2002). Individual differences in reasoning: Implications for the rationality debate? In T. Gilovich, D. Griffin, and D. Kahneman (Eds.), *Heuristics and Biases: The Psychology of Intuitive Judgment* (pp. 421–40). New York, NY: Cambridge University Press.

Stanovich, K. E., and West, R. F. (2007). Natural myside bias is independent of cognitive ability. *Thinking & Reasoning, 13*(3), pp. 225–47. doi: 10.1080/13546780600780796.

Sternberg, R. J. (1985). Implicit theories of intelligence, creativity, and wisdom. *Journal of Personality and Social Psychology, 49*(3), pp. 607–27. doi: 10.1037/0022-3514.49.3.607.

Tangney, J. P. (2000). Humility: Theoretical perspectives, empirical findings and directions for future research. *Journal of Social and Clinical Psychology, 19*(1), pp. 70–82. doi: 10.1521/jscp.2000.19.1.70.

Tenney, E. R., Small, J. E., Kondrad, R. L., Jaswal, V. K., and Spellman, B. A. (2011). Accuracy, confidence, and calibration: How young children and adults assess credibility. *Developmental Psychology, 47*(4), pp. 1065–77. doi: 10.1037/a0023273.

Todd, A. R., Bodenhausen, G. V., Richeson, J. A., and Galinsky, A. D. (2011). Perspective taking combats automatic expressions of racial bias. *Journal of Personality and Social Psychology, 100*(6), pp. 1027–42. doi: 10.1037/a0022308.

Twenge, J. M., Konrath, S., Foster, J. D., Keith Campbell, W., and Bushman, B. J. (2008). Egos inflating over time: A cross-temporal meta-analysis of the narcissistic personality inventory. *Journal of Personality, 76*(4), pp. 875–902.

van Inwagen, P. (1999). It is wrong everywhere, always, and for anyone to believe anything upon insufficient evidence. In E. Stump and M. J. Murray (Eds.), *Philosophy of Religion: The Big Questions* (1st ed.). Malden, MA: Wiley-Blackwell.

van Inwagen, Peter. (2010). We're right, they're wrong. In R. Feldman and T. A. Warfield (Eds.), *Disagreement* (pp. 10–28). Oxford, UK: Oxford University Press.

Van Pachterbeke, M., Keller, J., and Saroglou, V. (2012). Flexibility in existential beliefs and worldviews. *Journal of Individual Differences, 33*(1). doi: 10.1027/1614-0001/a000056.

von Hippel, W., and Trivers, R. (2011). The evolution and psychology of self-deception. *Behavioral and Brain Sciences, 34*(01), pp. 1–16. doi: 10.1017/S0140525X10001354.

Wallace, H. M., and Baumeister, R. F. (2002). The performance of narcissists rises and falls with perceived opportunity for glory. *Journal of Personality and Social Psychology, 82*(5), pp. 819–34.

Webster, D. M., and Kruglanski, A. W. (1994). Individual differences in need for cognitive closure. *Journal of Personality and Social Psychology, 67*(6), pp. 1049–62. doi: 10.1037/0022-3514.67.6.1049.

Wegener, D. T., and Petty, R. E. (1997). The Flexible Correction Model: The role of naive theories of bias in bias correction. In M. P. Zanna (Ed.), *Advances in Experimental Social Psychology* (Vol. 29, pp. 141–208). London, UK: Academic Press.

Westen, D., and Blagov, P. S. (2007). A clinical-empirical model of emotional regulation: From defense and motivated reasoning to emotional constraint satisfaction. In J. J. Gross (Ed.), *Handbook of Emotional Regulation* (pp. 373–92). New York, NY: Guilford Press.

Westen, D., Blagov, P. S., Harenski, K., Kilts, C., and Hamann, S. (2006). Neural bases of motivated reasoning: An fMRI study of emotional constraints on partisan political judgment in the 2004 U.S. presidential election. *Journal of Cognitive Neuroscience, 18*(11), pp. 1947–58. doi: 10.1162/jocn.2006.18.11.1947.

Whitcomb, D., Battaly, H., Baehr, J., and Howard-Snyder, D. (2015). Intellectual humility: Owning our limitations. *Philosophy and Phenomenological Research, 91*(1), pp. 1–31.

Williamson, T. (2004). Sosa on abilities, concepts, and externalism. In J. Greco (Ed.), *Ernest Sosa and His Critics* (pp. 263–71). Oxford, UK: Blackwell Publishing.

Williamson, T. (2009). Replies to critics. In P. Greenough and D. Pritchard (Eds.), *Williamson on Knowledge* (pp. 279–384). Oxford, UK: Oxford University Press.

Wilson, T. D., Centerbar, D. B., and Brekke, N. (2002). Mental contamination and the debiasing problem. In T. Gilovich, D. Griffin, and D. Kahneman (Eds.), *Heuristics and Biases: The Psychology of Intuitive Judgment* (pp. 185–200). New York, NY: Cambridge University Press.

Wittgenstein, L. (1980). *Culture and Value*. Amended 2nd ed. with English translation. Oxford, UK: Blackwell Publishing.

Wood, W. J. (2012). How might intellectual humility lead to scientific insight: Discussion summary. *The Big Questions Online*. https://www.bigquestionsonline.com/node/177/comment/summary/all.

Wranik, T., Barrett, L. F., and Salovey, P. (2007). Intelligent emotional regulation: Is knowledge power? In James J. Gross (Ed.), *Handbook of Emotional Regulation* (pp. 373–92). New York, NY: Guilford Press.

Wright, C. (2004). Warrant for nothing (and foundations for free)? *Supplement to the Proceedings of the Aristotelian Society, 78*(1), pp. 167–212. doi: 10.1111/j.0309-7013.2004.00121.x.

Wright, C. (2007). The perils of dogmatism. In S. Nuccetelli and G. Seay (Eds.), *Themes from G.E. Moore: New Essays in Epistemology and Ethics* (pp. 25–48). Oxford, UK: Oxford University Press.

Zagzebski, L. (1994). The inescapability of Gettier problems. *The Philosophical Quarterly, 44*, pp. 65–73.

Zagzebski, L. (1996). *Virtues of the Mind: An Inquiry into the Nature of Virtue and the Ethical Foundations of Knowledge*. Cambridge, UK: Cambridge University Press.

Zagzebski, L. (1999). What is knowledge? In E. Sosa and J. Greco (Eds.), *The Blackwell Guide to Epistemology* (pp. 92–116). Oxford, UK: Blackwell Publishing.

Zajonc, R. B. (1980). Feeling and thinking: Preferences need no inferences. *American Psychologist, 35*(2), pp. 151–75. doi: 10.1037/0003-066x.35.2.151.

INDEX

Lightning Source UK Ltd.
Milton Keynes UK
UKHW020620080223
416661UK00005B/316